George F. Wolz
St. Charles College
August 16, 1965

RICHARD SCHLATTER, GENERAL EDITOR

Humanistic Scholarship in America

&? THE PRINCETON STUDIES ?&

THE COUNCIL OF THE HUMANITIES
WHITNEY J. OATES, CHAIRMAN
PRINCETON UNIVERSITY

The Books and

ANTHROPOLOGY
Eric R. Wolf

ART AND ARCHAEOLOGY
James S. Ackerman   Rhys Carpenter

CHINESE PAINTING
Wen Fong

CLASSICS
Eric A. Havelock

ENGLISH LITERATURE
David Daiches

FOREIGN LITERATURE
Henri Peyre

HISTORY
John Higham
Leonard Krieger   Felix Gilbert

LINGUISTICS
Eric P. Hamp   Karl D. Uitti
Rulon Wells

Their Authors

MODERN AMERICAN CRITICISM
Walter Sutton

MUSICOLOGY
Frank Ll. Harrison   Mantle Hood
Claude V. Palisca

THE ORIGINS OF AMERICAN
HUMANISTIC SCHOLARS
Robert H. Knapp

PHILOSOPHY
Roderick M. Chisholm   Herbert Feigl
William K. Frankena   John Passmore
Manley Thompson

RELIGION
Paul Ramsey, ed.
Philip H. Ashby   Robert M. Grant
James M. Gustafson   J. H. Nichols
Harry M. Orlinsky   John E. Smith
Claude Welch

RELIGION, A HUMANISTIC FIELD
Clyde A. Holbrook

The aim of these volumes is to present a critical account of American humanistic scholarship in recent decades. They have been commissioned by the Council of the Humanities, Whitney J. Oates, Chairman, of Princeton University and were made possible by a grant from the Ford Foundation.

—Richard Schlatter, General Editor.

RELIGION

❧ ❧

PAUL RAMSEY
EDITOR

PHILIP H. ASHBY
ROBERT M. GRANT
JAMES M. GUSTAFSON
J. H. NICHOLS
HARRY M. ORLINSKY
JOHN E. SMITH
CLAUDE WELCH

PRENTICE-HALL, INC.   ENGLEWOOD CLIFFS   NEW JERSEY

FOREWORD

The Ford Humanities Project under the direction of the Council of the Humanities at Princeton University is looking at American humanistic scholarship of recent decades. We have commissioned about a dozen volumes by recognized scholars in each field. These volumes are giving us an account of humanistic scholarship, enabling us to see just what that scholarship has contributed to the culture of America and the world.

In the course of our discussions at Princeton about the volume having to do with scholarly work in the field of religion, we came upon a peculiar difficulty—peculiar that is to the field of religion scholarship. A number of American scholars maintain that religion is not a scholarly discipline like art history or musicology or classical studies because religion demands of its students creedal commitments incompatible with free scholarly inquiry. In the end we decided to have two volumes on the study of religion, and Clyde Holbrook's *Religion, a Humanistic Field,* which appeared first, is a full and wise discussion of this question. The present volume gets on with the task of describing and judging the work of American scholars who have studied various aspects of religion.

The wisdom of our decision to commission the volume by Professor Holbrook is sustained by this second volume: the problems of definition of the field, of methodology, and of the relation of belief to scholarly objectivity are raised here again and again. Professor Ashby describes at length the difficulties historians of religion have encountered in freeing themselves from provincial theological biases of the past. Professor Orlinsky remarks that scholars too often "mix together scholarship and apologetics" and states that "until the student of biblical theology learns to deal with his data as critically as the student of ancient Greek, or Roman, or Assyrian, or Egyptian religion does, he can hardly expect his studies to achieve validity in scholarly cricles." Professor Grant gives a lucid and sensible account of the perplexities of the historian who is also a Christian

vii

when he studies the New Testament accounts of miracles. And for anyone who is outside the Christian community, the essays on Christian theology and Christian ethics will seem, inevitably, sectarian and parochial compared to other essays in the volumes of the Princeton Studies. All of this was symbolized by the difficulty we had in finding a suitable title for this volume: one of our authors insisted that *Religion* or *Religious Scholarship* was an ambiguous title and that we should adopt something like *The Scholarly Study of Religions*.

But when all this is said—and Professor Holbrook's volume is strongly recommended to the reader who wants to pursue the matter further—we obviously do have a wealth of American scholarship having to do with religion that is good judged by any standards. Clearly, scholarship in this area has attained great maturity and is growing steadily in strength and importance. This volume records ferment, debate, problems, and very many positive achievements.

RICHARD SCHLATTER
General Editor

CONTENTS

ix

THE HISTORY OF RELIGIONS

PHILIP H. ASHBY
ASSOCIATE PROFESSOR OF RELIGION
PRINCETON UNIVERSITY

The late Professor Joachim Wach of the University of Chicago in 1955 prefaced his *The Comparative Study of Religions* with the following quotation from a European scholar of the nineteenth century:

> This present century will not come to an end without having seen the establishment of a unified science whose elements are still dispersed, a science which the preceding centuries did not have, which is not even yet defined, and which perhaps for the first time, will be named science of religions.[1]

This hope for a new discipline possessing integrity in its own right as a unified "science," and capable of gathering and interpreting data in a degree hitherto not attained, summarizes in large measure the history of scholarship during the past century in the history of religions. The optimistic forecast of the nineteenth century scholar has not materialized. The attempt at its fulfillment, however, has been the particular feature separating the scholar from the tradesman within the broad outlines that have dimly marked the area of this yet not fully conceived "science."

Every academic discipline is confronted with the periodic, if not constant, obligation to redefine its methodology, its independence from and dependence upon other areas of scholarship, and the criteria for its own boundaries of specific concern. Especially is this true for "new" fields in the study of religion. In company with the psychology and sociology of religion, the history of religions during the past decades has not possessed a self-definition that would be agreed upon by even a large minority of its scholars, nor one that would be accepted as legitimate by its critics. While often cognizant of the unsettled problems within even those disciplines that have long been recognized, the historian of religions has, nevertheless, frequently considered himself to be unique in the ambiguity of his situation. Historian, philologist, anthropologist, sociologist, philosopher, theologian, or student of human culture—is he one, or all, or some of

[1] (Columbia, 1958), p. 2; Quoted from E. Burnouf, *La Science des religions,* 3rd ed. (1870), p. 1; Wach's translation.

3

these? Can he claim with integrity to be an equal among colleagues to whom one or more of these designations can be applied without question? Is his sphere of scholarship an enterprise that is capable of establishing itself upon its own foundations while acknowledging the interdependent relationship all areas of knowledge have with each other; or is the undertaking suggested by the phrase *history of religions* at best only a synthetic and *ad hoc* pursuit wherein legitimate disciplines sometimes conveniently meet?

Further, is it possible to speak of a "unified" area of scholarship that considers data that have as yet no acknowledged boundaries in time, space, societies, peoples, or in human experience and aspiration? True, many of the normally established humanistic areas of scholarly endeavor have the totality of human experience, insight, and accomplishment within their domain, yet they have succeeded in gaining for themselves the status of equal partnership with other disciplines claiming the right of co-regency over an expanse which cannot allow a single sovereign. The claim of the history of religions has as yet not been acknowledged by those from whom it seeks recognition, and with whom it hopes to participate in academic, scholarly, and religious circles.

In assessing the scholarly endeavors and concerns within the history of religions in America in recent decades we are confronted by a series of problems still unanswered. We shall have occasion to note many of these problems, but it appears that the majority of them find their origin and their complexity within the broad areas already presented—is the history of religions by nature and, therefore, necessity a synthetic discipline in a degree others are not, and is the scope of its legitimate and mandatory concern unlimited to the extent that its data and the methods applied to them must of necessity be the borrowed products of scholarly pursuits not inherent to itself?

The foregoing suggests that we are discussing an area of scholarship that does not know its own raison d'être, nor the boundaries of its concern. At first glance it appears that the historian of religions is the cause of his own problems, an uncertain enthusiast who by his lack of scholarly rigor and his desire to cast his net widely has forfeited the very claim he is seeking to make for his discipline. Such a conclusion, however, misses the central nature of the problem that

4

continues to plague the field. The primary role and function of the history of religions is conceived to be that of describing and interpreting the "religious" data of the past and the present. Its reason for being arises out of a need to comprehend fully the religious forces of human history and to understand their significance for the past, the present, and for man himself. The vast nature of the object to be studied is the inevitable and necessary result of the emerging science itself, a responsibility that man's quest for knowledge will not allow to be ignored because of the complexities it produces.

The history of religions, therefore, must be said to be an area of scholarly pursuit in search for a definition of itself. Convinced of the need for its existence, its leading proponents have in many instances themselves been engaged in activities that appear to fall more properly within a classification other than *history of religions*. They have not, however, allowed the uncertainties of the field to undermine their judgment that they are engaged in an area that cannot be dealt with adequately by other disciplines separately or collectively.

The beginnings of the study of religions other than one's own are, of course, to be associated with the earliest descriptions and interpretations of other cultures on the part of ancient peoples. It is not within the province of this essay to chronicle the historical development of such interests and studies, but we should note that until the nineteenth century scholarly activities in this area were not considered to be separate from the established disciplines of the time. Sometimes related to political or military interests, they were more often associated with the development of antiquarian concerns in regard to the origins of human thought and activity, the search for truth, and/or the attempt of Christianity to establish itself as the one true religion. As a result of these motivations the study of the history of the religions of the world has until the past century and a half been the responsibility of the predecessors of the disciplines we now know as theology, philosophy, classics, and history. As a student of the thought and history of the world the scholar of the past did not make sharp distinctions between those areas that we today would group together under the category of *humanities*. Perhaps the greatest distinction to be made between scholars of the past and present in regard to their approach to the subject of religion lay in the degree of the former's personal involvement with a specific theology, which they often allowed to be the arbiter of decisions as to value and disvalue, as well as truth and falsity. Whatever their motivations and their shortcomings, contemporary scholarship is obviously indebted to them for factual information as well as for methodological procedures. The contributions of scholars whom today we would separate as theologians, historians, classicists, etc. combined to create a basis upon which, with the growing distinctions between areas of humanistic study, it was thought a new discipline could be erected.

The scholars concerned with religion in the middle decades of the nineteenth century, therefore, were confronted with the growing necessity to make a claim for a field of scholarly endeavor that was distinct and yet not separate from those disciplines that had more identifiable roots in the past as distinguishable and proper pursuits. They felt themselves equipped for the task by virtue of both rapidly increasing knowledge and the growing conviction that the various fields of scholarship collectively possessed the resources to reveal past and present fact as well as truth.

Theologians and, more frequently, philologists, archaeologists, students of foreign cultures, etc. began to conceive of a new discipline that they considered necessary for the adequate study of religion and that would be both the sum of their separate work and, yet, distinct in its own right because of the wider range of its inquiry and the necessary development of a methodology peculiar to its own total needs. True, there were not a few who saw in their own specialty the key to the total endeavor, and who maintained that other studies and methods of approach were peripheral at best. However, the ever increasing amount of material available for examination, and the variety of its contents inevitably demanded differing techniques of study, and the perceptive scholar could not remain firm in his championship of his own approach in total isolation from all others.

As a result, the middle and latter decades of the nineteenth century witnessed the rise of a discipline that was thought to be equipped to record, interpret, and evaluate the religious history of mankind. This was the minimal expectation shared by the proponents of what in this essay we are terming the history of religions. For them it was to take varying turns and to be known by different names.[2] It continues today to seek to achieve the minimal expectations of its earliest modern exponents; and, despite its own confusions and the tenuous status it still occupies in some scholarly circles, it is compelled to strive to be a unified science, the "science of religions."

⋙ 2 ⋘

In company with other academic pursuits in America, the study of the history of religions has in large measure been dependent upon the varying interests and accomplishments of European scholarship. The few native American shcolars in the general field during the nineteenth and early twentieth centuries were most often followers of European trends rather than pioneers in their own right. And, up until the present, a large number of the best-known scholars in the field in America have been European born and educated. Only in the more specifically church-oriented and theologically concerned academic circles did native-born and largely American-trained scholars attain much note. These, with certain exceptions, were engaged primarily in the "comparative" study of religion as it has waxed and waned in the interest of the Protestant churches and their seminaries.

The major themes bequeathed by earlier European scholarship to the development of the history of religions in America arose primarily out of the historical circumstance of the nineteenth century. In the area of cultural studies the century was one that furnished scholarship with precise and detailed knowledge of other peoples and their histories in a degree hitherto unknown. Ancient and contemporary religions, primitive and sometimes esoteric cults apparently differing in marked degree from Western religious practices, mythologies and theologies reflecting both the lowest and highest insights of the human intellect were available for investigation in a manner

[2] In America *the history of religions* has generally come to be preferred more than *comparative religions*. A leading university, however, has recently established a chair in *World Religions,* and some college courses are now given that title. In Germany the terms *Religionswissenschaft* and *Religionsgeschichte* are common, while in France *l'histoire des religions* and *l'étude comparée des religions* have been used. Confusion arises for the layman when the scholar uses these terms to indicate specific methodologies or areas within the larger study of religion. It is hoped that this essay will indicate the differences meant by the scholar and the difficulties of arriving at an adequate name or term in English.

that assured the collection and codification of data with, at least, a more advanced measure of precision than previously possible. In the majority of instances individual phenomena of religion and collective systems of religious thought and practice that had been at best only dimly known, and therefore often gravely misunderstood, were now beginning to be investigated on their home grounds under conditions demanding the use of scholarly tools and *disciplined* imagination.

In addition to the obvious political, military, and economic factors that contributed to this development, the equally apparent but often misunderstood religious element of missions must be given its proper place. It is essential to note that the beginnings of the modern study of the religions of the world largely paralleled in time and scope the period of Christian missionary activity which Professor Latourette called "the great century." We shall have occasion to refer later to the relation of Christian missionary theory to the development of the study of the "non-Christian" [3] religions. At this point it is necessary to correct the prevalent lay opinion that the Christian missionary enterprise was and continues to be in opposition to the scholarly objectives of the history of religions. It is true that the religious-theological commitment that was the ultimate raison d'être of Christian missions resulted in misunderstandings of other religions, both in fact and interpretation. Nevertheless the missionary activity of the past century and a half produced scholars of religion who possessed a sensitivity for the religious longings and attainments of other peoples frequently not present in the "objective" scholars who were their contemporaries.

As a result of the varied contributions to knowledge brought about by increased acquaintance with the non-Western world in the preceding decades, scholars in the last half of the nineteenth century had at their disposal a variety of tools essential to the study of the religions of the world. Primary among them were philology and comparative linguistics, archaeology, history, biblical studies, the

[3] Professor Wilfred Cantwell Smith has rightly pointed to the negative and misleading connotation of the term *non-Christian* from the perspective of an empathetic consideration of religions. See "Comparative Religion: Whither-and-Why?" in *The History of Religions,* ed. Mircea Eliade and Joseph M. Kitagawa (U. of Chicago, 1959), p. 33 n.

8

philosophy of religion, and the early forms of what were to become anthropological and sociological studies.

The name of Professor Friedrich Max Müller (1823-1900) of Oxford must be given prominence in any discussion of the modern development of the study of religion. Building upon his immense linguistic knowledge, particularly in Sanskrit, Max Müller devoted himself to the study of philology and comparative linguistics, paying particular attention to the naturalistic mythologies that he found in the literary deposits of human cultures. As one of the pre-eminent scholarly figures of his time, and a gifted popularizer of his theories among the cultured laity of England and the Continent, Max Müller is viewed by many as "the father of the history of religions." Despite the fact that many of his theories are no longer accepted by scholars, his role as editor of the monumental *Sacred Books of the East* assures him of a lasting place among leading historians of religions. While Max Müller and his followers greatly overemphasized the role of comparative linguistics and comparative mythology as the keys to the enigma of religious origins and relationships, the recognition of the central importance of linguistic and literary studies in the area of the history of religions has been a continuing emphasis since his time.

The role of archaeology in the study of the history of religions is evident, especially in areas of study devoted to religious history and expressions of the past. The ancient religions of the Western world were, in some measure, as unknown in their details as were the religions of the non-Western areas. The literary deposits that were common property of various Western humanistic studies, and the obvious monuments and ruins of ancient and classical cultures, did not in themselves combine to give the scholar a precise knowledge that would enable him to describe accurately and to interpret correctly. Archaeological discoveries followed by scientific methods of reconstruction and interpretation served an important corrective function in enabling Western scholarship to describe and evaluate the history and function of earlier Western religions. These had all too often been either ignored or depreciated as participants in the development of Western society and thought. Nor has the contribution of archaeological research been limited to the Western world and its areas of origin. As a result, modern scholarship has been able to document sources that were primarily traditional and literary in contemporary religions by means of the study of physical remains that are less subject to changes of circumstance and interpretation.

In similar fashion the greatly expanded area of world historical knowledge served as a direct and essential contributor to the study of religion. Obviously, the descriptive task fundamental to the study of religion is by definition historical in nature. The past century and a half has been marked both by the increased gathering of facts concerning the histories of areas and peoples and by the development of a variety of scholarly disciplines that contribute to the continuing accumulation of such knowledge. More importantly, during this period there has been an increasing number of scholars from the non-Western areas who have directed their attention to the history of their own area. This is of particular significance to the history of religions in that description of history from "outside" is now counterbalanced by "inside" historical description, and vice versa, to the benefit of both. Whether greater objectivity always results may be questioned, but the values arising from scholarly description of the history of one's own environmental and inherited traditions are readily apparent.

The prevalent lay habit of considering the study of the history of religions to be limited to the non-Hebraic-Judaic-Christian religions has often caused students to overlook the role played by biblical studies in the development of the history of religions as a scholarly pursuit. With the increase of technical studies of the Bible, its literary forms and development, the history it recorded, and the religious thought and practice it revealed, scholars of the Old and New Testaments were compelled to devote greater attention to the religious ethos in which these scriptures were produced. As a result, it was inevitable that they were led to an investigation of the adjacent religions and cultures of the Semitic world, and to a consideration of the religious themes, traditions, and cults within the broad arena of Christianity's early formulations. The knowledge thus gained of early Semitic religion and of the relationship of Hebraic-Judaic thought and cult to the Weltanschauung of the area and period serve to make more clear the interaction of local religions upon each other. So, too, not only were the religions of the Greco-Roman world more fully known, but the historic circumstances and religious influences present in the period of Christianity's beginnings were perceived with a clarity previously lacking. The result is to be seen in the continuing awareness from the perspective of the history of religions, and even of more theologically oriented studies, that the Hebraic-Christian religious experience and tradition is not to be isolated unto itself as a completely distinct and unique phenomenon in the religious history of the world. Earlier scholars and theologians, lacking detailed factual knowledge, had struggled with this problem, but it could now be confronted by scholars unhampered by theological provincialisms that had not been corrected by historical facts and wider theological perspectives.

The lines of demarcation between philosophy, theology, and the philosophy of religion have often been hazy. The identity among them during much of Western intellectual history is a prime example of the difficulty inherent in any attempt to separate humanistic disciplines. If theology be considered as "Christian reflection"[4] in a systematic and constructive manner upon the essential themes of the Christian faith, it still may remain a difficult matter to make a clear distinction between it and the other two disciplines, particularly from the perspective of the theologian. Again, philosophy and the philosophy of religion have differed much less between themselves as disciplines than they may seem to have varied in specific instances because of the concerns and predilections of a particular scholar. However, the philosophy of religion, or the philosophic inquiry that devotes itself to the recurring themes of religious thought found in a number of religions, may be singled out as a special collaborator with the history of religions. In many instances in the past, philosophers of religion have played the role of historians of religions, and historians of religions of necessity have been engaged in tasks that involved them in the role of the philosopher of religion. The major contribution of the philosophy of religion to the history of religions in past decades has been the philosophical inquiry into the nature of religious experience, conceptions of history, the divine, man, the world, etc. In other words, philosophy of religion has entailed reflection upon the fundamental concepts apparent within most, and perhaps all, of the religious expressions of history. In this

[4] See Claude Welch's essay on "Theology" in this volume.

function the philosophy of religion and the history of religions are dependent upon each other, both in the gathering of knowledge and the interpretation of it.

It is sufficient at this point to suggest that the beginnings of sociological and anthropological studies in the nineteenth century served to place before the student of religion information concerning peoples and societies that had previously been either unobtainable or erroneous to the extent that a little knowledge often was worse than none at all. Despite the temporary and often faulty enthusiasms brought about by the particular theory of a scholar or a school in which it was held to be *the* key to man's religious belief and organization, each of the theories contributed further insight into the phenomenon of religion. Animism, mana, totemism, *Kulturgeschichte,* the theory of the prelogical mentality of primitive or preliterate tribal man—these and other conceptions put forward by the predecessors of modern sociologists and anthropologists advanced the developing material and methodology of the historian of religions.

As a result of the foregoing developments during the nineteenth and early twentieth centuries, during the past decades the history of religions in America has developed upon a base which continues to reflect concerns and advancements primarily identified with non-American scholarship. Stated briefly, the foundation upon which the history of religions continues to operate in America and elsewhere consists of the following components: (1) a conviction that the phenomenon of religion, or the phenomena of religions, is a legitimate and necessary discipline of scholarly study, subject to the same or similar rules of scholarship employed in other humanistic areas; (2) a recognition of the variety within the totality of the human religious experience and expression, a variety that demands that the observer be able to rise above his own provincial limitations in order to perceive the value of a particular phenomenon within its peculiar religious and cultural setting; (3) an awareness of common or "classical" features and themes within the varieties of religious experience and expression that can neither be dismissed lightly nor quickly assumed to demonstrate the equality or basic unity of the separate religions; and (4) a growing appreciation of the richness and profundity of thought, insight, and modes of appearance to be found in religions associated with differing cultures.

The above list includes subjective matters relating to value and individual appreciation as well as the suggestion, implied throughout, that facts concerning religion must be known. The history of religions, despite its ambition to be known as a science, has not been able to divest itself of a subjective element that appears to qualify, if not to thwart, its claim to be a discipline descriptive in nature and objective in intent. Like the field of history, its role and purpose places it (perhaps with some inner discontent) within the humanities from which it seeks to venture forth into the fields of the social sciences, only to discover in so doing that its search for value and for truth demands that it bifurcate itself if it is to fulfill its raison d'être.

◈ 3 ◈

The study of the history of religions during the first three decades of the twentieth century in America was associated primarily with Protestant theological seminaries. Teaching of the subject, usually under the title of *Comparative Religion,* was also done in many of the church-related liberal arts colleges throughout the country and, occasionally, in a few of the large independent universities. In the latter, however, the study of religion was beginning to find a place for itself as a part of other disciplines concerned with the study of man and his culture. Religion, as such, generally continued to be excluded from the curricular offerings of independent and state colleges and universities. With the exception of a few scholars who were becoming increasingly aware of the relationship of religion to their primary pursuits, scholarship in the area was limited to teachers of the history of religions, or comparative religion, in theological schools and centers preparing students for the ministry or, occasionally, for the teaching of religion.

The Protestant theological atmosphere of the early decades of the present century in America was one that, particularly in the larger interdenominational theological schools, reflected the growing theological liberalism of the period. Among the many facets of this liberalism, a predominant theme was an appreciation of human accomplishment and potentiality in the spheres of individual and social religious attainment. It would be an error to assume, however, that this meant a depreciation of the role of the divine in human affairs.

It did, nevertheless, give to its exponents a conviction that the revelatory activities of God, and the responses of men to them, were not limited to the Hebraic-Christian tradition. Not only is God sovereign over all existence, but he has revealed himself to men in diverse ways in all times and places. This statement may appear to be too extreme a characterization of theological thought as it related to the non-Christian religions, but the emphasis that the leading historians of religions and missionary scholars of the period placed upon the general revelatory activity of God was, in fact, a primary motive behind their writings.

The extreme statement of this position in relation to the study of the religions of the world had been written by Professor Max Müller in 1865 when he claimed that from a comparative study of religions:

1. We shall learn that religions in their most ancient form, or in the minds of their authors, are generally free from many of the blemishes that attach to them in later times.

2. We shall learn that there is hardly one religion which does not contain some truth, some important truth; truth sufficient to enable those who seek the Lord and feel after Him, to find Him in their hour of need.

3. We shall learn to appreciate better than ever what we have in our own religion. No one who has not examined patiently and honestly the other religions of the world, can know what Christianity really is, or can join with such truth and sincerity in the words of St. Paul: "I am not ashamed of the Gospel of Christ." [5]

Over sixty-five years later, at the zenith of Protestant liberal theology in America, the Laymen's Foreign Missions Inquiry, under the chairmanship of Professor William Ernest Hocking of Harvard, reflected the prevailing theological liberalism of the major American Protestant denominations, their scholars, and educated laity by placing great emphasis upon the role of non-Christian religions and cultures as preparatory to acceptance of the Christian gospel. Holding that a period of creative relationship between the various religions and cultures of the world was at hand, their report concluded that it was necessary "that the modern mission make a positive effort, first of all to know and understand the religions around it, then to recog-

[5] Friedrich Max Müller, *Chips From A German Workshop*, vol. I (Scribner's, 1869), p. 48.

nize and associate itself with whatever kindred elements there are in them." [6]

Scholarship in the area of the history of religions inevitably reflected a comparative concern when such scholarship was intimately related to the theological and missionary task of the Christian church. As a result, with some major exceptions, much of the writing and instruction in the subject involved a comparative analysis of the non-Hebraic-Christian religions individually and collectively with Christianity. The descriptive task that had been at the center of the earlier attempts to found a science of religion was in America to a large degree smothered by the theological-missionary concern of scholars and teachers who were personally involved in the attempt to demonstrate the superiority of their own religion over all other religions. It would be erroneous to suggest that the great majority of European scholars and teachers in the field during the nineteenth century were not also theologically involved. American teachers and writers in the area of comparative religion, however, seldom devoted themselves to serious descriptive investigation and scholarship, contenting themselves for the most part with textbook production and comparisons between other religions and Christianity in which Christianity was demonstrated to be greatly superior. The exceptions are associated with the all too few American scholars whose works continue to have value today, such as Robert E. Hume's *The Thirteen Principal Upanishads* (1921), George Foot Moore's *Judaism in the First Centuries of the Christian Era* (1927), or James Bissett Pratt's *The Pilgrimage of Buddhism* (1928). The last-named achieves its primary value not because of scholarly specialization in Buddhism, which Pratt did not claim, but because of a degree of scholarly empathy seldom attained by the American historians of religion of the time.

A primary weakness behind the classroom activities and writings of the teachers of comparative religion was their lack of adequate scholarly training. Usually recruited from the ranks of the Christian clergy, and often having previously served a period as a missionary in a non-Christian area, few of them had undertaken formal academic work in the history of religions or in the specific non-Christian religion they claimed as their area of special knowledge.

[6] *Re-Thinking Missions* (Harper, 1932), p. 33.

It was assumed that their missionary experience, or their general interest in the subject of religion, equipped them to be adequate interpreters of the non-Christian religions and gave them the ability to weigh the values and disvalues of these religions for their adherents and mankind in general. With the exception of the few who held chairs in the leading universities or theological schools, they were not firmly grounded in the history of the various religions of the world nor were they adequately versed in the methodology of their discipline.

This lack of scholarship on the part of the great majority of American teachers of comparative religion during the first decades of this century contributed to the failure of comparative religion to gain a secure status in academic circles. Generally considered by their colleagues in theological seminaries to lack the scholarly rigor demanded in other theological disciplines, they were also distrusted by secular scholars, both for their lack of learning and for the presumed absence of objectivity in their view of the non-Western religions. The few who did possess the confidence of their colleagues found themselves unsupported by student interest; and this meant that they failed to provide for their own replacement in the theological-scholarly world.

It is essential to note the paucity of opportunity in America for the training of scholars in the history of religions during the first half of the twentieth century. Where there are few scholars there are limited opportunities to train more scholars. Even in academic centers where there were leading historians of religions—such as the University of Chicago, Harvard, Union Theological Seminary in New York, and Yale—it was recognized that the training given the occasional young scholar was not adequate unless it was greatly supplemented by studies in Europe. The history of religions had still not become an American discipline; unlike other humanistic studies that had succeeded in part to create their own scholarly resources in America, the field retained its European dependence. The seminal scholarly writing and creative attempts to establish productive methodologies essential to the continuing development of such studies continued to be European products.

The decline of comparative religion in the American theological-seminary world and in the liberal arts colleges was also related to the general temper and international outlook of the American people during the third and fourth decades of the twentieth century. While an individual scholar might pursue more intensive study, the general lack of student demand for training in the history of religions and the absence of lay support and recognition of the value of this field of study combined to weaken a scholarly discipline that was and still is dependent upon the educational process for its financial undergirding and general encouragement. The United States and Canada, and the United States in particular, had not as yet emerged from their isolation from the rest of the world. Concerned with their own internal development, and not yet deeply involved in the well-being and the actions of the non-Western peoples, there was little interest in the history, society, or religions of those areas. True, commercial interests were awakening to the value of scholarly studies and student training in the history and societies of areas in which they had vital interests, but the early support of commercial circles for area study programs in the large American universities did not, by and large, give direct encouragement to investigation of religion itself. The indirect benefits of these programs to the study of religion proved to be of great significance, but at the time neither a distinct nor a significant role was assigned to the study of the history, thought, or social function of religion per se.

Further, the one primary factor that supported the development of the study of non-Western religions, Christian missions, was itself in a period of relative decline in its general support among both church and nonchurch people. This decline was not evident so much in number of missionaries nor in direct church support of the total missionary program; rather, it was reflected in two developments of attitude that were mutually contradictory. First, there was the growing belief among American theologians and philosophers of missions that the religions of the non-Western world were not divinely inspired preparations for the reception of the Christian message, and that the contemporary religions of the East were doomed to rapid disappearance before the advance of Christian truth and the power of Western civilization. Second, there was a growing sentiment among church laity and the general public that the missionary effort of Christianity was a misplaced activity contributing to the destruction of indigenous values and freedoms in missionary areas, as well as an

17

assertion of Western uniqueness and pride unjustified in the light of the religious and cultural attainments of non-Western man. As a result of these two trends of thought, basic support of the study of the non-Western religions was weakened, and the teaching of the history of religions, or comparative religion, rapidly disappeared as a significant effort even in those theological seminaries and church colleges where it had achieved some measure of acceptance in previous decades.

Thus, the period of the 1930's in America witnessed the failure of the historical and comparative study of religion to continue the steady advance that had been confidently hoped for and predicted by its earlier advocates. The number of scholars and teachers exclusively devoted to work in the field was extremely limited; the interest of other scholars and academic leaders was greatly qualified; and religious and public support was almost nonexistent.

◄§ 4 §►

A basic problem for the study of the history of religions in the West arises from the inherent relationship between the field and Christian theological concern. The support given in America by the Christian missionary enterprise to the comparative study of the world's living religions was conducive to a close connection between such studies and theology, yet often the relationship was not clearly discerned even by teachers who sought to be scholarly in their teaching and writing. The Christian teacher of the subject, those who supported his presence in theological and academic communities, and the students themselves were generally Christian thinkers first and foremost, and students of other religious traditions second. Approaching their investigations of other religions from a background that was Christian in personal commitment and theological conviction, it is true that they understood their task to be descriptive in its initial and elementary stages. As a result of their basic theological orientation, however, they could not be content with simple description, nor could they detach themselves from their primary concern with religious truth to proceed to the objective evaluation they considered essential. The emphasis upon the preparatory values of the non-Christian religions for the Christian message, and the recognition of a general divine revelation available to all mankind, were conclusions that resulted from a Christian theological position. Only rarely were these interpretations arrived at from the study of the non-Christian religions themselves. The study of the religions of the world by Christian students, therefore, has been highly dependent upon the Christian theological ethos of a particular time for its method, emphases, and conclusions.

In the early periods of Christian interest in the pagan religions surrounding Christianity, the approach to them had been an apologetic one: the aim was at the least to demonstrate their insufficiency when compared to Christianity, while in the extreme the goal was to establish that the religious rivals of Christianity were the products of demonic activity directly counter to the truth revealed in Jesus Christ. The early argument that the content of the non-Christian religions did not measure up to the truth present in the Christian gospel had often been accompanied by a recognition that they possessed some, though limited, values in preparation for the reception of Christianity. It may be said that for nineteen hundred years the Christian theological understanding of religions other than itself had been, in one manner or another, a variation upon this basic theme developed by Christian theologians in the early centuries of the religion. Even with the development of new tools of study and increased familiarity with religions far removed from the area of Christian history and influence, these Christian views of the other religions underwent little change. At the most, there was a heightened awareness of the depths and values of the human perception and expression of the divine revelation in all existence, but even this was limited to the very few who had the necessary firsthand knowledge of another religion to arrive at such a conclusion.

The theological position of an important group of Western Christian scholars in the last decades of the nineteenth and early years of the twentieth century was a very liberal form of this traditional Christian attitude toward non-Christian religions. God was held not to have left himself without witness in the world and its history. However, this knowledge of God through general or natural revelation was not sufficient in itself to overcome the basic evil and ignorance of natural man. At the very best, like the pre-Christian revelation to the Hebraic-Jewish people, "natural religion" may have prepared men for an understanding and acceptance of the final and necessary revelation brought to the world in Christ. In all too many instances, however, natural religion had been perverted by human evil with the result that, rather than leading men to the truth, it was a barrier in their path.

During the 1930's this Protestant Christian theological understanding of the non-Christian religions began to undergo a radical change in theological circles in America. As in the study of the history of religions, American scholarship in Christian theology was profoundly influenced by European theological trends. The rise of what has been called neo-Reformation or neo-orthodox theology following World War I very quickly made itself felt in American theological thinking. Under the leadership of European theologians such as Karl Barth and Emil Brunner, this "new" theological position was soon brought to bear upon the missionary task of the church with inevitable results for the study of the non-Christian religions.[7]

Barth's theological position affirmed that there is no knowledge of God anywhere in the world except in the hearts of converted Christian believers. God has spoken to mankind only in the person of Jesus Christ; it is only through Christ that both knowledge of God and salvation come to man. Therefore, there is a clear distinction to be made between Christianity and all other forms of religion, or rather between *Christianity* and *religion*. The religions of mankind cannot even be classified with Christianity as being of the same general character, for Christianity is *the* revelation of God to man, whereas all other religions are merely the creations of man. Human religion, that is all religions except Christianity, should rightly be seen as unbelief. God, revealing himself to man, is confronted by men who are not able and do not want to accept God's self-revealing love. These human religions are the products of man's resistance to the divine revelation; they are the supreme examples of a positive unbelief on the part of man. It is only the specific revelation of God in Jesus Christ that is capable of penetrating fully into man's heart and thought; any general or natural revelation there may be is always repudiated by man.

The central statement of this theological position in relation to both the Christian missionary enterprise and the study of the non-

[7] See Claude Welch's essay on "Theology" in this volume.

Christian religions was put forward by Hendrick Kraemer, Professor of the History of Religions at the University of Leiden in the Netherlands. Kraemer held that "the Christian revelation as the record of God's self-disclosing revelation in Jesus Christ, is absolutely *sui generis.*" [8] All religions and systems of thought, Kraemer held, are seen as "clumsy or magnificent evasions when they are considered in the light of 'Biblical Realism.'" [9] By the term *biblical realism* Kraemer was seeking to convey the idea "that the Bible, the human and in many ways historically conditioned document of God's acts of revelation, consistently testifies to divine acts and plans in regard to the salvation of mankind and the world, and not to religious experiences or ideas." That is to say, the central message of the Bible is its witness to "God's creative and redemptive dealing with men and the world." [10] The whole emphasis is thus placed upon the view that the Bible must be considered as the record of God's thought and acts in regard to man. If the Bible is held to be "a tale about the pilgrimage of the human soul toward God," then the central message and concern of the Bible is lost; man, if he sees the Bible in this light, is merely continuing his resistance to divine revelation.

Recognizing that longings and dim insights of a religious nature are present in the religious history of humanity outside the Christian revelation, and that the revelation of and in Christ "may be termed in a certain sense the fulfillment" of these longing and vague insights, Kraemer insisted, however, that Christianity cannot be considered as a consummation of the religious pilgrimage or seeking of man. There is never fulfillment in the sense that Christianity perfects or completes the religious beliefs or insights that have existed before Christianity is made known. Man is in a state of hostility toward God, and all non-Christian religious beliefs are the creation of man. There is, therefore, no natural theology or general revelation in the sense that there is everywhere available for man, if he but seeks it, an intelligible knowledge of God. The special revelation

[8] Hendrick Kraemer, "Continuity or Discontinuity," *The Authority of the Faith,* vol. I, "The Madras Series" (New York: International Missionary Council, 1939), p. 1.
[9] Hendrick Kraemer, *The Christian Message in a Non-Christian World* (Harper, 1937), p. 75.
[10] Kraemer, "Continuity or Discontinuity," pp. 1 ff.

contained in Christ is not a superstructure that rests upon a foundation furnished by general revelation. While specifically stating that he is not denying that God has been working in the minds of men outside the sphere of revelation in the event of Jesus Christ, Professor Kraemer did maintain that any men who are men of faith under such circumstances are the products of the working of the Spirit of God, and not of the non-Christian religions in which they find themselves. Despite the imperfections of Christianity arising from its status as a historic phenomenon subject also to the demonic tendencies of man, Christianity is the only religion that is the result of a direct act or revelation on the part of God. It is the only religion that finds its roots in the *sui generis* revelation of God to man testified to by biblical realism. The other religions find their source in human aspiration alone.

It will be realized immediately that the acceptance of such a theological position in regard to the non-Christian religions of the world would have a profound effect upon the attitude with which the Christian scholar and student approaches the study of the other religions. While it would be incorrect to suggest that neo-orthodox theology, or its application to the problem of the relationship between Christianity and the other religions, was accepted universally by American Protestantism, nevertheless, Protestant theology and philosophy of missions did undergo a marked change as a result of its impact.

The inevitable result of this change in theological emphasis in Europe and America was that those involved in the Christian apologetic and missionary endeavor outside the West, who had been the chief supporters of comparative and historical study of religions, lost much of their interest in such studies. The decline of courses relative to the non-Christian religions in theological seminaries and church-related colleges appears to be directly related to the appearance in America of theological thought that either was a direct result of the "new" theological thought originating in European Protestant circles, or a reflection from other sources of a nonliberal attitude toward the non-Christian religions. As a consequence, the relatively small number of teacher-scholars was further reduced, and potential scholars in the discipline among theological students were attracted to other areas of teaching and research. With a few important exceptions, teaching and opportunities for scholarship in the history of religions were almost nonexistent in church-related academic centers. At the least, Christian theology saw in the study of the non-Christian religions nothing more than the historical record of man's dire plight and deep need for salvation through the Christian gospel; at the most, theologians acknowledged that the study of the history of religions demonstrated the need for the Christian missionary proclamation and that it might aid missionary thinkers and workers in the field to understand better the task that confronted them. In neither case were the religions to be considered to possess ultimate value in themselves as conveyors or depositories of truth.

This change in theological perspective and the resulting decline in theological interest in the study of the history of religions appears at first glance to have meant not only the ultimate disappearance of the study of the non-Hebraic-Christian religions, but also the dismissal of those religions by Christian scholars as viable forces in the contemporary world. For a brief period in the twentieth century, Christian theological scholarship thought itself able to return to the isolated and provincial outlook that had dominated Western Christian thinking during so much of the past.

The nadir of the comparative and historical study of religions in America was reached in the years immediately preceding World War II. The Protestant theological climate combined with the provincial and isolationist attitudes of the time to produce a lack of interest on the part of academic groups and students in the religions of the non-Western world. In religious circles the cause of this disinterest was primarily a theological one; in academic-scholarly centers a sustained concern with the non-Western world, its culture, society, and religion had yet to come into existence. The "science" of religion had all but disappeared from the American scene before it had had the opportunity to develop beyond its infancy. However, world events and the further development of scholarship that was not so closely allied with Christian theological thought combined to bring about a resurgence of teaching and scholarship in the area of the history of religions that has given the discipline an impulse for scholarly strength and vitality it did not possess before. While not freed from its relationship to theology, and not always seeking to be, the history of religions has nevertheless embarked upon a path that is

23

enabling it to express what it considers to be its own unique role as a scholarly discipline independent in its own right, free to declare for itself the terms of its relationship to theology.

✥ 5 ✥

The corrective to the low state of the history of religions in America, both as a field of academic instruction and as an area of scholarly pursuit, made its appearance as the result of scholarly activity that was primarily nontheological in nature. Throughout the latter part of the nineteenth century and the early decades of the twentieth century, scholarship in adjacent disciplines concerned itself more and more with studies related to religion in the non-Western world, and to research into the phenomenon of religion per se. Largely through the growing awareness by nontheological scholars of the central significance of religion in the history, culture, society, and total ethos of an area and its peoples, the study of the history of religions was not only revived but given a structure and form enabling it to begin again in its attempt to attain the stature envisaged by its nineteenth century proponents.

The collective expression of these studies in their direct relationship to the history of religions is best summed up in the term *Religionswissenschaft* as it was first used by Continental scholars. Combining the German conception of *Wissenschaft* as both "science" and "learning" or "knowledge," *Religionswissenschaft* did not mean a science of religion in the limited empirical sense so often erroneously assumed by Americans engaged in other disciplines. While the emphasis of scholars pursuing the study of the history of religions in the *Religionswissenschaft Schule* of thought was placed in large measure upon the ascertainment of historical and contemporary fact, the limits of the endeavor were, and are, much broader than the name itself might suggest.

Relying to a large extent upon the contribution of the many separate but allied scholarly disciplines concerned with the history of human society and culture, *Religionswissenschaft* from the beginning conceived one aspect of its task to be the gathering of knowledge concerning religious history, religious belief, and religious expression. In this endeavor there are no geographical or temporal boundaries, no limitations upon the nature of religious phenomena arising out of the predilections of the investigator, and no concern to establish the superiority of one religion over another. In each of the foregoing instances, certainly, the particular interest of the individual scholar often immersed him in concentration upon one period and/or area of religious history, one or a related group of religious phenomena, or involved him in an attempt to ascertain the contributive value of a particular religion, theological theme, or cultus to human life.

It is incorrect, however, to assume that *Religionswissenschaft*—knowledge and learning about religion—can be attained by description of religious history, or statements of what is believed by the adherents of a religion, or reports of how religious groups or individuals give expression to their religious beliefs and commitments. Such portrayals are basic to knowledge about religion; for scholars of the history of religions, however, they are but a preliminary step to the understanding of religious phenomena.

The impact of the scholarly methodology and concern embodied in the *Religionswissenschaftlich* approach to the study of the history of religions began to make itself felt in America in a decisive manner during the 1940's. Scholars involved in area and cultural studies that required attention to religion were aware that knowledge of their own specialties was not sufficient to give them the degree of understanding needed. Also, they were aware that the comparative study of religions as it had developed in this country was not adequate to the task that was demanded. The scene was thus set for the development in America of a scientific study of religion based upon European accomplishments, but now equipped by temperament and scholarly resources to proceed as a colleague rather than simply as a dependent of non-American scholarship.

The fundamental thrust of the scientific study of the history of religions as it had developed in the early decades of the present century, and as it has continued to evolve in Europe and America, has centered around three primary focal points: the nature of religious experience, the expression of that experience both collectively and individually, and the problem of interpretation. While the first and second of these may be said to be in large measure a matter of the collection of data wherever it may be found, the problem of interpretation lies at the center of the scholarly task of the historian of religions. It is, of course, trite to say that the accumulation of data in and of itself is of relatively little value without adequate principles of interpretation upon which they can be classified and properly understood. Nevertheless, questions concerning the appropriate role and method of interpretation are always present in humanistic and cultural studies.

The study of the history of religions, when pursued in the spirit of *Religionswissenschaft,* has become increasingly dependent upon another aspect of the study of religions, namely, the phenomenology of religion. While, again, arising primarily in Europe and dependent upon European scholars for the more advanced explications of its method and aim, the phenomenology of religion has become in large measure the tool that historians of religions, in America and elsewhere, now employ in their scholarly pursuits and conclusions. Generally held along with *Religionsgeschichte* (the specifically descriptive nature of the history of religions) to be an aspect of *Religionswissenschaft,* the phenomenology of religion is the "systematic treatment of History of Religion." [11] The attempt at a systematic treatment of religion demands that data be surveyed and classified so that the investigator can discern their nature as individual phenomena, as well as ascertain the religious values of specific beliefs, acts, or religious expressions. The data must first be gathered. They must then be placed in groups wherein the criterion for inclusion rests upon a conception of "types" of religious phenomena. Although the construction of a typology of religious phenomena may at first be rather arbitrary because of lack of knowledge of the essential nature of the particular phenomenon, it is a necessary first step, for classification of data enables the scholar to come to a more adequate understanding of his subject and thereafter be equipped to refine and redefine his categories. The study of the particular item is aided by attempts to place it in various groups; and a more precise definition of a group or type is brought about by the increased knowledge

[11] W. Brede Kristensen, *The Meaning of Religion,* trans. John B. Carman (The Hague: Martinus Nijhoff, 1960), p. 1. For a discussion of the phenomenology of religion see also Gerardus van der Leeuw, *Religion in Essence and Manifestation,* trans. J. E. Turner (London: George Allen & Unwin, 1938).

of separate items that may or may not have some common or essential relationship.

A basic problem in the development of the phenomenology of religion has been that of the degree to which the phenomenologist is limited to description only. Is the task of the phenomenologist simply that of gathering and classifying data? Is it possible to do even this adequately, if one limits himself to outward description and, perhaps, inward intent and meaning without seeking and interpreting the *value* present in the phenomenon itself? Some phenomenologists have placed their emphasis upon the descriptive pursuit; and they prefer to leave the problem of the value of the phenomenon or of the collective group of phenomena to the philosopher of religion, or, occasionally, to the theologian. Using the technical term *epoche* to imply the suspension of judgment in regard to value, they conceive their task to be that of seeing and describing the "thing in itself" as it stands as a phenomenon, and not as it stands in a world of intradependent and contingent objects. They do not mean by this that qualitative analysis and evaluation have no place in the study of religion; they do hold, however, that it must be separated from the phenomenological pursuit itself. Further, a misunderstanding results if it is not clear that all phenomenology rests upon the principle that "(1) Something exists. (2) This something 'appears.' (3) Precisely because it 'appears' it is a 'phenomenon.' " [12] But, it must be noticed that the appearance of a phenomenon is an appearance to someone, to a person who by his relation to the appearance is in a subject-object relationship to it. Therefore, it cannot be said that the phenomenon is a pure object, since it is related to a subject; and since it is an appearance to a subject, the phenomenon is also in some sense a subject related to an object.

It is at this point that the supposed weakness of phenomenology as an attempt at pure description is apparent unless it is clear that the attempt to get at the "thing in itself" is qualified by the one relational aspect that cannot be escaped in all human endeavor to gain understanding, namely, the human factor itself. For the phenomenologist the primary aim is to overcome the subjective element in himself as a scholar while allowing full status to the subjective element in the

[12] van der Leeuw, *op. cit.*, p. 671; see also pp. 671-78.

person or community to whom the appearance of the phenomenon is significant. Recognizing that phenomenology, albeit descriptive in nature, is a description of phenomena that have had value in some degree for individual persons and groups, some phenomenologists have sought to ascertain the value that the item or items had for those peoples involved in their appearance, and not the universal value the phenomena have for mankind as a whole. As a result, contemporary phenomenology of religion is engaged in a descriptive pursuit that demands that comparison be made between separate phenomena in order that they may be classified by their type and nature, and it is required to pay attention to their value for the religious individual or group involved.

It is the claim of phenomenologists of religion that their discipline is a return to the comparative study of religion as it was ideally conceived by their scholarly predecessors of the nineteenth century. Comparison is essential for the purpose of understanding the value relationships of religious phenomena among the human beings concerned. The scientific study of religions by the method of phenomenology is not to be pursued in order to establish the value supremacy of one religious system over another, or even the value of a particular religion for all mankind. This is a responsibility that can only be assumed by the theologian of a particular religion after he has at his disposal the facts and understanding furnished by *Religionswissenschaft*. By comparative study the phenomenologist of religion examines all phenomena that claim or appear to be legitimately in the sphere of the religious. Although dependent upon the history of religions as a historical discipline showing the development, context, and environment of the phenomena, he is, nevertheless, required to engage in a systematic analysis in which the phenomena are observed in their ideal connection. Separate historical data, which have no connection or relationship in geographic location or identity or continuity of time, are placed in relationship by their types and functions for the purposes of understanding the group as a whole in its structure and its role within the broader aspects of the science of religions. Cultus and belief within a particular historic religious tradition or complex falls within the province of the historian of that religion; the systematic analysis of a particular phenomenon in that religion is the task of the phenomenologist of religion. In this schol-

arly pursuit he is engaged in the comparative study of religious phenomena for the purpose of understanding the phenomena and their
role in the total sphere of religion. Understanding the data of religious history is his concern, and not the discovery of relative degrees
of ultimate value between phenomena which must differ in some degree because of the differing *Sitz im Leben* of each.

The contemporary study of the religions of the world, in America
and among scholars around the world, whether it be known under
the name of *comparative religion, the history of religions,* or *the
science of religions,* uses in large measure the method of approach to
its subject that is to be identified with the phenomenological study of
religion. While the phenomenology of religion is not the totality of
what is meant by *Religionswissenschaft,* it is today a primary scholarly discipline and tool being used to further the development of a
science of religion.

❧ 6 ❧

The relationship of a scholarly area of research to other areas clearly
adjacent to it in concern and purpose is often self-evident; however, the intradependent and reciprocal connection between disciplines that are in some measure different in their methods of approach and in their objects of study is not always apparent either to
the scholar or to the layman.

With the appearance of *Religionswissenschaft* the previously recognized, but often ignored, intrarelationship between the study of
the world's religions and other scholarly pursuits became more evident. A scientific study of religion was now fully understood to be
one that utilized all appropriate methods of research into the subject. No longer was religion solely in the province of the theologian
or historian whose views issued primarily from the perspective of his
own religious tradition and its accustomed categories. The scholar
might be a theologian or a religious historian, but his qualifications
for the investigation of religion different from his own personal faith
were not related primarily to these matters. Religious phenomena
that were familiar and strange, enticing and repellent, apparently
structured and apparently chaotic, possibly ennobling and possibly
debilitating, perhaps containing ultimate truth and perhaps nothing

but fantasy—all were now to be approached as empirical fact without preconception of their value. The strange and unfamiliar in religious practice were not to be depreciated, but studied, because of their alienism. The repellent, the chaotic, the debilitating, the non-rational—each required that the scholar probe until he had attained an empathetic knowledge sufficient to overcome the pejorative connotation inherent in the terms he would first apply to them. The scientific study of religion was in need of all possible aids to the understanding of its subject.

An obvious first requirement in the study of a religion is to have available to the scholar the oral tradition and/or the written documents of the religion itself. If the religion is that of a preliterate people it is incumbent upon the primary investigator that he come to know the oral means of expression used in the articulation of the Weltanschauung and cultus of the religion. So, also, must the oral and written language be known in the case of a religion of a more developed culture, where written expressions of the beliefs, teachings, and practices are not only available but central to the religion and its history. It is for this reason that the linguistic and philological disciplines are pre-eminent partners with the scientific study of religions.

Nineteenth century students of language played a significant role in making available to the Western world the literature of the East. The literature of the great religions of antiquity, and the living religions of the non-Western world, were brought to the attention of Western scholars who could not study all languages, but had to depend upon the linguistic specialist for much of their materials. At the present time this contribution continues through the activity of Western and Eastern scholars as they pursue their tasks of philological study and the better translation of writings. Recognizing that an individual scholar of religion cannot know all or even a small majority of the languages of the religions with which he must be concerned, the scientific study of religion is dependent upon the contribution of scholars who devote themselves to the endeavor to convey to others the essential thought of a religion by a study of its language or languages. The history of religions as a developing discipline in America and elsewhere could not continue to exist without the support they supply.

Linguistic scholarship in religion, however, is not only a matter of the translation of documents. Those scholars who devote themselves to the study of one or a group of the non-Western languages are frequently immersed in the ethos and thought processes of a culture to a degree completely impossible for the non-language specialist. Even when the primary interest is not in the religion of the area, studies of the culture as a whole enable scholars to understand and interpret the several components of the culture in a manner not open to the student who does not possess the basic linguistic tools, or who concentrates on only part of the culture and society. In America contemporary scholarship in the area of the history of religions possesses much of its present vitality and promise for the future as a result of the increasing opportunity for future scholars to be trained in the Eastern languages in Amercian colleges and universities.

This availability of instruction in the languages of the non-European world is a development of the recent past. With few notable exceptions, academic centers were greatly limited in offering courses in which the undergraduate or graduate student could become proficient in either ancient or contemporary languages of the Near, Middle, and Far East. As a result, graduate students wishing to embark upon the study of the history of religions found themselves far behind European students who had been able to begin their language training at an earlier stage of their academic careers.

With the increasing interest in the non-Western world that arose in America after World War I a few universities were able to establish courses of instruction in the languages and history of the major areas of Asia and the Near East. Not until the time of World War II and immediately afterward, however, did general public support, student interest, and academic policy combine to create in any significant number integrated and adequate departments and programs for the study of the regional cultures of the non-Western world.

As a result of this development of area study programs concerned with the Near, Middle, and Far East, the study of the history of religions now has the essential support of other academic departments. The historian of religions is the beneficiary of the specialized study of a total culture and its history that can only be done by the scholar who limits himself to one general cultural area in order that he may attain the depth of knowledge that is needed to understand the area

31

in its total variety and its essential unity. This the historian of religions cannot do without ceasing to be a historian of religions and becoming a historian of one religion only. If he did this his scholarly contribution to the scientific study of religion might be considerable, but he would not be engaged in *Religionswissenschaft* as it has come to be differentiated from the study of a particular religion.

An outstanding feature in American higher education during the past decade and a half has been the rapid development of intensified area study programs at leading academic institutions into international centers for the study of the areas of the program's major concern, and the undertaking of more limited but equally significant studies in many of the universities and colleges across the country. Not only have general courses dealing with non-Western cultural areas been made available to American undergraduates but, of equal importance, the basic foundation has been laid for the support of American scholarship in non-Western cultural and related studies. The undergraduate can now more easily take advantage of the invitation and opportunity to pursue graduate studies in the area or areas of his interest; and opportunities for a professional scholarly career are also more available in colleges and universities. Further, we must not overlook the contribution to scholarship on the part of individuals who after their academic training embark on careers under governmental or private auspices that require them to reside in non-Western areas.[13]

A feature of such programs that has contributed greatly to the increase of scholarship has been the degree to which they have encouraged the training of non-Western students in the scholarship and methodology developed in the West for the study of human culture and society. Generally speaking, non-Western scholars have not produced from their own resources techniques of historical and cultural studies that are suitable to the contemporary situation or that are in accord with the present stage of the science of religion. By the development of centers in the West for the study of cultures, however, the formal training that the non-Western student has often

[13] The work of Sir Charles Eliot, a British foreign servant, is an example of the contribution to scholarly studies that can be made by a nonprofessional scholar. See his *Hinduism and Buddhism: An Historical Sketch,* 3 vols. (London: Edward Arnold & Co., 1921).

lacked has been made available to him. It is interesting to note the number of young men and women from the Middle and Far East who are advanced students in American and European universities where they study the history and culture of their own native societies. While they would not have come to the West in order to study the religious history and thought of their own tradition, the broader, and yet intense, discipline offered by area study programs gives them a more objective basis for the study of their own religious traditions as well as their culture as a whole.

The foundations being laid for scholarly production by non-Westerners themselves in the study of non-Western cultures is a major benefit arising from area study programs. While a primary concern of the younger scholars from these areas is usually related to the economic, political, and technological development of their home areas, they are also being trained for a humanistic study of their traditional environments. Their linguistic background and their sensitivity to the nuances of the culture and tradition of their early environment equip them to produce scholarly descriptions and sensitive interpretations of the history and culture of the areas from which they come in a manner almost impossible for the foreigner. The result of this development is already apparent as Western scholars come more and more to depend upon Eastern scholars for objective scholarship in the areas of their primary competency.

This is of immeasurable significance for the development of cultural studies. Every humanistic discipline needs wherever possible the benefit of the experience and insights of people who are on intimate terms with the matter being studied. True, those who are constituents of the cultural area under consideration may lose some of the closeness of their identity with it if they are trained to study it as observers. For the most part, however, they retain a capacity for insight and for empathetic description and analysis that often outweighs any disabilities in the matter of scholarly objectivity that their origin may impose upon them.

The study of religion is particularly benefited by the participation of scholars who are closely associated with the various religions of the world by birth and continued affiliation. While the methodology and tools of research most often used are products of Western scholarly development, the resources and insights available to the non-

Westerner are equally needed; attempts to create typologies and theoretical structures in order to comprehend better the phenomena of religion are subject to the useful corrective judgment of qualified scholars who are more than observers. An increasing number of the outstanding scholars of the history of religions are non-Westerners who have received some of their training in the area study programs offered by Western universities. Parenthetically, it is interesting to note the degree to which they, like their Christian counterparts of previous decades and today, are confronted with the problem of overcoming or, at least, placing in proper perspective their own theological inheritance and convictions.

Just as the development of area study programs was in large measure the result of a growth of interest in the languages of non-Western peoples and societies, so the beginnings and subsequent expansion of those studies we now term sociology and anthropology were related at inception in a significant degree to the nineteenth century concern with the origin of religion. Scholars of the eighteenth and nineteenth century were especially interested in the beginnings of cultural and social forms among groups of peoples, and in the main were convinced that the key to an understanding of the individual items within society was to be found in the origin of the phenomena and their subsequent development. Stated generally, the positions of thinkers such as David Hume and Adam Smith in the eighteenth century, or Auguste Comte in the nineteenth, were based upon the presupposition that the institutions and related beliefs of a society are the direct outgrowth of the characteristics or elements to be found in human nature. Therefore, the student of human society and of its institutions and thought-forms must focus his attention upon the societies themselves, considering them as natural organisms that are the outgrowth of natural man.

A corollary of this emphasis upon natural man in his early state, and upon society in its earliest forms, was the belief that man and society were in a process of inevitable development as a result of basic laws or principles inherent in man and reflected in societies that are the result of man's own process of evolution. Comte's law of intellectual development reflects this by its insistence that the nature of man's intellect ensures that all areas of human knowledge will go through three different theoretical states: the theological or fictitious state, the metaphysical or abstract state, and the scientific or positive state.

By and large the writers of the nineteenth century who devoted themselves to human nature and development, and to social institutions and forms, reflected the enthusiasm for natural man and the conviction of inevitable human and social progress that was characteristic of the time. They were theorists, not empirical investigators, far more concerned with discovering the origins of social forms than with the contemporary function and structure of elements within a given society. Not questioning the evolutionary progress of man and society, and seldom revealing an awareness that adequate knowledge of early forms and prior origins lay completely beyond their capacity to discover, they presented their hypothetical conclusions as if they were established facts resting firmly upon fieldwork investigation. Fieldwork was, unfortunately, an activity subsequent rather than prior to their conclusions. It was only in the last decades of the nineteenth century that significant beginnings of "on the spot" studies of foreign societies, particularly primitive societies, were made. This development was to bring sociological and anthropological studies to their present positions as significant scientific disciplines in the twentieth century.

The comparative study of religions typical of the beginning of the twentieth century was closely allied with the studies and theories propounded by the sociologists and anthropologists of the time. Convinced of the primary importance of the origin of social phenomena, students of religion were greatly dependent upon the theories put forth by genetic and evolutionary anthropologists. William Robertson Smith, Sir Edward Tylor, and Sir James Frazer are notable examples of scholars who combined their study of religion with the anthropological theories of the time, or vice versa, with the result that their conclusions were all too often determined by the presuppositions from which they proceeded rather than by the materials that they studied. Nevertheless, since scholarship can also be advanced by its errors of method and theory when these are recognized by subsequent students, the contributions to the study of religion by these scholars and their contemporaries is of signal importance.

35

Their errors were primarily the result of the conviction that despite obvious complexities their search for beginnings, for relationships resulting from the given natural state and psychological structure of all men, and for relationships and similarities arising out of diffusion through numerous societies from a common source was assured of success as an inevitable consequence of the evolutionary progress which was central to their thinking.

The contribution of sociological and anthropological studies to the scientific study of religion at the present time is of paramount significance because each of the three disciplines has ceased to place its emphasis upon theories as such, and instead now stresses the primacy of objective descriptive analysis. True, theorists and their supporting schools of thought continue to engage in scholarly debate, but the significant development is that the theories are defended or attacked on the basis of empirical evidence to a greater extent than previously existed. It would be erroneous to suggest that any scholarly discipline worthy of the name is not constantly erecting theories that appear to be applicable to its subject matter and that appear to lead to a more adequate understanding of it. Those areas of study that we term humanistic and social, however, appear to achieve a measure of scientific status in direct proportion to their freedom from dogmatic theories that are not at every moment subject to the correction of observable fact. In this empirical emphasis they today find much of their strength and ability to contribute to the growth of human knowledge. This method is, without doubt, also a limitation upon a scholar's ultimate ability to probe to the core of those phenomena within his purview that do not disclose their ultimate natures to an examination of their structure and function only.

Fortunately, contemporary sociologists of religion, social anthropologists, and students of culture and society are often aware of the self-imposed limitations that they must maintain in their studies if their scholarship is to retain its integrity. When they are aware of the complexity of religious content and function within a social group and in the life of the individual person, when they even dimly perceive the nature of religious experience as it is expressed in theological and philosophical categories, they are quick to acknowledge that the value of their studies does not lie in the discovery of the *ultimate* nature of religion itself. "Those of us who study the sociolog-

36

ical implications of religion will err . . . if we imagine that our work will reveal the nature and essence of religion itself." [14] The anthropologist or sociologist is concerned with the values of a phenomenon as a part of the totality of a culture, and he is hopeful that the phenomenon will cast light upon the values of a comparable aspect in another society. It is to be questioned however, whether it is his scholarly function as an anthropologist or as a sociologist to arrive at universal social and cultural values as such.[15]

As a result of the emergence during this century of sociological and anthropological studies as scientific means for gathering factual information about social institutions and structures, the study of religion is able to ascertain in a degree hitherto unknown the interrelationship of religion with its corresponding components within a given society. Anthropology has centered its attentions upon preliterate and tribal peoples, while sociology has focused upon the more developed social structures of the world. In each case, the understanding of religion in its community expressions and forms has greatly benefited, and the history of religions has been enriched as an area of scholarly research.

A discussion of the interrelationship between the history of religions and other scholarly endeavors that complement and strengthen it must make mention, at least, of the potential contribution of psychology to the study of religion. It is necessary, however, to speak of the potential role of psychology in this matter because of its present failure to make the contributions that its advocates confidently expected at the beginning of this century. With the exception of the few psychologists of religion who are teaching in theological seminaries and a number of practicing psychologists who have written on the subject of psychology and religion, few psychologists in academic positions have devoted their scholarship to the psychology of religion itself.

In Europe the attempt of Friedrich Schleiermacher at the beginning of the nineteenth century to define religion in terms of "feeling" contributed to the growth of theological and philosophical interests in an investigation of the individual and his religious experience. The

[14] Joachim Wach, *Sociology of Religion* (U. of Chicago, 1944), p. 4.
[15] See the discussion on this problem in *An Appraisal of Anthropology Today*, ed. Sol Tax *et al.* (U. of Chicago, 1953), pp. 322-41.

interest of Hegel, Feuerbach, Fechner, Lotze, Brentano, and Wundt in the growing investigation of the psychological aspects of religion and religious experience is indicative of the rapidly developing conviction that in such studies the key to the *homo religiosus* is to be found. In general, however, psychology as it developed not only repudiated metaphysics but tended to give less and less attention to religious phenomena. While it would be too extreme to maintain that all psychologists have considered religion to be an aberration and have therefore approached it only in this light, it is true that the study of religion has not aroused the interest of psychological scholarship that was to be expected from the nature of the modern beginnings of psychological study.

In America the psychological study of religion received its greatest impetus from the work of William James, particularly by the publication of his *The Varieties of Religious Experience* in 1902. In the preceding decade there had begun to appear a number of articles and a few books by a group of scholars who were to be the pioneers in the development of the psychology of religion as an academic discipline in theological schools. Under the leadership of Professors Starbuck, Hall, Leuba, and Coe, the early years of this century witnessed a growing enthusiasm among church scholars for the psychological study of religion. This interest was not shared by professional psychologists as a group, however, and the contributions of psychology to the history of religions have been slight. With the exception of certain studies of religious mysticism, the majority of those who did devote themselves to studies in the psychology of religion came more and more to center their interests in religious nurture and problems related to religious education of the young. As a result, the few scholarly contributions of the psychology of religion to the history of religions in America have come more often from leading international theorists in the realm of psychology and psychoanalysis than from American academic psychologists.[16]

The foregoing references to the relationship between the history of religions understood as *Religionswissenschaft* and other scholarly

---

[16] The contribution of psychological theories and studies to the consideration of religious symbols is an instance of the increasing role that psychology can and should play in the study of *Religionswissenschaft*. See, for example, the studies by Mircea Eliade.

disciplines will serve, it is hoped, to indicate the degree to which the progress of the history of religions in recent years has been related to the advance of scholarship in these other areas. By their rapid achievement of academic position in American colleges and universities and by the contributions of additional knowledge and insight into human history and society, these sciences have supported the history of religions in America in its continued effort to become *Religionswissenschaft.* It is certainly to be hoped and confidently expected that other areas of study that have obvious correlations with the study of religion, and that in some instances have already made contributions to American historians of religions, such as the study of artistic and aesthetic expressions, will join with the historian of religions in his efforts to understand more adequately the phenomena that collectively constitute the religious dimension.

⋞ 7 ⋟

It has been evident throughout this essay that I have been confronted with the problem of finding the proper, or more preferable, term to use for the academic discipline that is the subject of my discussion. I have suggested that the *history of religions* or *comparative religions* —the two designations most often used in America—has been in the recent past an area of scholarship in search for an adequate definition of itself. The study of religion outside the Judeo-Christian tradition, with certain exceptions relating to the religions of antiquity, has been pursued under both of these titles. Properly understood and correctly pursued, historical and comparative studies of religion are recognized as being fundamental aspects in the study of religion that is now made possible by the available methods of scholarship and the requirements of humanistic studies in general. This essay has indicated, however, that the scope of the modern study of religion is not adequately designated by the use of either or both of the terms *historical* or *comparative;* nor does it reflect the essential character of the scholarship that is involved.

The growing use by European scholars of the phrase *the science of religion* indicated their realization that it was only through the use of a variety of disciplines, and the development of the "new" studies of their time, that the varied data which constitute the totality of the

39

phenomenon religion could be described and understood adequately. By the use of the term *science* they sought to divorce their studies from the theological elements and concerns that had marked the Western study of religions. They were convinced that it is possible for the scholar to arrive at conclusions about religion that are objective in both fact and interpretation.

Nevertheless, many of these scholars were conscious that the nature of religion is such that it can be neither described nor understood adequately solely by a description of the empirical in its historical structure or sequence. Further, some were aware that comparative analysis of the constituent elements of religion, no matter from what source or by what investigators, was not sufficient in itself to probe to the necessary depths demanded by the very nature of the subject matter. As students of religion trained for the most part in the classical tradition of the nineteenth century, they were cognizant of the new scholarly resources that promised greatly increased knowledge of their subject. By a combination of these new means of study, the historical and comparative methods already in process of development, and an as yet not fully conceived element, they hoped to create a science of religion.

In conjunction with the development of teaching and scholarship in the history of religions in America in the past few decades, scholars have increasingly devoted themselves to the attempt to create a workable definition of their enterprise. In so doing they have taken into account the several disciplines that have been mentioned as co-partners and contributors to the study of religion, and they have sought to give recognition to their essential role in a scholarly approach to the phenomenon of religion. In isolated instances they have succumbed to the claims of one of these disciplines to the extent that they have placed that particular approach at the apex of what they have then determined to be the science of religion. In such cases the science of religion has become the following of one particular avenue of scholarly research combined with the insights made available by other and adjacent means of study.

Both European and American scholars, however, have rightly objected that the science of religion cannot be any *one* of the disciplines that have come to be recognized as essential partners in the scholarly approach to religion. If it were primarily only one of them, such as archaeology, history, sociology, etc., the history of religions as a distinct pursuit would not have attained the needed scholarly approach to the complexities and varieties of religion, nor would it be capable of achieving the total insight and knowledge without which religion continues to be more unknown than known. Readily aware of the significant contributions of each of the means of study, those who have as their main concern religion itself have continued to maintain that no one of these is sufficient as the primary element to be used in conjunction with the others.

Nor, it is contended, can the science of religion be defined as the use of a combination of the disciplines discussed. Here, again, the separate and distinct yet interrelated contributions of the various areas of study are recognized. Even when the results of all the methods with their separate insights are placed together in a meaningful manner, however, there are those who hold that the ultimate aim, method, and results of the scientific study of religion would not thus be obtained. An element remains lacking, and without it the science of religion would continue to be a descriptive discipline restrained by its announced methodology and purpose from penetrating into the center of its subject matter. Description is essential, of course, and this is the foundation upon which a study seeking scholarly status must rest; yet the student of religion finds himself unable to be content with description alone.

The refusal by students of religion to be content with a discipline limited to description is found by some to be adequate ground for the exclusion of such studies from the academic curriculum. Misunderstanding this search for something more on the part of scholars of religion, the critics often assume that it must be the search for metaphysical truth whereby religious value and disvalue will be declared to have been established on objective scholarly grounds. In other words, they are of the opinion that the theological concern that was characteristic of the earlier comparative approach continues to be at the heart of any study of religion that demands something more than a descriptive analysis. They consider any claim that the study of religion can be pursued scientifically to be false because it will not give up an element of personal theological value judgment or subjectivity that they consider to be foreign to the scientific spirit; and, further, they dispute the contention that scholars in the field are able to detach themselves from an overriding solicitude for metaphysical matters that are more properly the province of theology and, perhaps, philosophy.

A significant attempt to meet this problem was made by Professor Erwin Goodenough of Yale University in 1959 at a meeting of American scholars called together for the purpose of considering the feasibility of organizing a scholarly society among those engaged in the study of the world's religions. In a paper entitled "Religionswissenschaft," he attacked the idea that "science, philosophy, and religion move on different levels of knowledge, and that through revelation we go beyond the whole scientific method, because science must draw its conclusions from analyses of material that can be counted and measured." [17] It was his contention that the science of religion aims to move from empirical religious data "to hypothesis, and from hypothesis back to data, and to correct hypothesis by data, as nearly as possible in scientific fashion." For Professor Goodenough there is a limitation to the scope of the science of religion, but that limitation does not impose itself within the realm of empirical data that, by definition, is the legitimate area of scientific investigation. The data are submissible to the application of present and future scientific methods and the only limitation is the inevitable result of present but not necessarily permanent inadequacy on the part of scholarship.

In company with those scholars who have succeeded in penetrating the exterior manifestations of the phenomena of religion, Goodenough is quick to point out that the serious student must look beyond the data. As a scholar who seeks to follow a scientific method, for him the basic approach to his subject matter must be one that is descriptive and that arrives at hypotheses as a result of the phenomena described. Nevertheless, recognizing that religion is not finally reducible to an element or essence that, given present tools of scholarship and method, can be fully understood by such an approach, he holds it to be the one available method whereby progress can be made *toward* the as yet unattainable objective of the study of religion, namely, total understanding.

> The tremendum about us and within us will still have n dimensions. Religionswissenschaft in the mid-twentieth century can take

17 ACLS *Newsletter,* X, 6 (June 1959), 5 ff.

us not to total understanding . . . , but to somewhat greater comprehension of man in his religious problem. It can do so only as we combine science and religion in our very marrow, combine them into a dedication to learning about religion by the slow, dogged approach of science.[18]

It is by the scientific approach that the essential element at present inaccessible to such a method will ultimately be brought to light.

Goodenough and others who would agree with him in his emphasis have not abandoned the underlying concern and conviction of the earliest exponents of a science of religion. They were convinced, and their successors remain hopeful, that by the use of a scholarly methodology that is essentially "scientific" not only will there be found new and significant insight into the nature of religious experience and its individual and collective expressions, but also (and this is of even greater importance) that discoveries will be made that will enable the scholar to achieve at least a beginning comprehension of the "tremendum." By the scientific study of religion the scholar can approach the problem of valuation with criteria that are free from the provincial theological biases of the past, criteria that are based upon the universal religious experience and history of mankind.

Two of the leading scholars in the history of religions in America in recent years, both European born and trained, have been the late Joachim Wach and his present successor at the University of Chicago, Mircea Eliade. Exhibiting the intense concern with problems of methodology that has characterized Continental scholars identified with *Religionswissenschaft,* both have reflected in their writings the realization that a primary effort must be devoted to the continuing problem of method. While not suggesting that the task of gathering data is complete, or ever will be while the human experience of religion continues, they have continued in their writings and lectures to challenge American historians of religions to direct their attention to the development of more adequate techniques and procedures.

Always stressing the necessity that the historian of religions must seek the goal of "integral understanding" of the religions he is studying, Wach placed emphasis upon the necessary personal equip-

[18] *Ibid.,* p. 18.

43

ment essential to the historian of religions.[19] He stated the need for the student of religion to have the "most extensive information possible." By this emphasis Wach was not only pointing to the obvious need for knowledge about a religion on the part of the scholar who is studying it; he meant also to indicate the importance to the historian of religions of a knowledge in depth of the phenomenon of religion wherever it is to be found. The expert in one religion must also be cognizant of the nature, history, and expressions of religion beyond the one religion he seeks to understand. Adequate understanding of one religion is seldom, if ever, achieved by knowledge about that religion only. The historian of religions needs to possess wide knowledge of his subject in its universal expressions if he is to fathom one religion in depth.

Further, when the scholar seeks to understand a religion that is not his own, his personal "emotional condition" is of paramount importance. This, of course, has been a serious problem in the area of hermeneutics for all humanistic and social studies. There have been those who have sought to maintain that the true nature of a religion is best discovered by the observer who is able to maintain himself aloof from a personal involvement in it and from religion in general. He may be convinced of its importance in human history as a phenomenon affecting individuals and societies; but, it has been argued, he is better equipped as a scholar to describe and interpret a religion if he himself is not involved or committed to that religion or any other. It was Wach's firm belief that there must be an engagement between the observer and the observed, an engagement wherein interest in the observed religion is not limited to a recognition of its importance as a social or cultural factor, but rather, is primarily focused upon the attempt to participate with its adherents in their experience and the resulting expressions of that experience. There must be an "engagement of feeling," and this can only be achieved when there is concern with the values that are held to exist within the religion by its adherents.

Closely related to this is Wach's emphasis upon the need for the student of a foreign religion to have a constructive purpose. In this he was pointing to the biased and, therefore, inadequate interpreta-

[19] See Wach, *The Comparative Study of Religions*, pp. 11ff.

tion of non-Christian religions that resulted from a theological or missionary attempt to establish their erroneous or defective nature. In addition, he was particularly aware that with the development of nontheological or nonreligious orientations in the study of religions, there are some scholars who, by their failure to appreciate the more subtle values of religion discernible to the religious person, produce erroneous analyses of the religions they seek to interpret. Recognizing that differences of understanding and appreciation are inevitable, and that there is a necessary place in scholarship for criticism founded upon scholarly evaluation, Wach nevertheless maintained that the purpose behind the study of the history of religions must be constructive. If this were not the case the results of the endeavor would be greater misunderstanding and perversion of the religion or religious phenomenon under investigation.

Wach's suggestions about the personal equipment of the historian of religions are applicable to most, if not all, humanistic studies. However, the layman who is not acquainted with the development of the study of the history of religions will fail to grasp the problems the discipline has faced, and continues to confront, if he does not recognize that these apparently obvious requirements of the historian of religions are often not met by those who study, teach, and write about the religions of the world. The variety of human religious experience and expression demands that the historian of religions understand the multiformed nature of his subject. If he does not, he may be a historian of Buddhism, or of Christianity, or of Islam, etc., he is not a historian of religions. If the student of religion is motivated only by idle curiosity or by a recognition of historical importance alone and lacks the necessary emotional condition that would enable him to achieve empathy with the matter under investigation, his "understanding" does not attain the depth demanded by his subject. Finally, if the purpose of scholarship is to destroy the subject that is studied and if the subject be religion, it is the contention of contemporary historians of religions that not only is objectivity lost as in any partisan prejudice, but an understanding of the essential nature of that about which understanding is sought is thwarted.

Professor Eliade in his numerous writings has pointed repeatedly to the basic requirement that the nature of his subject matter places

45

upon the historian of religions.[20] This, he contends, is the necessity that the historian of religions seek to understand religious experience and expression "on their own plane of reference." While many things are important, such as the efforts to gather historical fact, to gather and classify under types the various expressions of religion, to isolate a particular phenomenon and then, perhaps, to endeavor to determine its possible relationship to other similar phenomena, these do not constitute the whole task of the historian of religions.

The historian of religions must use the empirical method in approaching his subject. The facts of religion are to be discovered and studied within the historical context; there is, however, yet more depth and breadth to comprehend. The problem that we have continually noted remains, for, as Eliade remarks, the historian of religions has to "complete his historical work as phenomenologist or philosopher of religion." The scholar, if he is scientific in any acceptable sense of the term, is bound first to the task of ascertaining historical fact, but he must as a historian of religions "decipher in a 'fact,' conditioned as it is by the historical moment and the cultural style of the epoch, the existential situation that made it possible." Eliade would not deny that historians in general are also concerned with the existential situation of their data. By his emphasis upon it he is seeking to remind his readers that for the historian of religions to ignore this would be to defeat the purpose that lies at the very foundation of the study of religion.

Further, to state "that a religious datum is always a historical datum does not mean that it is reducible to a non-religious history. . . ." Religious phenomena are historical phenomena, but error is made when the historian of religions or others ignore the peculiarly "religious" quality of the phenomena by exclusive or major emphasis upon them as only aspects of economic, social, or political history. Again, the specific phenomenon must be understood on its "own plane of reference." If the phenomenon is a religious one, the plane of reference, no matter what other factors may be present, is fundamentally *religious*.

[20] The following discussion is dependent primarily upon Eliade's "Methodological Remarks on the Study of Religious Symbolism," *The History of Religions,* ed. Mircea Eliade and Joseph M. Kitagawa (U. of Chicago, 1959), pp. 86-107; and "History of Religions and A New Humanism," *History of Religions,* I (Summer 1961), 1-8.

In company with others, Eliade suggests that the attempt to consider the essence of a religious phenomenon is analogous to the problem that faces the student of aesthetics. The historical factors surrounding aesthetic production are of great significance; yet the totality of the aesthetic expression cannot be reduced to them without the loss of the "individual experiences" of the creator and of the observer and of the "transpersonal realities" inherent to the work. The fact that the particular universe of works of art, or of religious phenomena, "is not the physical universe of immediate experience does not imply their non-reality." The *homo religiosus* is not understood in his full nature as *homo religiosus,* nor is aesthetic expression understood in its fullness as *aesthetic* expression, unless the particular mode of being essential to each is recognized and accepted by the observer who seeks to understand them.

Maintaining that religiohistorical data can best be integrated by the methodology that is peculiar to the science of religion as it has developed in recent decades, Eliade is aware that contemporary historians of religions are extremely reluctant to formulate generalizations concerning religious phenomena. By this reluctance they are failing to perform the task for which their scholarship prepares them above all others.

In his consideration of the reasons for this reluctance Professor Eliade discusses two problems that have confronted the scientific study of religion since early in the present century. First, there is the fact that the history of religions covers all of human history and, therefore, puts before the scholar such an immense amount of data that it is obvious no one scholar can master even a minor portion of it. The individual student of religions who knows a little about a lot of religious phenomena cannot claim to be a scholar of the history of religions. Therefore, the scholar must purposely devote himself to what, in reality, is but a small portion of the discipline in which he claims scholarship.

The answer that Eliade gives to this problem is one that must be clearly recognized and accepted by historians of religions and their scholarly colleagues. "It is not a question, for the historian of religions, of *substituting himself for the various specialists,* that is to say, of mastering their respective philologies. . . . One is a historian of religions not by virtue of mastering a certain number of philologies,

47

but because one is able to integrate religious data into a general perspective." The historian of religions must demand of himself that he obtain a reasonable knowledge of the scholarly productions of his colleagues in all the disciplines that contribute to an understanding of religious phenomena, and it is incumbent upon him that, combining this knowledge with the fruits of his own studies of religion, he venture into the task of integrating the results that are in his possession. I suggest that this, ultimately, is his function as a historian of religions; it distinguishes him and his discipline from that of other scholars who study much that is of a common subject matter.

Second, Eliade notes the "philosophical timidity" of many scholars who are engaged in the detailed research essential to the historian of religions. Convinced that adequate study and understanding of religion on their part demands specialization and conclusions only in their speciality, and keenly aware of the many and varied theories that were so freely offered by their predecessors some decades ago, the contemporary historian of religions is content to leave to others, "linguists, anthropologists, sociologists, ethnologists, and philosophers," the presentation of general theories concerning religion.

This hesitancy to venture publicly into the pronouncement of integrating theories about religious phenomena is not unrelated to the desire of the historian of religions to gain the confidence of his academic colleagues in other disciplines. The decline of the teaching of the history of religions in America was undoubtedly related to the suspicion created by the association of comparative studies of religion with theological and missionary interests. Because of these interests it was inevitable that generalizations and theories were produced that did not reflect the scholarly objectivity that was claimed. Today, the historian of religions is often more shy of generalizations than he has scholarly reason to be, because of his desire to erase the false image of his discipline that remains from the past.

One of the most suggestive discussions of the present state and future development of the study of religions in recent years by an American scholar has been presented by Professor Wilfred Cantwell Smith of Harvard University.[21] He endeavors to make clear what appears to him to be the essential next step if the study of religions is to achieve the results that have been the hope of past and

21 Smith, *op. cit.*, pp. 31-58.

present historians of religions. It is, I think, an essential move in the direction toward the achievement of what Joachim Wach meant by "integral understanding." Professor Smith summarizes his argument as follows:

> The traditional forms of Western scholarship in the study of other men's religion was that of an impersonal presentation of an "it." The first great innovation in recent times has been the personalization of the faiths observed, so that one finds a discussion of a "they." Presently the observer becomes personally involved, so that the situation is one of a "we" talking about a "they." The next step is dialogue, where "we" talk to "you." If there is listening and mutuality, this may become that "we" talk *with* "you." The culmination of this progress is when "we all" are talking *with* each other about "us." [22]

Smith is suggesting what I believe to be the primary element that must be included in the scientific study of religions. This is the factor of the *personal* in religion, the fundamental constituent that, while amenable to scientific inquiry, continues ultimately to defy such investigation except as persons confront and are confronted by other persons. Today Western religion is not alone in its investigation of other religions. Each of the contemporary viable religions is now engaged in a consideration of itself as it increasingly sees itself in the light of the other religions and the totality of the human religious experience. But, even at the level of this confrontation, it is not a matter of one religious institution or system of belief facing others. It remains in essence the meeting of *persons* with *persons*. This is the element that cannot be confined to a description of the empirical in its historical structure or sequence.

In the study of religious phenomena of the past the science of religions, despite all of its present resources, will not be able to capture completely the personal element that is always at the center of religious expression. In the scholarly consideration of religion as it is now, and as it will be, the historian of religions must continue to seek the "integral understanding" that will result only as the religiously sensitive scholar meets the person of faith.

[22] *Ibid.*, p. 34. Dialogue, of course, cannot be achieved in studying archaic religions, and probably not in the instance of contemporary primitive religions. Much is gained, however, when scholars progress from the "it" approach to the "we–they" recognition of human religious aspirations present in such religions.

OLD TESTAMENT STUDIES

ᵈᵍᵇ

HARRY M. ORLINSKY

PROFESSOR OF BIBLE
HEBREW UNION COLLEGE–JEWISH INSTITUTE OF RELIGION
NEW YORK CITY

The writer acknowledges with pleasure the critical reading of this essay by Professors J. J. Finkelstein (University of California, Berkeley), Hyman Kublin (Brooklyn College), H. G. May (Graduate School of Theology, Oberlin College), and G. E. Wright (Harvard Divinity School). The essay was improved by their critical comments; the short-comings remain the writer's.

≈§§≈

Old Testament studies on this side of the ocean in the past three decades have differed radically from those of the decades preceding. The differences are due primarily to an older, growing tendency coming into contact with two entirely new factors. The Bible had for long been under severe attack. Nineteenth century European rationalism had seriously weakened the authority of the Bible as divinely revealed scripture; and, furthermore, the kind of analysis and discoveries that marked biblical research in pre-World War I days tended to lessen considerably the value of the Bible as history. Few scholars tended to accept biblical statements as correct without additional, extrabiblical proof. This rationalistic approach reached fruition in recent decades, though in a way hardly anticipated by its adherents, as a result of two far-reaching factors: (1) the unprecedented upsurge of archaeology, and (2) the sociopolitical conditions that developed as a result of the American and world depression that was ushered in by the Wall Street Crash of 1929. How this came to pass constitutes the essential theme of this essay.

≈§ 1 §≈

Old Testament Studies Prior to about 1930

Biblical research in the late nineteenth and early twentieth centuries —the term *biblical* (or *Bible*) will in this essay connote the Hebrew Bible, the Old Testament, alone—generally dealt with the philology, i.e., the grammatical and textual analysis of the Bible; or else it attempted to determine the authorship and the relative, or absolute, date of each section, often each chapter and even each verse, of each biblical book. And since extrabiblical data were then available in but rather meager measure, it was chiefly the biblical writings themselves that were closely analyzed. This was the period when the great introductions to the Bible were composed, when the standard grammars, dictionaries, and encyclopedias were worked up.

Among the introductions, the most notable were Julius Wellhausen and Friedrich Bleek's *Einleitung in das alte Testament,* 5th ed.

53

(1896), and S. R. Driver's *Introduction to the Literature of the Old Testament* (1891; last revised edition, 1913). In the other categories, the pre-eminent representatives were probably F. E. König's *Historisch-kritisches Lehrgebäude* and *Historisch-comparative Syntax der hebräischen Sprache* (3 vols., 1881-97) and F. H. W. Gesenius's *Hebrew Grammar,* 28th ed. (1910), edited and enlarged by E. F. Kautzsch and revised and translated by A. E. Cowley; Francis Brown, S. R. Driver, and C. A. Briggs' *Hebrew and English Lexicon of the Old Testament* (1906) and the thirteenth edition of Gesenius's *Hebräisches und aramäisches Handwörterbuch über das alte Testament* (1899) by F. P. W. Buhl (with Albert Socin and Heinrich Zimmern); the *Dictionary of the Bible* (4 vols. and Extra Volume, 1898-1904) edited by James Hastings (H. H. Rowley and F. C. Grant revised the *Dictionary* in one volume in 1963); and the *Encyclopaedia Biblica* (4 vols., 1899-1903) edited by T. K. Cheyne and J. S. Black. Nor should Carl Brockelmann's ambitious *Grundriss der vergleichende Grammatik der semitischen Sprachen* (2 vols., 1908 and 1913) go unmentioned.

But the time for reconstructing the career of biblical Israel had not yet come. Brave attempts had been made in that direction, e.g., in Bernhard Stade and Oskar Holtzmann's *Geschichte des Volkes Israel* (2 vols., 1887-88); Rudolf Kittel's *Geschichte des Volkes Israel,* 7th ed. (3 vols., 1923-25 and 1927-29); Eduard Meyer's *Die Israeliten und ihre Nachbarstämme* (1906), which has *Beiträgen* by Bernhard Luther; and especially—and even now still useful and most stimulating—Julius Wellhausen's *Prolegomena zur Geschichte Israels,* 6th ed. (1905) and *Israelitische und jüdische Geschichte,* 4th ed. (1901).

This was the heyday of philology and textual criticism in the lower and higher institutions of learning all over Europe. The classical and medieval areas of study—involving Greek and Latin essentially—revolved about philology; it was natural that the cultures of the ancient Israelites and other Bible peoples were studied along the same lines, with Hebrew and Arabic the chief languages involved. There was no reason for Semitic departments and theological seminaries to differ in this respect from their "Greco-Roman" counterparts.

ক্ষ 2 ৪৯

The Age of Archaeology

The consequences of archaeology for the new kind of study of the Bible have been so far-reaching that the adjective *revolutionary* comes to mind at once, and correctly so. Virtually all nontextual and many textual studies have become antiquated or obsolescent because of what archaeology has wrought.

Whence suddenly archaeology? Eighteenth and nineteenth century Europe was the scene of nationalistic growth and imperialistic expansion. By the time that most of Europe had been carved up among a few major and many more minor powers, several of the nations—notably England, France, and Germany—had extended their interests and claims into major regions of western Asia. One of the cultural aspects of European imperialism was the pursuit of knowledge not alone of the contemporary but also of the ancient peoples who inhabited the lands between the Tigris and Euphrates Rivers on the east and the Nile River on the west.

The physical remains of the past that were already exposed came first to be studied, sometimes even transported to one or another capital city or outstanding museum in Europe. Egypt, Sumer, Assyria, Babylonia—notable civilizations of the last three millennia B.C.—began to emerge from their graves of dust, even if yet only imperfectly and sporadically. Hieroglyphic and cuneiform inscriptions, along with other documents that, while not epigraphic, told their tale no less clearly and reliably—pottery, walls, floors, figures, statues, gods, frescoes, reliefs, and the like—provided the supplementary materials badly needed for scholars to begin to reconstruct the history of the Bible lands of old: "supplementary" because the Bible itself had long constituted a major primary source for this period and area, but "badly needed" because the Bible—in the absence of adequate extrabiblical data—was an inadequate and hence sometimes misleading source for the reconstruction of the history of the peoples it mentions.

Sporadic surface exploration, however, and what then passed for archaeology did not yet provide the historian of antiquity with sufficient data. Moreover, it was an antiquated and suspicious feudalist

55

society, characterized by the sprawling Ottoman Empire, that then dominated that part of the world and that made for additional difficulty for those who were beginning to devote themselves to the creation and development of a new branch of science, investigation by systematic excavation. Important as was the pioneering work of the early explorers and archaeologists—the name of W. M. Flinders Petrie, at the least, should not go unmentioned here—and valuable as were the monuments and other documents that were brought to light, e.g., the Rosetta Stone (1799), the Behistun Inscription (from 1835 on), the Moabite Stone (1868), the Siloam Inscription (1880), the Tell el-Amarna Tablets (1887), and the Code of Hammurabi (1901-02)—some accidentally discovered by ordinary people—it was only after World War I, when the Ottoman Empire collapsed and England and France came to occupy or otherwise control most of western Asia, that archaeology came into its own as a fully developed and refined discipline.

Scientific digging on an extensive scale became possible for the first time. For one thing, the enlightened attitude of the new European powers was encouraging to responsible scholars and institutions who were willing to spend time and money in excavation. Second, a new major power had arisen in the world as a result of the great conflict of 1914-18, the United States. Archaeologically speaking, this phenomenon was reflected in the coming to life of the American School of Oriental Research in Jerusalem (which had been in existence since 1900) and of the creation of a second School in Baghdad.

Prior to World War I the notable achievements of Americans in Palestinian research were Edward Robinson's epoch-making *Biblical* and *Later Biblical Researches in Palestine and in the Adjacent Regions* (3 vols., 1856; two volumes on the 1838 expedition with Eli Smith, one volume on the 1852 expedition), and G. A. Reisner and C. S. Fisher's excavation of Samaria (1908-10) for Harvard University. The new surge of activity coincided with the arrival of W. F. Albright at the American School in Jerusalem, first as Fellow (1919-20) and then as Director (1920-29, 1933-36). Other men and academies of learning joined in this intriguing area of investigation, e.g., the University of Pennsylvania's Museum (at Beth-shan), the University of Chicago's Oriental Institute (at Megiddo), and Haverford College (at Beth-shemesh).

But it was chiefly the American Schools and Albright, sometimes in association with Pittsburgh–Xenia Seminary and with McCormick (formerly Presbyterian) Theological Seminary, that stood out in this endeavor. It was they, along with such stalwarts as C. S. Fisher, Père H. L. Vincent of the Dominican École Biblique et Archéologique Française de Jérusalem, and Albrecht Alt, and alongside such institutions as the British Palestine Exploration Fund, that raised biblical archaeology to a high standard, attracted many fine talents, and provided a firm and broad basis for a new approach to the study of the Bible. Indeed, the history of biblical studies in the past three or four decades, in the United States and in Palestine–Israel, perhaps more than elsewhere, has largely been the history of biblical archaeology.

First and above all, there is the matter of biblical history. The darkest periods in ancient Israel's history had long been the second millennium B.C., covering Hebrew origins, the Egyptian experience, the conquest of Canaan, the period of the Judges, and the beginnings of the Israelite monarchy. It was not that the period of the first millennium was all light, or is even now all clarity—far from it!—but the history of the several major and minor societies among which Israel originated and took shape, and the historical setting—that is, the time and place and motivation of the composition—of the biblical texts dealing with Hebraic beginnings were either altogether unknown or vexingly elusive.

The first clear breakthrough, following several important excavations and scores of articles, was Albright's *The Archaeology of Palestine and the Bible* (1932; 2nd ed., 1933), in which new archaeological data were utilized to demonstrate that, far from being wholly or largely fictitious and the creation of a later period, the biblical accounts of the patriarchal period were to be taken, in their broad outline, quite seriously. Abraham, Isaac, and Jacob, their spouses and their experiences, were no longer to be dismissed as mythological; they were basically real, even if not established as literally historical. This point of view, derived altogether from the practice and results of archaeology, was nothing short of revolutionary in its approach

57

to the Bible as a source for history and in its influence on biblical studies from then on.

Up to then, and throughout the Thirties, only one serious history of biblical Israel had been produced in the United States, A. T. Olmstead's *History of Palestine and Syria* (1931). The author listed or described the archaeological data, both material and literary, that were then available; but the time had not yet come for the weaving together of pertinent archaeological data with biblical data discriminately employed. (In Europe, the only serious history produced was W. O. E. Oesterley and T. H. Robinson's two-volume *History of Israel* [1932]; though the Preface indicated that use was made of archeological data in the *History,* none really was.)

It was chiefly the excavations proper and the publication of the archaeological data themselves that were of prime importance for the biblical scholar in the Twenties and Thirties. It is thrilling to look back from the vantage point of our early Sixties and scan the quantity and quality of the initial reports and the more detailed analyses of excavations. The most important dig, not for spectacular finds but for helping to lay a solid foundation for excavator and interpreter alike, was probably that of Tell Beit Mirsim (perhaps biblical Kiriath-sepher) by Albright—four campaigns from 1926 to 1932. The dig itself, the presentation of it, and the use made of it in biblical analysis are clearly conveyed in his model volumes, *The Excavation of Tell Beit Mirsim* (1932), *The Bronze Age* (1937), and *The Iron Age* (1943). The most important organs in the field were easily the *Bulletin of the American Schools of Oriental Research* (henceforth simply *Bulletin*) and the *Annual,* both associated with the fine editorial work of Albright; they exhibit biblical archaeology at its best, from its serious beginnings in the earlier Twenties to its high level of deserved authority at the present. (In Europe, the *Palestine Exploration Fund Quarterly Statement* stood out, joined in time by such fine journals as *Révue biblique, Palästinajahrbuch, Bulletin of the Israel* [formerly *Jewish Palestine*] *Exploration Society,* the *Israel Exploration Journal,* and the annual *Eretz-Israel.*) For the less initiate, the Schools have been publishing since 1938 the excellent and unique *Biblical Archaeologist* under the imaginative editorship of G. E. Wright, with whom, in 1952, F. M. Cross Jr. became associated as co-editor and F. V. Filson as assistant in New Testament matters; in 1959 E. F. Campbell Jr. replaced Cross and has now (1963) become sole editor.

Several fine works have been written in this country on what biblical archaeology is, and on its rise and present scope. Among the older works, Millar Burrows' *What Mean These Stones?* (1941), C. C. McCown's *The Ladder of Progress in Palestine* (1943), and Jack Finegan's *Light from the Ancient Past* . . . (1946; rev. ed., 1959) are most noteworthy; Nelson Glueck's *The Other Side of the Jordan* (1940) covers a more limited area. More recently, there are W. F. Albright's *The Archaeology of Palestine* (Penguin Book, 1949; reprinted several times and revised), G. E. Wright's *Biblical Archaeology* (1957; 2nd, rev. ed., 1962; also abridged as *An Introduction to Biblical Archaeology* [1960])—and see his learned survey of "The Archaeology of Palestine" in the Albright Festschrift, *The Bible and the Ancient Near East* (1961), edited by G. E. Wright—and J. B. Pritchard's *Archaeology and the Old Testament* (1958). G. E. Wright and D. N. Freedman have edited *The Biblical Archaeologist Reader* (1961), a fine cross section of the field, though some of the articles might have been brought up to date. G. W. Van Beek has contributed a fine survey of "Archeology" to *The Interpreter's Dictionary of the Bible,* Vol. I (1962). G. F. Owen's *Archaeology and the Bible* (1961) is a good example of the conservative approach to the discipline. A clear and informative "biography of a dig" is now available in J. B. Pritchard's *Gibeon* (1962). A sort of archaeological-topographical history of Canaan –Israel may be acquired from Nelson Glueck's *The River Jordan* (1946) and *Rivers in the Desert* (1959; now a Grove paperback).

Among the several biblical atlases that have made their appearance, G. E. Wright and F. V. Filson's *Westminster Historical Atlas to the Bible* (1945; 2nd ed., 1956) has been the standard work since it first came out. E. G. Kraeling's *Bible Atlas* (1956) and especially *The Oxford Bible Atlas* (1962) edited by H. G. May deserve mention. The most recent work (1957) on *The Geography of the Bible* is that by Denis Baly; and see also his *Geographical Companion to the Bible* (1963).

Not untypical of the way in which archaeology helped set scholarship straight in its use of biblical data was the case of the three broken jar handles with the same seal impression on them. Plausible arguments had been advanced persuasively by C. C. Torrey, chiefly in his *Pseudo-Ezekiel and the Original Prophecy* (1930), that the biblical statements about a widespread Babylonian devastation of Jerusalem and Judah in 586 B.C. and an extensive Babylonian captivity of many of the conquered Judeans were greatly to be discounted; in other words, that portions of such books as II Kings, Jeremiah, and Ezekiel were not to be taken at the face value accorded them by tradition. But in 1928 at Tell Beit Mirsim, and in 1930 at Beth-shemesh and again at Tell Beit Mirsim, jar handles were excavated bearing the inscription "Pertaining to Eliakim steward of (King) Jehoiachin." This archaeological datum, along with some other pertinent data, was cleverly used by Albright in an article entitled "The Seal of Eliakim and the Latest Preëxilic History of Judah, with some Observations on Ezekiel" (*Journal of Biblical Literature,* LI [1932], 77-106) to prove that the biblical material was essentially reliable: the destruction of Judah's capital city and Temple and sovereignty was substantial, and the fact of the Babylonian captivity was stranger than any scholarly fiction. It was almost as an anticlimax that a group of neo-Babylonian cuneiform tablets came to light a decade later, with specific reference to Judah's King Jehoiachin in exile in Babylon. (See Albright's article in the *Biblical Archaeologist,* V [1942], 49-55, based on E. F. Weidner's initial article in *Mélanges . . . René Dussaud,* II [1939], 923-35.) One could multiply such instances readily.

Excavation of sites outside the Holy Land made no less significant contributions to the better understanding of the Bible. Mesopotamia, Asia Minor, Syria, and Egypt disgorged important, sometimes sensational, materials for the biblical scholar. A significant discovery, for example, occurred in 1930, when a peasant ploughing his field at Ras esh-Shamrah in Syria found himself stopped by a heavy stone slab and removed the obstruction, exposing the entrance leading to a room. In the excavations that ensued—conducted by a French group under C.F.-A. Schaeffer—the ancient Canaanite city of Ugarit was uncovered, and a number of fifteenth century B.C. Canaanite texts of capital importance for the Bible were brought to light.

In the analysis of these texts, American scholarship has been in the forefront of activity. Among the better studies are those by H. L. Ginsberg (articles chiefly in the *Bulletin,* and its *Supplemen-*

tary Studies, Nos. 2-3), J. A. Montgomery and Z. S. Harris (*The Ras Shamra Mythological Texts* [1935] and numerous articles), W. F. Albright (in the *Journal of the Palestine Oriental Society,* 1934, and in a series of articles in the *Bulletin* from 1932 on), T. H. Gaster, Albrecht Goetze, and C. H. Gordon (his *Ugaritic Manual* [1955] is standard). Their contributions—and those by several other scholars—appear in scattered journals both here (especially in the *Bulletin, Journal of the American Oriental Society, Journal of Biblical Literature,* and *Journal of Near Eastern Studies*) and abroad. Psalm 29, for example, was clearly demonstrated to be of Canaanite origin, with Israel's God, *YHWH* (LORD), replacing the Canaanite deity, Baal, of the original. Parts of such poems as the Balaam Oracles (Num. 23-24) and the Song of Moses after the Crossing of the Sea of Reeds (Exod. 15), not to mention the Song of Deborah (Judg. 5)—because they were now recognized as exhibiting older (Ugaritic–Canaanite) characteristics of poetry—have come generally to be regarded as ancient compositions, dating from the late second millennium. (See Albright's "The Role of the Canaanites in the History of Civilization" in *The Bible and the Ancient Near East* [1961], ed. G. E. Wright; esp. pp. 338-39 and notes 60-61 on p. 357. M. J. Dahood has now published a useful survey of "Ugaritic Studies and the Bible" (*Gregorianum,* XLIII [1962], 55-79).

Hebrew origins, especially in relation to the Habiru (or Hapiru), have been the subject of much study, though the problem has eluded solution. Julius Lewy has written on "Ḫābirū and Hebrews" (*Hebrew Union College Annual,* XIV [1939], 587-623). T. J. Meek devoted Chapter I to "The Origin of the Hebrew People" in his *Hebrew Origins,* 2nd ed. (1950). In 1954 and 1955 there appeared respectively, virtually simultaneously, *Le Problème des ḫabiru à la 4ᵉ rencontre assyriologique internationale* (*Cahiers de la Société Asiatique,* XIII), edited by Jean Bottéro, and Moshe Greenberg's *The Hab/piru.* And now Mary P. Gray has analyzed "The Ḫâbirū-Hebrew Problem in the Light of the Source Material Available at Present" (*Hebrew Union College Annual,* XXIX [1958], 135-202).

~§ 3 §~

Extrabiblical Research

Since it is virtually impossible to comprehend biblical Israel's society outside its Near Eastern setting, perhaps something should be said here about recent research in the lands of the Fertile Crescent of old. It is probably not wrong to assert that the history of ancient Egypt, Assyria, and Babylonia is now better known—better in the sense that there are more data of a reliable character pertaining to their history—than that of Israel, even if detailed up-to-date histories of those countries have not been made available in recent years. Among the older works, special mention should be made of Eduard Meyer's *Geschichte des Altertums,* 2nd ed. (2 vols., 1907-09 and 1928-31), A. T. Olmstead's *History of Assyria* (1923), and Volume 3 of *The Cambridge Ancient History* (1925), which is now in the process of considerable revision, in part by American scholars.

J. A. Wilson's *The Burden of Egypt* (1951; now a Phoenix paperback under the title *The Culture of Egypt* [1956]) is a clear and stimulating interpretation of ancient Egypt's culture. *When Egypt Ruled the East* (1942; rev. ed., 1957) by Georg Steindorff and K. C. Seele gives a fine survey of the period of the New Kingdom (about 1500-1100 B.C.) and is instructively and attractively illustrated. In 1946, Henri and H. A. Frankfort edited *The Intellectual Adventure of Ancient Man,* with a long Introduction and Conclusion by the editors, and chapters on Egypt by J. A. Wilson, Mesopotamia by Thorkild Jacobsen, and the Hebrews by W. A. Irwin. The volume reappeared in 1949—without the chapter on the Hebrews (which Irwin worked up separately as *The Old Testament: Keystone of Human Culture* [1952])—as a Pelican paperback, under the title *Before Philosophy.* In 1948 Henri Frankfort published a penetrating study of *Ancient Egyptian Religion,* and three years later a brilliant study of *The Birth of Civilization in the Near East* (a Doubleday Anchor Book in 1956).

Following his *Sumerian Mythology* (1944) and numerous preliminary studies, S. N. Kramer published *History Begins at Sumer* (1959, Anchor Book; constituting essentially his earlier book, *From the Tablets of Sumer* [1956]), probably the best in the field. A. T.

Olmstead has written a fine *History of the Persian Empire* (Achae-menid Period [1948]; now a Phoenix paperback), marred only by malicious—as well as historically impermissible—references to twentieth century (A.D.!) Zionism (e.g., on pages 466-67). And even if he did not succeed in determining the relative date of Ezra and Nehemiah (cf. John Bright's "The Date of Ezra's Mission to Jerusalem," in the *Yehezkel Kaufmann Jubilee Volume* [1960]), it is the fault of no one; our data are simply inadequate.

As a supplement to its *Journal,* the American Oriental Society published in 1954 a fine monograph (fifty-five pages) on *Authority and Law in the Ancient Orient,* with relevant chapters on Egypt by J. A. Wilson, Mesopotamia by E. A. Speiser, the Hittites by H. G. Güterbock, and Canaan–Israel by Isaac Mendelsohn. A year later R. C. Dentan edited *The Idea of History in the Ancient Near East,* which includes full treatments of Egypt by Ludlow Bull, Mesopo-tamia by E. A. Speiser, and Israel by Millar Burrows.

The Albright Festschrift (1961) offers a fine survey of the Near East of old: "South Arabian History and Archaeology" by G. W. Van Beek, "Sumerian Literature, a General Survey" by S. N. Kra-mer, "Formative Tendencies in Sumerian Literature" by Thorkild Jacobsen, "Egypt: Its Language and Literature" by T. O. Lambdin, "Egyptian Culture and Religion" by J. A. Wilson, and "Hittite and Anatolian Studies" by Albrecht Goetze. And for *The Interpreter's Dictionary of the Bible* (1962), now come to hand, A. L. Oppen-heim contributed an extensive survey of Assyria and Babylonia; J. A. Wilson wrote on Egypt, I. J. Gelb on the Hittites, and S. N. Kramer on Sumer. The lamented R. T. O'Callaghan's volume on *Aram Naharaim* (1948) is still the best study in the field. On the name (*Aram*) *Naharaim,* see J. J. Finkelstein's illuminating article, "Mesopotamia" (*Journal of Near Eastern Studies,* XXI [1962], 73-92).

Considerable portions of the documents of the ancient world that have special relevance to the Bible have been made accessible in English translation. Outstanding is the volume edited by J. B. Pritch-ard, *Ancient Near Eastern Texts Relating to the Old Testament* (1950; 2nd ed., 1955), with contributions by W. F. Albright, H. L. Ginsberg, Albrecht Goetze, Albert Jamme, S. N. Kramer, T. J. Meek, A. L. Oppenheim, R. H. Pfeiffer, Franz Rosenthal, A. J. Sachs,

E. A. Speiser, F. J. Stephens, and J. A. Wilson. The companion volume, *The Ancient Near East in Pictures* (1954), is superbly executed; together they constitute the American counterpart to *Altorientalische Texte und Bilder zum alten Testament* that Hugo Gressmann edited in 1926-27. For more popular usage, *Ancient Near Eastern Texts* was abridged for *Religions of the Ancient Near East: Sumero-Akkadian Religious Texts and Ugaritic Epics* (1955), edited by Isaac Mendelsohn; and both the *Texts* and the *Pictures* were excerpted for *The Ancient Near East: An Anthology of Texts and Pictures* (1958), edited by J. B. Pritchard. See also I. M. Price, O. R. Sellers, and E. L. Carlson's *The Monuments of the Old Testament: Light from the Near East on the Scriptures* (1958).

Prominent among the major collections of Aramaic documents brought to light in recent decades is the batch of Jewish Elephantine papyri (mostly fifth century B.C.) that R. J. Williams came upon and identified in 1949 in the basement of the Brooklyn Museum— where they had been lying unknown in a tin biscuit box for a number of years—and that were subsequently published by E. G. Kraeling in *The Booklyn Museum Aramaic Papyri* (1953). H. L. Ginsberg has been especially active in the elucidation of Aramaic inscriptions; see his studies in the *American Journal of Semitic Languages,* L (1933), 1-9; LII (1935), 95-103; *Journal of the American Oriental Society,* LXII (1942), 229-38; LXXIV (1954), 153-62; *Journal of Near Eastern Studies,* XVIII (1959), 143-49. R. A. Bowman has published articles in the *American Journal of Semitic Languages,* LVIII (1941), 302-13, 359-67; and the *Journal of Near Eastern Studies,* VII (1948), 65-90.

Some Canaanite–Phoenician, Aramaic, and Old Hebrew texts are conveniently available in English translation in *Ancient Near Eastern Texts,* 2nd ed. (1955), edited by J. B. Pritchard; or in the abridged version, *The Ancient Near East* (1958). And see the nice survey of "Inscriptions" by R. J. Williams in *The Interpreter's Dictionary of the Bible.* Williams also contributed the introduction, translation, and notes for "The 'Israel Stele' of Merenptah," "The Hymn to Aten," and "A Penitential Psalm" in the section "Egyptian Documents" to the excellent *Documents from Old Testament Times* (1958; now a Harper Torchbook), edited by D. Winton Thomas.

The publication from the Thirties on of the Canaanite (Ugaritic) texts of the middle of the second millennium B.C., together with the appearance of new Sumerian texts and studies, has given an impetus to the renewed study of the mythology of the ancient world in which biblical Israel grew up. A significant work in this area is T. H. Gaster's *Thespis: Ritual, Myth and Drama in the Ancient Near East* (1950; now, in revised form, a Doubleday paperback). The best collection of "Myths, Epics, and Legends" (Egyptian, Sumerian, Akkadian, Hittite, and Ugaritic) is to be found in *Ancient Near Eastern Texts Relating to the Old Testament,* edited by J. B. Pritchard. And S. N. Kramer has edited a fine statement of the *Mythologies of the Ancient World* (1961; both in Quadrangle Books and as a Doubleday Anchor Book), which includes chapters on Egypt by Rudolf Anthes, Sumer and Akkad by S. N. Kramer, the Hittites by H. G. Güterbock, and the Canaanites by C. H. Gordon. R. J. Williams has written on "The Fable in the Ancient Near East" in the W. A. Irwin Festschrift, *A Stubborn Faith* (1956), edited by E. C. Hobbs.

A new dimension has been added by C. H. Gordon to the study of the Bible, viz., the east Mediterranean setting that helped shape early Israel's culture.

> The meeting of many peoples in the Levant during the second millennium B.C. converted the East Mediterranean into the focal point of world history and produced the synthesis that gave birth to Western Civilization. The peoples involved were varied. Some contributed the heritage of Mesopotamia and Egypt. At the center were the Minoans who stimulated their less developed neighbors such as the Greeks and Hebrews to produce civilizations of their own. . . . The Greeks and Hebrews started on their historic careers in different but interrelated segments of the East Mediterranean. . . . Ugarit at last provides the literary link connecting Israel and Hellas.

This view is expressed in Gordon's detailed study of "Homer and Bible" (*Hebrew Union College Annual,* XXVI [1955], 43-109) and has been enlarged in his recent book, *Before the Bible: The Common Background of Greek and Hebrew Civilizations* (1963).

◆§ 4 §◆

Negative Aspects of Archaeology

To such an extent had archaeology become a primary factor in the clarification of so many biblical problems, i.e., in putting them into proper historical setting, that in more recent years it has even threatened to become a harmful factor in biblical research.

There are two aspects to the worthwhileness of archaeology for the scholar. First, and perhaps more important, archaeology provides very considerable and useful material for the reconstruction of a culture of bygone days. The material is permitted to speak for itself, and sizeable segments of that culture come to light for the first time. "The most extraordinary advance in Palestinian archaeology," Albright noted in *The Archaeology of Palestine*, "has certainly been in the field of prehistory. In 1920 this branch of our science was wholly undeveloped . . ." (p. 37). Second, if, in addition, some of this new information—usually only a minor quantity of it—sheds light on something or other in the Bible, that is all to the good. Naturally, biblical historians and philologians stress the second aspect; to them, archaeology in and about the Holy Land is important not so much as a discipline, as a branch of science per se, but as a handmaid, a tool for the better understanding of the Bible and the Holy Land. Unlike the Sumerologist, Akkadiologist, Hittitologist, Egyptologist, and the like, who have been interested chiefly in laying bare the history of their areas from the beginning of time to the end of the *floruit* of the civilizations that interest them, the biblical scholar has been interested in archaeology mainly for its help in elucidating the Bible. To be sure, the prehistory of Palestine was studied and the new knowledge of it was appreciated per se, as were the excavated materials that shed light on the history of the Holy Land in general, if not on the Bible in particular.

But during this same period, especially since the "Cold War" of the post-World War II period set in, conditions on the North American continent, as in the world generally, had become increasingly troublesome. World War I had hardly saved the world for democracy, or vice versa. The rise of totalitarianism and the inability of the great democratic countries to resolve the problems of societal insecurity and conflict made for increasing vexation. Reason and science had not succeeded in bringing to people, as individuals or as members of larger groups, the kind of contentment they had been seeking. So a renewed interest in numerous forms of religion developed on a large scale. People began once again to seek out what had long been regarded as the Word of God.

This Word, however, was no longer an isolated phenomenon in the midst of history; no longer was it a static event, independent of time and place. For biblical criticism had come to pass, and archaeology had come to pass, and it had become possible and necessary to comprehend the Word of God, the Bible, much better than heretofore as part of the historical process in general. (See, e.g., M. S. Enslin's contribution, "Biblical Criticism and Its Effect on Modern Civilization," to the ACLS collection of *Five Essays on the Bible* [1960], edited by Frederick Burkhardt.)

Thus the historical circumstances that had brought archaeology into being now combined with those that brought the Bible once again to the fore of man's attention; the result has been an extraordinary increase of popular interest in the Bible and—i.e., in the light of—archaeology. Increasingly during the Forties and Fifties, and there is no sign of a let-up, people began to seek out the "truths" of the Bible as "proved" by archaeology. They could not go back to the Bible in the spirit of their ancestors of the nineteenth century and earlier, to whom every word in the Bible was literally the word of God, divinely revealed. Mid-twentieth century man wants to know the Bible as regards its historical origins, its reliability, its authority.

Consequently, when scholars noted this or that archaeological datum as substantiating this or that statement in the Bible, it was easy for undisciplined journalists and popularizers not only to exaggerate beyond reasonableness the scope of substantiation but to take a giant, and utterly unjustified, step beyond that and assert that this substantiation demonstrated the Bible as the revealed word of God! Nothing could be more of a non sequitur in disciplined reasoning than the juxtaposition of these two completely independent phenomena. This is the theme of Nelson Glueck's essay "The Bible and Archaeology" (in the above-mentioned ACLS symposium on the Bible and the humanities, *Five Essays on the Bible*), which is something of a sequel to earlier articles by G. E. Wright (*Biblical Archaeolo-*

gist, XXII [1959], 101-08) and J. J. Finkelstein (*Commentary,* XXVII [1959], 341-50). This widespread confusion between the Bible as a religious document and the Bible as a historical document will be discussed below from another angle.

~§ 5 §~

The Decline of Biblical Philology;
The Dead Sea Scrolls

The rise of biblical archaeology in the several decades following World War I coincided with—indeed was in part responsible for— the decline in biblical philology. In the general educational pattern of the United States, the humanities began to give way to the pure, applied, and social sciences. The number of students studying Greek and Latin in high school and college has decreased considerably in the past two or three decades—though the number has more re- cently been on the increase, especially in private schools; and these subjects are no longer required of students in some theological semi- naries. So that by the time a student has acquired the B.A. (and even the B.D.) degree and decides to specialize in Bible, he must begin the study of Greek and Latin, of Hebrew, Aramaic, and Syriac, of Arabic and Akkadian and/or Egyptian. And since it is much easier to do original work in such expanding disciplines as archaeology and Ak- kadian, it is the latter areas that have been attracting the research ef- forts of promising young scholars who might otherwise tend toward biblical philology. So that E. C. Colwell, in his presidential address for the Society of Biblical Literature, on "Biblical Criticism: Lower and Higher" (*Journal of Biblical Literature,* LXVII [1948], 1- 12) could begin right off with the assertion "Biblical criticism today is not the most robust of academic disciplines . . . , [it] is relatively sterile today. . . ." And it is surely symptomatic that in his survey of the *Old Testament in Modern Research* (1954), H. F. Hahn left philology and textual criticism unsurveyed.

It was in this atmosphere that the Dead Sea Scrolls first came to the attention of biblical scholars here and abroad, at the end of the For- ties. Scholar and layman alike were thrilled to read in the press that ancient scrolls of the Bible, about two thousand years old, had been discovered in caves—soon to be associated with the name of the nearby site, Qumran—at the northwestern end of the Dead Sea. Seven major manuscripts were involved in the find, two of them biblical and two others bearing directly on the text of the Bible: (1) a virtually complete manuscript of the book of Isaiah, all sixty-six chapters; (2) a sizeable fragment of Isaiah (chiefly from Chapter 38 on); (3) an interpretation (*pesher*) of Habakkuk 1-2, in which the biblical text is quoted, usually a few words at a time, and commented on; and (4) a collection of psalms of thanksgiving (*hodayot*) in which passages from Psalms and some other biblical books are quoted. The remaining three Scrolls are quite extrabiblical: (1) a tract dealing with the beliefs and practices (the so-called Manual of Discipline) of the sect; (2) a legendary elaboration in Aramaic of some of the stories in Genesis (the so-called Genesis Apocryphon); and (3) a text dealing with a war between the righteous (children of light) and the wicked (children of darkness).

In view of the fact that the oldest dated Hebrew manuscript of the Bible—containing the Latter Prophets—was written at the beginning of the tenth century, and the oldest manuscripts of the Septuagint translation of the Bible were of the fourth and fifth centuries, scholars naturally were most eager to get at these ancient biblical texts that were written in the days of the Second Temple, when sovereign Judea had not yet passed into history.

The Julius Wellhausens and S. R. Drivers, the G. F. Moores, M. L. Margolises, and J. A. Montgomerys would have known how to deal with the biblical texts and quotations. Alas, the treatment that the Scrolls, notably the complete Isaiah, received at the hands of the current generation of scholars generally was not calculated to win friends among textual critics. In addition, one of the prominent personages in the Scrolls, referred to as the "Right(eous) Teacher" (*moreh haṣ-ṣedeq*), was identified by some as the immediate forerunner, even prototype, of Jesus. Whether this identification was true or not—and it was not—many saw in it a menace to Christianity, both of the first century and of our own twentieth. Lots of excitement was naturally generated by these factors, and for a time the scholarly argument and analysis took place in an air of unreality and popular hysteria.

The situation as a whole was not helped any by the additional fact that the date of the Scrolls was in dispute. Most scholars accepted a pre-Christian date (second-first centuries B.C.), others a date in the Mishnic period (first-third centuries A.D.), and a few in the Karaite period (from the eighth century on). To the textual critic of the Bible, the matter of date was secondary; it was the character and inherent worthwhileness of the text of the Scrolls that mattered. In the first detailed "Studies in the St. Mark's Isaiah Scroll" (*Journal of Biblical Literature,* LXIX [1950], 149-66), I asserted that "from the broader point of view in textual criticism, the relative age of a manuscript is not at all necessarily a criterion of its 'textual' proximity to the original whence it ultimately derived, and, what is even more important, it need not at all indicate the value of the text of the manuscript."

Now, more than a decade later, the debate is virtually over; see, e.g., the symposium of the American Textual Criticism Seminar (December 29, 1958), *Recent Developments in the Study of the Text of the Bible: Qumran and the Present State of Old Testament Text Studies,* with articles by P. W. Skehan on "The Masoretic Text" and H. M. Orlinsky on "The Septuagint Text" (*Journal of Biblical Literature,* LXXVIII [1959], 21-25; 26-33). The views set forth in my article on the St. Mark's Isaiah Scroll (see esp. pp. 151-52) have prevailed, and they may be summarized as follows. (1) The scribes responsible for the complete Isaiah Scroll, and other Scrolls, were not particularly careful; in addition, these scribes—unlike the masoretes —were not always interested in copying the text faithfully, since it was their interpretation of the text that was of paramount importance to them. (2) Where the Septuagint and other versions (e.g., the Targum, Peshiṭta, and Vulgate) of Isaiah go their own way from the traditional Hebrew (so-called masoretic) text, the Isaiah Scroll agrees with the masoretic text; the text of the Scroll cannot be associated with the Hebrew *Vorlage* of the Septuagint or the other ancient versions. This is true of all the biblical texts among the Scrolls thus far published, save those of Samuel and Jeremiah. (3) When the text of Isaiah and all the other biblical Scrolls, except Samuel and Jeremiah, goes its own way from the traditional text—the peculiar spelling of the Scroll's text is not involved here—it is from a text from which the traditional text derives that the deviation occurs; in other words, the Scrolls represent the same text-tradition— even if frequently in corrupt or otherwise inferior form—that is preserved in the traditional text. (4) In extremely few instances have the Isaiah and related Scrolls—in contrast to the corresponding readings preserved in the traditional text—preserved readings that are original, or closer to the original readings. (5) The Scrolls will have their greatest value in helping convince more biblical scholars that the traditionally preserved text of the Hebrew Bible must be treated with far greater respect than it has been. (6) At the same time it should be noted clearly that the Septuagint does not always represent a misunderstanding of the Hebrew when it diverges from the traditional text; at least in some cases it rests upon a genuine variant text.

Perhaps a few specific cases in point will help illustrate the picture. When the Revised Standard Version's Old Testament Committee of translators was at work on the book of Isaiah, the majority of the Committee voted in favor of a reading in the Scroll, as against the reading preserved in the traditional text, in thirteen instances. Several years later, however, at least one member of the majority —Millar Burrows in *The Dead Sea Scrolls* (1955), pp. 305 f.— stated publicly: "For myself I must confess that in some cases where I probably voted for the emendation I am now convinced that our decision was a mistake and the Masoretic reading should have been retained. . . ." And since the majority sometimes numbered exactly one more than the minority, the worthwhileness of the Scroll even in these few instances was hardly overwhelming. More recently, the *New York Herald Tribune* (August 20, 1962; pp. 1, 9) reported a statement made by G. R. Driver, director of the ten-man panel responsible for the British *New English Bible: The Old Testament:* "They [i.e., the Dead Sea Scrolls] are very disappointing indeed from our point of view."

This is not to say that the biblical fragments among the Scrolls did not here and there preserve an original reading, or a reading that— while itself not original—might lead the alert textual critic to such; a striking instance of the latter may be found in Samuel Iwry's analysis of *"Maṣṣēbāh* and *Bāmāh* in IQ Isaiah^A 6₁₃" (*Journal of Biblical Literature,* LXXVI [1957], 225-32) and "The Qumran Isaiah and the End of the Dial of Ahaz" (*Bulletin,* CXLVII [1957], 27-33).

For the better appreciation and evaluation of such biblical texts among the Scrolls as the complete Isaiah, very much work remains to be done. For example, I have long been convinced that the Isaiah and other Scrolls (e.g., one of the Psalms fragments; see my comment in note 39 of "The Textual Criticism of the Old Testament" in the Albright Festschrift, pp. 130 f.) were—at least in part—copied from dictation and probably also from memory; for numerous erroneous readings in these texts are due to *hörfehler,* whereas far fewer errors than most scholars think are due to letters of the alphabet looking alike. Neither Malachi Martin in his two-volume work on *The Scribal Character of the Dead Sea Scrolls* (1958) nor any of his reviewers has drawn attention to this important matter.

Or, again, before adequate study had been made of the orthography and grammar of these biblical texts—so that proper use of them could be made for the better understanding of the morphology and pronunciation of biblical Hebrew prior to the turn of the Christian era—some scholars rushed to announce that the Scrolls manifested a dialect of Hebrew that was older than that manifested by the traditional text; for some details, see my article "The Textual Criticism of the Old Testament," pp. 121-24 and notes 34-45 on pp. 130-32. This gratuitous elevation of the Isaiah Scroll has now been effectively dealt with by E. Y. Kutscher (an Israeli scholar who has taught and written much in the United States) in *The Language and Linguistic Background of the Isaiah Scroll* (1959; in Hebrew); and there has just come to hand D. N. Freedman's study of "The Massoretic Text and the Qumran Scrolls: A Study in Orthography," in *Textus* (Annual of the Hebrew University Bible Project), II (1962), 87-102.

There are, too, the fundamental questions: What attitude did the scribes of the Scrolls manifest in the matter of reproducing as faithfully as possible a biblical text? Were they interested in receiving and transmitting the text accurately, or was it primarily interpretation—naturally to help demonstrate and justify their own practices and beliefs—that guided them? These questions, fundamental as they are, cannot as yet be answered for lack of close analysis of the texts. In short, the textual criticism of the biblical texts among the Scrolls, "that necessary introduction to the study of the Bible" as put recently, remains to be done.

Recent surveys of the Scrolls in relation to the Bible may be found in Millar Burrows' *More Light on the Dead Sea Scrolls* (1958), Part III, "Results for Old Testament Studies"; and F. M. Cross Jr.'s

The Ancient Library of Qumran and Modern Biblical Studies (rev. ed., 1961; Anchor Book), Chapter IV, "The Old Testament at Qumrân." A general guide to the *Multipurpose Tools for Bible Study* (1960) has been worked up by F. W. Danker; and an earlier, less complete work, *Tools for Bible Study* (1956), was edited by B. H. Kelly and D. G. Miller from a series of articles that appeared in the 1947-49 issues of *Interpretation.*

◆§ 6 §◆

Bible Translations

The rise of archaeology gave a tremendous impetus also to the renewed interest in Bible translations. The universally accepted and respected Authorized (King James) Version of the Bible (AV or KJ; 1611) had begun already in the nineteenth century to undergo revision, in the form of the British Revised Version (RV) of 1885 and the American Standard Version (ASV) of 1901. But during the decades that followed, this revision proved inadequate: (1) the English language, on both sides of the Atlantic, had undergone too much change for the average reader of the English Bible to be content with the words and style of the revision, and (2) the popular interest in biblical archaeology had made everyone aware of the need to retranslate the Bible more accurately in the light of the new discoveries. Consequently, considerable scholarly activity in the Old Testament in recent decades has been devoted to the making of new English translations of the Hebrew Bible.

Individual organizations and persons, in a position to act swiftly and unilaterally, were quick to produce new translations that would satisfy the needs of various segments of society. Easily the outstanding of these "unauthorized" new versions was *The Complete Bible: The Old Testament, An American Translation* (1927), by J. M. Powis Smith, T. J. Meek, Leroy Waterman, and A. R. Gordon. Known popularly as "the Chicago translation," this version has been eminently successful, has gone through numerous printings, and has been revised by T. J. Meek. Its popularity is due to the simplicity and directness of its language and to its fine scholarship.

In 1937, after several meetings held in 1930-32, the International Council of Religious Education authorized the making of a new trans-

73

lation of the Bible. The Council, consisting of the educational boards of forty major Protestant denominations of the United States and Canada, was truly the representative body of American Protestantism. The Council appointed a committee of scholars to produce a version that would "embody the best results of modern scholarship as to the meaning of the Scriptures, and express this meaning in English diction which is designed for use in public and private worship and preserves those qualities which have given to the King James Version a supreme place in English literature."

Much of the best scholarship available in the United States and Canada was devoted during the Thirties and Forties to the making of the revised Old Testament, which appeared in 1952 (together with the New Testament that had appeared in 1946). The committee of actual translators consisted essentially of the following: Dean L. A. Weigle (chairman), J. A. Bewer, Millar Burrows, George Dahl, J. P. Hyatt, W. A. Irwin, Fleming James, H. G. May, James Moffatt, James Muilenburg, H. M. Orlinsky, W. R. Taylor, Leroy Waterman, and K. M. Yates. J. A Montgomery and C. C. Torrey made a substantial contribution to the translation in its earlier stages. The Revised Standard Version is distinguished from the British and American Revised Versions chiefly by four features: (1) the words and style employed in current literary English were usually substituted for those in the older versions; (2) the newer knowledge made available by archaeology was frequently incorporated in the RSV; (3) the consonantal text was sometimes emended, either on the authority of one or another ancient version or by conjecture; and (4) the vocalization of the traditional (so-called masoretic) consonantal text was sometimes changed—but without the reader being told of it. The new revision has generally been received warmly the world over by scholar and layman alike, even though it has been considered by some to have departed from the Revised Version too much and by others not enough.

Essentially the same needs that moved the Protestant community of the United States to request and receive a new English Bible motivated also the Roman Catholic and Jewish communities. Following the appearance of the New Testament in 1941, the Episcopal Committee of the Confraternity of Christian Doctrine authorized a new translation of the Old Testament, to be made by members of the

Catholic Biblical Association of America. (The actual translators, close to forty in number, came to be headed by L. F. Hartman, P. W. Skehan, and S. J. Hartdegen as editors-in-chief.) "The supreme goal to be sought in rendering the word of God into the vernacular," says the Letter of the Episcopal Committee, "is rigorous fidelity to the meaning of the original, expressed in simple and intelligible language." Of *The Holy Bible Translated from the Original Languages with Critical Use of All the Ancient Sources,* Volumes I (*Genesis to Ruth*), III (*Sapiental Books: Job to Sirach*), and IV (*The Prophetic Books: Isaiah to Malachi*) appeared in 1952, 1955, and 1961 respectively. Each biblical book is preceded by a brief introduction, the text is accompanied by explanatory footnotes, and a list of textual notes is provided at the end of each volume.

In 1955 the Jewish Publication Society of America appointed a committee of seven scholars to prepare a new translation of the Hebrew Bible. As the King James and Revised Versions of the Protestants and the Douay Version of the Roman Catholics, so did the well-known Jewish Version of 1917 that the Society had published cease to satisfy the needs of those who had not been raised on the older— sometimes obsolete or obsolescent—idiom and who demanded the more correct translation that the newly discovered materials now helped to make possible. For the Pentateuch the actual translators were H. M. Orlinsky (editor-in-chief), H. L. Ginsberg and E. A. Speiser (fellow editors), and Max Arzt, B. J. Bamberger, Harry Freedman, and Solomon Grayzel.

The first part of the new translation, *The Torah* (i.e., the five books of Moses), appeared in 1962. Unlike the new Protestant and Catholic translations, the new Jewish Version adheres to the traditional Hebrew text. In numerous instances, however, where the translators were convinced that the correct meaning was uncertain or the originality of the traditional Hebrew text was in doubt, they said so in a footnote. Probably more than any other authorized translation, whether the traditional Hebrew text was followed or emended, the authors of the new Jewish Version felt free to abandon the literary format and Hebraisms of its predecessors. It also appears that this new translation has made much more use both of the best of medieval Jewish exegesis and of the more recent extrabiblical materials that have come to light. An important reason for this may be

75

found in the fact that, unlike the Protestant and Catholic versions, which were authorized by authoritative religious bodies, the Jewish Version was sponsored by a Jewish cultural organization made up of individuals drawn from and responsible only to the Jewish community at large, both religious (Orthodox, Conservative, and Reform) and secular. See now my detailed article on "The New Jewish Version of the Torah: Toward a New Philosophy of Bible Translation" (*Journal of Biblical Literature*, LXXXII [1963], 249-64).

Among the numerous recent surveys of modern English versions of the Bible are S. I. Rypins' *The Book of Thirty Centuries* (1951); H. G. May's *Our English Bible in the Making* (1952); I. M. Price's *The Ancestry of Our English Bible*, 3rd rev. ed. (1956) by W. A. Irwin and A. P. Wikgren; and D. N. Dow's "Twentieth Century Translations of the Bible into English," in the 1961 *Bulletin* of Austin Presbyterian Theological Seminary.

⊸§ 7 §⊸

Biblical Theology

The popular interest in religion in general and in the Old Testament in particular that has become increasingly intense since the end of World War II is reflected also in recent Old Testament research.

For several decades after its appearance in 1904, the posthumous volume on *The Theology of the Old Testament* by A. B. Davidson of Great Britain dominated the field. In Europe the renewed interest in biblical theology was already manifest in the Twenties and Thirties. In this country it was not really until the Forties that this subject attracted the interest of scholars. It constituted an integral part of W. F. Albright's two important works: *From the Stone Age to Christianity: Monotheism and the Historical Process* (1940; now, in revised form, an Anchor paperback) and *Archaeology and the Religion of Israel* (1942). A few years later there appeared Millar Burrows' *An Outline of Biblical Theology* (1946) and O. J. Baab's *The Theology of the Old Testament* (1949; now an Anchor paperback). Other works that deserve mention are R. B. Y. Scott's *The Relevance of the Prophets* (1944); G. E. Wright's *The Old Testament Against Its Environment* (1950), *God Who Acts: Biblical*

Theology as Recital (1952), and *The Biblical Doctrine of Man in Society* (1954); and, most recently, James Muilenburg's *The Way of Israel: Biblical Faith and Ethics* (1961). The list might readily be expanded—by adding, e.g., Wright's *The Challenge of Israel's Faith* (1944) and "The Faith of Israel" (in *The Interpreter's Bible,* Vol. I [1952]) and Muilenburg's "The History of the Religion of Israel" (*ibid.*)—and might be made to include American editions in English translation of foreign works, e.g., Yehezkel Kaufmann's *The Religion of Israel from Its Beginnings to the Babylonian Exile* (1960), abridged and translated from the Hebrew by Moshe Greenberg; Walther Eichrodt's *Theology of the Old Testament,* Vol. I (1961), translated from the German by J. A. Baker; and Gerhard von Rad's *Old Testament Theology,* Vol. I (1962), translated from the German by D. M. G. Stalker.

Yet it would not be easy to regard any of these works as standard, let alone definitive. For one thing, we do not have as yet—and may well never have—sufficient extrabiblical data to provide the pertinent background for the history of ancient Israel's religious beliefs and practices. In addition, the more recent analysis of the Hebrew Bible itself has not made many objective scholars confident that the last word has been said on the date and provenance of the vast majority of passages that bear on our problem. Finally, there is the purely subjective and environmental element according to which the Christian scholar will sometimes tend to see the Old Testament essentially as the beginning of a process that logically and inevitably achieved fulfillment in the New Testament; or, again, according to which Christian and Jewish scholars will tend to seek out in the Bible beliefs and practices—in short, values—that are relevant, vital, and even authoritative for present-day society. It is one thing for a scholar to devote his talents to the detailed study of the Old Testament in its historical development during the second and first millennia B.C., or else to specialize in the study of our own twentieth century society; it is something else again, however, for the same scholar to attempt scientific conquest of these two distinct areas of research. Such scholars, as put recently by someone, "tend often to mix together scholarship and apologetics."

To what extent a change of attitude and methodology may be expected in this area of research in the foreseeable future may be gauged by these two, quite typical expressions of one and the same sentiment:

> Upon the basis of a thoroughly critical approach to the Old Testament, whereby the literature, its setting, history and text are rigorously scrutinized and its awareness of a supernatural order is given as much weight as its record of sociological and historical data, a true Old Testament theology may be formulated. This theology will be both descriptive of a particular culture and normative for a religious faith which transcends all cultures. Here is an area of research in which biblical scholarship of today must apply itself with increasing diligence and passion, lest the religion of tomorrow be severed completely from the biblical revelation which gave it birth. [O. J. Baab, "Old Testament Theology: Its Possibility and Methodology" in *The Study of the Bible Today and Tomorrow,* ed. H. R. Willoughby (1947), p. 418.]

> A theology of the Old Testament will be worthy of the attention of men today in the measure in which it keeps close to life and does not operate merely at the academic level where thought and action are apt to be divorced. [N. W. Porteous, "Old Testament Theology" in *The Old Testament and Modern Study,* ed. H. H. Rowley (1951), p. 344.]

And when Millar Burrows, for example, published his *Outline of Biblical Theology* (1946), his position had been made quite clear already five years earlier, when he stated in the Preface to his *What Mean These Stones?*—a book that deals with archaeological material—as follows:

> Only readers concerned with the religious values of the Bible will find anything of interest in these pages. The volume has been written with a frankly and definitely religious interest. It has also, of course, been written from a particular religious point of view, that of a liberal Protestant Christian. At the same time the facts presented and much of the interpretation put upon them will, it is hoped, be helpful to Catholic and Jewish students of the Bible and to Protestants whose theological presuppositions differ from those of the author. [P. xi.]

Clearly, until the student of biblical theology learns to deal with his data as critically as the student of ancient Greek, or Roman, or

Assyrian, or Egyptian religion does, he can hardly expect his studies to achieve validity in scholarly circles.

Perhaps a specific case in point will be illuminating. It is universally believed by scholars that the last three verses of Isaiah 52 and all of 53 deal with the Suffering Servant of the Lord who is a person (or the people Israel, perhaps personified) who took it upon himself, even though he was innocent of transgression, to suffer punishment in place of others who had committed transgression and who were deserving of punishment. The Suffering Servant suffered vicariously (from Latin *vicarius,* "substitute") for others. In addition, some scholars sought, and found extrabiblical parallels and other data, chiefly neo-Babylonian (seventh-sixth centuries B.C.), to provide pertinent historical background for Isaiah 53.

And yet this universally accepted belief has by no means been demonstrated. For one thing, strange as it may seem, no one has actually proved—indeed, virtually no one has ever bothered to offer proof—that the Second Isaiah (the author of Chapters 40 ff. is generally referred to as such) had in mind any such notion as vicarious suffering. Second, hardly any attention has been paid to the question of whether the *servant* in question really deserves capital *s* in the universally employed term *Suffering Servant.* Third, the alleged literary parallels have not been subjected to close scrutiny. In short, a concept of major significance has been gratuitously assumed for sixth century B.C. Israel, and data of various kinds have been adduced to explain it and support it. In point of fact, this whole concept belongs to the category of *Q.E.D.* (See my Goldenson Lecture of 1964 [Hebrew Union College, Cincinnati], *The So-Called "Suffering Servant" in Isaiah 53.*)

Examples of this approach to biblical theology could readily be multiplied to point up the increasingly urgent need for studying anew the religious beliefs and practices of ancient Israel—in short, biblical concepts in their historical development—without regard to the interests of those to whom such postbiblical developments as Rabbinic Judaism, Christianity, Gnosticism, Islam, and Karaism have special appeal.

G. E. Wright sees the problem and poses the question differently: Is there a biblical theology, and if so, what is it? In the nineteenth century, biblical theology constituted essentially the search for the ideas and ideals that evolved in the biblical period; the approach in general was Hegelian. In our own generation the two most important works on biblical theology are those of Walther Eichrodt and Gerhard von Rad. Both answer the question "Is there a biblical theology?" in the affirmative, but they differ in their comprehension of the term. Eichrodt would use the concept of covenant as the central and organizing principle in his systematic reconstruction of biblical theology; von Rad, on the other hand, regards Eichrodt's reconstruction as far too systematic, unjustifiably creating an integrated whole where none obtained. Rather does von Rad view the most important or core content of the Bible as a series of events that have been integrated in cultic confesions. These confessions furnish the schema that holds the disparate material in the Hexateuch together so that the whole has become a great confessional document.

⋘ 8 ⋙

Biblical History

Archaeology has greatly stimulated fresh studies in biblical history and has made it necessary for all textbooks on the subject to be written anew; revision no longer suffices.

In 1936 T. J. Meek published a fresh analysis of *Hebrew Origins* (rev. ed., 1950; now a Harper Torchbook) against the ancient Near Eastern background, dealing topically, in successive chapters, with "The Origin of the Hebrew People," "Law," "God," "Priesthood," "Prophecy," and "Monotheism." Four years later Albright's *From the Stone Age to Christianity* made its appearance. Its primary purpose—as the title, the subtitle (*Monotheism and the Historical Process*), and the chapter titles (from III to VI they are: "Praeparatio," "When Israel Was a Child . . ." [Hos. 11:1], "Charisma and Catharsis," and "In the Fulness of Time . . ." [Gal. 4:4]) indicate —was to explain the history of the Near East, Israel included, as leading naturally to Christianity; but it did, nevertheless, constitute the first organized attempt to deal chronologically with the history of biblical Israel in the light of the archaeological and related data then available. This book is now a landmark in the field. It is true that specialists have found fault with the book, each in his own field: the philosopher of history, the cuneiformist, the New Testament specialist, the specialist in the Second Jewish Commonwealth, etc. But the book as a whole is a tour de force in the best sense of the term; and its influence—in conjunction with the same author's *Archaeology and the Religion of Israel* (1942)—has been deservedly profound.

The chief contribution of this work—apart from scores of valuable individual observations—is the systematic manner in which the author weaves together the extrabiblical data with the biblical to achieve a pattern of biblical history according to which the biblical text, analyzed critically, emerged as a generally reliable document for the reconstruction of ancient Israel's career. This attitude of critical appreciation of the Bible as one of the most valuable sources in antiquity for the modern historian found generally ready acceptance. What would have been quite new and controversial a decade previously was now met by dwindling opposition. Albright's work set the tone for historical studies thereafter.

Historians and philosophers outside the biblical field were generally slow to take cognizance of the revolutionary developments in the writing of biblical history. Thus the noted historiographer R. G. Collingwood, in his (posthumous) book on *The Idea of History* (1946), dismissed the biblical material in less than a page (p. 17) as but "theocratic history and myth." Two years earlier the well-known social philosopher Bertrand Russell wrote in his *History of Western Philosophy* (1944): "The early history of the Israelites cannot be confirmed from any source outside the Old Testament, and it is impossible to know at what point it ceased to be purely legendary. David and Solomon may be accepted as kings who probably had a real existence, but at the earliest point at which we come to something certainly historical there are already two kingdoms of Israel and Judah [ninth century B.C.]" (p. 309).

In 1954 I published the first popular history of *Ancient Israel* based upon the new discoveries and analyses. Apart from Albright's chapter on "The Biblical Period" (now, in revised form, a Harper Torchbook) in *The Jews: Their History, Culture, and Religion* (2 vols., 1949; 2nd ed., 1955) edited by Louis Finkelstein, my book remains the only up-to-date manual available in the field. It was not until 1959 that there appeared, finally, the first full-length, fresh *History of Israel,* by John Bright. Influenced throughout, as he readily admits, by the work of his mentor, Albright, Bright's detailed textbook has made fine use of the vast amount of material now available for his subject, both the extrabiblical data and the extensive secondary literature. Unlike the detailed histories of the Twenties and Thirties, and even of the Forties and Fifties among several written by European scholars—e.g., Martin Noth's *Geschichte Israels* (1950), which was reprinted without substantial change of the text as a second edition in 1954 and translated into English in 1958 as *History of Israel*—Bright has recognized the great value of the biblical text when discriminately employed.

From the foregoing it would seem possible, at long last, to write a thoroughly acceptable history of ancient Israel, one that will conform to the highest standards of modern scientific historiography. Yet the fact is that the time has not yet come, and well may never come, when such a work can be achieved, for there are two major problems that confront the modern historian in handling the sources of the biblical period.

First, the historian cannot fulfill his task when his sources are inadequate and of uncertain authorship and date. The sources for biblical history are even now neither sufficient nor chronologically secure. It is only occasionally that a biblical book, or its component parts, can be ascribed to a definite time, place, author, and purpose; and even though the extrabiblical material has become extensive, it generally suffices only for the broadest sort of understanding. European—chiefly German—scholarship is less inclined than American to regard archaeological and other extrabiblical data from the ancient Near East as pertinent for "proving" biblical statements and for reconstructing Israel's biblical career in any detail. But this difference in *Anschauung* may not be pursued here. On "the German school" of Albrecht Alt and Martin Noth as against "the American school" of W. F. Albright, see, e.g., John Bright's *Early Israel in Recent History Writing* (1956) and the chapters in the Albright Festschrift on "Modern Study of Old Testament Literature" by John Bright, "Biblical History in Transition" by G. E. Mendenhall, and "The Archaeology of Palestine" by G. E. Wright, all of whom are disciples of Albright. It need scarcely be added, however, that even when the two schools agree, there is no assurance that their common viewpoint is correct. Thus, e.g., the American school accepted uncritically the view of the German that the political structure of

Israel before the rise of the monarchy was that of an amphictyony, a confederacy of tribes centered about and held together by a common religious shrine. Yet in point of fact there is no evidence in favor of this view and much that is against it; see my discussion of "The Tribal System of Israel and Related Groups in the Period of the Judges" in *Studies and Essays in Honor of Abraham A. Neuman* (1962), edited by Meir Ben-Horin, B. D. Weinryb, and Solomon Zeitlin (reprinted in *Oriens Antiquus,* 1 [1962], 11-20).

The second serious difficulty is that in the handling of the biblical material there is the major problem of discovering the fundamental economic, social, and political forces from documents couched almost exclusively in religious terminology and given to interpret all human experience as manifestations of divine intervention. As I pointed out in the Introduction to *Ancient Israel:*

> Those who are responsible for the composition of the Hebrew Bible believed that what they uttered and wrote derived from the God who had entered into a mutual covenant with Israel. According to the terms of the covenant, God loved and protected Israel and no other people, and Israel worshiped and loved no other God but Him. The modern historian, however, cannot accept such an interpretation, but must seek—behind the religious terminology— the same kind of documented human story, with an examination of its underlying dynamics, that would be his proper objective in any other field. Otherwise he would achieve no more than a compilation of myths, chronicles, annals, oracles, autobiographies, court histories, personal apologia. The historian cannot regard any human activity or statement, be it religious or secular, sacred or profane, as beyond his domain. His competence is limited only by the nature and adequacy of his sources. [P. 9.]

Not so, for example, in Bright's philosophy. His *History,* he states in the Foreword, "has . . . been prepared with the particular needs of the undergraduate theological student in mind" (p. 10). His view is that "the history of Israel is the history of a people which came into being at a certain point in time as a league of tribes united in covenant with Yahweh. . . . The distinguishing factor that made Israel the peculiar phenomenon that she was, which both created her society and was the controlling factor in her history, was of course her religion. Since this is so, Israel's history is a subject inseparable from the history of Israel's religion" (pp. 9-10). And see his clear summary of "Hebrew Religion, History of" in *The Interpreter's Dictionary of the Bible;* also the article on "History" by C. R. North.

As for the significance and end-product of Israel's history, Bright concludes in his "Epilogue: Toward the Fulness of Time" that three aspects stand out: (1) "The Old Testament presents Israel's history as a history of redemption and promise, a 'salvation history' (*Heilsgeschichte*). Yet, also, and at the same time, it presents us with a history of rebellion, failure, frustration, and most bitter disappointment, in which hope is often dashed, ever deferred, and at best only partly realized. It is, in short, a *Heilsgeschichte* that never in the pages of the Old Testament arrives at *Heil* (salvation); it is a *Heilsgeschichte* that is also not yet a *Heilsgeschichte*—a story without theological terminus." (2) For the Jew, "in the end, Judaism gave the only answer possible for it . . . it was that pointed out by the Pharisee, the way that led to normative Judaism, to the Mishnah and the Talmud. The history of Israel would continue in the history of the Jewish people, a people claimed by the God of Israel to live under his law to the last generation of mankind. . . ." (3) For the Christian "there is another answer, the one the Christian gives, and must give. It is likewise historically legitimate, for Christianity did in fact spring from the loins of Judaism. That answer is that the destination of Old Testament history and theology is Christ and his gospel. . . . In Christ, and because of Christ, the Christian sees [Israel's] history, which is 'salvation history' (*Heilsgeschichte*), but yet also a history of disappointment and failure, made really and finally *Heilsgeschichte*." In fine, "Israel's history leads straight on to the Talmud— or the gospel. It has in fact led in no other direction" (pp. 446-53).

This matter of philosophy of history is crucial. It was a central feature in the discussion that followed the papers of E. R. Goodenough and M. S. Enslin in the symposium on "The Bible and the Humanities" sponsored by the American Council of Learned Societies at its Annual Meeting, January 21, 1960. The penultimate paragraph in Goodenough's paper, "The Bible as Product of the Ancient World," published in the ACLS collection of *Five Essays on the Bible,* asserts:

The Church preserved this burst of highly individual books with all their different points of view and made them into a single Bible.

84

Here we have what we began with, the miracle of a canonical collection which, once accepted as such, was preserved with almost superhuman care for textual integrity. It put with this collection, as a single revelation of the one God, the books of the ancient Jews. Churchmen of all denominations have worked since that time on the endless problem of showing how they present a single faith. Faith that our problems are solved in the person of the risen Lord is the faith in which traditional Christianity unites, but the problems Jesus seemed to solve have essentially, from the very beginning, been each man's own. Jesus could become the model monk, crusader, public school gentleman, Marxist leader, captain, bridegroom through the ages, precisely because he was given so many roles from the start. [P. 19.]

M. S. Enslin, in his discussion of "Biblical Criticism and Its Effects on Modern Civilization," also in the ACLS collection, stated:

Briefly, then, biblical criticism has destroyed the tyranny of the Bible and made evident its lasting values. Gone is the either-or approach: (a) accept it as the complete and final word of God, which, if anything seems to conflict with it, thereby proves that other to be false, if not blasphemous; (b) reject it as a false and fraudulent fabrication with which the enlightened can and need have no part. . . . For myself, I have no slightest intention of doing either—there are many signs that the Bible, freed from its graveclothes, is destined to remain in our culture as an imperishable asset. No longer a book of ready answers, by no means free from trivia and unwise pronouncements, errors and contradictions. Because it is a series of human books, written by human beings, groping their way to discoveries by the only path by which men and women ever seem to have made any discoveries, namely, through their own experiences and the experiences of their predecessors and fellow searchers, it is surely not surprising it should be. . . . [Pp. 30-44.]

R. H. Bainton, in his paper on "The Bible and the Reformation" in the same symposium, put it this way:

[When Luther designated both the Old Testament and the New as a unity,] the modern reader will say that this unity was achieved by imposing upon the Old Testament a sense which was not there. But this is precisely the point at issue. Luther, following LeFevre, said that the plain historical sense of Scripture is what the writers

85

of Scripture intended to say. Now if they intended to prophesy, then prophecy is the literal sense. If they intended to foreshadow Christ, then their clairvoyance is the historical meaning. This problem was not restricted to the sixteenth century. Even today one who believes in a religious philosophy of history will interpret the events differently from one who sees in the Old Testament only the fortuitous clashing of nomads emerging from the Syrian sands. [Pp. 20-29.]

American scholarship has generally ignored A. J. Toynbee's attempt at *A Study of History* so far as the ancient Near East, Israel included, is concerned. The very few scholars in this area who reacted to Toynbee found his assertions unacceptable; see my essay "On Toynbee's Use of the Term *Syriac* for One of His Societies" in the A. H. Silver Jubilee Volume, *In the Time of Harvest* (1963), where *inter alia* the self-confessed ignorance and irrationality of Toynbee in matters biblical (and Jewish) are dealt with. I should have cited there and made use of the devastating critique of Toynbee's *Study* in Henri Frankfort's penetrating analysis of *The Birth of Civilization in the Near East* (1951; Anchor Book, 1956).

◦§ 9 §◦

Social, Economic, and Legal Institutions

Sociology has come rapidly to the fore since World War I, and it is not surprising that the Bible has undergone sociological analysis in recent decades. Back in 1912, Louis Wallis published *Sociological Study of the Bible* and he returned to the subject in later years: *God and the Social Process* (1935), *The Bible Is Human* (1942), and *The Bible and Modern Belief* (1949). David Jacobson wrote on *The Social Background of the Old Testament* (1942), and Joachim Wach on *Sociology of Religion* (1944). By far the best is Max Weber's *Das antike Judentum* (1921), translated and edited by H. H. Gerth and Don Martindale as *Ancient Judaism* (1958).

In general, however, these works could hardly have hoped to become authoritative, for none of them demonstrated the control of the biblical and comparative material that the discipline demands; also, the material available to them hardly sufficed for reliable sociological treatment. Their merit lay chiefly in the fact that they tended to present the biblical and related data within a secular framework. Much more useful have been the numerous articles, in scattered journals, dealing with specific phenomena, for no over-all pattern can be discerned for any society unless sufficient individual aspects of its culture are correctly identified. In the light of the but freshly recovered Hurrian (Nuzi) texts of the mid-second millennium B.C., C. H. Gordon published new analyses of such social phenomena as "Fratriarchy in the Old Testament" (*Journal of Biblical Literature,* LIV [1935], 223-31) and "The Status of Women as Reflected in the Nuzi Tablets" (*Zeitschrift für Assyriologie,* XLIII [1936], 146-69). In 1937, Gordon and Millar Burrows both wrote on the Genesis (Chapters 29 and 31) account of Jacob, Laban, and Laban's daughters, using the new Nuzi data (respectively: *Bulletin,* LXVI, 25-27, and *Journal of the American Oriental Society,* LVII, 259-76); but Moshe Greenberg has now urged "Another Look at Rachel's Theft of the Teraphim" (*Journal of Biblical Literature,* LXXXI [1962], 239-48). Gordon's *The World of the Old Testament* (1958) is a useful repository of this and other extrabiblical material.

Much recent study has revolved around such institutions as the family and marriage: e.g., Raphael Patai's *Sex and Family in the Bible and the Middle East* (1959), Millar Burrows' *The Basis of Israelite Marriage* (1938), L. M. Epstein's *Marriage Laws in the Bible and Talmud* (1942), and Ephraim Neufeld's *Ancient Hebrew Marriage Laws* (1944). A somewhat earlier work was Julian Morgenstern's "Beena Marriage (Matriarchat) in Ancient Israel and Its Historical Implications" (*Zeitschrift für die alttestamentliche Wissenschaft,* Neue Folge, VI [1929], 91-110; VIII [1931], 46-58). Isaac Mendelsohn has utilized recently discovered Mesopotamian data for his articles on "The Family in the Ancient Near East" (*Biblical Archaeologist,* XI [1940], 24-40) and "On Marriage in Alalakh" in *Essays on Jewish Life and Thought* . . . (1959), the S. W. Baron Festschrift. Levirate marriage, still not yet comprehended adequately for lack of sufficient data, has been discussed chiefly by Millar Burrows (*Journal of Biblical Literature,* LIX [1940], 23-33, 445-54; *Bulletin,* LXXVII [1940], 2-15). A bird's-eye view of family institutions in biblical Israel, with bibliography, is available in Roland De Vaux's *Ancient Israel: Its Life and Institutions* (1961);

Isaac Mendelsohn's forthcoming book on the subject will be more analytical.

The political, social, and economic structure of ancient Israel is now better known than before, though there will always be, as stated above, the major problem of discovering the fundamental economic, social, and political forces from documents couched almost exclusively in religious terminology and given to interpret all historical experiences as manifestations of divine intervention. This caveat can scarcely be overemphasized when one notes De Vaux's comment in the bibliography of his *Ancient Israel*. In dealing with Part II, "Civil Institutions"; section 2, "The Free Populations: Its Divisions"; subsection 4, "Rich and Poor"; he says (p. 524): "On the rich and the poor: the question has been studied chiefly from the religious angle." (!) What more need be said?

Isaac Mendelsohn has contributed much to the enlightenment of this area: "Gilds in Babylonia and Assyria" (*Journal of the American Oriental Society*, LX [1944], 68-72) and "Guilds in Ancient Palestine" (*Bulletin*, LXXX [1940], 17-21); his *Slavery in the Ancient Near East* (1949) incorporates several *Vorstudien*. In 1941, Millar Burrows wrote on "Democracy in the Hebrew-Christian Tradition: Old and New Testaments" in the Second Symposium of *Science, Philosophy and Religion,* and C. U. Wolf has since recognized "Traces of Primitive Democracy in Israel" (*Journal of Near Eastern Studies,* VI [1947], 98-108), as has Robert Gordis in "Democratic Origins in Ancient Israel—the Biblical *'Ēdāh*" in the *Alexander Marx Jubilee Volume* (1950). Ephraim Neufeld has traced "The Emergence of a Royal-Urban Society in Ancient Israel" (*Hebrew Union College Annual,* XXXI [1960], 31-52) and has written other articles in the area of economics, among them "The Prohibition Against Loans at Interest in Ancient Hebrew Laws" (*Hebrew Union College Annual,* XXVI [1955], 355-412) and "Socio-Economic Background of Yōbēl and Šemiṭṭā" (*Rivista degli studi orientali,* XXXIII [1958], 53-124). Julius Lewy has published a study of "The Biblical Institution of *Dᵉrôr* in the Light of Akkadian Documents" (*Eretz-Israel,* V [1958], 21*-31*), and Isaac Mendelsohn has made a study "On Corvée Labor in Ancient Canaan and Israel" (*Bulletin,* CLXVII [1962], 31-35), an important institution; he made an earlier analysis of "Samuel's Denunciation of Kingship in the Light of the Akkadian Documents from Ugarit" (*Bulletin*, CXLIII [1956], 17-22).

Scattered among journals or imbedded among other archaeological data, there has gradually accumulated a considerable quantity of reliable data pertaining to industry and trade in ancient Israel. Back in 1937, Samuel Yeivin edited a fine study, in Hebrew, of *Trade, Industry and Crafts in Ancient Palestine* (Volumes IX and X of the excellent "Library of Palestinology" of the Israel [formerly Jewish Palestine] Exploration Society), with contributions by Benjamin Maisler (now Mazar), Immanuel Ben-Dor, Nelson Glueck, Samuel Klein, Michael Avi Yonah, and Mordecai Narkiss. What is needed now, and is quite realizable, is a detailed up-to-date volume many times greater in size.

There has been no archaeological expedition in the territory of biblical Israel and her neighbors of old that has not added new data on industry and trade and brought clarification to this fundamental aspect of human activity; and the same applies, of course, to ancient Near Eastern strata, which have yielded thousands of economic and related texts. A good idea of some of these may be obtained from such works as *Trade and Market in the Early Empires: Economies in History and Theory* (1957), edited by Karl Polanyi, C. M. Arensberg, and H. W. Peason. Note, especially, Chapters II-IV: "Marketless Trading in Hammurabi's Time" by Polanyi, "A Bird's-Eye View of Mesopotamian Economic History" by A. L. Oppenheim, and " 'No Man's Coast': Ports of Trade in the Eastern Mediterranean" by R. B. Revere. Also of particular interest are Oppenheim's article on "The Seafaring Merchants of Ur" (*Journal of the American Oriental Society*, LXXIV [1954], 6-17); W. F. Leemans' studies of *The Old Babylonian Merchant* (1950) and *Foreign Trade in the Old Babylonian Period* (1960) as revealed by texts from southern Mesopotamia; and J. B. Curtis and W. W. Hallo's "Money and Merchants in Ur III" (*Hebrew Union College Annual*, XXX [1959], 103-39). C. H. Gordon recently described Abraham the Patriarch as "a merchant prince; a *tamkârum*" in "Abraham and the Merchants of Ura" (*Journal of Near Eastern Studies*, LXXV [1958], 28-31), on which see W. F. Albright's discussion of "Abram the Hebrew" (*Bulletin*, CLXIII [1961], 36-54; see especially sections II and III).

Albright's excavations at Tell Beit Mirsim revealed evidence of extensive activity in dyeing and weaving (see "Dyeing," with bibliography, by R. W. Funk in *The Interpreter's Dictionary of the Bible*), and important information was made available by Nelson Glueck's excavation of a copper refinery at Solomon's port of Ezion-geber (at the head of the Gulf of Aqaba) and of the copper mines in the vicinity. Glueck discusses his excavations in Chapters III and IV of *The Other Side of the Jordan* (1940), pointing out that "Ezion-geber was the Pittsburgh of Palestine, in addition to being its most important port." Benno Rothenberg has also made a study of this area in "Ancient Copper Industries in the Western Arabah" (*Palestine Exploration Quarterly*, XCIV [1962], 5-71), which includes Appendixes by Yohanan Aharoni and B. H. McLoed.

G. W. Van Beek has worked up a useful survey of "Frankincense and Myrrh" and their pertinence for the "cultural, economic, and political effects of the demand for these substances" (*Biblical Archaeologist*, XXIII [1960], 69-95). J. B. Pritchard has had much to say about "Industry and Trade at Biblical Gibeon" (*ibid.*, 23-29); and in Chapter IV of his *Gibeon* (1962), "The Makers of Wine," he points out that "at least one reason for Gibeon's prosperity was the success of some of its enterprising citizens in the making and the export of fine wine. Gibeon may be said to have been an ancient 'Bordeaux' of Palestine."

Another beverage industry has been the subject of a study by L. F. Hartman and A. L. Oppenheim, who cooperated to produce a monograph *On Beer and Brewing Techniques in Ancient Mesopotamia* (1950; Supplement 10 to the *Journal of the American Oriental Society*). Beer played a more important role in ancient Israel, as well as in Philistia, than is generally realized. The Hebrew word *shekar* (cf. *shikkor*, "drunkard"), traditionally translated "strong drink" (or "[hard] liquor" in some modern, "unauthorized" versions of the Bible), has sometimes been rendered "ale" (at Lev. 10:9, Num. 6:3, Deut. 14:26) in the new Torah translation (1962) of the Jewish Publication Society.

There is considerable economic material in the Bible, and a closer scrutiny of the text in the light of the kind of data adduced above will help to ferret it out and make proper use of it.

The past decade and a half has witnessed the discovery of no less than three major collections of laws from the Mesopotamia of about 2000 B.C., thus antedating the great Code of Hammurabi (about 1725 B.C.) by from about one to three centuries: the Ur-Nammu body of laws, the laws of Lipit-Ishtar, and the laws of Eshnunna. Considering these together with the legal material previously brought to light (e.g., the Middle Assyrian, Hittite, and neo-Babylonian collections of laws, and sundry other legal documents), one must feel gratified that so great a quantity of data has become available to the biblical scholar, as well as to the historian of law in general. A fine sampling of these materials is now available in English translation, the work essentially of Albrecht Goetze, S. N. Kramer, and T. J. Meek, in *Ancient Near Eastern Texts* (1950), edited by J. B. Pritchard.

Withal, it is still too early to think in terms of a detailed and standard work on biblical law in the light of Mesopotamian law; we simply lack sufficient details, especially in the Bible, for so refined a comparative analysis. Not only that, there is sometimes the tendency to elaborate on the "superiority" of biblical law, both in the letter and in the spirit, to the disadvantage of Sumer, Babylonia, Assyria, etc. J. J. Finkelstein has criticized this attitude in general in "Bible and Babel: A Comparative Study of the Hebrew and Babylonian Religious Spirit" (*Commentary*, November 1958, pp. 431-44). And he has come back to this theme—though without dealing specifically with biblical law, on which see his long article in Mesopotamian law, s. *mishpaṭ,* to appear in Volume V of Israel's excellent Hebrew *Encyclopaedia Biblica*—in his review-article on "Ammiṣaduqa's Edict [edited by F. R. Kraus, 1958] and the Babylonian 'Law Codes'" (*Journal of Cuneiform Studies,* XV [1961], 91-104):

The "Edict" of the title . . . serves mainly as a point of departure for a series of excursuses on a whole range of social and economic institutions of the Old Babylonian period. Real penetration into many of these institutional phenomena thus submitted to analysis, such as the precise status of the social strata . . . the rôle of the Crown in economic and commercial life, the form of private credit and loan transactions and their control, have long been appreciated as of fundamental importance to a secure grasp of the live social organism that was the relatively homogeneous civilization of Southern Mesopotamia from ca. 2000 to 1700 B.C. Yet for all the information accumulated about such matters from the thousands of private documents and letters of the period, the so-called "law-codes," allusions in other sources, and the numerous studies devoted to them of greater or more modest scope, there are still very few of such institutions which have warranted the feeling that we have penetrated their living reality, and not merely the words or terms that symbolize and, in effect, obscure them. . . . [Kraus] is all too aware of the near impossibility of attaining such definitive understanding of the basic social, legal, and economic institutions of the period under discussion with the amount and kinds of source material at our command. . . .

One of the older works on *The Origin and History of Hebrew Law* is that of J. M. P. Smith; first published in 1931, it has recently been reprinted, unfortunately without drastic revision. A useful survey of "The Origin of Hebrew Law" constitutes Chapter II of T. J. Meek's *Hebrew Origins*, 2nd ed. (1950), from which one interesting statement may be quoted here: "There is no doubt but that there is great similarity between the Hebrew and Babylonian codes. . . . There must be some connection between the two codes, but the connection is not such as to indicate direct borrowing. No one today argues that. Whatever borrowing there was came indirectly, either through common inheritance or through Canaanite influence, or much more likely through both ways" (pp. 68-69). Background material may be found in E. A. Speiser's "Early Law and Civilization" (*Canadian Bar Review*, October 1953, pp. 863-77) and "Authority and Law in Mesopotamia" (Supplement 17 to the *Journal of the American Oriental Society* [1954], pp. 8-15). Isaac Mendelsohn's chapter on "Authority and Law in Canaan-Israel" (*ibid.*, pp. 25-33) and G. E. Mendenhall's "Ancient Oriental and Biblical Law" (*Biblical Archaeologist*, XVII [1954], 26-46) are more specific.

During the past years, however, it has been specific legal matters that have been subjected to close analysis, and this has been all to the good. Mendelsohn has discussed such problems as "The Disinheritance of Jephthah in the Light of Paragraph 27 of the Lipit-Ishtar Code" (*Israel Exploration Journal*, IV [1954], 116-19), "A Ugaritic Parallel to the Adoption of Ephraim and Manasseh" (*Israel Exploration Journal*, IX [1959], 180-83), and "On the Preferential Status of the Eldest Son" (*Bulletin*, CLVI [1959], 38-40). M. R. Lehmann analyzed "Abraham's Purchase of Machpelah and

Hittite Law" (*Bulletin,* CXXIX [1953], 15-18), and G. E. Mendenhall discussed "Puppy and Lettuce in Northwest-Semitic Covenant Making" (*Bulletin,* CXXXIII [1954], 26-30). Ephraim Neufeld discussed, in the light of ancient western Asiatic law, *"Ius redemptionis* in Ancient Hebrew Law" and "Inalienability of Mobile and Immobile Pledges in the Laws of the Bible" (*Revue internationale des droits de l'antiquité,* VIII [1961], 29-40; IX [1962], 33-44). Moshe Greenberg has written on "Some Postulates of Biblical Criminal Law" and E. A. Speiser has discussed some socioeconomic and legal terms in "Leviticus and the Critics"—both in the *Yehezkel Kaufmann Jubilee Volume* (1960)—and W. F. Albright has made a fine analysis of "The Judicial Reform of Jehoshaphat" in the *Alexander Marx Jubilee Volume* (1950).

◄§ 10 §►

Psychology-Psychoanalysis

Mention at least must be made of the fact that psychoanalysis and psychology, increasingly dominant disciplines since World War I, have made their presence felt also in the study of the Bible. In the *Hebrew Union College Annual,* Abraham Cronbach published "The Psychoanalytic Study of Judaism" (VIII-IX [1931-32], 605-740) and "New Studies in the Psychology of Judaism" (XIX [1945-46], 205-273), with reference to other studies that pertain to the Bible.

But it has been chiefly some outstanding biblical personages who have been analyzed so that their underlying motivations and drives have been laid bare. Moses, David, Hosea, Jeremiah, and Ezekiel have been, as it were, laid out on the analyst's couch. Most recently Samuel has been treated neuropsychologically, in *Samuel and the Beginnings of the Prophetic Movement* (1961), a twenty-eight page monograph by W. F. Albright. Having assumed, *inter alia,* that Samuel was a reformer and had rejected the priestly ritual of Shiloh, Albright assumed further that "there may also have been a very human element in Samuel's reform movement. As a youth he presumably suffered from the persecution of other boys at Shiloh who belonged to priestly and Levite families. Our own experience of the cruelty of the young is here reinforced by many systematic studies, ranging from phenomena of gang psychology to social parallels with the so-called 'peck hierarchy' of barnyard fowls. We need have little doubt that Samuel's recorded harshness and refusal to compromise received part of it's impetus from unhappy experiences as a boy in Shiloh." It seems that anyone can analyze anyone else in any period in whatever region and circumstances by assuming whatever event, experience, motivation, or reaction will fit the supposed problem at hand. Actually Samuel was a typical diviner-priest and a member of the guild of seers; the problem is sociological, not psychological. See my discussion of "The Seer in Ancient Israel" in *Oriens Antiquus* (to appear in 1965, pp. 1-21).

Of interest is the fact that in Europe after World War I, and especially as a consequence of the breakdown of the economic and social order in the Twenties and early Thirties, a host of modern novelists, mostly German, began to write on biblical themes and personalities. Joseph and his brothers, Jeremiah, Job, the Nile River, David, Joshua, Moses—these were the themes on which Mann, the Zweigs, Werfel, Ludwig, and others wrote. But of course none of these works had any scholarly justification or merit; unable to comprehend and confront the postwar situation in the milieu in which they grew up and functioned as writers, these men leaped over— i.e., escaped—time and place, and expressed their twentieth century A.D. hopes and frustrations in terms of a second or first millennium B.C. environment, which they themselves created out of a woeful lack of adequate data. Probably the best of this genre, not only well written and thoughtfully reasoned but straying little from the basic Hebrew text, is Maurice Samuel's *Certain People of the Book* (1955).

In general, the psychologist-psychiatrist knows neither the Bible nor its background, and the biblical scholar is equally amateurish in the discipline of psychology. And while it may be possible and worthwhile in theory for a trained psychologist and a competent biblical scholar to join efforts in working up psychological analyses of biblical persons and themes, in practice there is always the great danger that the result will recall the alleged fear of Bernard Shaw that a union with Isadora Duncan could well produce an offspring who danced like the father and reasoned like the mother. The nonsense that pervaded Freud's attempt to psychoanalyze *Moses and Mono-*

theism (1939) should constitute a grave warning to those who would recreate a personality and a set of circumstances in the absence of sufficient and reliable data. On the other hand, E. C. Broome Jr.'s analysis of "Ezekiel's Abnormal Personality" (*Journal of Biblical Literature*, LXV [1946], 277-92) is one of the superior efforts.

Commentators on the Bible have generally attempted to recreate, more or less within the limits of the pertinent material available, the life, times, and teachings of the person credited with having written the biblical book on which they were commenting. Sheldon Blank's *Jeremiah: Man and Prophet* (1961) is a good case in point. A sympathetic and popular work that has been enjoying considerable favor is Fleming James's *Personalities of the Old Testament* (1939; frequently reprinted). But success in this area will never be achieved. As I have had occasion to remark, after striving mightily to work up sufficient data for a brief biography of Moses (in *Great Jewish Personalities in Ancient and Medieval Times,* ed. Simon Noveck [1959], pp. 10-39), "There is no single work on Moses that is satisfactory; and unless—most unlikely—new materials of some substance come to light, none need be expected. The full-length biographies are essentially fiction" (p. 39).

⊸§ 11 §⊱

Chronology

Without chronology there can be no writing of history; an undated document may be useful to the homiletician, but hardly to the historian. So it is a source of gratification that the chronology of the Fertile Crescent of antiquity, the Hebrew Bible included, is now much better known than in the days prior to archaeology. The standard work now, following on such earlier works as F. X. Kugler's *Von Moses bis Paulus* (1922) and J. Lewy's *Die Chronologie der Könige von Israel und Juda* (1927), is E. R. Thiele's *The Mysterious Numbers of the Hebrew Kings: A Reconstruction of the Chronology of the Kingdoms of Israel and Judah* (1951). For the Near East during the second millennium B.C., see the bibliography and charts worked up by E. F. Campbell Jr. in the Albright Festschrift, *The Bible and the Ancient Near East* . . . (1961).

The subject is an intricate one, and only the barest statement may be made here. In general, it is Mesopotamia and Egypt that provide several absolute dates that help fix certain biblical events—*synchronisms* is the technical term employed. The Egyptian data, involving the reigns of Ramses II and Merneptah (about 1290-1210 B.C. in all), help determine a thirteenth century date for the Exodus from Egypt. In turn, the approximate dates for David and Solomon, in conjunction with Egyptian data, help us date the Egyptian invasion of Judah by King Shishak (about 920). For the period of the Divided Monarchy (about 925-722) Assyrian documents are extremely helpful chronologically; see the fine survey by W. W. Hallo, "From Qarqar to Carchemish: Assyria and Israel in the Light of New Discoveries" (*Biblical Archaeologist,* XXIII [1960], 34-61). And most recently the publication of the *Chronicles of Chaldaean Kings* (626-556 B.C.) *in the British Museum* (1956) by D. J. Wiseman has shed much light on the last years of the Kingdom of Judah and the First Temple.

With the aid of Babylonian data, much of the last decades of Judah's history can now be dated with confidence. For example, the biblical statement (II Kings 23:29) that King Josiah of Judah was killed at Megiddo by Pharaoh Necho when he tried to stop the Egyptian army from marching north and east against the Assyrians must now be corrected to indicate that Necho was really marching to aid weakened Assyria against the growing power of Babylonia, and that Josiah, to prevent this powerful coalition from coming to pass, marched against Necho—and thus against Assyria and in behalf of Babylonia. A discussion of this incident may be found in M. B. Rowton's "Jeremiah and the Death of Josiah" (*Journal of Near Eastern Studies,* X [1951], 128-30).

Archaeology, too, has come very much to our aid in helping determine more precisely some biblical data. The partial conquest of Canaan by the Hebrews-Israelites under Joshua is now somewhat more clearly understood as the result of the excavation of several sites; clear summaries have been written by G. E. Wright—Chapter V, "Conquest," of his *Biblical Archaeology* (1957)—and by G. E. Mendenhall—"The Hebrew Conquest of Palestine" (*Biblical Archaeologist,* XXV [1962], 66-87). And see in this connection E. F. Campbell Jr.'s fine survey of "The Amarna Letters and the Amarna Period" (*Biblical Archaeologist,* XXIII [1960], 2-22). The temple of Baal (or El)-berith mentioned in the Abimelech story in Judges 9 (vv. 4, 46) has recently been identified and dated in its several phases and lengthy history (seventeenth-twelfth centuries B.C.) in the ruins of Shechem—see L. E. Toombs and G. E. Wright's "The Third Campaign at Balâṭah" (*Bulletin*, CLXI [1961], 11-54), especially pages 11 ff. and 28 ff.; and even the sacred area mentioned in verse 6 seems now to have been identified archaeologically and chronologically—see now pages 5-32 of their report on "The Fourth Campaign at Balâṭah (Shechem)" (*Bulletin*, CLXIX [1963]).

Even the patriarchal period is beginning to emerge from chronological obscurity. A recent study is W. F. Albright's stimulating analysis of "Abram the Hebrew: A New Archaeological Interpretation" (*Bulletin*, CLXIII [1961], 36-54), based in part on material acquired by Nelson Glueck in his explorations of the Negeb (see, e.g., his *Rivers of the Desert* [1959], pp. 60-110). The Persian and early Hellenistic period (about 500-200 B.C.), on the other hand, is still very much a no man's land, and even the relative—let alone the absolute—chronology of Ezra and Nehemiah remains uncertain.

J. A. Montgomery worked up a fine bibliography and survey of "The Chronology" (of the Hebrew Kingdom) for his *International Critical Commentary on the Books of Kings* (1951), with references to the works of Julian Morgenstern (whose work on *The Chronological Order of Ezra and Nehemiah* was published in 1962) and others; and there is also a fine survey of "Chronology of the O.T." by S. J. De Vries in *The Interpreter's Dictionary of the Bible*, Vol. 1 (1962). All in all, one can look forward to continued progress in the attempt to unravel the complexities of chronology in its relation to Israel's career and the Bible.

ᵛᵍ 12 ᵍᵛ

Commentaries, Introductions, and Textual Studies

The writing of detailed full-length commentaries on biblical books, a feature of European scholarship, has not caught on on this side of the ocean. When this activity was in full swing in Germany and England in the nineteenth and early twentieth centuries, American scholars were drawn into cooperative efforts with their British colleagues.

The "International Critical Commentary" series, begun before the turn of the century, was a joint British-American project and easily the most ambitious and worthwhile undertaking of American biblical scholarship. Of the "American" volumes written prior to the Age of Archaeology, *Judges* (1895; reprinted several times) by G. F. Moore and *Amos and Hosea* (1905) by W. R. Harper perhaps stood out; but even these have long been in need of drastic revision. Since World War I, two "American" volumes have appeared, both by J. A. Montgomery and both of superlative quality: *The Book of Daniel* (1927) and *The Books of Kings* (1951; the manuscript was completed in 1941 and was edited by H. S. Gehman). Rarely have philological and archaeological and other extrabiblical data been utilized and woven together in the scientific exposition of a biblical book in the manner that Montgomery achieved in these two volumes.

The indefatigable Julian Morgenstern, last of the great practitioners of literary criticism in this age of archaeology, has published in the *Hebrew Union College Annual* what really constitute full-length commentaries: "The Book of the Covenant" (Exodus 22-23) (V [1928]; VII [1930]; VIII-IX [1931-32]; and XXXIII [1962] —a total of close to 600 pages); "Amos Studies" (XI [1936]; XII-XIII [1937-38]; XV [1940]; and XXXII [1961]—a total of some 375 pages); and "The Message of Deutero-Isaiah in Its Sequential Unfolding" (XXIX [1958], 1-67; XXX [1959], 1-102), with which compare his study of "The Suffering Servant—a New Solution" (*Vetus testamentum,* XI [1961], 292-320, 406-31).

Moses Buttenwieser has written commentaries on *The Book of Job* (1922) and *The Psalms: Chronologically Treated with a New Translation* (1938); Robert Gordis has dealt with *Koheleth: The Man and His World* (1951); and C. C. Torrey's commentary on *The Second Isaiah* (1928) is an outstanding achievement.

The American reading public of detailed critical commentaries on biblical books—unlike even the European, let alone the Israeli—has always been extremely meager, and institutions and individual patrons who would pay for the publishing losses incurred by these "worst" sellers have been exceedingly few in number; nor have our major publishing houses been prone to ignore the profit motive. During the past few decades, however, the very large and inquisitive middle class that has emerged in the United States and that has become interested in matters biblical-archaeological has attracted the interest of publishers. This middle class is biblically ignorant, and can react positively only to popular presentation. And so Abingdon-Cokesbury Press undertook and issued *The Interpreter's Bible* (1952-57), a twelve-volume commentary on the Old and New Testaments, six for each Testament. Each biblical book is provided with an introduction, both the King James Version and the Revised Standard Version, some scholarly exegesis, and homiletical exposition; general articles on the Bible and on the Old Testament occupy just over a third of Volume I. In a way this work made publishing history in the biblical field, since the volumes are bulky (in quarto format and averaging 1,000-1,200 pages each) and are priced at $8.75 each. Yet even though most of the contributors rank high in the field, the scholarly merit of the work could hardly be notable when such a relatively small proportion of the space was allotted to exegesis—on the average, hardly one-fourth of a page.

A few full-length introductions to the Bible have been produced in the past couple of decades. The most successful, so far as popularity is concerned, is R. H. Pfeiffer's *Introduction to the Old Testament* (1941; frequently reprinted), the most detailed and systematic to appear in English since the great *Introduction to the Literature of the Old Testament* by Britain's S. R. Driver (9th ed., 1913) and corresponding to Otto Eissfeldt's *Einleitung in das alte Testament* (2nd ed., 1956). In his detailed review of Pfeiffer's *Introduction* (*Journal of Biblical Literature*, LXI [1942], 111-26), W. F. Albright correctly stated that "it marks the end of an era of systematic research in this field. . . . The most unexpected characteristic of Pfeiffer's work is the insignificant part occupied by archaeology . . . [or] any of the new linguistic data or new philological techniques. . . ."

Among the more popular introductions are B. W. Anderson's *Understanding the Old Testament* (1957; frequently reprinted) and N. K. Gottwald's *A Light to the Nations: An Introduction to the Old Testament* (1959).

The book of Ezekiel experienced sudden and intensive analysis in the Thirties and Forties. Throughout the heyday of literary and textual criticism, when book after book was being analyzed into smithereens, so that the traditional author of a book was left with relatively little of the text as his own—the remainder being distributed among redactors, glossators, and the like—the book of Ezekiel managed to escape unscathed. Then scholarly activity, begun in Europe, descended here too upon the book, to the point where C. C. Torrey, for example, claimed that he had isolated *Pseudo-Ezekiel and the Original Prophecy* (1930)—he later reaffirmed his claim in "Certainly Pseudo-Ezekiel" (*Journal of Biblical Literature,* LIII [1934], 291-320)—and W. A. Irwin, in his detailed study of *The Problem of Ezekiel* (1943), commenting on the work of Gustav Hölscher (who had retained for the prophet less than 170 out of a total of 1,273 verses), observed wryly: "At the worst, Hölscher is by a safe margin of some 170 verses, in whole or in part, less radical than certain other famous critics, for they delete the *entire* Book of Ezekiel; still worse, they delete Ezekiel himself also!" (p. 12). Scholarly opinion today generally recognizes the book of Ezekiel (although Chapters 40-48 are more moot than others)—as well as Ezekiel himself—as substantially historical. H. G. May's study of the book in *The Interpreter's Bible,* Vol. VI (1956) and C. G. Howie's article on "Ezekiel" in *The Interpreter's Dictionary of the Bible,* Vol. II (1962) are representative of current opinion.

An interesting aspect of text analysis has been raised about the book of Ecclesiastes (Koheleth). According to H. L. Ginsberg, the traditional Hebrew text is a translation from an original Aramaic; the most vigorous supporter of the conventional belief that no Aramaic original was involved is Robert Gordis. Frank Zimmermann has participated in the controversy, and has extended the translation theory to other books, e.g., to "Chronicles as a Partially Translated Book" (*Jewish Quarterly Review,* XLII [1951-52], 265-82, 387-412). The problem is not a new one—any more than it was for the New Testament when C. C. Torrey promulgated an Aramaic (and in part Hebrew) original for *The Four Gospels* back in 1933—but it is argued now with greater knowledge and acumen. Full bibliographies will be found in Gordis's *Koheleth: The Man and His World* (1951) and Ginsberg's *Koheleth* (1961; in Hebrew).

Very little research has been done in recent decades on the origin and character of the so-called masoretic text; Israel, however, is a beehive of activity in this field. It seems that the Hebrew text of the Bible had never been fixed, in the manner that the number of the major divisions and of the books of the Bible had been fixed. Consequently, the term *masoretic text*—the Hebrew text as fixed by the masoretes, the Jewish scribes of old—is a misnomer; the term *preserved* or *traditional Hebrew text* is preferable. This is why the Jewish Publication Society's new translation of the Torah is described on the cover as "A New Translation of the Holy Scriptures According to the Traditional Hebrew Text."

Solomon Zeitlin has published "Some Reflections on the Text of the Pentateuch" (*Jewish Quarterly Review,* LI [1960-61], 321-31); his earlier essay, "An Historical Study of the Canonization of the Hebrew Scriptures" (*Proceedings of the American Academy for Jewish Research,* III [1931-32], 121-58), set many aspects of canonization in a new light.

In my essay "On the Present State of Proto-Septuagint Studies" (*Journal of the American Oriental Society,* LXI [1941], 81-91), I observed:

> Of course there was at one time more than one text-tradition of the Hebrew Bible. The Hebrew manuscripts used by the several Septuagint translators of the various books in the Old Testament differ at times not in minor details alone, but, as is the case in such books as Jeremiah, Job, Esther, *recensionally* from the masoretic text-tradition. But those text-traditions have long perished, driven out by the Hebrew text that was used by the Mishnah and Talmud, by Theodotion, Aquila, Symmachus, Origen, Jerome, from the first-second to the fifth centuries A.D. . . . [so] that all *extant* [italics in original] Hebrew manuscripts of the Bible go back to one text-tradition. [Pp. 85-86.]

This statement, made over two decades ago, has been demonstrated to the hilt by the Dead Sea Scrolls: (1) the biblical fragments among the Scrolls overwhelmingly are either identical with or represent a (usually inferior) variation on the theme of what came to be known as the masoretic text; (2) the Scroll fragments of Samuel and Jeremiah are *recensionally* different from the preserved Hebrew text, and what had previously been "long perished" has now become "extant." I have since made a fuller statement (*Journal of Biblical Literature,* LXXVIII [1959], 31-33; reprinted in the Albright Festschrift), which includes notes and references to earlier publications and especially to the clear statement by F. M. Cross Jr.

Moshe Greenberg has discussed "The Stabilization of the Text of the Hebrew Bible, Reviewed in the Light of the Biblical Materials from the Judean Desert" (*Journal of the American Oriental Society,* LXXVI [1956], 157-67).

An area of masoretic activity that has been worked in recent years is that of Kethib-Qere, where the consonants of one word are written (*kethib*) in the text proper together with the vowels of another word or form, while the consonants of the other word or form are written in the margin, and the vowels in the text and the consonants in the margin are read together (*qere*). Robert Gordis wrote on *The Biblical Text in the Making: A Study of the Kethib-Qere* in 1937 and I have subsequently taken exception to the thesis and details of his work in several articles: "Problems of Kethib-Qere" (*Journal of the American Oriental Society,* LX [1940], 30-45); "The Import of the Kethib-Qere and the Masoretic Note on *Leḵāḫ,* Judges 19:13" (*Jewish Quarterly Review,* XXXI [1940-41], 59-66); "The Biblical Prepositions *Táḥaṯ, Bēn, Bá'aḏ,* and Pronouns *'Anû* (or *'Ánū*), *Zō'ṯāḫ*" (*Hebrew Union College Annual,* XVII [1943], 267-92); and "The Origin of the Kethib-Qere System: A New Approach" (Supplement 7 to *Vetus testamentum,* Oxford Congress Volume [1960], 184-92).

Since the first half of the book of Daniel (2:4–7:28)—probably the original half—sizeable portions of Ezra (4:8–6:18; 7:12-26), a passage in Jeremiah (10:11), and two words in Genesis (31:47) are in Aramaic, and because biblical Hebrew and Aramaic are cognate languages, it is worth noting that Aramaic studies, too, have made considerable progress in recent decades. In 1927, J. A. Montgomery had made full use of the data then available in his commentary on *The Book of Daniel.* The state of Aramaic studies a decade later was the subject of the Lidzbarski Prize winner, Franz Rosenthal's *Die aramaistische Forschung seit Th. Nöldeke's Veröffentlichungen* (1939); and the same scholar has now published *A Grammar of Biblical Aramaic* (1961).

Alexander Sperber's critical edition of *The Bible in Aramaic, Based on Old Manuscripts and Printed Texts* constitutes an important textual aid to the study of the Bible. Volumes I-III have appeared to date: *The Pentateuch According to Targum Onkelos* (1959), *The Former Prophets According to Targum Jonathan*

(1959), and *The Latter Prophets According to Targum Jonathan* (1962); Volume IV will deal with "General Conclusions." The project is an expensive one, and—not uncharacteristically—it is a foreign publisher (Brill of Leiden) rather than an American who has undertaken it.

◄§ 13 §►

Paleography and Alphabet

Paleography is another aspect of biblical research to which American scholarship has made a notable contribution. Already in 1937 W. F. Albright had gone quite beyond his predecessors in setting forth systematically the typology of Old Hebrew scripts in "A Biblical Fragment from the Maccabaean Age: The Nash Papyrus" (*Journal of Biblical Literature,* LVI, pp. 145-76). And more recently his talented disciple F. M. Cross Jr. has produced probably the standard work for some time to come on "The Development of the Jewish Scripts," constituting Chapter 6 in *The Bible and the Ancient Near East* (1961). Almost a decade earlier, Cross, in full cooperation with D. N. Freedman, had published a standard work on *Early Hebrew Orthography: A Study of the Epigraphic Evidence* (1952; vol. 36 in the "American Oriental Series"). Matitiahu Tsevat has criticized Cross and Freedman's treatment of the *'aleph* in "A Chapter on Old West Semitic Orthography" in the *Joshua Bloch Memorial Volume* (1960).

Cross and T. O. Lambdin, following earlier discussions by half a dozen other scholars, have dealt with "A Ugaritic Abecedary and the Origins of the Proto-Canaanite Alphabet" (*Bulletin,* CLX [1960], 21-26) and have concluded that "the tablet supplies . . . confirmation of other evidence that the names of the Proto-Canaanite signs as well as their order are at least as old as the fourteenth century B.C., and adds additional support to the view that the acrophonic principle, integral to the names of the signs, went back to the invention of the script." One of the earlier discussions was Ignace Gelb's *A Study of Writing* (1952).

∝§ 14 §∝

Septuagint Studies

In the area of textual criticism, most of the relatively meager work done by Americans in recent decades has dealt with the Septuagint. Both as the oldest translation of the Bible (third-first centuries B.C.) and as the only translation that was made before the Hebrew text of the Bible had become more or less standardized, the Septuagint (Old Greek) version is far and away the most important witness to the biblical text of old.

Up to 1930 the major contribution was made by that master scholar M. L. Margolis; see my chapter on "Margolis' Work in the Septuagint" in *Max Leopold Margolis: Scholar and Teacher* (1952) for a detailed account and a full bibliography. J. A. Montgomery, Margolis's contemporary and friend, was the other notable Septuagint scholar in this country; his publications will be readily located in his two major works, *The Book of Daniel* (1927) and *The Books of Kings* (1951), both in the "International Critical Commentary" series.

Since 1930, Septuagint research in this country has been carried on chiefly by the disciples of these two scholars, and their students. H. S. Gehman, trained by Montgomery, published several studies involving the recensional affinity of Septuagint manuscripts and of translations (daughter versions) of the Septuagint, e.g., the Old Latin, Armenian, Ethiopic, and Arabic. He has also written on the theological-exegetical character of the Old Greek translation. His students have generally pursued the latter aspect: C. T. Fritsch published a dissertation on *The Anti-Anthropomorphisms in the Greek Pentateuch* (1943) and "The Concept of God in the Greek Translation of Isaiah" in *Biblical Studies in Memory of H. D. Alleman* (1960), edited by J. M. Myers *et al.;* D. H. Gard wrote on *The Exegetical Method of the Greek Translator of the Book of Job* (1952); J. W. Wevers has analyzed some of the textual data in the books of Kings (for bibliography see *Theologische Rundschau,* XXII [1954], 85 ff., 171 ff.).

I am a follower of Margolis and I have dealt with the problems of the Proto-Septuagint, recensional aspects of the Septuagint and its daughter versions, the Hebrew *Vorlage* of the Septuagint, the exegesis of the Septuagint, and the alleged antianthropomorphic character of the Septuagint translators. The main articles, with full reference to the extensive and scattered literature, are probably "On the Present State of Proto-Septuagint Studies" (*Journal of the American Oriental Society,* LXI [1941], 81-91; no. 13 in Offprint Series); "The Septuagint—Its Use in Textual Criticism" (*Biblical Archaeologist,* IX [1946], 21-34); "Current Progress and Problems in Septuagint Research" (chap. VIII in *The Study of the Bible Today and Tomorrow* [1947], ed. H. R. Willoughby); a twenty-page essay on *The Septaugint: The Oldest Translation of the Bible* (1949); "The Hebrew Text and the Ancient Versions of the Old Testament" (chap. IV in *An Introduction to the Revised Standard Version of the Old Testament* [1952]); and "Studies in the Septuagint of the Book of Job," Chapters I-V to date (*Hebrew Union College Annual,* XXVIII-XXXV [1957-64]). M. S. Hurwitz and Arthur Soffer, students of mine, have published master's dissertations on "The Septuagint of Isaiah 36-39 in Relation to That of 1-35, 40-66" and "The Treatment of Anthropomorphisms and Anthropopathisms in the Septuagint of Psalms" respectively (*Hebrew Union College Annual,* XXVIII [1957], 75-83 and 85-107).

Alexander Sperber has dealt with the Septuagint in some of its aspects. In *Septuagintaprobleme* (1929); "The New Testament and the Septuagint Translation of the Old Testament" (in Hebrew; *Tarbiz,* VI [1934], 1-29); "The Problems of the Septuagint Recensions" (*Journal of Biblical Literature,* LIV [1935], 73-92); and "Wiederherstellung einer griechischen Textgestalt des Buches Ruth" (*Monatsschrift für Geschichte und Wissenschaft des Judentums,* LXXXI [1937], 55-65), he tried to prove essentially that Lagarde, Rahlfs, Margolis, and Montgomery were in error a priori in assuming that the extant manuscripts of the Septuagint and the daughter versions of any given book in the Bible could be grouped recensionally and that the text of the main recensions could then be analyzed so as to produce approximately the original Septuagint translation. Indeed, postulated Sperber, there never was a single original Septuagint translation of any biblical book; there were, at the outset, many independent such translations. In this approach, Sperber was trying to prove in some detail the unproved hypothesis of his teacher, P. E. Kahle.

Suffice it here to say that the Kahle-Sperber hypothesis has convinced no one, and now the data from the Dead Sea Scrolls have given it the coup de grâce. For some detailed criticism and bibliography, see my studies "On the Present State of Proto-Septuagint Studies" (*Journal of the American Oriental Society*, LXI [1941], 81-91; especially 86 ff.) and "The Textual Criticism of the Old Testament," Chapter V in *The Bible and the Ancient Near East* (1961).

It is to be hoped that with the publication of the Dead Sea Scroll material on Samuel and Jeremiah, containing texts that seem to show some affinity to the Hebrew *Vorlagen* of the Septuagint version of these books, some interest in Septuagint research will be aroused; see my "Qumran and the Present State of Old Testament Text Studies: The Septuagint Text" (*Journal of Biblical Literature*, LXVIII [1959], 26-33).

⤙ 15 ⤚

Grammars, Lexicons, and Dictionaries

Our knowledge of the linguistics of biblical Hebrew, both per se and as an integral part of comparative Semitic linguistics, has made considerable progress in recent decades, chiefly because of the many important documents brought to light by excavation. Indeed, all Hebrew lexicons and grammars now in use have been rendered in great measure obsolete by the new discoveries.

Biblical Hebrew, it is well known, grew out of the Canaanite branch of Semitic languages. The discovery since the beginning of the Thirties of the Ugaritic texts of the fifteenth century B.C. and of many other Canaanite and related texts, e.g., Phoenician, Moabite, Palestinian Hebrew inscriptions (Lachish Ostraca, Seals, etc.), the new Aramaic inscriptions, the more penetrating analysis of such previously known texts as the Tell el-Amarna Tablets, the Sardinian inscriptions (Nora Stone, etc.), the Samaria Ostraca, and the Gezer Calendar—all this has led to a much more precise understanding of the Bible than was previously possible.

Several excellent *Vorstudien* and monographs and scores of first-class articles have now been achieved by American scholars; at least some of them may be mentioned here specifically. Z. S. Harris set a high standard in the Thirties with his *Grammar of the Phoenician Language* (1936) and *Development of the Canaanite Dialects: An Investigation in Linguistic History* (1939). Prior to their appearance, and subsequently too, much important work in northwest Semitic linguistics was done by W. F. Albright and H. L. Ginsberg; nor should the more recent work by W. L. Moran on the Canaanite elements in the Tell el-Amarna Tablets go unnoted. A pretty full bibliography will be found in the second of Harris's two works just cited and in Moran's chapter on "The Hebrew Language in Its Northwest Semitic Background" in the Albright Festschrift.

So that while the time may not yet have come for something of an up-to-date comparative Semitic grammar to be written, a historical grammar of biblical Hebrew is possible; indeed, it is an urgent desideratum.

The grammars in general use are approximately half-a-century old: F. H. W. Gesenius's *Hebrew Grammar,* 28th ed. (1910), edited and enlarged by E. F. Kautzsch and revised and translated by A. E. Cowley; and Hans Bauer and Pontus Leander's *Historische Grammatik der hebräischen Sprache des alten Testamentes* (2 vols., 1918-22). The very much superior *Hebräische Grammatik* by Gotthelf Bergsträsser (intended as the twenty-ninth edition of Gesenius's grammar) was never completed; only Parts I (*Lautlehre,* 1918) and II (*Verbum,* 1929) appeared; the syntax—as in Bauer and Leander's work—remained untouched.

F. R. Blake has proposed *A Resurvey of Hebrew Tenses* (1951), and has included an appendix on "Hebrew Influence on Biblical Aramaic" and references to earlier grammatical studies of his. Moses Buttenwieser has discussed "The Importance of the Tenses for the Interpretation of the Psalms" ("The Precative Perfect" and "Conditional and Temporal Sentences") in the *Hebrew Union College Jubilee Volume* (1925). T. J. Meek has sometimes dealt with the problem of tenses when writing about the difficulties that confront the translator of the Bible, e.g., in "Translating the Bible" (*Journal of Biblical Literature,* LXXIX [1960], 328-35); Albrecht Goetze has written on "The Tenses of Ugaritic" (*Journal of the American Oriental Society,* LVIII [1938], 266-309); and I have written "On the Cohortative and Jussive after an Imperative or Interjection in Biblical Hebrew" (*Jewish Quarterly Review*, XXXI [1940-41], 371-82; XXXII [1941-42], 191-205, 273-77) and "Notes on the Qal Infinitive Construct and the Verbal Noun in Biblical Hebrew" (*Journal of the American Oriental Society*, LXVII [1947], 107-26; no. 22 of Offprint Series).

Scores of studies of individual problems have appeared in the past several decades, scattered in journals, Festschriften, and the like, frequently as incidental footnotes in nongrammatical works.

What is true of the grammars is no less true for the lexicons. The widely used *Hebrew and English Lexicon of the Old Testament* (1906), edited by Francis Brown, S. R. Driver, and C. A. Briggs, and the seventeenth edition of F. H. W. Gesenius's *Hebräisches und aramäisches Handwörterbuch über das alte Testament* (1915) by F. P. W. Buhl (with Heinrich Zimmern, W. M. Müller, and Otto Weber), are both in very urgent need of wholesale revision; the former has undergone only modest revision at the hands of G. R. Driver (1952). Even the best of the recently published lexicons, Ludwig Koehler's *Lexicon in Veteris Testamenti Libros* (1948-53; *Supplementum*, 1958)—unlike the Aramaic part, done by Walter Baumgartner, which is first class—is hardly adequate in etymology or in comparative linguistics or in textual criticism. The sort of data compiled in Wolf Leslau's *Ethiopic and South Arabic Contributions to the Hebrew Lexicon* (1958) and related publications remains to be exploited. The same may be said of such studies as T. O. Lambdin's fine survey of "Egyptian Loan Words in the Old Testament" (*Journal of the American Oriental Society*, LXXIII [1953], 145-55; J. C. Greenfield's "Lexicographical Notes" (*Hebrew Union College Annual*, XXIX [1958], 203-28; XXX [1959], 141-51); and M. J. Dahood's numerous textual-linguistic studies during the past decade or so in such journals as *Biblica*, *Catholic Biblical Quarterly*, and *Zeitschrift für die alttestamentliche Wissenschaft*. In *A Study of the Language of the Biblical Psalms* (1955), Matitiahu Tsevat has gone beyond literary analysis into linguistic analysis to determine the idiom of the Psalms as compared to that of classical Hebrew as a whole; and see also his "Alalakhiana" (*Hebrew Union College Annual*, XXIX [1958], 109-34/36).

It would be a big boon for biblical scholarship if a foundation would subsidize such a major and time-consuming project as a Hebrew and Aramaic lexicon of the Bible. With a competent scholar at the head of a committee, each member a recognized specialist in his field (Biblical Hebrew, Northwest Semitic—i.e., Canaanite–Phoenician, Aramaic, etc.—Sumerian, Babylonian, Assyrian, Arabic, Ethiopic, Egyptian, and Syriac; such primary versions as the Septuagint, Targum, Peshiṭta, and Vulgate; textual criticism; etc.), and a staff of younger men to compile critically the numerous and manifold data—all the scholars in various degrees to be paid for their work so as to be freed from other time-consuming and income-producing chores—and publication of the opus assured, a definitive lexicon for decades to come could be produced in about eight to ten years at the most. And by then a comparative Semitic grammar would probably become realizable.

THE STUDY OF EARLY CHRISTIANITY

৽৳৽

ROBERT M. GRANT
PROFESSOR OF THE HISTORY OF EARLY CHRISTIANITY
THE DIVINITY SCHOOL
UNIVERSITY OF CHICAGO

The author is grateful for help in revising his manuscript to Professors F. W. Young and, especially, A. N. Wilder, though they are of course not responsible for his errors in matters of fact or judgment.

1

INTRODUCTION

The trouble with describing recent American work in the New Testament and other early Christian literature is twofold. First, there is not a great deal of material for study from the first century of our era or from the early second. The body of literature in the field—even if about a dozen writings of the apostolic fathers are added to the twenty-seven books of the New Testament—does not enable us to set forth a really adequate picture of the origin and early growth of the Christian religion. New discoveries have illuminated the background of early Christianity; they have shed little light directly upon it. The second point is related to the first. Because of the importance of the materials we possess, they have been intensively studied from the second century to our own day, though relatively exact philological methods have been employed more frequently since the seventeenth century than in earlier times. The enormous volume of New Testament studies means that nearly every possible permutation and combination of interpretations has been set forth at one time or another, and the graduate student who now ventures to write a thesis on some New Testament topic is forced either to produce an essay in bibliography or to run the risk of repeating what has already been said.

Insofar as the study of the New Testament is related to the tradition of exegetical work, it seems to recapitulate the history of earlier generations. Very roughly, it can be said that the period just before the Depression of 1929-32 was characterized by the peak of enthusiasm for sociohistorical study, with strong emphasis upon environmental influences. Two books that can be regarded as symptomatic of this age came from the "Chicago school": S. J. Case's *Jesus: A New Biography* (1927) and D. W. Riddle's *The Martyrs: A Study in Social Control* (1931).

Immediately after the Depression came a period of renewed concern for the Christian church, and historical-theological study of the New Testament came to be marked by considerable enthusiasm for "form criticism," the study of the oral tradition underlying the written gospels. This kind of study had been developed in Germany during and after World War I and began to flourish there during the economic crisis of the Twenties. The form-critical method led in turn to a renewed emphasis not only upon the church but also upon early Christian theology.

During the Forties theological interpretation became increasingly important, and historical studies were to some extent under a cloud (just as in Germany after World War I). Scholars did not always recognize the extent to which their interpretations of the New Testament or of the apostolic fathers were conditioned by the kind of modern theology they espoused, but it cannot be denied that by insisting upon the theological significance of the materials with which they were dealing they were able to view these materials (to some extent) in the light of early Christian presuppositions and thus could interpret them more adequately.

By the end of the Forties, however, it had become fairly clear that the word *theological* could not serve as a key for unlocking historical doors. At the same time the recovery of new materials related to the New Testament background provided fresh insights into historical problems. From Qumran came the Dead Sea Scrolls, necessitating a new look at Jewish apocalyptic thought; from Nag-Hammadi came a library of Gnostic documents that reflected not only the heterodoxy of Coptic Egypt but also that of earlier times and other places.

During the Fifties most scholars continued to pursue the interests first developed in the Thirties or Forties, modifying their ideas to some extent in relation to the new discoveries. It looks as if the Sixties will be marked by further concern for history and historical problems, though it may be hoped that the insights of earlier periods will not be lost.

Is it possible to speak of the progress of New Testament studies during the last generation? Probably it is not, except insofar as individual scholars have made contributions related to specific subjects or areas of investigation. Another area in which some advance may come is very likely that of method. Perhaps the shifts in emphasis, decade by decade, have induced a certain measure of caution in regarding the latest word as the last word; perhaps they have encouraged a closer adherence to the texts being studied and have resulted in less enthusiasm for a particular kind of method than for other kinds.

For instance, modern scholars are not likely to explain the life of Jesus as Case did when he laid great weight upon the possible participation of Jesus, as a young man, in the building program going on at Sepphoris in Galilee. According to Case, it was there that he learned that Jewish exclusiveness was alien to the purpose of God. His mission could be explained in relation to this hypothetical environment. Yet we cannot be sure that modern scholars will not go just as far in another direction. They are likely nowadays to explain the mission of Jesus as based either upon what he had learned at Qumran (if he was actually there) or upon his reaction against the Dead Sea teachers.

Again, modern scholars are unlikely to agree with the words of Riddle: "Agreement with known environment is the criterion by which a datum is identified as authentic, that is, having actually come from Jesus or as having been produced by a Christian community" (*The Martyrs,* p. 210). Such an axiom is based upon greater confidence in the "rigidity" of human history than is warranted. Sociologists can often predict social development in relation to large groups. Their methods are not adequate for dealing so precisely with particular individuals. And it is by no means certain that the differences among various kinds of "known environments" are so striking that by paying attention to them one can separate Jesus from early Christian communities in this way.

One reason for what we regard as the absence of progress in New Testament studies lies in the nature of the materials. If there were to be progress, what would it be? Presumably it could involve the interpretation of new documents; but by definition the New Testament consists of twenty-seven canonical books. The alternative to this kind of progress could be based on new interpretations of the old documents; the documents could be placed in various kinds of contexts and thus be understood in new ways. Certainly scholars have followed the latter path. But the question that then arises is whether or not progress in scholarship is actually thus achieved.

To a considerable extent American scholars tend to agree with the words of Goethe's Mephistopheles: "Grau, meiner Freund, ist aller Theorie." They are relatively slow to accept the radically liberal or radically conservative ideas that are produced especially in Germany, and for this reason their work usually represents a kind of mediating position between older and newer views, one might almost say between what the New Testament text says and what its latest exegetes make it say. In all scholarship there is this kind of time lag. In American New Testament scholarship the time lag is regarded as beneficial.

This characteristic of American scholars has tended to prevent the creation of "schools" with special points of view. Perhaps the only exception to this rule was provided during the period between 1914 and about 1940, when the Chicago school flourished. Case's pupil H. R. Willoughby has described it thus: "In the midwestern area, specifically centered in Chicago, there developed the most coherent social-history group to emerge among the biblical researchers of America. Their applications of social-historical methodology to the investigation of the environments, the literature, and the history of the early Christians have been quite extensive" (*The Study of the Bible Today and Tomorrow*, pp. xiv f.). The influence of the school on American scholarship was very considerable. At the same time, however, those who were influenced rarely accepted the methodology of Case or Riddle, the school's foremost teachers; and there were many scholars whose concern for the environment of early Christianity was not derived from Chicago. Among them such creative individualists as A. D. Nock and H. A. Wolfson of Harvard and E. R. Goodenough of Yale.[1]

Even at Chicago not everyone adhered to the principles of the school. The most conspicuous example was E. J. Goodspeed, who was primarily concerned not with social history but with problems of text, translation, and literary history.

This is to say that New Testament scholarship in America, as not in Germany, is the product chiefly of individuals. They work in relation to the international study of early Christianity, not primarily in relation to that of other Americans or even to that of their colleagues. To some extent this feature of American scholarship is a weakness, overcome only in part by the efforts of such groups as the Society of

---

[1] Though belonging to a somewhat older generation, the work of B. W. Bacon of Yale cannot be neglected; he wrote an important book on New Testament theology (*The Apostolic Message*, 1925), as well as significant studies of two gospels (*Studies in Matthew*, 1930; *The Gospel of the Hellenists*, 1933).

Biblical Literature and Exegesis, its various regional sections, and the Chicago Society of Biblical Research. On the other hand, such individualism is the inevitable product of the geographical extent of North America and the cultural and religious diversity that still flourishes. Beause of these environmental factors, American scholarship has been relatively free of domination by any particular school of thought. It is likely that in the future it will remain free, especially since efforts are being made to correlate the work of Protestant and Roman Catholic scholars.

It is also important to recognize that in general the individual scholars of whom we speak have tried to make use of various kinds of approaches and have not limited themselves to any one line or angle. For this reason all sorts of checks and balances are present in American scholarship. One might suppose that in the late Twenties and early Thirties there was universal confidence in the historical method as then understood. Such was not the case, as an article by James Moffatt on "The Limitations of Historical Method" shows, as do books and articles by such scholars as H. J. Cadbury and B. S. Easton. When form criticism was used in America, it was not the radical method employed in Germany. The American theological treatment of the New Testament in the Forties was less thoroughgoing than this kind of treatment elsewhere, and American scholars generally were less prone than others to regard either the Dead Sea Scrolls or the Nag-Hammadi documents as providing final solutions to New Testament problems.

In spite of all these qualifications, it can probably be said that three avenues of approach are especially prominent in American study of early Christianity today. (1) There is a considerable emphasis upon what may be called a theological understanding of the New Testament. This approach is generally viewed as an indispensable part of historical study, just as historical work is an indispensable part of theological understanding. The reason for so viewing the theological approach is that theology (understood rather broadly) represented the basic concern of the authors of the documents involved, as well as that of their earliest readers. (2) There is an increasing emphasis upon the relation of the New Testament writings to those of the apostolic fathers and the apologists, not to mention such later fathers as Irenaeus. This emphasis is due to recognition of the historical and theological links between the primitive church and the church of later times. (3) There is a continuing emphasis upon the relation of early Christianity to its various environments, though the idea that all early Christian phenomena can be explained as derivatives from environment has become less popular.

These three approaches can be reduced to two. The theological approach is essentially equivalent to dealing with the documents themselves; it may be viewed as a kind of internal criticism. The other approaches are concerned with the environments of the documents—the first, with the Christian environments, the second, with the non-Christian environments. These can be regarded as types of external criticism.

Both of these approaches are reflected in *The Study of the Bible Today and Tomorrow* (1947), edited by H. R. Willoughby for the Chicago Society of Biblical Research. A. N. Wilder, writing on "New Testament Theology in Transition," claimed that it was necessary to set forth the unity of New Testament thought by concentrating upon the canonical books and looking for the "history of salvation" in them, guided always by the best historical science available, as a control against subjectivity. The New Testament is to be read in the light of its authors' own presuppositions. On the other hand, P. Schubert insisted upon "the abiding and ever-urgent task" of reconstructing the history of the earliest Christianity; he recommended greater concentration upon environmental study and the correlation of early church history with history in general. Only one essay in the volume was specifically devoted to early Christian literature outside the New Testament; in it S. E. Johnson remarked that "nothing is antecedently more likely than variety in early Christianity," and he proceeded to prove its existence.

These attitudes have remained essentially unchanged during the last fifteen years, and the study of early Christianity will presumably continue to derive its impetus from both of them, although individual scholars will naturally concentrate their attention upon one or the other.

It should be pointed out, of course, that American study of early Christianity is only one branch, and not the most important branch, of international scholarship in this area. Sometimes graduate students are reluctant to add both French and German to the "biblical languages" with which they are acquainted. Such reluctance leads only to lack of awareness of the major issues confronting scholarship; for the most important work in the New Testament and early Christian literature is published in German and French, not to mention Italian, Swedish, Dutch, and sometimes Spanish. For this reason an account of American scholarship by itself is necessarily one-sided. Especially in recent years the participation of Americans in international conferences and projects has become increasingly important.

Furthermore, as I have already hinted, American scholarship, like the United States itself, has been predominantly Protestant in the past. There is every likelihood that this situation is changing and that full recognition of the international nature of the study will be accompanied by increasing recognition of the significance of Roman Catholic work. Such recognition will result in reconsideration both of the premises and of the methods of New Testament scholarship, and, out of the impending ferment, it may be hoped that more valuable and lasting results will be achieved.

Such, in the broadest of outlines, is the way American study in this field looks to one participant. We now turn to assess some of its methods and results in more detail, relying upon three traditional headings (Canon and Text, Literary Criticism, Historical Criticism) and two sets of conclusions (Some Results of New Testament Study, Environment and Early Church History).

◄§ 2 §►

METHODS AND RESULTS

Canon and Text

Much American study of the canon has been carried on by scholars related to the University of Chicago. Thus E. J. Goodspeed, in his book *The Meaning of Ephesians* (1933), developed the theory that this letter, not written by Paul, was composed by a Paulinist who, upon reading Acts, visited the principal places mentioned in the book, collected and edited nine letters by Paul, and added Ephesians at their head. His pupil John Knox added the hypothesis that the Paulinist was the Onesimus mentioned in Philemon and that he was perhaps the later bishop of Ephesus mentioned by Ignatius.

These theories, obviously of considerable importance for the history of the New Testament canon, have been vigorously debated. The question about the authenticity of Ephesians has been raised in acute form by H. J. Cadbury in an article entitled "The Dilemma of Ephesians" (*New Testament Studies,* 1959). Here he asks the question "Which is more likely—that an imitator of Paul in the first century composed a writing ninety or ninety-five per cent in accordance with Paul's style or that Paul himself wrote a letter diverging five or ten per cent from his usual style?" That this is a genuine dilemma can be shown by rephrasing the question. Which is more likely—that we can determine the authenticity of a letter written ninety or ninety-five per cent in accordance with Paul's style or that we cannot? It would appear that a negative answer must be given to the rephrased version and, therefore, that the original question cannot be answered, at least on the grounds on which it was asked. Moreover, if it cannot be answered, the foundation of the theories of Goodspeed and Knox must be called in question.

Another problem arises in relation to the pastoral epistles (to Timothy and Titus). Since the early nineteenth century it has been generally agreed that these epistles were written not by Paul but by a Paulinist who lived later and did not quite understand his model. In

120

1921 it appeared that the case against Pauline authorship was settled by the work of P. N. Harrison, who claimed that the vocabulary of the letters was (1) not Pauline and (2) close to that of early second century writers. In recent times the statistical foundation of Harrison's work has been challenged, notably by B. M. Metzger in a brief but important study (*Expository Times,* 1958). The nonauthenticity of the pastoral epistles must be proved on some ground other than the nature of their vocabulary, though all can agree that they present historical and theological difficulties when compared with the major letters of Paul.

Similarly the history of the collection of the gospels has had to be revised because of the questioning of old axioms. The fact that the gospel of John appears on the Christian scene rather late does not prove that it was not written, and used, at an early date. Moreover, the thesis of Helmut Koester concerning the use of oral tradition rather than written gospels by the earlier apostolic fathers removes a good deal of the "evidence" for the use of the synoptic gospels (and, by inference, for the non-use of John) in the early period. At the present time we do not know either when or where the four gospels were first used together, though it remains possible that some or all of them were employed at Antioch by the end of the first century.

Generally speaking, modern *docta ignorantia* supports a more conservative position in regard to the history of the canon. Scholars are less often prone to say that because in our fragmentary evidence for early Christian literature and history a particular book is not quoted that book was not in existence or use. Some of the boldness and even rashness has departed from the study of the canon.

At the same time, we are coming to know a bit more about the books that early Christians rejected, and we can see why they were rejected. The Greek papyri discovered during the last seventy years have included pieces of several gospels, epistles, acts, and apocalypses, usually reflecting a naïve and unreflective theology but sometimes rather explicitly Gnostic in nature. The Coptic gospels of Mary (Magdalene), Thomas, and Philip are largely Gnostic, while the Gospel of Truth is probably semi-Gnostic but not a gospel.

It should be added that very recently Morton Smith of Columbia University discovered near Jerusalem a manuscript (written on the end papers of an early edition of Ignatius) that contains part of a letter by Clement of Alexandria. In this letter Clement criticizes the Carpocratian Gnostic version of the gospel of Mark and quotes from the "authentic" secret version of the gospel that was known only to a few members of the church of Alexandria. The excerpts from the "secret" Mark suggest that like other Gnostic documents it was composed by using words and phrases from the canonical gospels and arranging them in novel contexts. The importance of Smith's discovery lies in the light it casts on Alexandrian Christianity in the second century and on the transmission of the gospels. It proves that the true history of the canon is quite different from the history previously expounded by scholars. Smith's manuscript also illuminates a dark corner of the history of the New Testament text.

The study of the text of the New Testament has benefited greatly from discoveries of papyri and, to a lesser degree, from continuing investigations of late manuscripts, versions, and patristic citations. In this area the work of E. C. Colwell has been exceedingly important, largely because of his ability not only to organize research but also to re-examine problems of theory. A generation ago it was generally agreed that there were four "families" of New Testament texts, based upon texts current in the third or fourth century at Alexandria, Caesarea (in Palestine), Antioch, and Constantinople. Colwell vigorously criticized the notion of "families" as such, pointing out that it was derived from areas of philology in which, because of the paucity of manuscripts, genealogies could be traced and "stemmas" created. Such a situation does not exist in the New Testament field, and therefore it is far better to speak simply of "text types." A particular instance of the failure of the older theory has been found in relation to the writings of Origen. Older scholars believed that they could show that the New Testament text used by Origen at Alexandria before A.D. 231 was different from the text he later used at Caesarea. Further research showed that Origen (1) sometimes used a text called Caesarean in Alexandrian writings and (2) sometimes used a text called Alexandrian in Caesarean writings. The theory was not only wrong in general but incorrect in relation to the evidence.

Again, the discovery of the papyri has led to considerable embarrassment for the theory that there were four text types, if not families. Very few of the papyri, which come largely from the third century (though in some instances from the second), present us with the pure text types that, according to the theory, they should present. It would appear that the study of the early text, originally based on a combination of the major fourth century manuscripts with the evidence of versions and of early fathers, has to be undertaken *de novo,* beginning with the papyri that actually provide our earliest evidence. Colwell has pointed this out (in *Early Christian Origins,* ed. A. P. Wikgren, 1961), and has set forth ten propositions that are highly significant for future study.

1. A texttype is a process, not the work of one hand.
2. The Vulgate Versions were the work of one hand and were editions as well as translations.
3. The Greek Vulgate—the Byzantine or Alpha texttype—had in its origin no single focus as the Latin had in Jerome. Like Jerome's Vulgate it had several revised editions.
4. Origen did not make an edition (create a texttype) of the Greek New Testament.
5. The so-called Western text or Delta texttype is the uncontrolled popular text of the second century. It has no unity and should not be referred to as the "Western text."
6. The Beta texttype (Hort's "Neutral") is a "made" text probably Alexandrian in origin, produced in part by the selection of relatively "good old MSS" but more importantly by the philological editorial know-how of Alexandrians.
7. The so-called Caesarean texttype is not Caesarean and is at least two types, the earlier of which is a proto-type, an early stage in the process which produced the mature Beta and Delta texttypes.
8. It follows from number 1, as also from the textual data, that the earliest witness to a texttype is never the archetype of the texttype.
9. The textual history of the New Testament differs from corpus to corpus, and even from book to book; therefore the witnesses have to be regrouped in each section.
10. As in dating documents, so in dating texttypes what is needed is a datable witness to the type, not only to some of its readings, for the overwhelming majority of readings were created before the year 200. But very few, if any, texttypes were established by that time.

Colwell's ten points prove two things: (1) the vitality of American study of the New Testament text, and (2) the necessity for reworking textual criticism along new lines.

Literary Criticism

Literary criticism of the New Testament in America, as elsewhere, has suffered from its employment for theological-dogmatic purposes, especially in the hands of those who have used it to show that most of the New Testament books were not written by their presumed authors and that most of them have also suffered from interpolation in "orthodox" directions. What has been neglected—though a notable exception is provided by the work of H. J. Cadbury—is the examination of the style and literary method of the New Testament authors. This is to say that questions of authorship are, when not insoluble, secondary, and that the primary task of literary criticism is the analysis of what the document in question says. What did its author intend to convey to his earliest readers, whoever they were?

The analysis can begin with the smallest units of the document, the words the author used. But since the meaning of these words in a particular document is ascertainable chiefly in relation to their immediate context, it is probably more satisfactory to begin with the sentences the author employed and to examine their structure. In other words, in an articulated language like Greek (perhaps more than in other kinds of language), the first object of investigation should be the writer's grammar and syntax. By beginning at this point we can proceed from what can be fairly well known to what cannot be so well known.

For example, some of the verses in the first epistle of John may be printed in "sense lines" as follows:

1 John 1:5-7

God is Light,
and in him is no darkness at all.

If we say that we have fellowship with him
but walk   in the darkness,
we lie, and

do not do the truth; but
if we walk in the light
  (as he is in the light)
we have fellowship with one another, and
the blood of Jesus his Son cleanses us from all sin.

1 John 2:9-11

He who says he is in the light and
    hates his brother
  is in the darkness even until now.
He who loves his brother
  abides in the light, and
  there is no cause for stumbling in it (him). But
he who hates his brother
  is in the darkness and
  does not know where he goes
              because the darkness has blinded his eyes.

1 John 3:4-10

Everyone who commits sin
              commits lawlessness also; and
sin is lawlessness.
And we know
          that he was manifested to take away sins; and
          in him is no sin.
Whoever abides in him sins not;
  whoever sins   has not seen him and
                does not know him. . . .
He who does righteousness is righteous, just as
He   is righteous;
he who commits sin   is of the devil. . . .

Whoever is begotten of God commits no sin, because
          His seed   abides in him;
therefore he   cannot sin,   because
    he is begotten of God. . . .
Whoever does not righteousness is not of God, nor
  he who does not love his brother.

1 John 4:8, 12, 16, 18, 20

He who does not love
   does not know God; for
      God is Love. . . .
If we love one another,
  God abides   in us, and
  his love is made perfect in us. . . .
      God is Love;
   and he who abides in love
      abides in God, and
     God abides in him. . . .
There is no fear in love; but
  perfect love casts out fear,
      because fear has torment; and
he who fears is not made perfect in love. . . .
If a man says, "I love God," and
  hates his brother,
  he is a liar; for
  he who does not love his brother
     whom he has seen
   cannot love God,
     whom he has not seen.

It is obvious that in many instances the arrangement of sentences in this fashion is open to question; but it is also obvious that when arranged in sense lines an author's sentences convey their meaning rather more clearly than would otherwise be the case. Since the ultimate purpose of New Testament study is, or should be, the exegesis of what the New Testament authors intended to say, some method like this may well lead to such understanding—or at least toward it. The method itself is, of course, not new; something like it was employed in the ancient church and by such critics as G. Heinrici and Johannes Weiss, and somewhat differently by Rudolf Bultmann. It has achieved conspicuous success and recognition in relation to 1 Corinthians 13 and Colossians 1:15-20, to mention no other passages. But its use deserves to be extended. Among American scholars who have employed a similar method are N. W. Lund (*Chiasmus in the New Testament,* 1940) and J. M. Robinson (*Journal of Biblical Literature,* 1956).

It is difficult to classify the methods loosely designated as form criticism and tradition criticism, for in general they are concerned in much the same ways with much the same materials, but reflect different emphases. Form criticism deals with oral traditions, or more precisely with the literary records of oral traditions, and attempts to classify the various forms being employed; tradition criticism, or tradition history, tries to analyze the stages through which the traditions passed before reaching the stage of writing. Form criticism becomes tradition criticism at the point where the analysis of forms is used as a ground for historical criticism. Often the point of metamorphosis is overlooked, and it is assumed that literary analysis can produce historical fruits. To a considerable extent this assumption is based upon a rather rigid historical differentiation of forms and ideas supposedly Jewish (hence early) from forms and ideas supposedly Hellenistic (hence late).

We can raise little objection to the use of form criticism as such. It is evident that Jesus employed the parable, the short saying, and other forms of speech, and that his words, or the words ascribed to him, can be understood more fully if their content is interpreted in relation to their form. It is not so evident that the forms are as clearly definable as is often supposed; for example, parable is not always distinct from allegory, and there is no reason to suppose that, although Jesus preferred parable, he always avoided allegory. It is not at all evident that he was the only early Christian to employ the forms he used. For instance, the presence of "Semitic parallelism" in a sentence does not prove that Jesus spoke it.

When form criticism crosses the line into tradition history our questions multiply. Some form critics have sharply differentiated Jewish and Greek forms and ideas and have assumed that this differentiation provides a key to unlock problems of authenticity. Since they are now in the field of historical analysis, they should be aware that such sharp distinctions are rarely possible in historical study. The Judaism of Jesus' time was pervaded by Greek elements, as two American scholars have clearly shown—Saul Lieberman *Greek in Jewish Palestine,* 1942; *Hellenism in Jewish Palestine,*

1950) and E. R. Goodenough in his monumental work on Jewish symbols (*Jewish Symbols in the Greco-Roman Period,* 1953 ff.). Similarly such a "Hellenist" as Philo was more closely related to Palestinian Judaism than might be supposed, as Samuel Belkin has shown (*Philo and the Oral Law,* 1940). The existence of Hellenistic Judaism, and the difficulty of classifying its components, suggests that the classification scheme is too rigid. (The same observation can be made in regard to the study of the early fathers, who owe much both to Jew and to Greek.)

Our conclusion in regard to form criticism must be that it rightly draws attention to the fact that the tradition circulated in oral form before it was written down, and that it was written down for the use of the church. Form criticism goes beyond the limits of our knowledge when it attempts to show exactly how and why traditions were modified as they were transmitted. For instance, it is not possible to say that later Christians added all the moralizing conclusions that often stand at the end of the parables of Jesus—sometimes such was the case, sometimes not; and often we cannot tell. Similarly it cannot be said that every saying of Jesus originally possessed specific relevance to a specific situation in his time, and that during transmission his sayings were generalized. We cannot know if this process always occurred.

Another important question related to literary criticism but on the border line between it and historical analysis is concerned with the original language in which Jesus spoke. In the Thirties and Forties a prior question was often discussed: In what language were the gospels written? In America the chief proponent of Aramaic originals for the gospels was C. C. Torrey of Yale; his views were severely criticized by E. J. Goodspeed and E. C. Colwell (*The Greek of the Fourth Gospel,* 1931), and it is now established that the gospels were Greek books. On the other hand, Torrey and others certainly showed that behind the gospels lie Aramaic sources and that Jesus himself spoke Aramaic. This fact means that a partial test of the historical authenticity of Jesus' sayings can be provided by translation into Aramaic. For example, the play on the Greek word *anōthen* in John 3:3 has no Aramaic equivalent, and in Mark 14:22 no emphasis can be laid upon the word *is* ("this is my body"), for in Aramaic no verb would be used. This is to say, on the one hand, that sayings not translatable into Aramaic have been influenced by the process of transmission more than others have been, but not, on the other, that a translatable saying is necessarily genuine.

Historical Criticism

The term *historical criticism* is not altogether satisfactory, for it is sometimes regarded as implying that some kind of attack upon the documents is being undertaken. Actually such an attack is often involved in efforts to test the reliability of documents, but it is only a part of the test. Historical study necessitates both analysis of documents, events, and environments and synthesis of the results in relation to (1) the history of the church and to (2) the history of the Hellenistic world and the Roman empire, as well as to (3) the history of religion in the Roman period or more generally.

On the whole, the results of historical study are determined in advance by the goals that the historian sets for himself, though the goals are modified by the preliminary conclusions that he reaches. For this reason his analysis is closely related to the presuppositions with which he starts. Why does he deal with the New Testament documents and not with others? What does he hope to find in the course of his investigations? What methods is he going to employ?

Since the eighteenth century, historians have been especially concerned with one significant aspect of the New Testament writings, an aspect that is central to the gospel narratives but is also to be found in other parts of the tradition. This aspect is that of the miraculous. Most students of the New Testament, especially those strongly influenced either directly or indirectly by modern world views, have refrained from denying the possibility of miracle but have rejected the more striking miracles of the gospels. One reason for not denying the possibility of miracles lies in the history of criticism. In the eighteenth century many rationalists rejected the stories of exorcisms and healings, but their successors have found that a newer understanding of psychosomatic factors restores the credibility of these accounts. At the same time, there are some New Testament miracles that cannot be satisfactorily related to the course of human events as a whole. These include the stories of virginal conception, changing water into wine, multiplying bread and fish, walking on water, and resurrection. Since the resurrection of Christ obviously lies at the center of the Christian gospel, as the apostle Paul stated in 1 Corinthians 15:1-19, few Christian critics have directly criticized this miracle.[2] Instead, they have concentrated their attention upon the stories of "lesser" miracles, usually explaining them as products of piety or misunderstanding but not treating them as accounts of events.

In this regard ideas about environment have played an important part. The primary distinction that has been drawn is between ancient and modern ideas. Case began a book with the words "The sky hung low in the ancient world." What he meant was that ancient cosmology and ancient ideas about angels, demons, and other spirits belong only to the past; modern man does not share these ancient views and must resolutely reject ideas organically related to them. Bultmann has expressed this criticism even more sharply. Others have agreed with it, often with less consistent conclusions.

It is at this point that further historical analysis is needed, not in order to reject the conclusions of Case or Bultmann but in order to refine and correct the method of argument. It is not true to say that all ancient men accepted miracles; I have adduced evidence that shows that some did while others did not (*Miracle and Natural Law,* 1952). It may be added that to treat some miracle stories as Jewish and early (exorcisms, healings) and others as Hellenistic and late (miraculous feedings, walking on water, virginal conception) is not altogether satisfactory when one bears in mind the "mixed" situation in which early Christians found themselves.

But when we have made qualifications of this sort, we still face the problem of dealing historically with miracles that, almost by definition, lie outside the sphere of history as ordinarily understood. If the miracle stories had not seemed remarkable they would not have been told. For this reason it is impossible or nearly impossible to coordinate them with the usual course of history, understood as the narrative of human events.

The miraculous is one part (perhaps the most important part) of a more general problem, that of the significance of unique events. The modern emphasis on environmental study has often meant that a synthetic picture of a particular environment has been used to de-

[2] See the theological study by R. R. Niebuhr, *Resurrection and Historical Reason* (1957).

termine what could or could not have taken place or been believed in that environment. For example, in Judaism cannibalism was viewed with abhorrence; therefore, in a Jewish environment Jesus could not have spoken of eating his flesh or drinking his blood (John 6:54; cf. Mark 14:22-24). The conclusion has therefore been drawn that the words were ascribed to Jesus under the influence of a theme drawn from some of the mystery religions of the time, in which the dying and rising god was eaten by his devotees. We do not know, however, that in this period such meals actually existed; furthermore, the accusation of cannibalism levied against second century Christians suggests that the idea of eating the god was not especially popular among Greeks and Romans, at least in official circles. It is true that there are various different statements about the eucharist in early Christian documents, but the conclusion that has been drawn does not explain the differences satisfactorily.

Some warnings about method have been provided by E. R. Goodenough in a lecture delivered at the 1960 Annual Meeting of the American Council of Learned Societies. Three important fallacies that he mentioned deserve especial notice. (1) It is often supposed that "an earlier document about either ideas or a historical incident will more correctly report the true events or original teachings than a later document" will. Such a rough-and-ready judgment is not correct, for it neglects the intentions of the writers of the documents, as well as their use of different kinds of sources. For instance, the official naval histories of World War I are often inadequate or misleading because of propagandist purposes and inadequate research. At the same time, it must be maintained that eye-witness accounts are usually preferable as sources to materials provided by those who were not witnesses of the events. (2) It is often supposed that an idea encountered in an early document must have influenced the expression of the same idea, or a similar one, in a later document; conversely, it is supposed that a statement that is more complex or better coordinated than another must be later than the simpler or less adequate version. The fallacy found here is twofold: (*a*) it can be expressed as *post hoc, propter hoc,* whereas only *propter hoc, post hoc* is true; and (*b*) a rather naïve form of genetic evolutionism does not necessarily illuminate the history of ideas. (3) It is often supposed that in a particular location all people thought alike; a document regarded as Hellenistic must come from a Hellenistic city. In actual fact the diversity characteristic of modern cities was characteristic of Rome, Antioch, Alexandria, and the smaller cities of the Roman empire. Rigid geographical constructions are no more useful than rigid chronological ones.

The basic difficulty seems to lie in the inveterate tendency of scholars to provide generalizations that more or less fit the facts and then to argue on the basis of the generalizations. Goodenough also points out that "we have not a good understanding of arguing *e silentio*," and he claims that "to draw any conclusions at all in this field we must all argue largely from silence." The trouble arising at this point is related to what the silence means. Very often it seems that modern students of early Christianity assume the truth of one of two notions and proceed to treat the one they prefer as axiomatic. (1) The early Christians wrote down practically every thought they had, and most of these thoughts have been preserved. Therefore first century Christianity is fully reflected in the New Testament. (2) The early Christians were bound by a *disciplina arcani* and therefore kept secret many of their thoughts and acts; what they kept secret was either (*a*) the same as later thought and practice or (*b*) radically different from what came later. Actually the situation was considerably more complex. For instance, the Lord's Supper is explicitly mentioned in one letter by Paul but in no other New Testament epistle; it is discussed in the Didache, in the letters of Ignatius, and in the first apology of Justin, but in no other Christian writing before Irenaeus. Was the eucharist of Ignatius and Justin the same rite as that found in 1 Corinthians? How important was it to early Christians in general? At this point a prior judgment of the nature of the early Christian church is obviously essential to reaching a conclusion.

To Goodenough's points must be added another related to the approach to rather contradictory evidence. Suppose that Jesus is reported to have said that (1) the reign of God is in the future and (2) the reign of God is already present. Suppose also that, in general, later Christians held that the reign of God is present. In the opinion of many New Testament scholars the idea that the reign of God is present must have been ascribed to Jesus—wrongly—by later transmitters of his words, for (1) the two ideas cannot be reconciled, (2) "authentic" tradition cannot have contained reports of both, and (3) Jesus cannot have held both views. Furthermore, since the reign of God did not come, no one would have reported Jesus as predicting that it would come had he not actually made such a prediction.

The logic of this argument is more apparent than real. (1) It is not certain that the two ideas are not reconcilable, since in later Christian writings (as well as earlier ones) both are often found. (2) It is hard to see why those who transmitted the traditions were unable to suppress statements with which they disagreed, especially if they were willing to invent traditions that they found edifying. (3) Why should it be the case that passages that disagree with later attitudes provide the foundation for genuine history? Perhaps at the base of such a notion lies a view that the seemingly improbable is the historically true; but all that can really be said is that sometimes the seemingly improbable is true, sometimes not.

It would appear more probable that if apparently discordant views are ascribed to Jesus both should be regarded as expressions of what he himself proclaimed; the emphases may be those of the transmitters of tradition, but behind both kinds of views lies the teaching of Jesus.

A similar problem arises even in regard to such a valuable study as that by H. J. Cadbury, *The Peril of Modernizing Jesus* (1937). The author vigorously maintained that Jesus was a man of first century Palestine and that what he said in his setting has no direct relevance to various situations in the twentieth century. Cadbury was well aware that as the tradition about Jesus was handed down it was given shape by those who tended to make it more general and to adapt it to situations beyond Palestinian ones. In Cadbury's view, however, the only authentic interpretation of Jesus was a historical one that gave due recognition to "unpalatable" historical features of his teaching. It is certainly true that some aspects of the tradition have not seemed edifying to modern critics. It is not certain, however, that unpalatability is a valid criterion either for history or for theology.

Similarly, in regard to the questions of authorship that we have called secondary, the basic problems are not as simply solved as earlier scholars believed they were. We have already seen some of the difficulties involved in regard to Ephesians and the pastoral epistles. Further difficulties arise when one tries to apply critical principles to early Christian traditions about authorship.

Cadbury, for example, has tried to provide such principles. "The fact that in early 'tradition' a document was ascribed to a particular author does not prove that he wrote it." His grounds for this statement lie primarily in the fact that when early Christian authors defend "tradition" they usually rely on information derived from the document in question; therefore this information is the source of the tradition. While it is possible, of course, that the tradition was based upon such internal evidence, we do not actually know that it was so based. Therefore to Cadbury's principle must be added another: the fact that in early "tradition" a document was ascribed to a particular author does not prove that he did *not* write it. Irenaeus argued that Luke, the companion of Paul, wrote Acts, and he relied on internal evidence for his proof; but we do not know either (1) that Luke did not write Acts or (2) that Irenaeus' view that he did was derived from the internal evidence as examined either by him or by a predecessor.

Another principle stated by Cadbury is directed against some groups of modern scholars. "The fact that a document provides no indication that it was written by a particular author does not suggest that he wrote it." Again, however, this statement must be supplemented by another: the fact that a document provides no such indication does not suggest that such an author did *not* write it. Principles of this kind have a function that is primarily negative; they remind us of how little we really know about the authors of many New Testament books.

In dealing with the prospective audience of Luke-Acts, Cadbury has set forth another principle that is more directly based upon comparisons with other ancient writings. "The fact that an individual is addressed in a preface to a literary work clearly indicates that the work was addressed not to him but to a wider audience." Certainly the examples that he provides from Greek and Roman writers show that in general this principle is true. It is not always easy to decide, however, whether a general rule holds good in a specific instance. A parallel may be found in the writings of some of the Greek apologists. It is true that their writings were read and preserved by Christians, even when the writings were addressed to specific Roman emperors. Nonetheless, it is by no means certain that the apologies of Justin and Athenagoras were not addressed precisely to Antoninus Pius and Marcus Aurelius. Here the form used for petitions overlaps the form used for dedications; and it may be that the Theophilus addressed in Luke-Acts was in a position to receive a petition as well as a dedication, though we do not know who or what he was. All one can say is that he was probably a real person.

In general, therefore, we can conclude that the use of general principles in analyzing particular historical phenomena is subject to considerable limitation. In antiquity the rhetorical schools taught the methods of "refutation" and "confirmation" in regard to myths and historical materials. Too often, modern scholars confine their activities to one aspect or the other. In many cases the use of both methods would reveal that the balance of "probability" is very difficult to establish.

Indeed, one may reasonably suspect that the starting point of this kind of analysis is to be found in a determination to get rid of tradition as such. Consider the alternatives: (1) The internal evidence disagrees with the tradition. Therefore *ipso facto* the tradition is valueless. (This view is essentially correct, and can be applied to the question of the authorship of Hebrews.) (2) The internal evidence agrees with the tradition. Therefore the tradition is based on the internal evidence and is valueless. In either case, tradition is rejected. Perhaps there is a third possibility. (3) The internal evidence partly agrees, partly disagrees, with the tradition. In such a case the elements in agreement would presumably be viewed as based on internal evidence, while those not in agreement would be regarded as simply erroneous. The basic presupposition lies in the notion that those who transmitted the tradition had no sources of information beyond those that we possess now.

The presupposition is subject to the criticism given by Goodenough in his 1960 ACLS lecture. "There is the danger," he writes, "that in our ignorance of the past we project our own desires and patterns into the material when we try to interpret it. This, may I say, is worse than a danger—we do it more or less inevitably." The only safeguard against this inevitable process is to be found in an element of detachment from the subject involved, as well as from the methods used by our teachers or even by ourselves. There must be a close relationship between the student and the subject matter; at the same time, he must recognize that he is not identical with it.

One pattern often imposed on the materials by historical critics is that of "development." In order to trace development it is necessary to understand (1) the chronological sequence of the writings and (2) their environmental settings. The temporal sequence is used to establish a measure of the distance between different writings; the environmental analysis is used to explain why the differences exist.

This kind of pattern can be expressed in another way. As phenomena, the writings are obviously discrete if not disparate. One begins with the discrete phenomena, then interprets them synthetically by imposing some general framework on them. Development can then be applied to the various phenomena by arranging them chronologically and considering the environments. The development is set forth in the chronological arrangement and explained environmentally.

For example, it may be that some early Christian writings speak of Jesus as a man, while in later ones he is regarded as God. The development can then be explained in relation to the more Jewish, monotheistic environment of the earlier writer and the more Greco-Roman, polytheistic environment of the later writer. There are several difficulties in regard to such a picture. (1) The chronology is essential in the use of the method. But only a few of the New Testament books can be given any secure date. (2) The existence of development is assumed. But it cannot be traced in such documents as the Pauline epistles, much less in the various gospels. The actual picture, in view of the chronology, is not one of development but of remarkable variety, even at the same time and in the same place. (3) The explanation in terms of environment is not altogether satisfactory, since we know little about the specific environments of the various New Testament writers, and what we do know does not enable us to explain what they wrote.

In addition it must certainly be pointed out that when development is assumed without proof and used as a clue to chronology the results are extremely fragile. To date a book by its presumed location in the hypothetical development is not to date it at all.

In the light of our criticisms of historical criticism as ordinarily

136

employed, it is now possible to understand the nature of the situation in which New Testament study finds itself. A test case is provided by the gospel of John, the historical situation of which has been a matter of debate since the second century. A generation ago it was widely agreed that this document was properly called the fourth gospel, since it was written after the composition and circulation of the synoptics, some or all of which its author knew and used. It was also widely agreed that the author—who cannot have been the apostle John, since the book was written late and some ambiguous evidence from the second century suggests that he died early—did not write the book as we have it; the existence of displacements and interpolations by an editor must be postulated. On the provenance of the gospel, opinion was sharply divided. A minority held that the book was primarily addressed to Palestinian Jews; a majority held that it was influenced, if not by stoic thought or Philo, at least by Hellenistic religious ideas, perhaps by Gnostic thought.

Perhaps it would be too much to speak of a revolution in the study of this book, but at least there has been a considerable change of direction or emphasis. (1) The question of the date of the gospel must be left open, since the arguments for and against its use of the synoptics suffer from the absence of a workable method of analysis. We do not know if John knew the synoptics, though we do know certainly that he was familiar with the traditions behind them. (2) We do not know if the apostle John was primarily responsible for writing the book. (3) Since we are in no position to appeal to the idea of development in support of a late dating, we can better assess the new parallels to Johannine thought that have been found in the Dead Sea Scrolls. These suggest that an audience for John's gospel could have existed either at Qumran or in the Essene communities elsewhere. The parallels provided by Gnostic thought remain significant, but our knowledge of Gnostic origins does not provide much assistance in dealing with chronological matters.

Finally, the fact that the earliest witness to the distinctive Johannine style and thought is Ignatius of Antioch (c. A.D. 110) does not help to date the book. (1) Ignatius may have known either the book or its author, but the evidence does not permit us to judge this question. (2) There is no reason to suppose that at Antioch Ignatius was the first Christian to encounter Johannine thought; Ignatius is simply the first Christian writer from Antioch whose writings have been preserved. (To a certain extent they were preserved by chance, that is, because of the admiration for Ignatius felt by his younger contemporary Polycarp.) (3) The passage that may allude to the future destruction of the temple (John 4:23) does not prove that the temple had been destroyed when John wrote, any more than a statement that Christians are put out of the synagogue (9:22) proves that the book was written after A.D. 70. (4) It remains striking that in the non-Johannine literature of the New Testament there seem to be no allusions to Johannine doctrines (there may be an exception in 1 Timothy 3:16), while echoes of synoptic teaching are found in the Pauline epistles and elsewhere. This shows, however, not that John had not written, but that his work was not widely known.

In consequence of observations like these, we must conclude that a new picture of "the rise of early Christianity" needs to be drawn and that the method to be employed must remain closer to fact and logical inference from fact than older methods have.

What is involved in genuine historical analysis is the study of the relation of a document to its setting in time and place and, in the case of a historical document (one that deals with events before the time it was written), its relation to the earlier settings that are discussed in it or that can be inferred from it. In part the purpose of such analysis is to correlate the document with other data from its period so that we may assess the resemblances and differences that exist. Usually this kind of study begins with the discovery of what seem to be parallels, and their importance is then exaggerated, with the result that the document is regarded as just like that to which it is parallel. Only at a later stage of investigation can the differences be recognized and assessed. The purpose of assessing resemblances and difference is to delineate the nature of the particular document in relation to contemporary documents and thus to achieve deeper understanding of it. At the same time, a Christian document, for example, is related not only to other contemporary documents from the non-Christian world but also to other documents in the Christian tradition. Its relationships with other Christian documents are just as important as those with non-Christian documents, and indeed, in view of the purposes for which Christian documents were written, more important.

Religious-historical analysis, then, has as its goal the understanding of a document in relation to its environment, partly in the world in general, partly in the Christian context. The ultimate goal, however, lies in the realm of theological understanding at a point where historical and theological understanding intersect. This is so because what binds the Christian documents together is the proclamation of the gospel by the church. Were it not for the gospel and the church there would be no Christian documents.

American contributions linking historical analyses in the various senses of which I have spoken have been less impressive than the environmental studies by American scholars. Too often there has been a tendency to view environmental study as untheological or theological analysis as unhistorical; and to a considerable measure such a view of the products of critical work is correct. Why is this so? One may venture the hypothesis that it is largely because of the success of liberal Protestantism in the earlier years of this century and the consequent limitation of historical study to "the life and times of Jesus" and modern church history. Ancient and medieval church history fell under a cloud, and ancient and medieval theology went with it. Theologies that jumped from Jesus to the latest modern notions were necessarily unhistorical, and the scholars who supported them were likely to hold that historical analysis and theological understanding had nothing to do with each other.

Despite "the canonization of modernity" and the conception of theology as unrelated to the life and tradition of the church, scholars have recovered more historical views of theology and more theological views of history (especially church history). It is again becoming possible to correlate environmental study with theological understanding.

Some Results of New Testament Study

During recent decades there has been no American work comparable in scope and excellence to *The Beginnings of Christianity, I,* the five-volume work on Acts that was finished in 1933. (It was numbered *I* because its editors hoped to go on beyond Acts to a study of the subapostolic age, but their hope was never fulfilled.) Indeed, apart from the rather brief exposition in *The Interpreter's Bible,* the commentary genre has been somewhat neglected. Exceptions to this rule have been provided by studies of Philippians (F. W. Beare, 1959), Mark (S. E. Johnson, 1960), and Matthew (F. V. Filson, 1960) in a series edited by Henry Chadwick of Oxford, and by the excellent independent commentaries by Beare on 1 Peter (1947; revised 1958) and B. S. Easton on the pastoral epistles (1947). The more recent commentaries tend to lay more emphasis on an author's theological ideas than on linguistic and historical matters; Filson states his own purpose thus: "My primary attempt has not been to reconstruct sources but to grasp and state the meaning of the Gospel author."

The study of the historical Jesus was summed up by C. C. Mc-Cown in 1940 when he published *The Search for the Real Jesus* and appealed to "empirical religious realism" as a means to finding "the social Jesus." With the continuing decline of the social gospel after the war, this kind of search did not appeal to most scholars, and the work of S. E. Johnson (*Jesus in His Homeland,* 1957), while described as written "in the light of his geographical, cultural and religious background," is directed not toward "the social Jesus" but toward a figure who is historically comprehensible. Interest in the historical Jesus is motivated by theological considerations in J. M. Robinson's *A New Quest of the Historical Jesus* (1959); his book is chiefly devoted to German works and is addressed to an audience influenced by German theology. Americans are likely to regard the quest not as new but as renewed, especially since they continue to meditate upon H. J. Cadbury's *The Peril of Modernizing Jesus* (1937).

Relatively complete studies of the apostle Paul or of his thought have been rather rare, though mention should certainly be made of the "mediating" and perceptive *St. Paul* (1938) by A. D. Nock and the more radical works by D. W. Riddle (*Paul, Man of Conflict,* 1940) and John Knox (*Chapters in a Life of Paul,* 1950), both of which regard the testimony of Acts as nearly useless or in need of drastic revision. In addition, M. S. Enslin's study of *The Ethics of Paul* (1930) remains significant because of its correlation of Paul's ideas with Greco-Roman thought.

In part, the lack of full studies of Paul seems due to the lack of adequate frames of reference in which to set his views. H. J. Schoeps (*Paulus,* 1959) has classified various frames as Hellenistic, Hellenistic Jewish, Palestinian Jewish, and eschatological; he claims that all must be taken into account. The problem arises when one tries to see how they are interrelated, and the difficulty of the task is increased by the fact that modern ideas of all four "patterns" are in flux.

In a brief study of *Paul and His Recent Interpreters* (1961) E. E. Ellis lays emphasis on the Palestinian Jewish factors, interprets the crucial eschatological passage in 2 Corinthians 5:1-11 in relation to Jewish thought, not Hellenistic, and points out the phenomena that favor Pauline authorship of the pastoral epistles. These rather conservative views may well, as Ellis suggests, represent "the future trend." If so, statements about Paul based only on the major epistles or on his relation to the Greco-Roman world will have to be revised. (Compare the English work of W. D. Davies, *Paul and Rabbinic Judaism*, 1948.)

At the same time, the pendulum action characteristic of New Testament studies will have to be guarded against. I, to whom Ellis refers as a "mediating" scholar, believe that the historical and theological phenomena are too complex to be regarded as exclusively Jewish or Greek; and the linguistic studies (*The Semantics of Biblical Language*, 1961) of James Barr, now of Princeton, suggest that sharp distinctions of this kind owe their existence primarily to modern analysts, not to ancient writings.

With such qualifications in mind, it must still be said that the study of Paul needs to be carried on in new ways, with greater attention paid both to what he says (and what he means by it) and to what Acts says about him. In particular, the question of the authenticity of the pastoral epistles needs to be re-examined, in spite of the commentary by Easton. The older statistical methods are not satisfactory (see pp. 120 f.), and other approaches based upon rather hypothetical reconstructions of early church history are not entirely persuasive.

American study of the book of Acts, however, has been highly significant, chiefly because of the work of one man: H. J. Cadbury. (This point is clearly made in Dom. J. Dupont's *Les sources du livre des Actes: État de la question,* 1960; to Cadbury's work he adds that of A. D. Nock.) Cadbury's sense, both critical and common, has given his studies a permanent value. He began with *The Style and Literary Method of Luke* (1920), continued with *The Making of*

Luke-Acts (1927) and the commentary on Acts in *The Beginnings of Christianity* (1933), and added further observations in *The Book of Acts and History* (1955). His work owes a good deal of its solidity to the painstaking literary analysis, especially stylistic, with which it began and to the sober and cautious historical judgments that characterize it.

American work on the rest of the New Testament has not been conspicuously important, though one should mention *The Primitive Christian Catechism* (1940) by Philip Carrington of Quebec; in this book an attempt was made to find a pattern of common teaching behind several of the epistles. Similarly Carrington's *Primitive Christian Calendar* (1952) looks for the origin of the arrangement of the gospels in early lectionary systems. In part the lack of American work in this area may be due to the view that Jesus and Paul are more important than the life and thought of the later church. If so, it may be expected that over a period of time more work will be done.

There have been relatively few significant introductions to New Testament literature as a whole, but one should mention the studies of Samuel Sandmel (*A Jewish Understanding of the New Testament*, 1956), H. C. Kee and F. W. Young (*Understanding the New Testament*, 1957), and J. L. Price (*Interpreting the New Testament*, 1961). These three books are written from history-minded points of view; all testify, in various ways, to the theological importance of the materials studied. Writing an introduction is an extraordinarily difficult task, partly because of the ever increasing range of modern critical and theological work, and it may be that eventually the question of the nature of an introduction will have to be raised; perhaps it should do no more than provide a general introduction to the study of religion, or perhaps it should assume a more specialized purpose.

Apart from studies of special subjects, there seems to be only one major study of New Testament theology from this period; this is the *Introduction to New Testament Thought* (1950) by F. C. Grant, which approaches the topic in a rather eclectic way, largely thematic but partly chronological. The book is less systematic than Bultmann's *Theology of the New Testament* (translated by the American scholar Kendrick Grobel) and does not employ the *heilsgeschichtlich* approach of Ethelbert Stauffer (*New Testament Theology*).

Indeed, one of its many merits may be that it does not attempt to impose a system upon the New Testament materials. In this regard it resembles two earlier American works whose titles reflect their authors' views: *The Religion of the New Testament* (E. W. Parsons, 1939) and *The Varieties of New Testament Religion* (E. F. Scott, 1943). Americans have not tended to favor the idea that there is a single New Testament theology; instead, they have either emphasized diversity in the New Testament or reserved the title *theology* for systematic constructions.

Two highly individual studies by Kierkegaard-influenced P. S. Minear deserve more attention than they have received from New Testament scholars; these are his *Eyes of Faith* (1947), emphasizing subjectivity in the approach to the Bible, and *Images of the Church in the New Testament* (1960), reflecting a strong concern for the ecumenical movement.

More closely related to systematic theology are three small books by John Knox: *The Man Christ Jesus* (1941), *Christ the Lord* (1945), and *On the Meaning of Christ* (1947), republished together as *Jesus, Lord and Christ* (1958). Knox prefers, partly on philosophical grounds, to speak of the "event" rather than of the "person" of Christ; in his view, knowledge of this event (and participation in the event) is mediated to believers by the community of faith that is grounded on a memory historically determined. Obviously he intends to link Jesus with the church, and it is therefore not surprising that in his lectures on *The Early Church and the Coming Great Church* (1955) he points to the unity of early Christianity as based on canon, creed, and ministry; "early Catholicism . . . was a fulfillment, even if only proximate and quite imperfect, of hopes as old as the church itself."

Knox's studies reflect the characteristic American concern for the practical consequences of academic work. In *The Early Church* he advocates acceptance of "the historic episcopate" by all Christians. This plea may seem to mark a considerable swing away from such a book as his radically "scientific" *Marcion and the New Testament* (1942), in which he claimed that Marcion's Luke was an earlier version of the canonical gospel; but as he himself points out, his concern for the episcopate is already foreshadowed in his *Philemon Among the Letters of Paul* (1935), in which he argued that the Onesimus of

Philemon later became bishop of Ephesus. Knox's studies are also significant because of their double concern for New Testament and patristic studies. In my view, this concern will become increasingly important.

Environment and Early Church History

One of the most striking features of recent New Testament study has been the way in which the area of investigation has tended to be enlarged, not only backward toward the Old Testament and the Jewish and general Hellenistic backgrounds but also forward toward the early church fathers and their Jewish and general Greco-Roman backgrounds. Just as the study of Judaism and the Hellenistic world has been expanded by archaeological discoveries—of which the most striking has been the Dead Sea Scrolls and the Qumran buildings—so the study of the background of the early church has been given considerable impetus by the Gnostic documents from Nag-Hammadi in Egypt. In both situations the discoveries have come after a period of preparation in which emphasis was already being placed upon materials like those that were found. The earlier background materials had come to include Jewish apocalyptic literature and Hellenistic texts and monuments of various kinds; the later background materials had been enriched by studies of the literary, political, social, and religious environments of early Christianity. And in each case the new discoveries have tended to overshadow, if only temporarily, the importance of the older ones. Enthusiasts have supposed that the New Testament could finally be "explained" in relation either to Qumran or to Nag-Hammadi, or to a combination of elements revealed at both sides. The Christian attitude toward Jesus was to be interpreted primarily, if not exclusively, as based upon Essene views of their "Teacher of Righteousness," while the reliability of the gospels was to be checked by comparing some of their contents with that of the gospel of Thomas. In both cases such notions have tended to be tempered by criticism. Though the discoveries, and their application as well, remain extremely important, it cannot be said that New Testament scholarship has entered a new era.

At the beginning of the period we are considering, G. F. Moore produced his monumental study of *Judaism in the First Centuries of the Christian Era* (2 vols., 1927; notes, 1930). Moore's subtitle, *The Age of the Tannaim,* was often neglected, although he made his point clear in the last volume of his work. He was writing on Palestinian Judaism as reflected in the Tannaite sources of the second century of the Christian era; he was not writing on either the Diaspora or on the Judaism of New Testament times—nor was he primarily concerned with "parties, sects, schools, or looser groups." He intended to deal with "the continuity and the progress of the main current of what is called rabbinical Judaism." This current, prominent before the fall of Jerusalem in A.D. 70, achieved "exclusive supremacy" after it.

While Moore's work contains materials that parallel and illuminate some aspects of the New Testament, especially the synoptic gospels and the epistle of James, it cannot be used as a complete representation of "varieties of Jewish experience" in the early first century. Moore did not intend it to be used in this way. Indeed, *Judaism* is potentially more valuable for the study of early church history than for the study of the New Testament. At the same time, the New Testament scholar neglects it at his peril; not every Jew was either a Hellenist or a devotee of exotic groups like the one at Qumran. Modern scholarship is afflicted by a tendency to pay attention to the bizarre and the new at the expense of the representative and the old. Moore looked in another direction. "For the task I have set myself the continuity . . . is of greater importance than the diversity and dissent." One of Moore's virtues was that he explicitly stated what he was doing.[3]

There are other Jewish documents that, long known and often studied, reflect important influences upon the thought of early Christians. Among such writings must be mentioned (1) the Septuagint (the principal Greek translation of the Old Testament), (2) the fragments of Greco-Jewish writers preserved chiefly by the church fathers, (3) the works of Philo of Alexandria, and (4) the works of Josephus. These writings are especially significant because

[3] See also the invaluable guide to haggadic exegesis provided by Louis Ginzberg, *The Legends of the Jews,* 7 vols. (1909-38)—useful also for patristic studies.

it can be shown that early Christians used them, whereas such proof can rarely, if ever, be provided in regard to the Qumran or Nag-Hammadi books.

In dealing with Philo's writings (including his *Questions,* translated from the Armenian version by Ralph Marcus, 1953), two main lines of approach have been taken. E. R. Goodenough (*By Light Light,* 1935; *An Introduction to Philo Judaeus,* 1940) has claimed that for Philo Judaism was essentially a mystical mystery religion; H. A. Wolfson (*Philo,* 1947), on the other hand, regards Philo as a Hellenizer "in language only, not in religious belief or cult." If one views Palestinian Judaism as providing criteria for a decision on this point, three possible conclusions have been indicated by Samuel Sandmel (*Philo's Place in Judaism,* 1956). (1) The rabbinic Judaism of Palestine was regarded as authoritative in Alexandria, and Philo provided "surface" Hellenization of its teachings. (2) "Alexandrian Judaism was . . . self-contained and almost self-sufficient." (3) Each kind of Judaism "developed along its own lines of creativity but without the complete loss of communication." Sandmel himself favors the last solution and speaks of "cross-fertilization," insisting upon the use of the Old Testament by both Philo and the rabbis and also upon the diversity in their use of common motifs.

As a parallel to this kind of conclusion one may refer to recent studies of the gospel of John and of the epistle to the Hebrews, as well as to analyses of some of the earlier church fathers. In these studies emphasis is being laid upon the multiplicity of possible environmental factors, for example in John. No single key such as "Judaism" or "Hellenism" will unlock all doors.

For the study of early Christian thought Philo remains exceedingly important. One may not agree with Wolfson that the early apologists used his works directly; conclusive evidence of Christian use first occurs in the writings of Clement of Alexandria. On the other hand, it is unlikely that Justin's logos-doctrine owed nothing to the Jewish philosopher. The Philonic bridge between the Old Testament and Greek philosophy provided a way of thinking that the early fathers reflect. Similarly Josephus was important to them because of his apologetic approach to history, and his influence upon Christian writers was significant from the late second century onward. In other words, these witnesses to Greek speaking and Greek writing Judaism show us that early Christians did not need to invent completely new modes of communication with the Greco-Roman world.

None of what I have said is intended to suggest that either rabbinic Judaism or Hellenistic Judaism was necessarily more important than what we now know from the Dead Sea Scrolls. It is only intended to point out that in our pursuit of the new we cannot ignore what has already been discovered, even though our understanding of the old may well require drastic modification because of information later acquired.

An important collection of essays on *The Scrolls and the New Testament* was edited by Krister Stendahl in 1957, and while most of the contributors are European, there are valuable articles by American scholars as well. Of these the ones most closely related to the New Testament are W. H. Brownlee's study of John the Baptist, S. E. Johnson's correlation of the Manual of Discipline with the Jerusalem church of Acts, W. D. Davies' discussion of Paul, and R. E. Brown's analysis of the parallels between Johannine thought and that reflected in the Dead Sea Scrolls. All four present sober statements in which both resemblances and differences are clearly indicated—as they are in Stendahl's own "introduction and perspective." [4]

A more radical use of Qumran materials is explained by Joseph A. Fitzmyer in the *Catholic Biblical Quarterly* (1961), in which he deals with 2 Corinthians 6:14-7:1. This passage (1) is out of place in its present context, (2) is not characteristically Pauline in style, vocabulary, or thought, and (3) contains ideas and expressions characteristic of the Qumran group. Therefore, Fitzmyer concludes, it was not written by Paul but was interpolated into 2 Corinthians. Since other reasons suggest that 2 Corinthians may be a composite document, his view deserves careful attention.

The Dead Sea Scrolls provide a highly significant example of the kind of apocalyptic thought that, by the end of the nineteenth century, had been recognized as illuminating the New Testament documents and their historical setting. This kind of thought, it can now

---

[4] At this point one should mention the important *John the Baptist* (1951) by C. H. Kraeling, important in spite of, or because of, the relatively minor use made of the scrolls.

be seen, was even more influential than had been supposed, and more variegated in its expression as well. The Qumran manuals of discipline, hymns of thanksgiving, and exegetical books provide valuable analogies to various New Testament books; the theological ideas and the concrete practices of the Dead Sea group are often analogous to their New Testament counterparts. Indeed, Qumran influences have been traced not only in Johannine thought, in the mission of John the Baptist and parts of the teaching of Jesus, in the church at Jerusalem, and in some of the Pauline communities, but even in such a document as the *Shepherd* of Hermas.

The success of tracing these influences is questionable. Sometimes the tracers seem to be convinced that parallels prove dependence, one way or the other, and that the presence of parallels excludes the possibility of either the absence of direct relation or the presence of a common viewpoint. For instance, a Qumran parallel to something in the New Testament does not necessarily diminish the importance of other parallels (e.g., Hellenistic or Gnostic), nor does it necessarily prove that the early Christians were converts from the Dead Sea group. In the continuing examination of the relationships, more rigorous methods must be employed and more emphasis must be laid upon what we do not, and perhaps cannot, know.

Similar observations should be made in regard to the new Gnostic materials as well as to the older ones. Not every parallel between a statement made by Paul, John, or Ignatius and a statement found in a Gnostic book shows that the New Testament writer had come under Gnostic influence. Indeed, it might better be argued that since the kinds of Gnosticism we know are largely Christian, the influence was the other way; the value of Gnostic documents for the study of the New Testament may lie chiefly in their witness to early New Testament exegesis.

The problems posed by Gnosticism itself have not received a great deal of attention from American scholars, though one should certainly mention the thesis of C. H. Kraeling, *Anthropos and Son of Man* (1927); the significant study by Hans Jonas, *The Gnostic Religion* (1958); and perhaps my own *Gnosticism and Early Christianity* (1959). The principal problems that arise in relation to Gnosticism are (1) how to define it, (2) how to analyze its origins, and (3) how to assess its relation to the early church. The three problems are interrelated, since the phenomenon that scholars call Gnosticism was actually expressed in a variety of systems, often inconsistent, and the definition given will largely determine the answer provided for questions about sources, dates, and relation to Christianity. The earliest kinds of Gnosticism we know were somehow related to the early church, and if Gnosticism includes a Savior who brings saving knowledge and/or rites to his followers, it would appear that this religion was essentially a heterodox form of Christianity. If Gnosticism could exist without such an agent of revelation and redemption, its primary sources could be traced elsewhere—to Judaism or Irenian religion or to Greek theosophy.

Again, few Americans have studied particular kinds of Gnostic thought; but the exceptions are important, including the late R. P. Casey (*The Excerpta ex Theodoto of Clement of Alexandria*, 1935) and Kendrick Grobel (*The Gospel of Truth*, 1960).

The significance of Jonas's book lies in the fact that he has given a picture of Gnosticism as a whole. Should Gnostic thought be regarded as derived from early Christian theology, a full study of early Christian thought would be required in order to test this hypothesis. Meanwhile Gnostic exegesis of the Bible is important for the history of interpretation. If we want to know how early readers, or some early readers, interpreted the New Testament books we have the testimony of the Gnostics—to be taken into account, however, only in relation to the interpretation provided by early Christians more orthodox in temper.

An example of this use of Gnostic thought (C. D. Morrison, *The Powers That Be*, 1961) occurs in relation to the controversial words of Paul about the *exousiai* to which everyone is to be subject (Romans 13:1-7). It can be shown from a criticism by Irenaeus that some Gnostics regarded the *exousiai* as spiritual powers. This fact shows that such exegesis was possible in the second century, or even the first. Against the testimony of the Gnostics, however, must be placed the unanimous testimony of the early fathers that the *exousiai* were primarily, if not exclusively, political in nature. For modern understanding of the passage both views are important, but presumably more weight should be given the patristic interpretation.

The reason for this conclusion lies in the modern study of the early Christian writers themselves. It is possible, to be sure, that all the writings of the apostolic fathers come from a time later than any New Testament book. Even if this be so (and it is by no means certain with respect to such documents as the Didache and 1 Clement), the interval between the New Testament and the apostolic fathers, as a group, is insignificant. Some scholars have tried to show that there is a much greater theological gulf; but this gulf seems to have been created by assigning normative significance to certain polemical passages in the Pauline epistles and by neglecting the New Testament passages that are exceedingly close to the later writings. If the view of Helmut Koester is accepted—that the earlier apostolic fathers relied not upon the synoptic gospels but upon oral traditions like those underlying the synoptic gospels—these fathers stand as close to the earliest Christian tradition as do these evangelists, and a preference for the evangelists over the fathers can be justified only by an appeal to the history of the canon; but the canon was the creation of the church that transmitted the books, and this church appealed to the authority not only of the Bible but also of the fathers.

The study of the early fathers resulted in much greater appreciation of their work as theologians and much greater understanding of their relation to the Greco-Roman and Jewish cultures in which they participated. For instance, the Jewish background of the Didache has been thoroughly investigated by J.-P. Audet (*La Didaché,* 1958, a book written largely at Harvard); the Hellenistic environment of 1 Clement is discussed in Werner Jaeger's *Early Christianity and Greek Paideia* (1961); the relation of Ignatius to his environment is ably handled by Virginia Corwin in her *St. Ignatius and Christianity at Antioch* (1960). K. W. Clark has recently dealt with the mysterious personality and attitudes of Hermas (in *Early Christian Origins,* ed. A. P. Wikgren, 1961). My own studies in the writings of the apologists may be mentioned in passing, as well as my investigations into early Christian analyses of the life of Jesus (*The Earliest Lives of Jesus,* 1961).[5]

It need hardly be said that studies of this sort are not peculiarly American, but it seems undeniable that toward the end of World War II a renaissance of patristic study began in America, and that its effects have been felt in both Roman Catholic and Protestant theo-

[5] See also "The Study of the Early Fathers Today," *Anglican Theological Review,* XLIV (1962), 280-94.

logical circles. On the Catholic side should be mentioned first of all the series of translations, with very full notes, entitled "Ancient Christian Writers," and the magnificent *Patrology* of Johannes Quasten of the Catholic University in Washington, D.C.

The result of this renaissance has been the treatment of the New Testament in less isolation from the early church. There has been a renewed emphasis upon the continuity of Christian life and thought as compared with earlier attempts to sever the gospel from the church. This emphasis is already requiring a fresh look at the ideas of the Protestant reformers about the relation of scripture to tradition, as well as a fresh look at the ideas of their Roman Catholic contemporaries. Most of the writings of the early fathers that we know today were ignored by, or unknown to, the men of the sixteenth century.

During the period with which we are concerned there has appeared only one treatise that covers the whole area of early church history; this is the very full treatment of *The Early Christian Church* (1957) by Philip Carrington. As the author says, "the 'tendency' in this history is to trust the evidence, and the tradition of the church in which it was produced and preserved; and to tell the story as the evidence presents it after it has been fairly examined and criticized." The book thus does not represent a new hypothesis except insofar as this confidence in the honesty of early Christian writers must, unfortunately, be regarded as novel.

In addition, early church history in America can derive benefit from the valuable *History of Antioch in Syria* (1961) by Glanville Downey, since much of the city's history is the history of the church there. There is no such study of the city of Alexandria, although one should mention the excellent survey by E. R. Hardy, *Christian Egypt: Church and People* (1952).

◄§ 3 §►

CONCLUSION

In my view there has been a considerable change in the atmosphere of New Testament study in America during the last generation. It is resulting in new directions not always close to those followed previously.

1. There is coming to be a fresh awareness of the limitations of criticism and critics, something that might be called a retreat from fancy to fact. The ancients were not always stupid; our contemporaries are not always intelligent. It is to be hoped that the interpretation of the New Testament will be more closely related to the phenomena involved and that it will be linked with linguistic analysis in general.

2. There is coming to be a fresh awareness of the need for logical analysis of the principles of criticism, and again this approach will limit the range of critical imaginativeness about the past.

3. There is a renewed interest in the historical background of the New Testament, not as expressed in handbooks about the ancient world view but as found in the actual phenomena that survive from New Testament times. Impetus has been given this concern by archaeological discoveries.[6]

4. There is a renewed recognition of the fact that the New Testament environment was not only the ancient world in general but the ancient church in particular, and that therefore the New Testament cannot be understood apart from church history. What is meant here by *church* is not any modern form of Christianity, but the ancient Catholic church (along with its concomitant heretical groups) whose life can be reconstructed from existing historical phenomena. Without consideration of the continuing historical existence of a visible church the New Testament remains fragmentary. It points to-

[6] A somewhat similar emphasis has been expressed by A. N. Wilder in various articles and especially in his *Otherworldliness and the New Testament* (1954). One cannot neglect F. C. Grant, *The Economic Background of the Gospels* (1926).

152

ward a context surrounding itself; but we do not know what the context is unless we go not only backward to the Old Testament but also forward to the early fathers, and even to the Gnostics, in order to see what Christianity did not become.

5. There is also recognition of the fact that the New Testament writers and the early fathers pointed to something, or rather to someone, beyond themselves; and this someone is the God who, they believed, had revealed, was revealing, and would reveal himself in Jesus Christ. No understanding of the New Testament, then, is adequate unless it finally takes this revelation into account. There would be no New Testament and no fathers had the faith of early Christians in Jesus not existed. This faith was faith in a particular historical person, and it was expressed in particular historical forms. The study of the New Testament, reaching its climax in the study of New Testament faith, cannot immediately prove that the student should share this faith.

This is to say that the philosophical or theological question as to the truth of the basic proclamation of the New Testament lies outside the scope of New Testament study as I have described it. In my view it is necessary to find out what the New Testament says before trying to determine if what it says is true. There will, of course, be a prior reason for investigating what the New Testament says, and such a prior reason can be found in (a) the investigator's existing faith or disbelief in relation to the Bible, the Christian religion, or some other religion, or (b) his relation to the history of culture, especially the Western cultures in which the Bible has played a significant role, or (c) a combination of these factors.

As we understand the situation, however, the investigator cannot assume a priori that the New Testament proclamation is either absolutely true or absolutely false. If he assumes that it is true, he must try to allow for the possibility that both he and the early Christians may have been mistaken; if he assumes that it is false, he must try to allow for the possibility that the early Christians may have been right. The investigator's goal is primarily that of sympathetic understanding.

In the context of the study of the humanities, the study of the New Testament has an important part to play, simply because the New Testament has had a very great influence upon the minds of human

153

beings, both in the East and in the West. Since other documents of human history are studied by means of textual, literary, and historical analysis, the New Testament must be studied by the same methods, so that its resemblances to other literatures and its differences from them will become clear. Some investigators will lay more emphasis upon common ideas and attitudes; others will lay stress upon what seems to be unique. Both alike, however, must remember that it is the New Testament that they are interpreting. A certain "loyalty" to the text is required.

Naturally the investigator-interpreter lives in the modern world, just as the early Christians lived in the ancient world. No one is exempt from contemporaneousness. But we must beware of reading ourselves and our problems into the literature. Not everything in the New Testament is directly relevant to the modern situation, and we distort its statements when we try too hard to relate it to ourselves. A historical perspective helps us to keep from overemphasizing certain aspects of the New Testament at the expense of others. Krister Stendahl has recently pointed out that the problems faced by Martin Luther were not identical with those faced by the apostle Paul, and that Paul's ideas are distorted when they are interpreted as if they were Luther's. Similar dangers occur in other situations.

This is not to say that insights derived from theology, philosophy, sociology, or psychology are irrelevant, only that they must be tested and retested in relation to the New Testament text itself. Like the history of religions, which is often in danger of becoming a branch of anthropology or sociology, New Testament study must be on its guard against surrendering its primary responsibility to others. This responsibility involves dealing with the materials in relation to the historical purpose or purposes for which they were written.

THE HISTORY OF CHRISTIANITY

J. H. NICHOLS
PROFESSOR OF CHURCH HISTORY
PRINCETON THEOLOGICAL SEMINARY

◄§ 1 ß►

GENERAL OBSERVATIONS

History of Christianity is a term probably more characteristic of the 1930's than of the 1960's for the subject of this essay, since there is now perhaps less timidity in using the older terms, *church history* or *ecclesiastical history*. During the generation of 1930-60 there was a rediscovery of the actuality and importance of the church among Christians and an increase in awareness of its dimensions. But however much one may wish to support the rehabilitation of the term and conception *church,* to talk of *church history* is to court misunderstanding still. To many or most it conveys a notion of a rather esoteric specialization in the history of certain ecclesiastical institutions, doctrines, and rites that presumably are marginal interests of some of the less alert and progressive strata in society. Some church histories do bear a resemblance to this description, but they scarcely set the standards in the literature of the discipline. *History of Christianity* probably seems a more inclusive and less technical term to most people. The whole difficulty no doubt reflects the modern situation of the Christian society as a historical community that has been overlaid by other communities and, if one may use the analogy, partially "denationalized," so that its self-consciousness has become dim and its corporate character fragmentary and tenuous. The renewed sense of that corporate character, that common heritage and destiny, is the basis for the revived insistence in scholarship on *church* history, rather than on a history of Christianity, which might be construed as a history of Christian ideas or practices in abstraction from the life of a distinct historic community.

One may also usefully distinguish church history, or history of Christianity, from Christian history, or history written from a Christian perspective. It is possible, for example, to write first-class military and diplomatic history, or history of science, visibly strengthened by Christian insights and perspectives, but such histories are somewhat marginal to church history, and much more narrowly special-

157

ized. Even a general historian whose sensitivities and inquiries derive unmistakably from Christian sources will not necessarily be a church historian. Good church history will have the breadth and scope of general history, no doubt, but will find its focus in the self-consciously Christian community immersed in all the multifarious relations and activities of the common life. It is possible, on the other hand, and indeed not uncommon, to write of Christian institutions, ideas, and activities from other than a Christian perspective, to subsume them under the perspectives of cultural and social history, to write a secularized church history. Many of the publications on the more recent history of American Christianity are of this character.

One conspicuous feature of the state of American scholarship in church history emerges from a survey of a few critical bibliographical articles on major periods. Whether one has to do with the early church in the Roman Empire, or the Middle Ages, Byzantine or Latin, or the Reformation, or the church in modern Europe, Protestant or Roman Catholic, the situation is the same: the writing of church history is essentially a facet of British and Continental scholarship. Here and there one comes across a creditable American achievement, but the shape of the continuing discussion is defined on the other side of the Atlantic. In this respect the American mind is still a colonial extension of the European. American production is generally of minor significance in both quantity and quality. Only in the study of American Christianity, and some closely related phases of British Christianity, does American scholarship play a leading role.

Beside the recognition of prevailing American dependence on Europe, a second observation obtrudes itself. American scholarship in this field is very unevenly distributed over the terrain. For four-fifths and more of the sweep of the life of Christianity one will find only a lonely handful of Americans scattered about, but when one comes to the church in America, and contiguous British territory, the American historians are as crowded as trout fishermen on opening day. Well over half of all American scholarly production in the whole discipline seems concentrated on American and British subjects; less than half of the available resources and energies are left to deal with everything else.

No one can quarrel with American interest in American topics. If Americans do not write the history of American Christianity, who will? But the American Christian experience is only a minor portion of the whole. The first Christian foundations in what is now the United States rested on a millenium and a half of prior Christian history in Asia, North Africa, and Europe. A competent teacher of church history planning a comprehensive course on the subject would surely have to allot at least two-thirds of the time available to the developments in Christian history before the church ever reached America. One who does not know the earlier story will not understand American Christianity. For the investigation of that first millenium and a half American scholars will obviously be at a disadvantage as compared to European scholars. The American contribution to general church history prior to the seventeenth century has been, in fact, even less impressive than one might expect in view of this disadvantage.

The inadequacy of scholarly personnel in America for the investigation and teaching of the history of Christianity outside America is dramatized by the obsolescent condition of the teaching tools of the discipline. Imagine teaching American or European or English or medieval history from a basic textbook half a century old! Church history is generally taught on the introductory level from such a textbook, Williston Walker's *History of the Christian Church* (1918), probably still the best single-volume text available. (Latourette's 1,516-page *History of Christianity* [1953] cannot be used as a single-volume text, despite Harper's ingenuity at bookbinding.) Historians of Union Theological Seminary, Wilhelm Pauck, Cyril Richardson, and Robert Handy, have refurbished Walker in a revised edition published in 1959, but you can only do so much with an old law tenement building. A good up-to-date textbook is needed.

Most teachers of the history of theology apologize as they refer their students to the *History of Christian Thought* (1932) by A. C. McGiffert, who was perhaps the dean of American church historians for the generation before 1930. After indicating many inadequacies of the book they conclude: "It's still the best thing we have." Harnack's *History of Dogma* is of course available in English, but does not cover the history of thought generally, and Seeberg's *Textbook of the History of Doctrine* is more of a manual for reference than a textbook. These works are of much higher quality than that of Mc-Giffert, but they are also a generation or more older.

One of the reasons that church history courses are generally taught in a pedestrian textbook-and-lecture fashion is that inexpensive editions in English of primary sources, source problems, and the like are lacking. For ancient church history, to be sure, there are three or four great English language series of the writings of the fathers ("Ante-Nicene, Nicene and Post-Nicene Fathers," series one and two; "Ancient Christian Writers"; and "Fathers of the Church") and five or six source books (Ayer, Gwatkin, Kidd, Stevenson, and Bettenson; not all, however, in print). But how is one to organize courses around the analysis and discussion of documents from the Middle Ages, the Reformation, or modern church history? Some help is given by the "Library of Christian Classics" (Westminster Press), one of the significant achievements of the generation at work during 1930-60, and the projected "Library of Protestant Thought" (Oxford University Press) will help still more. But none of these publications is really cheap enough for extensive classroom use like the German *Kleine Texte.*

In what other branch of history would one consider reissuing an encyclopedia of the vintage of the *Schaff-Herzog Encyclopaedia of Religious Knowledge* (1889), even with a couple of supplementary volumes? Where else would one find professors actually commending to students such an antique as Philip Schaff's *History of the Christian Church* (1858-92) as the most comprehensive single work in the field?

The American graduate student of the history of Christianity has never had in English a book such as Karl Heussi's *Kompendium der Kirchengeschichte,* which defines the minimum acquaintance with the whole field that might be expected of him. Nor is there in English any set of manuals like the four-volume *Handbuch der Kirchengeschichte für Studierende,* edited by Gustav Krüger, which supplies advanced students with an orientation to the problems and bibliography of all periods of church history. In the place of such tools the American graduate student lays end to end a set of textbooks on various periods, of diverse quality and authority, and with generally inadequate bibliographical indications. Perhaps the best-advised use

Heussi, but the majority know only enough German to pass the "reading examinations" given in our graduate schools.

American church historians have been unable to equip themselves adequately with the basic teaching tools, or even to keep reasonably up to date with translated adaptations of European tools. They have been torn between the backlog of postponed chores and the challenge of fresh inquiry, and they have not really accomplished very much with either task.

What is the matter with them? Some illumination is shed by the sociology of the discipline. The greater part of American scholarly production in the history of Christianity comes from men who are not church historians by profession. If this phenomenon be disregarded for the moment, professional church historians can be grouped in three classes: college teachers, teachers in denominational seminaries, and teachers in theological faculties related to universities. The third category is the smallest numerically, but it produces the great bulk of the solid scholarship. All told, the producing church historians of America in the last generation could be numbered off on the normal complement of fingers and toes or comfortably assembled in a large living room. Their chief fault is that they are so pathetically few.

A comparison with the related field of biblical studies brings out some of the practical problems of the discipline of church history. When a graduate student acquits himself creditably in a doctoral program in biblical studies, there is a good likelihood that he can find a post in which to devote a lifetime of scholarship and teaching to the Bible. Nearly all college departments of religion, and all Protestant seminaries have major Bible assignments in their programs.

Very few college religion departments, in contrast, include chairs in the history of Christianity. Some of them offer a course or two in the subject, but the man who teaches these is usually expected to teach ethics, comparative religion, or Bible courses as well. Along this path it is very difficult to acquire enough mastery of anything for creative scholarship. And if the aspiring scholar of the history of Christianity is sufficiently grounded in general history to secure a post in the history department, or can persuade the dean that he is, there again the better part of his energies will be directed to studies other than the history of Christianity. From men so situated little more can be expected than a textbook, or an occasional article or monograph of limited scope.

Most of the teaching of the history of Christianity is carried on in this country not in undergraduate liberal arts colleges, but as part of the training of ministers in theological seminaries. The seminary setting usually ensures the minimum of sympathy with the materials that is essential to good history, and that is not always present in the average university, but, on the other hand, it often imposes rather utilitarian directives on the church historian. The most widespread pattern is probably that of the introductory survey, taught generally after the style and at the level of the freshman survey course in history in the liberal arts college. Few seminary students take more than this survey, except perhaps an equally elementary conspectus of American church history or the modern history of the particular denomination to which the seminary is related. The interests of the students and the structure of the B.D. curriculum do not stimulate the faculty to fresh inquiry or creative scholarship in church history as much as in, for example, Bible or theology.

Certain geographical considerations also have a significant bearing on scholarly work or the lack of it. Many American seminaries were founded before the Civil War in accordance with the then current notion that they should be located some distance from worldly distractions. The result of this notion has been that many seminaries suffer from intellectual isolation and stagnation. Few of the denominational schools have libraries adequate for serious historical research. It is much easier to accumulate the requisite tools for biblical scholarship than it is to assemble any significant body of documents illustrative of the two milleniums of Christian history. Most seminary professors of church history do not have access to extensive sources other than those on American subjects; college teachers, of course, often have the same problem. As is to be expected, significant work in church history is concentrated around the major research libraries of the country. Where else can the historian work?

This brings us to the graduate theological faculties in university centers, where most of the scholarship of professional church historians has been carried on—in terms of providing basic tools, of training graduate students, and of fresh research and writing. Here are to be found the libraries, the provision for advanced and specialized courses, the debate of diverse theological, philosophical, and methodological tendencies, and the constant critical scrutiny of cognate disciplines, such as even the strong liberal arts college or denominational seminary can scarcely be expected to provide. In sharp contrast to the numerous university centers in Europe, especially in Germany, there are in the United States barely half a dozen such scholarly centers where research in church history is systematically pursued.

Church history as a university discipline in a recent development in the English speaking world. In 1845, in his *Essay on Development*, John Henry Newman observed, in what was no doubt a calculated slur at Milner: "It is melancholy to say it, but the chief, perhaps the only English writer, who has any claim to be considered an ecclesiastical historian, is the infidel Gibbon." In his inaugural lecture at Cambridge, *The Study of Ecclesiastical History* (1945), Norman Sykes surveyed the establishment of university chairs in the British Isles, Oxford in 1842, Trinity in 1850, Kings in 1863, Cambridge in 1882, and Durham in the twentieth century. University studies in Scotland began early in the eighteenth century, but the body of what was then taught was biblical history.

In the United States the university-related theological faculties have only begun to maintain a continuous and significant graduate program in the twentieth century. Early in the century a seminary professor of church history was not usually trained as such. He was more often a pastor called back to the school and given a certain amount of time to get up his subject. One did not identify himself, as did the Germans, by saying "I was a member of Karl Holl's seminar"—or Harnack's, or Lietzmann's. The established and competently led American graduate faculties of theology barely antedate World War I, at least as far as church history is concerned.

In the generation after 1930, American professional scholarship in church history was predominantly identified with one or another of a mere handful of graduate centers. The largest concentration in 1930 consisted of the group on the campus of the University of Chicago who published the *Bibliographical Guide to the History of Christianity* (1931)—Shirley Jackson Case, John T. McNeill, William Warren Sweet, Wilhelm Pauck, and Matthew Spinka. Next to

Chicago one should probably mention Yale, with Roland Bainton and Kenneth Latourette and later, at the nearby Berkeley Divinity School, Edward Hardy. By 1960, McNeill and Pauck had transferred to Union Theological Seminary in New York where they were colleagues of Cyril Richardson. After these three chief centers, Duke, with Ray C. Petry and H. Shelton Smith; Harvard, especially its Dumbarton Oaks group of Byzantine specialists such as Glanville Downey; and the Catholic University of America in Washington, D.C., with Richard Purcell and John T. Ellis, also deserve mention. There were, of course, other scholars of stature, such as Robert Calhoun of Yale and Giorgio La Piana of Harvard, who wrote very little but who shaped the minds of numerous graduate students. Here and there one also found distinguished and productive writers in the seminaries. But one could still say that the existence of the discipline as such in America virtually depended on these six graduate schools.

A survey so nationally delimited, however, is unnatural, irritating to compose, and probably to read. The community of scholars to which American church historians belong is international (apart from the specialists in the American church). Ask a church historian about the best works in his field and he will name titles and authors with scarcely a thought of nationality; to pick out the Americans among these is as impertinent and as artificial as it is to single out the albinos. Among them there are certainly no great church historians of the stature of Ferdinand Christian Baur, Adolf von Harnack, or Ernst Troeltsch. America has produced none such as they in any generation. Indeed a significant number of the notable church historians classified as American have been imported. To this day the American educational system does not produce its own replacements in this discipline. Deans and presidents, Protestant and Roman Catholic, are driven to Europe in their search for scholars with adequate equipment and gifts. And an account of the literature put in terms of the Americans alone is like a play whose full cast has been reduced to two minor characters and a horse; the plot has probably disappeared altogether.

There is, moreover, a serious problem as to the meaning of the term *American*. Americans have always been dependent on Europe for the best part of the historical literature they have used, but proba-

164

bly never before 1930 was there such a massive migration to America of European scholars. Hitler, Mussolini, and the Bolsheviks sent large numbers of refugee scholars to this country before the war, and the movement continued thereafter. In the field of church history, where there had been so few productive American scholars, the newcomers actually came to dominate the publishers' lists in terms of works of maturity and distinction.

At what point should the work of these immigrant scholars be accounted "American"? Many had already published major works in Europe, e.g., Vasiliev's *Byzantine Empire* or Kantorowicz's *Frederick the Second* or Kristeller's *Marsilio Ficino*. These works then frequently appeared in new American editions—this was true also of dissertations by younger men who wished to establish themselves on the American scene—but these publications tell us nothing of the tendencies of American scholarship.

Is there a point at which one might expect to find significant traces of the American environment in the work of such scholars? After ten years perhaps? In some cases the chief influence seems to have been signaled by a sharp decrease in production, as men became absorbed in learning to teach in the new context and found their sources less accessible. Most of those who were already mature scholars before their migration probably changed the fundamental pattern of their work only slightly. From this point of view one should probably include in a survey of American scholars only men who moved to America in their twenties or early thirties before they had developed their individual style or crystallized their understanding of the nature of the church.

So strict a criterion would falsify the situation. Many of the immigrants built their characteristic methods and interests into graduate programs and journals involving young American scholars. Take Roman Catholic institutions for illustration. The graduate program in early and medieval church history at Catholic University was transformed by Quasten, much as Gurian left an impress on Notre Dame or Halecki on Fordham. Holborn at Yale and Werner Jaeger at Harvard similarly built something identifiable from their publications into the graduate teaching of historians at these institutions. Very likely it will be another generation before it is apparent how much American universities have been able to assimilate and maintain of the wealth of perspectives, problems, and techniques brought to them between 1930 and 1960. Some will surely drop by the wayside and prove incapable of growth on American soil, but it does not seem unreasonable to hope for a permanent enrichment of the American scholarly tradition.

The better part of American scholarly writing about the history of Christianity, however, has come from outside the ranks of the professional church historians altogether. Church history has profited notably from the rise of interest in history faculties in the last generation of the history of ideas. Any serious attention to the history of Western philosophy, ethics, political theory, literature, or art will necessarily become deeply involved in the study of Christianity. The inner life of European and American culture is unintelligible apart from its historical faith. The church historian's natural ally, and often his instructor, has been the historian of ideas and literature. America has yet to produce such a master as Wilhelm Dilthey, or even a Paul Hazard or Basil Willey. But scholars like Ralph Gabriel, Perry Miller, William Haller, Arthur Lovejoy, and Franklin Baumer were unavoidably encroaching much of the time on church history. Any investigation of the literature and art of the West that is concerned with ideas as well as aesthetic form, or any inquiry into social, economic, and political ethics and theory will be dealing much or most of the time with consciously Christian formulations. In the United States between 1930 and 1960 the historians of culture and thought contributed more to the literature of church history than did the occupants of chairs assigned to the discipline. Because of the cultural segregation of theological faculties, these men also presented the perspectives of church history more effectively to the college and university community.

The weakness of professional church history in the United States is both cause and effect of a widespread religious illiteracy in American academic circles. This illiteracy expresses itself on the philosophical level in the very widespread adoption of reductionist theories of a quasi-Marxist variety among historians as well as social scientists. It is also apparent on the level of sheer factual information. Historians of reputation will commit really crashing bloopers in references to religious events or ideas and feel no need for apology. Had they exposed themselves to the same extent in, say, military or technological history, they would have felt constrained to resign and enlist in the French Foreign Legion. There are just not enough competent scholars to keep the profession as a whole up to the mark in these matters or to redeem it from a recurrent tendency to reductionist vulgarity.

Even among the ablest and best-informed scholars there is a perceptible uneasiness and embarrassment in the treatment of religious phenomena, a great reluctance to call a spade a spade. In his history of Harvard, Morison strains visibly to reassure his readers that early Harvard was not really *that* deeply interested in theology. Perry Miller acknowledges the stature of Jonathan Edwards, not as a great philosophical theologian but as one of America's greatest *artists*. Whitney Cross remarks how extremely difficult it is, "now that theology is a very nearly dead subject," to realize the extensive appeal of theological journals in the generation before the Civil War. He describes various factors that helped their circulation, but cannot explain away the mystery. "It seems an inescapable conclusion that a considerable proportion even of laymen read and relished the theological treatises" (*Burned-over District,* pp. 108 f.). It is symptomatic of an aspect of American intellectual life that such gifted scholars as these must discover in their mature years, often with pained surprise, what any competent church historian could have told them.

As soon as anyone specifies a weakness in American culture the usual sequel is to blame the educational system. It is hard to deny that the older stress on the classical languages and the humanities generally made for better-trained church historians. Every teacher of graduate students today is familiar with the candidate who has majored in electrical engineering or landscape architecture and who belatedly discovers a passion for the history of religious ideas. Even the average college graduate in the liberal arts, if there is one, is usually underequipped in the knowledge of languages, literature, general history, and philosophy needed as a preparation for the discipline of church history.

The weaknesses of the American educational system from this viewpoint, and the lack of adequate institutional support of the discipline of church history, rest on a deeper ground. After all, American resources are adequate to transform both situations radically. We do not have to remain in the humiliating status of dependence on Europe. The problem is that American religion is unconcerned in the matter.

The American churches themselves provide much of the explanation. In general they are anti-intellectual; perhaps more so than the American Chambers of Commerce. They will tolerate a certain amount of hard thinking in religious matters, but will not encourage or support it. It is un-American to love God with the mind. A Christian scholar in America is considered as eccentric as one who wears a beret, or rides a bicycle, or gathers wild mushrooms.

Of all forms of intellectual activity, history probably appeals least to the highly individualist American Christian. Biblical studies of a sort, yes, and some theology, perhaps. But the evangelicalism dominant in America has characteristically lacked a sense of community or of history. In *Law and Public Opinion in England During the Nineteenth Century,* Albert V. Dicey described vividly an attitude more influential in America than in his own country.

> The appeal of the Evangelicals to personal religion corresponds with the appeal of Benthamite Liberals to individual energy. Indifference to the authority of the Church is the counterpart of indifference to the authoritative teaching or guidance of the State or of Society. A low estimate of ecclesiastical tradition, aversion to and incapacity for inquiries into the growth or development of religion, the stern condemnation of even the slightest endeavor to apply to the Bible the principles of historical criticism, bear a close resemblance to Bentham's contempt for legal antiquarianism, and to James Mill's absolute blindness to the force of historical objections brought by Macaulay against the logical dogmatism embodied in Mill's essay on government. Evangelicals and Benthamites alike were incapable of applying the historical method, and neither recognized its value, nor foresaw its influence. The theology, again, which insisted upon personal responsibility, and treated each man as himself bound to work out his own salvation, had an obvious affinity to the political philosophy which regards men almost exclusively as separate individuals and made it the aim of law to secure for every person freedom to work out his own happiness. [P. 402.]

Church history is a very marginal interest to the habit of mind that has been dominant in American religion for most of our history.

There are many signs that the relevance and significance of church history is more widely sensed today, but inertia is still mighty. The generation from 1930 to 1960 does seem to have crossed a geological divide of significant dimensions. Thought about Christian history seems to have undergone more marked developments in these years than, for example, in the period from 1900 to 1930. The break is perceptible in the years of the war, from 1940 to 1945. The major publications of the Thirties were the work of men whose minds had been essentially shaped between 1910 and 1930, men such as S. J. Case, W. W. Sweet, P. K. Guilday, Roland Bainton, K. S. Latourette, J. T. McNeill, and Matthew Spinka. During and after the war a younger generation emerged whose writings seemed in various ways to reflect the Great Depression, the totalitarianism, the theological revival of the Thirties. This generation can be suggested by the names of Winthrop Hudson, S. E. Mead, G. H. Williams, Ray C. Petry, Wilhelm Pauck, L. J. Trinterud, J. T. Ellis, J. H. Nichols, Jaroslav Pelikan, and E. R. Hardy.

The older generation reacted in various ways to the cultural experiences of the 1930's. Some changed, some did not. Some retained or increased their authority and relevance, others seemed to diminish in stature. Case and Sweet dated rapidly; McNeill and Richard Niebuhr gained a more comprehending public.

Another way of suggesting the changes in these decades is to pair Parrington's *Main Currents of American Thought,* especially the sections on the colonial period, with Perry Miller's volumes on *The New England Mind.* There is an analogous contrast between the interpretation of the beginnings of the Christian church as found in Shirley Jackson Case's *Experience with the Supernatural* and that in Archbishop Carrington's *Early Christian Church.* Or again the central religious concerns of the Reformation receive quite different treatment in Preserved Smith from that in the comparable works by Holborn, Harbison, and Grimm. No doubt other pairs could be cited that would be less convenient for the argument, but these do seem to have some representative value. There is an enormous gain in each of the later studies in the capacity to enter appreciatively and intelligently into the religious experience under investigation. As Miller once said of Parrington: "He just didn't know what he was talking about."

169

The theological revival of the Thirties was not really "neo-orthodoxy" in America. In Europe, Barthianism often signified flight from historical thought to systematics, and between wars in Germany church history suffered in theological faculties. This does not seem to have happened in America. There was here also a new interest in systematic theology, a subject that had almost ceased to be taught about 1930 in the stronger theological faculties. But the new interest did not come at the expense of history; it was in some centers manifested as a new interest precisely in the history of theology. Augustine, Aquinas, Luther, Calvin, and Schleiermacher increased in actuality and authority. The classical soteriological teachings, especially, of sin, grace, and atonement increasingly seemed more impressive than evolutionary idealism and humanism. Church history, and especially the history of theology as handled by such great teachers as Robert Calhoun at Yale and Wilhelm Pauck at Chicago, played a significant role in the education of a rising generation. This more diffused influence is not always sufficiently appreciated. Church history was now playing a substantive role in the nurture of the church in contrast to its primarily critical role in the hands of a man like Case. The new openness to traditional Christian tenets, in turn, qualified historians better for their task of interpreting the past.

The recovery of specifically Christian understanding of human fulfillment as in part distinguishable from social progress was related to an increasing tension between church history and cultural or social history. If one took this seriously it was no longer possible to treat church life as merely the religious dimension of this or that national culture. Similarly, the totalitarian attempts to claim the minds and hearts of citizens absolutely stimulated the awareness of the dimensions of Christian obedience in all aspects of the common life. The church, the community and "culture" of those acknowledging the Christ, suddenly rose to the consciousness of Christians in these years with novel force. Church history could not but be deepened and enriched by a heightened perception of the character and significance of its subject matter.

As individual Christians were by the events of the 1930's made newly conscious that they belonged, not just to this or that national community, but to a universal society transcending cultural barriers, so it was with church history. Church history had been in danger of fragmentation into numerous national social and cultural histories, losing sight of its own unity and its own distinctive transnational tradition.

In contrast to general history as taught in a good university, church history has a definite shape. A university department of history must be in principle thoroughly relativist. There are pragmatic arguments for emphasizing European and American history, but in principle no one can say that any period or region is more important than any other. There is an indefinite number of possibilities of specialization with an equal right to claim attention. A good department is made up of a judicious balance of momentarily popular specializations.

Church history, on the other hand, has some built-in dimensions that are wider than one is likely to find in single history department specializations. Church history, in fact, is the chief heir to the great tradition of universal history as practiced by a Ranke or a Burckhardt. Even Toynbee ended up by writing something analogous to church history. The church historian *must* cross the boundaries of national cultures. He must be at home in at least two great civilizations, that of ancient Greece and Rome and that of the modern West. No one can be expected to master all this from the sources, of course, but in whichever region of church history one specializes, he should see it ever in the frame of the whole historic Christian community and especially its origins. The comparisons and contrasts that come to light in this frame of reference define the criteria and emphases proper to church history more than those deriving from this or that national culture. All this now seemed clearer to many American scholars than it had in earlier decades of the century.

There was a sudden spate of works on the Christian "philosophy of history." One of the preparatory study volumes for the ecumenical Conference on Life and Work at Oxford in 1937 was a symposium on *The Kingdom of God and History*. The most conspicuous writers on these themes, men like Tillich, Berdyaev, MacMurray, Reinhold Niebuhr, Dodd, Butterfield, Dawson, and Löwith, were rarely historians and rarely Americans. Most of them were philosophers or theologians and it is hard to see that their writings had much effect on the writing of church history.

For one thing few of them had much to say about the historical church. Reinhold Niebuhr, for example, seemed to have a view of history oriented more to Hebraic prophetism than to the New Testament. There was much here to learn about the ambiguity of all human aspiration and endeavor, the futility or at least fragmentariness of the historical process apart from a transcendent dimension of forgiveness. But little was said about the manifestations of redemption and the release of new life in the concrete historical community of the church.

There was a large degree of consensus in the repudiation of progress as a verifiable pattern of historical change. Against this consensus the most vigorous challenge came from K. S. Latourette. In his great history of the Christian mission and in several shorter writings, such as *Anno Domini* and *The Unquenchable Light,* Latourette vigorously defended the theory of the progressive advance of the church. He admitted a certain periodicity, an alternation of phases of expansion and recession, as proposed in E. C. Moore's *Spread of Christianity in the Modern World* (1919). But each successive advance more than recovered the ground lost, so that the whole fitted the pattern of postmillenial optimism of the evangelical missions of what he called "the great century," the nineteenth.

In this conception Latourette was surely representative of the main tradition of American Protestant thought up through the 1920's. He admitted the serious character of the anti-Christian movements of his day, but refused to let them shake his confidence in the visible realization of the Kingdom of God in history. He titled his volume on the generation of the dictators *Advance Through Storm.*

Latourette's thought had been shaped before the storms broke. What views could be expected of the younger American church historians whose formative years were those of the Great Depression, the rise of Hitler and Mussolini, the Soviet persecution of Christianity, and World War II? It would be dangerous to generalize from writings published before 1960, but there seems to have been a certain tendency to turn from developmental schemes on a grand scale to cross-sections or typologies as models for historical synthesis. Richard Niebuhr's *Christ and Culture,* for example, did not venture to lay down any pattern of advance down the generations, or even a hierarchy of solutions to the perennial problems of the faith. In this panorama of types of response there seems to have been a strong strain of relativism or skepticism when viewed from the developmental perspective. Yet the unity and continuity of the Christian society in its diverse situations was vividly sensed and exhibited, and the relevance of a fulfillment not identifiable with cultural achievement became clearer.

Church historians now found themselves also in a new relation to general history. American historians in general had been philosophically rather naïve in the 1920's. In the 1930's European reflection on the presuppositions of historical thought, ethical and epistemological, hit home to the American practitioners with sudden and shattering effect. Charles Beard, for example, was awakened from his positivist slumbers and delivered a presidential address to the American Historical Association in 1933 entitled "Written History as an Act of Faith." Carl Becker turned his devastating wit on the customary claim to disinterested objectivity. Every historian, it appeared, was in fact making certain intellectual and moral commitments whether consciously or not. It was still somehow more respectable in most faculties to write diplomatic history as a national apologist, or to read Western history as the progressive triumph of liberalism or scientific humanism, or, alternatively, to explain everything by economic determinants, than to interpret the past from the perspective of Christian faith. But at least the church historian was no longer in a wholly exceptional position when he admitted to certain a priori biases.

Theory *about* history, or church history, may be important, but it is not history, any more than literary criticism is poetry. A certain number of historians can sometimes be teased into a discussion about the presuppositions of their craft, but facility in this exercise is not to be equated with one's capacity as a historian—the best poets are not always, or even often, the best critics of poetry. Our concern is with history, or rather histories, in all their incredible variety. For this there seems to be no alternative to a survey of actual written histories, at least in a representative sampling.

The literature has been classified into two categories: that of works for which the language of the sources is modern English, and that of studies in the more basic but less popular sources written in other languages. In the latter case especially, it is very difficult to bring the account into the form of dramatic confrontation, or even to generalize at all. Anyone who has visited the professional meetings of historians knows the difficulty of engaging historians in a general discussion. Occasionally a topic will provide occasion for a lively debate, but more frequently it is quickly apparent after a learned paper has been read that only two or three people in the room are qualified to discuss it. On English language themes, some generalizations may be attempted, but for the larger sweep of Christian history it is hard to do more than mention or characterize one work after another.

2

CHURCH HISTORY THROUGH THE REFORMATION
AND SINCE OUTSIDE AMERICA

Putting aside American church history for later discussion and considering all the rest of the history of Christianity together, I find it difficult to make generalizations about the tendencies of American writers. The determinations of the issues and the alternatives are normally formulated across the Atlantic. The Americans are like snipers scattered about on a battlefield—now and then one of them makes a hit, but they scarcely ever take a major stronghold or hold one against attack. That is done by the marshaled legions of European scholarship, who, to be sure, are in most instances writing about their own countries, denominations, and heroes.

Among the chief repositories for scholarship in early church history are the *Anglican Theological Review,* the *Harvard Theological Review,* and *Church History. Vigiliae Christianae* is an international venture including American contributions and is, like the revived *Archiv für Reformationsgeschichte,* a testimony to the international character of such scholarship.

In 1930 Shirley Jackson Case was one of the most conspicuous American writers on early Christianity. He was at that time nearly sixty and had published half a dozen or more volumes on the period. His *Experience with the Supernatural in Early Christian Times* (1929) illustrates his *Tendenz,* a kind of evolutionary humanism, perhaps best understood as an extreme reaction to fundamentalism. Case continued to publish through the Thirties and even through World War II, but from the same viewpoint, unaffected by events or the new climate of opinion. His *Origins of Christian Supernaturalism* (1946) restates the position of his work of 1929. Neither is sufficiently sympathetic to the sources to be a first-rate historical interpretation. In 1930, Case was a leader of the militant modernists, but long before his last work he had come to seem dated and irrelevant. More than one of those who shared his perspective gave up church history altogether.

Kenneth Scott Latourette launched his seven-volume *History of*

175

the Expansion of Christianity in 1937 with a volume on *The First Five Centuries*. This volume perforce retraces much of Harnack's masterpiece on *The Mission and Expansion of Christianity in the First Three Centuries*. Latourette's more original contributions were to appear in the later volumes on the modern period.

Two of the three most distinguished scholarly works of the generation on this period were produced by Canadian Episcopalians. Charles R. Cochrane, Professor of Classics at the University of Toronto, published his masterful *Christianity and Classical Culture* in 1944 in America, and Archbishop Carrington his *Early Christian Church* (2 vols.) in 1957. Cochrane's theme is the transformation of the political tradition of Rome under the influence of Christianity; his book traces the story with rich learning and philosophical breadth from the reorganization of the Roman state by Augustus through the conversion of Constantine and the Catholic state of Theodosius, and culminates in the majestic synthesis of Augustine. Some of the experience of Cochrane's generation seems to have found expression through his perception of the limits of classical political idealism and his sharpened feeling for the transhistorical meanings disclosed by the Christian faith.

Philip Carrington's *Early Christian Church* (1957) is a notable synthetic achievement. The revulsion from the hypercriticism of the previous generation is apparent, but Carrington's respect for his sources is still highly sophisticated. As a readable presentation of mature digested historical judgment on the first two centuries, this work deserves to stand near to Cochrane's in significance.

The only work on the early church written in the United States that can be compared in breadth and scope with that of these Canadian scholars was written by a Jew, Harry A. Wolfson. Wolfson was interested in a comparative analysis of the adjustments made by the three "religions of the book" to the philosophical and cosmological heritage of Greece. In 1947 he published *Philo: Foundations of Religious Philosophy in Judaism, Christianity, and Islam* (2 vols.), which contends that Philonic thought is "the most dominant force in the history of philosophy down to the seventeenth century." He has pursued Philonic themes and motifs in his *Philosophy of the Church Fathers,* Volume I, *Faith, Trinity, Incarnation* (1956), a study designed to be completed by a second volume extending the analysis to Augustine and John of Damascus. Wolfson's "hypothetico-deductive" method puts the focus of interest on the constraints of logic rather than on the theological and religious dynamics in patristic thought, but his massive work has set many things in a new light.

In 1959, a transplanted European Roman Catholic, G. B. Ladner, launched a volume of ambitious scope, *The Idea of Reform: Its Impact on Christian Thought and Action in the Days of the Fathers,* a study so comprehensive and elaborately documented that the unifying theme sometimes seemed rather elusive.

During World War II, Roman Catholicism successfully challenged Protestant leadership in the American study of early Christianity. Johannes Quasten, who had made his reputation as a historian of the liturgy in Germany, moved to the Catholic University of America as Professor of Ancient Church History and Christian Archaeology. There he edited a series of dissertations entitled "Studies in Christian Antiquity" that appeared at the rate of about one each year from 1941. It is doubtful that any other single American graduate center has rivaled this production in early church history, at least in quantity. Since 1944, Quasten has also led the periodical *Traditio: Studies in Ancient and Medieval History, Thought, and Religion.*

With his colleague J. C. Plumpe, Quasten edited a new series of English translations of the fathers as "Ancient Christian Writers." Two years after its initiation his colleague Ludwig Schopp published the first volume of a parallel series of translations, the "Fathers of the Church." By 1960 both series included thirty or so titles. The duplication is unfortunate in view of the need for translations throughout the sweep of church history. The series are not strictly American; many of the translations are by Americans, but a number are by scholars from elsewhere in the English speaking world— not all, indeed, Roman Catholics. The editorial introductions and apparatus vary in fullness and quality from volume to volume. Between them, however, the two big Roman Catholic series make available a substantial number of texts hitherto inaccessible to Americans without knowledge of the classical languages.

There are a handful of major monographs of greater maturity than dissertations, but lacking the comprehensiveness of major historical syntheses. Their very diversity is perhaps characteristic of American scholarship, for example, Edward Hardy's *Christian Egypt, Church and People* (1952), J. C. Plumpe's *Mater Ecclesia* (1943), Virginia Corwin's *St. Ignatius and Christianity in Antioch* (1960), and Robert Grant's *Miracle and Natural Law in Graeco-Roman and Early Christian Thought* (1952) and *The Sword and the Cross* (1955). Arthur Vööbus has explored Syriac sources, publishing besides numerous articles *Celibacy: A Requirement for Admission to Baptism in the Early Syrian Church* (1951) and a *History of Asceticism in the Syrian Orient: A Contribution to the History of Culture in the Near East* (1958). Quasten produced the first two volumes of a superb *Patrology* in 1950.

The shift in theological climate in the latter half of the generation worked to the advantage of early church history perhaps more than to that of some other periods. The problems of Christianity as a minority in an indifferent or even persecuting society now again had actuality in the West as well as in Asia and Africa. Form criticism in New Testament studies put new emphasis on the role of tradition in the early church as did the ecumenical confrontation with Eastern Orthodox thought. Then the Nag-Hammadi discoveries of 1945 promised to revise substantially our understanding of Gnosticism and its place in the life of the ancient church. The sources for early church history are so scanty that any new discoveries are likely to be of revolutionary character. Unless one can classify Hans Jonas as American, Robert Grant is the chief American interpreter of the Gnostic materials, with his *Gnosticism and Early Christianity* (1959) and *The Secret Sayings of Jesus* (in collaboration with N. S. Freedman and W. R. Schoedel, 1960). As with the Dead Sea discoveries, the full significance of the new sources was not yet apparent in 1960.

Byzantine studies sharply pose the problem of classification. Is one to include Vasiliev? Florovsky? Dvorník? Vasiliev's *Byzantine Empire* (2 vols., 1928-29; 2nd ed., 1958), the most comprehensive account in English, was first published in Russian. Dvorník won distinction at the University of Prague, and America had little share in his revolutionary *Photian Schism: History and Legend* (1948), which radically revised the standing view of Photius and the "Second Schism." But Vasiliev's *Justin the First* (1950) and Dvorník's *Idea of Apostolicity in Byzantium and the Legend of the Apostle Andrew* (1958) both appear in the "Dumbarton Oaks Studies."

The most conspicuous native American in the field is doubtless Glanville Downey, who had a share in the translation of parts of John Malalas and Procopius. Downey has published studies of two great Christian centers, *Constantinople in the Age of Justinian* (1960) and the more extensive *A History of Antioch in Syria: From Seleucus to the Arab Conquest* (1961).

The annual *Dumbarton Oaks Papers* are the chief outlet for Byzantine studies, but valuable studies have also appeared as monographs, as Peter Charanis's *Church and State in the Later Roman Empire: The Religious Policy of Anastasius the First, 491-518* (1939) and D. J. Geanokoplos's *Emperor Michael Palaeologus and the West, 1258-1282: A Study in Byzantine-Latin Relations* (1959).

In America, the history of art as a discipline is perhaps even more exotic than the history of Christianity. Two works that are distinguished representatives for the ancient period are C. R. Morey's *Early Christian Art: An Outline of the Evolution of Style and Iconography in Sculpture and Painting from Antiquity to the Eighth Century* (1942) and Otto von Simson's *Sacred Fortress: Byzantine Art and Statecraft in Ravenna* (1948).

Before 1930, that half of Christian history known as the Middle Ages drew the attention of two of America's most notable amateur historians, H. C. Lea and H. O. Taylor. A considerable amount of editing and translating has been published since 1930, but, in general, American scholars of church history have not concentrated on medieval studies. On the other hand, any medievalist of general interests will perforce occupy himself to some degree with church history. The Mediaeval Academy of America has been the chief association of such scholars and has published significant scholarship in its quarterly *Speculum* and its *Bulletin of the Progress of Mediaeval and Renaissance Studies in the United States and Canada.* Since 1943, *Medievalia et Humanistica* has also presented medieval research with some regularity. As yet, however, there is no satisfactory authoritative and comprehensive history of the medieval church written in English, although there are more or less adequate textbooks of an introductory sort and valuable studies on various periods, areas, and subjects.

John T. McNeill—perhaps the most notable American-trained, professional church historian of the generation of 1930-60—began as a medievalist. His own dissertation of 1923, *The Celtic Penitentials,* was later followed by a contribution to the Columbia "Records of Civilization" series, *Medieval Handbooks of Penance: A Translation of the Principal Libri Penitentiales and Selections from Related Documents* (with H. M. Gamer; 1938). McNeill established the role of the Celtic monks in the transition to the system of private penance in the medieval church. Most of McNeill's later writing, apart from a couple of important essays on conciliarism, has been devoted to the Reformation and the modern period, but he has directed some useful dissertations in medieval church history.

Ray C. Petry, now at Duke and formerly one of McNeill's doctoral students, has proved to be one of the most productive Protestant historians of the medieval church. Petry's chosen themes have been largely aspects of piety or the Christian life—as is perhaps appropriate in a Methodist institution. Since his dissertation on Francis, as apostle of poverty, he has published two volumes on sermons: *No Uncertain Sound: Sermons That Shaped the Pulpit Tradition* (1948) and *Preaching in the Great Tradition: Neglected Chapters in the History of Preaching* (1950). In 1957 his "Library of Christian Classics" volume appeared, called *Late Medieval Mysticism,* with selections from Bernard of Clairvaux and the Victorines to Nicholas of Cusa and Catherine of Genoa. His most extended study on *Christian Eschatology and Social Thought: A Historical Essay on the Social Implications of Some Selected Aspects in Christian Eschatology to A.D. 1500* (1956) also draws extensively on homiletical and other sources related to practical Christianity.

Some significant work in monasticism has been done by Protestant historians. Catherine Boyd has published a thesis on *A Cistercian Nunnery in Medieval Italy: The Story of Rifreddo in Saluzzo, 1220-1300* (1943) and Lynn White another on *Latin Monasticism in Norman Sicily* (1938). The freer developments of a later period have been set forth in a very thorough study on the *Beguines and Beghards in Medieval Culture* (1954) by E. W. McDonnell.

A similar interest, further spurred by some Dutch nationalism, has shaped Albert Hyma's writing in church history. *Christian Renais-*

sance: A History of the "Devotio Moderna" (1924) developed from a dissertation and in 1950 he returned to the theme in *The Brethren of the Common Life.*

C. G. Loomis drew on an enormous hagiographic literature for his *White Magic: An Introduction to the Folklore of Christian Legend* (1948). Lynn Thorndike labored half a century on his *History of Magic and Experimental Science* (1923-58), which takes four volumes to reach the Reformation.

The intellectual history of the early Middle Ages has been usefully organized by the ancient historian M. L. W. Laistner in his *Thought and Letters in Western Europe, A.D.* 500-900 (1931), which appeared in a new edition in 1957. Allen Cabaniss, one of the editors of the "Library of Christian Classics" volume on *Early Medieval Theology,* has also published two separate monographs, one on *Agobard of Lyons* (1953) and the other on *Amalarius of Metz* (1954), and his co-editor, G. E. MacCracken, has edited a work each of Augustine and Arnobius.

The Protestant "Library of Christian Classics" contains two volumes on the scholastics from Anselm to Ockham, edited by E. R. Fairweather, and Richard P. McKeon has edited two small volumes of *Selections from Medieval Philosophy,* but the bulk of the publication of translations and of discussions of medieval theology and philosophy has been done by Roman Catholics. Thomas Aquinas has received the lion's share of attention and A. C. Pegis has edited several sets of selected translations. To be sure, there has been no American Gilson or even DeWulf, but Gilson lent himself to the founding of the St. Michael's Institute of Medieval Studies in Toronto. Medieval studies have also been promoted at Catholic University, at Notre Dame, and elsewhere. Journals such as *Traditio, Franciscan Studies,* and *New Scholasticism* contain many articles on scholasticism, often narrowly technical.

Notable contributions have been made to the exposition of medieval political thought. The most original and valuable part of Charles McIlwaine's *Growth of Political Thought in the West* (1932) is his long section on the Middle Ages. Another work of great distinction is Ernst Kantorowicz's *The King's Two Bodies: A Study in Medieval Political Theology* (1957). Kantorowicz's earlier study on Frederick the Second was originally published in German, but there might be some basis to claim *The King's Two Bodies* as American.

Alan Gewirth, a Jewish philosopher, has published a massive monograph on *Marsilius of Padua: The Defender of Peace* (2 vols., 1951, 1956), a study in the secularization of medieval political theory.

On the side of economic institutions there are two valuable studies by W. E. Lunt, the *Papal Revenues in the Middle Ages* in two volumes (1934) and the *Financial Relations of the Papacy with England to 1327* (1939). For the parish level, Catherine Boyd has set forth the fruits of long research in *Tithes and Parishes in Medieval Italy: The Historic Roots of a Modern Problem* (1952).

David Schaff, in an earlier generation, had written on John Hus and the reforming movement in Bohemia in the early fifteenth century, a subject calculated to interest students of the Reformation. The subject has been further explored by S. Harrison Thomson, who was trained in Prague, and by Matthew Spinka, himself of Czech background. In the 1920's Thomson published several articles on Wyclif and Hus, and in 1930 an edition of Wyclif's *Summa de ente*. In 1956 he edited critically, for the first time, *Magistri Johannis Hus Tractatus de Ecclesia,* effectually disposing of Loserth's thesis of Hus's dependence on Wyclif. Spinka meanwhile published a little study on *John Hus and the Czech Reform* (1941) and in 1953 the "Library of Christian Classics" volume entitled *Advocates of Reform, from Wyclif to Erasmus,* which presents texts of the conciliarists as well as of Wyclif and Hus. Joseph Dahmus also set forth with precision *The Prosecution of John Wyclif* (1952). Some of the violent consequences of Hus's execution are described in F. A. Heymann's *John Zizka and the Hussite Revolution* (1955). A rising Hussite literature seems to draw on Czech nationalism as well as on Protestant interest in backgrounds for the Reformation, and, since the communist revolution in Czechoslovakia, a polemic with Marxist historiography has grown in importance.

Roman Catholic scholars have also made important contributions to the study of conciliarism. The British-trained Brian Tierney sets forth a new perspective on the theoretical side in his *Foundations of the Conciliar Theory: The Contributions of the Medieval Canonists from Gratian to the Great Schism* (1955). The documents of the Council of Florence were prepared by Joseph Gill for publication in two volumes in 1953 and served as a basis for his authoritative study, *The Council of Florence* (1959). Oscar Halecki, another imported scholar, has traced the relation of the Ruthenian church to Rome in *From Florence to Brest, 1439-1596* (1959) as a local and partial realization of the reunion efforts of Florence.

Two publications by art historians dealing with themes of great importance to church history can be singled out. Cluny, long the greatest church in Latin Christendom and the site of movements of wide significance, has been explored archaeologically by Kenneth J. Conant, who published his *Carolingian and Romanesque Architecture, 800 to 1200* in 1958. Otto von Simson, Munich-trained, is the author of an important and well-written work on *The Gothic Cathedral: Origins of Gothic Architecture and the Medieval Concept of Order* (1956).

For the transition to modern times two journals should be noted, *Renaissance News,* and the internationally conducted *Archiv für Reformationsgeschichte.* The *Journal of the History of Ideas* also carries articles that cover a long chronological span and that are of interest to church historians.

The Reformation of the sixteenth century is the theme of more major histories by American-trained scholars in the generation under review than any earlier period. One could scarcely say, on the other hand, that Americans have participated significantly in the Luther or Calvin renaissances. These European movements have been reported or reflected in such dissertations as those of Edgar Carlson, John Dillenberger, and George Forell with regard to Luther, and of Edward Dowey in the case of Calvin. But the more mature American studies, those by Bainton, McNeill, and Schwiebert, have not been informed primarily by new theological insight and excitement. Americans have read and discussed Holl, Nygren, Niesel, and Torrance as interpreters of the great reformers, but this interest does not seem to have been a major force in the religious thought of the country. One might suppose that such a movement would be both liberating and deepening for that large section of American Protestantism that understands the Reformation only through the confessions, and that both pietism and evangelicalism, on the one hand,

and liberalism on the other, would have much to learn here, but it does not seem to have happened.

Roland Bainton's *Here I Stand* is a brilliant literary achievement, setting forth an impressive and engaging Luther able to win the interest of the general public. The interest, however, is less theological than psychological. Luther is studied as a man wrestling with his *Anfechtungen* or in the trials and joys of his marriage more than as theologian, prophet, or churchman. The human figure that emerges is unforgettable, but his meaning for the history of Christianity is less forcibly stated. It is a portrait perhaps well adapted for the unchurchly and unhistorically minded American religious individualist.

R. H. Fife launched a study of *Young Luther* in 1928 and in 1957 returned to his theme in a massive volume, *The Revolt of Martin Luther*. Rich in reference to the sources, Fife's study, like the slighter one by Blayney, *The Age of Luther* (1957), illustrates vividly the difficulties of an approach from the history of literature to a figure who was primarily a religious prophet and theologian. Both these works seem—and are—a generation out of date in their interpretation, because they are not adequately oriented in the theological debate about Luther's development and position.

The "Library of Christian Classics" devotes four volumes of translations and editions to Luther and four to Calvin. A new translation of Luther's complete works, in some fifty-five volumes, is well under way under the editorship of Jaroslav Pelikan and H. T. Lehman. One may wonder whether it will be an unmixed gain for biblical exegesis and understanding in America to have Luther's commentaries in English widely distributed among Lutheran preachers, or those of Calvin in the reprinted edition among Presbyterians and the Reformed. Pelikan's study of *Luther's Exegesis,* on the other hand, and the "Library of Christian Classics" volumes on Luther's *Romans,* by Pauck, or Calvin's commentaries, by Haroutunian, provide major texts and searching interpretations of the reformers as biblical expositors, a theme opened in America by J. M. Reu with his works on *Luther's German Bible* (1934) and *Luther and the Scriptures* (1944).

Luther and His Times: The Reformation from a New Perspective (1950) by Ernest G. Schwiebert is another history of major proportions. The new perspective is focused on the University of Wittenberg, its inner transformation by the reforming ideas, and its role as the center of propaganda and dissemination of influence by its students.

On the Reformed side there has been no new major study of Calvin, except that in John McNeill's *History and Character of Calvinism* (1954); the section devoted to the French reformer is, of course, the climax of that study. McNeill's knowledgeable work, which follows the movement from Switzerland, Germany, and France to Great Britain and the New World, is one of the major achievements of the generation for American scholarship. Similarly, his edition of the *Institutes,* in the "Library of Christian Classics," is a great editing accomplishment and constitutes the first critical edition in English, a significant fact in itself. Probably no major theologian has suffered such disadvantages in America as has Calvin. He has been very little known or read and has been almost universally deplored by historians as well as by the public generally.

McNeill's *Unitive Protestantism* of 1930 came just too early to profit by the rising ecumenical interest. McNeill had actively participated in the formation of the United Church of Canada in the 1920's and had then explored the ecumenical concern of the reformers, with results quite startlingly unlike the current view of the Reformation. These discoveries, related to his studies of medieval conciliarism, constituted a contribution of major importance to the understanding of the nature of the church and its historical development. Only gradually, however, did the American church catch up to McNeill, and his volume of 1930 has not yet been adequately digested.

Much of the recent interest in Calvinism and the Reformed tradition—like that of H. D. Foster of the preceding generation—seems to focus on their political influence. Robert Kingdon's *Geneva and the Coming of the Wars of Religion in France, 1555-1563* (1952) is a study of the operations of Geneva-trained pastors compared to modern methods of subversion. Maurice Lee Jr. has pursued political maneuvers in another area in his *James Stewart, Earl of Moray: A Political Study of the Reformation in Scotland* (1953). Winthrop Hudson's *John Ponet* (1942) brings to light an overlooked British political writer and studies the time with more interest in the religious substance of the issues and in the political ethic involved in political and military activities.

The English sixteenth century does not seem to have called forth any major historical work by an American, if we except Knappen's *Tudor Puritanism*. Franklin Le Van Baumer's thesis, *The Early Tudor Theory of Kingship* (1940), demonstrates that the medieval idea of the "body" of Christendom was still a live force through the century. L. B. Smith has analyzed *Tudor Prelates and Politics, 1536-1558* (1953); A. G. Chester has published a biography of *Hugh Latimer, Apostle to the English* (1954), and P. M. Dawley an account of *John Whitgift and the English Reformation* (1954) that is in effect an analysis of the Elizabethan church administration. There are literary studies, such as Charles Butterworth's volume on *The English Primers, 1529-1545* (1953) and Helen C. White's *Tudor Books of Private Devotion* (1951). Cremean's *Reception of Calvinistic Thought in England* (1949) provides a useful survey of the dominance of Reformed theology in the Elizabethan church, although with insufficient discrimination of the differences among Calvin, Zwingli, Bucer, and Bullinger.

On secondary figures there are Hastings Eells's *Martin Bucer* (1931) and Clyde L. Manshreck's *Melanchthon* (1958), neither of which is wholly adequate to the theological debates centering about these figures. In this respect they are representative of a conspicuous general weakness of American historians of the Reformation.

American Roman Catholics do not seem to have interested themselves much in the sixteenth century. Perhaps it is significant that Lortz's notable history of the Reformation has not yet found a translator, and that Grisar is still widely recommended as the best authority. One important Roman Catholic contribution, however, is Father Tavard's *Holy Writ or Holy Church: The Crisis of the Protestant Reformation* (1959), which sets forth a long perspective on the relative authority of scripture and of church. But again, can this be considered a work of "American" scholarship?

Spanish materials in libraries of the Southwest have been used to advantage by J. C. Longhurst in two case studies of the Spanish Inquisition, that of Juan de Valdés (1950) and of Diego de Uceda (1953). Maurice Boyd has similarly explored *Cardinal Quiroga, In-*

quisitor General of Spain (1959). The third volume of Latourette's *History of the Expansion of Christianity* is largely an account of the great Roman Catholic missionary effort of the sixteenth and seventeenth centuries.

Probably the most distinctive aspect of American scholarship in the history of the sixteenth century has been its contribution to the study of what has come to be called the left wing of the Reformation. In this limited area American scholars of the Reformation have played nearly as great a role as did the Europeans of the time, so that one finds here a situation approaching that of Puritanism studies, which were actually dominated by Americans.

The reasons for this development seem to have been varied. To a degree the left wing of the Reformation of the sixteenth century seemed to foreshadow the English Puritanism of the seventeenth century and the whole free-church tradition that has dominated American Christianity. There were apparently even some tenuous connections between the two. In any case, some Americans have explored the left wing with an interest in such themes as the voluntary church, separation of church and state, and religious liberty. A similar kind of historical interest in the ancestry of the laic, biblicist, unsacramental, and unecclesiastical type of Christianity led T. C. Hall back to Wyclif and the Lollards in his suggestive if not wholly convincing *Religious Background of American Culture* (1930). The Waldensians and Hussites of the late Middle Ages have had something of the same attraction.

Roland Bainton of Yale is the most conspicuous representative of this tendency, and he has given currency to McNeill's phrase *left wing of the Reformation.* In part animated by the interest in the struggle for religious liberty that had been nurtured in him by G. L. Burr, Bainton is a pacifist who has found a kindred mind in Erasmus and some of the Anabaptists. He has published major monographs on four individualists who had difficulties in finding a home in any of the state churches of the sixteenth century: *Concerning Heretics, Castellio* . . . (1935); *David Joris* (1937); *Bernardino Ochino* (1941), *Michel Servet, hérétique et martyr* (1953; English title: *Hunted Heretic*). Bainton's *Travail of Religious Liberty* (1951) includes brief popular summaries on each of these figures, with persecutors as foils, as well as on Locke, Milton, and Williams from the Puritan movement of the seventeenth century. His sketch *The Reformation of the Sixteenth Century* (1952) is especially notable for its informed and sympathetic handling of the left wing figures, and indeed views those of the "right wing" from that perspective.

Bainton's affinities are with the spiritualists and rationalists of the Reformation rather than with the biblicistic Anabaptists. But perhaps partly on the basis of their common pacifism, he has struck an alliance with the Mennonite historians of Anabaptism. The Mennonites have exhibited in this generation a vigor in historical studies unequaled, in proportion to their size, by any other Christian tradition in America. This has been an international movement, with followers in Switzerland, Germany, the Netherlands, and America. It seems to have arisen in part from the international crisis of identity of the Mennonites and their need to identify a viable tradition. Most of the leaders, even in America, are European in origin, but not all.

Harold Bender, an American Mennonite, was perhaps the most energetic organizer. He built up the Goshen College library to contain the largest collection of Anabaptistica in the world. Cornelius Krahn, a German immigrant scholar, emulated his work at the library of Bethel College. Bender edited from 1927 the *Mennonite Quarterly Review*, a denominational journal rivaled in the United States only by the *Catholic Historical Review*, which of course has vastly larger resources to draw on. For a full generation the *Mennonite Quarterly Review* has published sources, bibliographies, and articles on the left wing. In the 1950's this scholarship was organized for the production of the *Mennonite Encyclopaedia*, of which Volume I appeared in 1955, Volume II in 1957. Since 1930, the various volumes of the "Täuferakten" have been published on the Continent, providing the most important core of Mennonite source materials.

Monographs of importance that have emerged from the Mennonite activity are Cornelius Krahn's *Menno Simons* (1936), John Horsch's *Hutterian Brethren, 1528-1931* (1931), Robert Friedmann's *Mennonite Piety* (1949), and Harold Bender's *Conrad Grebel* (1950). *The Recovery of the Anabaptist Vision,* edited by G. F. Hershberger, is a Festschrift presented to Bender in 1957 by some twenty Anabaptist scholars. Franklin Littell, not himself a Mennonite, contributed in 1952 a thesis that was widely read, *The Ana-baptist View of the Church.* The stream of dissertations, articles, and studies is still increasing in the 1960's.

George Williams of Harvard has emerged as the heir apparent to Bainton's mantle as the leading non-Mennonite historian of the left wing. He edited much of the "Library of Christian Classics" volume on the left wing and wrote excellent introductions. The book, *Spiritual and Anabaptist Writers* (1957), comprises some thirteen items newly translated and edited, including writings by Anabaptists proper, spiritualists, and "evangelical rationalists."

Williams is also in a sense heir to Earl Morse Wilbur, who used materials in a dozen languages for his monumental *History of Unitarianism: Socinianism and Its Antecedents* (1945); *History of Unitarianism: In Transylvania, England, and America* (1952). Wilbur's work is uneven in quality, not always up to current scholarship or thoroughly digested, but is still a scholarly achievement of major dimensions.

The period of the last three hundred years is the time of the national fragmenting of the church and of the nationalizing of church history, and there has been an overwhelming concentration of American historians on their national church. Most of them have not had much interest in modern Christianity outside America. Surprisingly, this seems to be even more true of American Roman Catholics than of American Protestants, at least as far as publications go. No American has written a major comprehensive history of the church in Great Britain, Germany, France, Scandinavia, the Netherlands, Italy, Spain, or Russia. Most seminary surveys of church history peter out after the seventeenth century or narrow to mere denominational history, and until well after World War II there was no satisfactory textbook treatment of modern church history in English.

Far and away the outstanding American writer on modern church history is Kenneth Scott Latourette. Aside from his works there is little but a scattering of monographs on random aspects of the subject. Measured by sheer mileage on the page, Latourette is surely the most productive writer of church history in his generation. He is the author of two multivolume works, *A History of the Expansion of Christianity* in seven volumes (1937-45), and *Christianity in a Rev-*

olutionary Age: A History of Christianity in the 19th and 20th Centuries in five volumes (1948-62). He published an extended History of Christian Missions in China in 1929 and in 1953 produced a general text, A History of Christianity, with dimensions that would normally have appeared in two large volumes.

Despite his extensive volumes on earlier periods one might well argue that Latourette is essentially a historian of the modern period, and indeed, primarily of "the great century," the nineteenth. His history of Christian missions reveals little new source analysis and contains few important reinterpretations in its first three volumes, which are essentially a résumé of the existing literature. The surprise comes with Volume IV, the first on The Great Century, A.D. 1800–A.D. 1914, and its successors. Latourette gives as much space to that century as to all the eighteen that precede it. He justifies these proportions in terms of the unprecedented activity of the nineteenth century missions and the variety and size of the populations involved. No such comprehensive world-wide panorama had been previously attempted, and for several regions of the world Latourette's study is the first general description of their Christian life; for the United States, it is one of the best general accounts available.

Something of the same proportions, if not as extreme, is to be found in his History of Christianity. The work breaks in even halves at A.D. 1500, and 40 per cent or better is allotted to the three hundred years since the end of the religious wars (although Latourette does not mark a period at that point). The period since 1815 receives practically 30 per cent of the total, compared with 50 per cent in his history of missions. Such proportions would be inconceivable in England, where church history mainly emphasizes patristics with a minor interest in the sixteenth century and the Tractarians. On the Continent no such cursory dismissal of the Reformation would be acceptable.

Latourette's conception of Christianity is well suited to a historian of missions, and in that subject he has made a greater contribution than in general church history. He is fundamentally an evangelical individualist who visualizes Christian history as the ever widening impact of Jesus on individuals and his transforming power in their lives. Such an orientation is more effective in the interpretation of American church history than in dealing with more churchly, sacramental, theological, and institutionalized expressions of the faith, as in Europe generally.

Besides Latourette, two other Americans have attempted general expositions of modern Christianity. The brevity and readability of McNeill's volume on *Modern Christian Movements* (1954) cannot conceal his massive learning. J. H. Nichols' *History of Christianity, 1650-1950: The Secularization of the West* (1956) seeks to combat the general tendency toward cultural nationalism with a balanced survey of the universal church, analyzed in its relation to state, society, and culture.

From the small body of monographs and special studies in the modern period by Americans some representatives may be selected, moving from Roman Catholic subjects through the Protestant to the Orthodox. Only a few of them were written by professional church historians.

Literature on Roman Catholicism in Europe of the *ancien régime* is especially scanty. *The Heavenly City of the Eighteenth-Century Philosophers* (1932) is Carl Becker at his witty best—which is very good indeed—and R. R. Palmer has contributed an excellent matching piece with *Catholics and Unbelievers in Eighteenth Century France* (1939). These two works are highly illuminating on the debate of Christianity and the Enlightenment. There seem to have been no significant American studies on the relation of the French Revolution to the Roman Catholic Church, although R. W. Collins has written a thesis, *Catholicism and the Second French Republic* (1930), on a later phase of the revolutionary movement.

Carleton J. Hayes stimulated a number of theses at Columbia on the social Catholic movement in various countries, notably those of P. T. Moon on France and G. P. McEntee on England. More recently, J. N. Moody has edited *Church and Society: Catholic Social and Political Thought and Movements, 1789-1950* (1953), which ranges over Catholic Europe.

The more violent controversies of the Vatican with modern states have excited some interest. Concentrating on the years 1870-78, S. W. Halperin published in 1939 his *Italy and the Vatican at War,* which was followed some ten years later by L. P. Wallace's *The Papacy and European Diplomacy, 1869-1878* (1948). Still a decade later came a Roman Catholic study on *Vatican Diplomacy:*

A Study of Church and State on the International Plane (1959) by R. A. Graham, S.J. Unlike the two preceding, this work is more a systematic or theoretical investigation than a historical narration.

Among other special studies in modern church-state relations by Americans are E. M. Acomb's *French Laic Laws, 1879-1889* (1941), a study of an episode in the French controversy of church and state in education; Halperin's *Separation of Church and State in Italian Thought from Cavour to Mussolini* (1934), a useful survey on the theme stated, presupposing of course some command of the political and ecclesiastical history; and J. L. Mecham's *Church and State in Latin America* (1934), an attempt at a comprehensive survey.

On the Protestant side, the British churches have drawn more American attention than have the Continental Lutherans and Reformed, about whom there is very little good literature in English. The history of Protestant ecumenics, initiated by McNeill's *Unitive Protestantism,* has been continued in two studies devoted to the seventeenth century, *John Amos Comenius: That Incomparable Moravian* (1943) by Matthew Spinka and *John Dury: Advocate of Christian Reunion* (1944) by J. M. Batten, one of McNeill's former students.

The history of science became an established discipline in the generation of scholars at work during 1930-60, and the relations of science and Christianity, it soon appeared, had been grossly caricatured in A. D. White's old *History of the Warfare of Science with Theology in Christendom* (1910). The "war" has since been reappraised by two substantial studies, P. H. Kocher's thorough *Science and Religion in Elizabethan England* (1953) and R. S. Westfall's *Science and Religion in Seventeenth-Century England* (1958). John Dillenberger, a historian of theology, has attempted a general account, *Protestant Thought and Natural Science: A Historical Interpretation* (1960), and F. L. V. Baumer, a historian of thought, has silhouetted Christianity against its critics in *Religion and the Rise of Scepticism* (1960).

There are two or three studies of Continental Reformed churches with a view to church and state relations and political ethics—continuing interests of historians who specialize in the sixteenth century. G. H. Dodge has discussed *The Political Theory of the Huguenots of the Dispersion* (1947) and B. C. Poland has covered a larger period with *French Protestantism and the French Revolution: A Study in Church and State, Thought and Religion, 1685-1815* (1957).

In British church history one might have expected some scholarly work on the eighteenth century by American Methodists. There have been a number of popular books, of which Umphrey Lee's biography of Wesley and G. C. Cell's *Rediscovery of John Wesley* (1939) are among the weightier. The serious history of Methodism, on the whole, has been carried on in other countries.

For the nineteenth century there are again a few scattered works on church and state relations, mostly theses such as O. J. Brose's *Church and Parliament: The Reshaping of the Church of England, 1828-1860* (1959) and D. O. Wagner's *Church of England and Social Reform Since 1854* (1950). The latter seems to be an extension to England of an interest in social ethics that is distinctively American. J. A. Reynolds' *The Catholic Emancipation Crisis in Ireland, 1823-1829* (1954) illustrates the interest in religious liberty.

Because of the almost total lack of English language works on German Protestantism one may be especially grateful for W. O. Shanahan's *German Protestants Face the Social Question*, Volume I, *The Conservative Phase, 1815-1871* (1954). The interest, again, is a characteristically American one but the treatment is sufficiently full to make the work useful in several relations.

Shanahan's touch is least sure in theology and philosophy, where few Americans have done good work. Kierkegaard finally reached the United States in the generation after 1930 and had a notable influence in the American theological revival just when his stock seemed to be declining on the Continent. Swenson and Lowrie have been especially helpful in interpreting his work to Americans, but in general few Americans have attempted to interpret the great theological movement from Schleiermacher and Hegel through Kierkegaard, Ritschl, and Harnack to Barth. The idealist or at least post-Kantian tradition that lay behind this movement is not widely familiar to Americans.

The Bolshevik Revolution kindled an interest in North America in the Russian church. Most of the writing, however, has been quasi-journalistic. J. S. Curtiss has made the most important scholarly contribution with his two solid books, *Church and State in Russia*

. . . , *1900-1917* (1940), and *The Russian Church and the Soviet State, 1917-1950* (1953). P. B. Anderson has set forth a brief popular interpretation in *People, Church and State in Modern Russia* (1944) and Matthew Spinka has made things Russian one of his chief concentrations, beginning with *The Church and the Russian Revolution* (1927), followed by *Christianity Confronts Communism* (1936) and *The Church in Soviet Russia* (1956). Spinka has also made a special study of the life and thought of a striking figure of the revolutionary generation, *Nicholas Berdyaev: Captive of Freedom* (1950). N. S. Timasheff's *Religion in Soviet Russia, 1917-1942* (1942) is a particularly lucid outline, but with more dubious claim to represent American scholarship.

No doubt some works of comparable significance have been overlooked, but this admittedly arbitrary selection may at least illustrate the general character of the American literature and the distribution of scholarly interest within it.

◅§ 3 §►

AMERICAN CHRISTIANITY

The subject of the history of American Christianity, and the related topic English Puritanism, is the sole instance of a specialty of church history dominated by American writers, where, as a consequence, the American literature has within itself the shape of a coherent discussion.

Since an analysis of this literature will have to record some startling weaknesses on the part of professional church history, it is only fair to note that American church history is generally an avocation for scholars. There are almost no positions in the American academic world where one can earn a living by studying American church history. Chicago made the first full-time appointment at the end of the 1920's and Catholic University followed suit; Yale and Union made do with part-time arrangements. Most of the writing on American church history, apart from theses, has consequently been done by people who were primarily responsible for other matters.

There is no lack of interest in the subject; there has been, in fact, almost too much. By the end of the generation nearly half the articles on church history in the journals and nearly half the doctorates had to do with American themes. There has been a flood of writing in such journals as *Church History,* the *New England Quarterly,* the *William and Mary Quarterly,* the *Mississippi Valley Historical Review,* dozens of state historical reviews, and a handful of denominational journals, most important among them the *Catholic Historical Review.*

Too much of this extensive literature, however, is inferior in quality. Graduate students have sometimes turned to the American field to avoid foreign languages, or for lack of adequate historical and philosophical equipment, or because their historical imagination and curiosity had narrow limits. And with mountains of untouched source materials on American Christianity at hand, why venture into topics that might well require a visit to European libraries? To be sure, gifted and industrious men as well as many weak sisters have sought doctorates in American church history. Hence the flow of theses from the presses, constituting so large a proportion of the literature on the subject. For most the thesis is the first and last excursion into American church history. Once the doctorate is granted scarcely one in thirty can hope to teach and study American church history full time.

Basic tools are lacking for the teaching of American church history. W. W. Sweet has provided the most widely used text, *The Story of Religions in America* (1930), but it has been unsatisfactory in important respects since its publication. P. G. Mode's *Source-Book and Bibliographical Guide for American Church History* (1921) was not replaced until the recent publication of the collection by R. T. Handy, L. A. Loetscher, and H. Shelton Smith, *American Christianity: An Historical Interpretation with Representative Documents* (1960), and Nelson Burr's *Critical Bibliography of Religion in America* (1961) in two volumes. No attempt was made in 1930-60 to replace the Schaff series of denominational histories published in the 1890's in thirteen volumes. New denominational histories were written, some respectable, of which perhaps the most distinguished was L. J. Trinterud's *Forming of an American Tradition: A Re-examination of Colonial Presbyterianism* (1949). But the comprehensive vision of the church in America as a whole found no adequate expression.

The most impressive result of American scholarly research into church history has surely been the rediscovery of Puritanism. This is perhaps the one case in which American scholarship dominates a European subject. To be sure English and American Puritanism was an indivisible unit in the seventeenth century, but one might have expected English scholars to have controlled their side of the story. Most of the English historians, however, are Anglicans and have a vested interest in deprecating the whole business.

The Puritan renaissance, which began in the 1930's, followed a decade in which historians had been prevailingly hostile. There had been quasi-Marxist attempts to explain Puritanism as an ideology concealing economic interests. Much popular literature represented Puritanism as intellectually obscurantist, prohibitionist, and sexually repressive. Parrington's caricature of colonial thought was taught in hundreds of college classrooms.

It would make a neat pattern if one could claim that the renaissance of the 1930's was a kind of American equivalent to the Luther-renaissance then in progress in Germany and Sweden. After all, the Puritan movement represented the real popular-religious reformation of the English and from it came the mainstream of American Protestantism. The historical consciousness of American Baptists, Congregationalists, and Presbyterians had never retained a very vivid connection with the Continental Reformation, but such seventeenth century Puritan authors as Bunyan, Baxter, Owen, Howe, and Leighton had remained living forces in the American churches through the eighteenth and the nineteenth centuries. When the most influential and firmly entrenched American churches would recover their roots they might be expected to do so in terms of Puritanism.

The revival of Puritan studies would then have been the normal and predictable development when the American churches would seek to recover their soul. But it did not happen that way. It was not a matter of churchmen rediscovering theology, but of teachers of literature trying to understand the American literary heritage and finding themselves forced into theology. One striking work, to be sure, clearly reflected a new religious and theological mood and sensitivity —Joseph Haroutunian's *Piety Versus Moralism* (1932) revealed a capacity to penetrate Puritan theology and religion that had been absent from American historical writing for decades. But the churches generally evidenced no such deepening of historical insight. In fact the most direct heirs of the New England Puritans, the Congregationalists, displayed almost as much distaste and embarrassment with the subject as did the Anglicans. It was comical at the tercentenary of the Cambridge Platform of 1638 to see the Congregationalists celebrate the event while holding the document at arms' length with tongs. In England there was some perceptible connection between historical studies of Puritanism and the theological movement in the free churches associated with the name of Forsyth, but in America the Puritan heritage remained an undigested lump in the Congregationalist craw. It was very much the same case with the Unitarians. There is a string of Unitarian lives of Jonathan Edwards, for example, reaching a climax with Ola Winslow (1940), that all read like lives of Beethoven or Mozart by the tone deaf—they are

197

unable to leave him alone, and they are unable to understand him. No, the sudden flood of Puritan studies came generally without benefit of clergy or of church historians. One suspects in fact that some of its leading exponents may have occasionally broken out in a cold sweat in the night with the realization that they were writing church history.

W. K. Jordan was continuing an older tradition with his *Development of Religious Toleration in England* (3 vols., 1932-40). Studies of the progress of religious liberty and toleration were favorite themes of the older liberals before the days of the dictators put such matters in a more complicated light and rendered their achievement less a matter of the natural course of things. After the 1930's a mere compilation of materials would seem less satisfactory as a history of the achievement of toleration.

William Haller, of Columbia, began with three volumes of *Tracts on Liberty in the Puritan Revolution* (1934), but in 1938 his *Rise of Puritanism* took seriously what the Puritans had to say about central matters. Haller interpreted Puritanism as essentially a preaching movement, and he undertook to characterize the themes of the Puritan pulpit and related forms of literature with more precision than one found in the conventional generalizations about "Calvinism." A sequel, *Liberty and Reformation in the Puritan Revolution* (1955), follows the movement through the 1640's, contending that the very freedom of the Puritan pulpit precluded the possibility of theocratic reform, by producing such diversity that no ultimate alternative to religious toleration and liberty was possible.

M. M. Knappen had meanwhile published *Two Elizabethan Puritan Diaries* (1933) and a major comprehensive study in his *Tudor Puritanism* (1939). No doubt the Puritans, whose earnest effort it was to face ultimate realities without illusion, would have been shocked to hear themselves described in terms of "idealism," but the historian had a long bridge to build between Puritanism and the generation of the New Deal.

Puritanism and Liberty, first published in England in 1938, is a volume of documents on the political thought of Cromwell's soldiers, edited with a brilliant introduction by a Canadian historian of literature, A. S. P. Woodhouse. D. B. Robertson has argued the importance of the religious basis in his thesis, *Religious Foundations of Leveller Democracy* (1951), and the whole subject of *Puritanism and Democracy* (1944) has been analyzed with learning and judicial balance if with considerable diffuseness by R. B. Perry.

Perry Miller of Harvard has made the greatest contribution to the understanding of the colonial Puritans. *Orthodoxy in Massachusetts, 1630-1650* (1933) revolutionized the current understanding of the intentions of the founders of Massachusetts Bay with its delineation of the rationale and organization of the "Non-Separatist" Congregationalists. Five years later, in 1938, Miller and T. H. Johnson published the best anthology available, *The Puritans,* which among other things disposes of any notions that the Puritans were fundamentalist obscurantists. The same year, Miller took a serious look at the structure of federal theology in a very important essay, "The Marrow of Puritan Divinity." L. J. Trinterud has been most helpful in placing federal theology in the whole background of medieval and Reformation theology in another major article, "The Origins of Puritanism," *Church History,* XX (1951), 37-57. In this connection, incidentally, one should note what is probably the only significant Roman Catholic contribution to this whole movement— and, again, by a historian of literature—Walter J. Ong's *Ramus: Method, and the Decay of Dialogue; From the Art of Discourse to the Art of Reason* (1958). Ramus belongs of course to the sixteenth century but his influence was a major force in colonial New England.

Miller's *The Puritan Mind: The Seventeenth Century* (1939) is an attempt at systematic exposition of the intellectual world of New England, and *The New England Mind: From Colony to Province* (1953) traces the internal dissolution of this scheme of things through a succession of historical events. Studies of individual figures, such as *Roger Williams* (1953) and *Jonathan Edwards* (1949), have added significant reassessments in each case. From the viewpoint of the historians of theology or of Christianity, Miller's lineaments are sometimes erratic and impressionistic, but the church historians are hardly in a position to complain.

Several of Miller's Harvard colleagues also figure in Puritan literature. Samuel Eliot Morison contributed in 1930 the biographical sketches of *Builders of the Bay Colony* and in 1936 *Puritan Pronaos,* which, with N. B. Murdock's *Literature and Theology in Colonial New England* (1949) delineates the characteristic literary and artistic expressions of the Puritan mentality. In his *Increase Mather* (1925) Murdock had earlier studied the representative figure of the turn of the eighteenth century. E. S. Morgan of Yale published a biography of a comparable figure, John Winthrop, in his *Puritan Dilemma* (1958) and Conrad Wright supplied an intellectual and social analysis of the moralizing and rationalizing opposition in his *Beginning of Unitarianism in America* (1955).

Morison, meanwhile, had become the historian of the intellectual center of early New England. He wrote three books, *The Founding of Harvard College, Harvard College in the Seventeenth Century* (2 vols.), and *The Development of Harvard University, 1869-1929,* that were stitched together by a summary volume, *Three Centuries of Harvard, 1636-1936.* Clifford K. Shipton has continued the volumes of *Biographical Sketches of Graduates of Harvard University.*

The stream of publication on Puritanism shows no signs of diminution in the 1960's. The works listed are representative only of a considerably larger body of materials, and numerous graduate students are being trained as historians of Puritanism. There is no lack of sources or of promising leads. The new edition of the works of Jonathan Edwards under the general editorial supervision of Perry Miller may be taken as a kind of symbolic culmination of the movement. *The Freedom of the Will,* edited by Paul Ramsey, appeared in 1957 and the *Treatise Concerning Religious Affections,* edited by John E. Smith, three years later. Readers have been promised future publications from extensive unpublished manuscript materials. It would have taken a credulous man in 1930 to believe that such an undertaking would ever be attempted.

The church history of the national period is less indebted to the historians of literature. Mathiessen, to be sure, helped to set Melville and Hawthorne in some intelligible relation to their Puritan heritage, and transcendentalism, which belongs somewhere on the fringes of church history, has continued to fascinate historians of American literature. But, on the whole, it is rather the social historians, or the historians of social and political thought, to whom church historians interested in the nineteenth century owed most. Morison, Gabriel, Commager, and Schlesinger have done much for church history, although their contributions are not so direct as those of the interpreters of Puritanism.

The leading church historian of the pre-Civil War period is William Warren Sweet, who was called to the first chair of American church history at Chicago in 1927. In fact, however, Sweet belongs with the men I have mentioned rather than with the church historians proper. He was a social historian of McMaster's school who specialized in religious institutions and movements as a major aspect of the American social pattern. Both in his choice of materials and in his own method and orientation, he avoided theology, describing religious aspects of national culture rather than the American expression of the church catholic.

While Sweet continued to publish until 1955, his work essentially belongs to the 1930's and the prewar generation. In fact his intellectual outlook was that of the 1920's and, like that of his colleague Case, never really changed. He was not, to be sure, a militant modernist like Case; rather he was a typical Methodist, anti-intellectual in his own view of religion.

Sweet's contributions are less interpretations than accumulations of materials organized in preliminary fashion. He blocked out his assignment with his *Story of Religions in America* (1930). To write a comprehensive history of American Christianity—the *religions* of the title is revealing of the period—was a bold venture. The spade work had not been done—it has not been done yet—for any mature and digested, comprehensive church history in America. Probably Sweet lacked the equipment to produce such a work, but to attempt one would at least pose challenges and stimulate further monographic study. This service Sweet performed. The result is not one of real distinction, but for thirty years it has been the most widely used single-volume history.

Sweet's next and probably greatest contribution is his series of volumes on the westward movement of the churches into the Mississippi Valley in the first half of the nineteenth century. He dug up and published revealing documents of this great movement in the series "Religion on the American Frontier." He began with *The Baptists*

(1931) and proceeded through *The Presbyterians* (1936) and *The Congregationalists* (1939) to *The Methodists* (1946). This aspect of the pre-Civil War era he made peculiarly his specialty.

Sweet then moved on to a more extended, comprehensive treatment of the American Christian experience, originally planned in three volumes. *Religion in Colonial America* appeared in 1942 and ten years later, after two or three slighter publications, came *Religion in the Development of American Culture, 1765-1840*. No more volumes appeared. Sweet's strength was failing by the mid-1950's, but there was a deeper problem. He had concerned himself little with the period after the Civil War, and it was little amenable to his methods and the theories, such as the frontier hypothesis, that he had made peculiarly his own. Nonetheless he had contributed the most substantial history for the period up to 1840.

Other social historians of the same period have concerned themselves extensively with religious matters. Alice Felt Tyler's *Freedom's Ferment* (1944) provides a colorful panorama of the idealistic, socialist, reforming, and religious movements of the generation before the Civil War. Although more limited in scope, W. R. Cross's *Burned-over District* (1950) is perhaps even more instructive to the church historian. Revivalism especially fascinated the social historians. Earlier writers were often chiefly eager to exploit its sensational possibilities, but a more intelligent treatment is provided in C. A. Johnson's *Frontier Camp Meeting* and B. A. Weisberger's *They Gathered at the River* (1958). C. R. Keller's *Second Great Awakening in Connecticut* (1942) brings out the relations of revivalism to many other aspects of church life, and W. G. McLoughlin's *Modern Revivalism: Charles Grandison Finney to Billy Graham* (1959) is an acute critique.

For the period after the Civil War there are popular sketches by Garrison, Atkins, Schneider, and E. T. Thompson's *Changing Emphases in American Preaching* (1943), but no solid full history of the church in America. Arthur Schlesinger of Harvard probably has done as much as anyone to stimulate study of the period. In his "Critical Period in American Protestantism, 1875-1900" (*Mass. Hist. Soc. Proc.*, LXIV, 1930) Schlesinger identifies a twofold crisis, the one a challenge to the social structure of Protestantism, the other to its theology, both posed by the new urban industrialism and its technology. This is a specification of sociological determinism that was at least as illuminating for the end of the century as Turner's frontier hypothesis had been for its beginnings.

A number of theses have developed these suggestions, although the theological side has not stirred a great deal of interest. There have been, to be sure, some studies of evolutionist thought, like I. V. Brown's *Lyman Abbott, Christian Evolutionist* (1953), but evolution was less disturbing to the churches than the historical study of the Bible and its implications for the doctrines of inspiration and revelation. There are a couple of theses on fundamentalism by S. C. Cole (1931) and N. F. Furniss (1954), but these are quite too superficial from the viewpoint of church history. The most intelligent and suggestive study of these issues is directed, not to American controversies, but to parallel developments in Great Britain. W. B. Glover's *Evangelical Nonconformists and Higher Criticism in the Nineteenth Century* (1954) proved to be another instance of a historian of literature giving lessons to the church historians.

The theological side of recent American Christianity has drawn few interpreters. It is the challenge of the social programs of the church that has attracted the graduate students. Even the discussion of evolution has found most interest where it has borne on social and political ethics, as discussed in R. H. Gabriel's *Course of American Democratic Thought* (1940) or Richard Hofstadter's *Social Darwinism in American Thought* (1945).

Schlesinger's suggestion about the challenge to Protestant social thought found a lively response in a generation informed by New Deal idealism, and a flood of theses resulted. Not all, of course, can be assigned to Schlesinger's stimulus. One of the first and best is a Yale dissertation, Howard Hopkins' *Rise of the Social Gospel in American Protestantism* (1940). A. I. Abell's *Urban Impact on American Protestantism* (1943), however, and H. F. May's *Protestant Churches and Industrial America* (1943) are Schlesinger theses.

The social gospel was pursued into the postwar period in three or four more theses, R. M. Miller's *American Protestantism and Social Issues, 1919-1939* (1958), Paul A. Carter's *Decline and Revival of the Social Gospel, 1920-1940* (1956), and J. N. Hughley's *Trends in Protestant Social Idealism* (1948). With D. B. Meyers' *Protestant Search for Political Realism, 1919-41* (1960) the perspective has significantly changed and we have a study of social ethics that no longer fits the pattern of Progressivist and New Deal idealism.

In this connection two excellent studies on the social ethic of American Roman Catholicism should be noticed: H. J. Browne's thesis, *The Catholic Church and the Knights of Labor* (1949) and A. I. Abell's long-awaited *American Catholicism and Social Action . . . , 1869-1950* (1960).

The social gospel interest seems to have been responsible also for some recent dissertations in the pre-Civil War period. In 1954, two appeared on very similar themes: John R. Bodo's *Protestant Clergy and Public Issues, 1817-1848* and C. C. Cole's *Social Ideas of the Northern Evangelists, 1826-1860.* Timothy L. Smith's *Revivalism and Social Reform in Mid-Nineteenth Century America* (1957) is refreshingly different in its approach to the subject, even though some of its main contentions are not convincing. C. I. Foster's *Errand of Mercy: The Evangelical United Front, 1790-1837* (1960) is another Schlesinger thesis. The topic is a major one for church history and worth a treatment a little less committed to the theory of ideology.

The abolitionist movement has been the subject of several studies. Those of G. H. Barnes, especially *The Antislavery Impulse, 1830-1844* (1933), and the publication of the two volumes (1934) of the Weld-Grimké letters of 1822-44, edited by Barnes and D. L. Dumond, have moved Garrison and the Unitarians from the leading role in the abolitionist drama and have replaced them with Weld and the evangelicals. W. S. Jenkins has supplied one of the best expositions of *Pro-Slavery Thought in the Old South* (1935).

This widespread interest in the social influence and activities of the churches in the 1930's and since contrasts sharply with German scholarship of the same period. Social ethics and its history seem to have been a distinctively American concern, or perhaps a concern of the English speaking world. The literature is overwhelmingly of a single orientation, and as monotonous as the innumerable Roman Catholic theses on nativism. One begins to wonder if there were no anti-New Deal church historians, and to inquire what had been going on in the majority of the churches that had not participated in the social gospel.

For historians of the post-Civil War period in American Christianity, among the most important subjects are the religious aspects of the enormous immigration. The problems of "Americanization," of unification of diverse national groups into larger church bodies, and the final emergence from cultural isolation are common to Roman Catholicism and Lutheranism in particular.

The most influential as well as the largest of the American denominations was in the last generation unmistakably the Roman Catholic Church, and there was impressive historical activity in the communion. The chief center was Catholic University in Washington where J. T. Ellis directed graduate students and edited the *Catholic Historical Review,* the most important Roman Catholic church history journal. Curiously enough, the Roman Catholic historians resemble the nineteenth century American Protestant scholars in their preoccupation with the early church and the American church.

There is as yet no comprehensive scholarly history of American Roman Catholicism to replace Shea's *History of the Catholic Church in the United States* (1886-90), although Theodore Maynard has written a popular *Story of American Catholicism* (1941) and J. T. Ellis an outline of *American Catholicism* (1952). Ellis has also edited a source book of *Documents of American Catholic History* (1956).

No doubt considerable spade work must be done before a comprehensive history can be written. Important in this connection are the regional, i.e., diocesan, histories. Of these perhaps the best is the *History of the Archdiocese of Boston . . . , 1604-1943* in three volumes (1944) by R. H. Lord and others. Another important diocese has been described by George Paré in his *Catholic Church in Detroit, 1701-1888* (1951).

Another approach to the general subject is through the chief tributary nationality groups. Giovanni Schiavo has compiled a large volume on the *Italian Contribution to the Catholic Church in America* (1949) as the second volume of his *Italian-American History.* Better digested and more enlightening is C. J. Barry's *Catholic Church and German Americans* (1953), which expectedly emphasizes especially the controversies of the 1890's over Cahenslyism, the school question, and Americanism. Similarly, an earlier sociological analysis of *The Polish Peasant in Europe and America* (1918) by W. I. Thomas and Florian Znaniecki is also of great value to the church historian. Most useful of all, of course, would be an interpretation of the Catholicism of Ireland and its adaptation in America.

From 1930 to 1960 numerous contributions were made to the already large literature of biographies of founders of various orders and institutions. Two that belong to history rather than hagiography are A. M. Melville's *Elizabeth Bayley Seton, 1774-1821* (1951) and V. F. Holden's *The Yankee Paul: Isaac Thomas Hecker* (1958).

Although the author is not a Roman Catholic, R. A. Billington's *Protestant Crusade, 1800-1860: A Study of the Origins of American Nativism* (1938) belongs to the genre of Catholic studies on nativism; in it all opposition to Roman Catholicism is lumped together as prejudice and no serious attempt is made to discriminate and evaluate the grounds and levels of disagreements generated in the Protestant community by Roman Catholic immigration.

The greatest concentration of historical interest has been on the period between the Civil War and World War I. The literature of this period exhibits a curious parallel to the one-sidedness of the corresponding Protestant concentration on liberalism and the social gospel. J. T. Ellis has devoted two volumes to the leading prelate and liberal champion in his *Life of James Cardinal Gibbons, Archbishop of Baltimore, 1834-1921* (1952). As supporting figures have come J. H. Moynihan's *Life of Archbishop John Ireland* (1953) and P. H. Ahern's *Life of John J. Keane: Educator and Archbishop, 1839-1918* (1955). The story of *The Catholic University of America* has been told in four volumes, beginning with J. T. Ellis's *Formative Years* (1946), followed by volumes by Ahern (1948), Hogan (1949), and Barry (1950). R. D. Cross has attempted a synthesis in his *Emergence of Liberal Catholicism in America* (1958), a sympathetic treatment by an outsider. The anti-Gibbons wing, of such figures as Corrigan, McQuaid, Messmer, and O'Connell, has not received comparable attention, but T. T. McAvoy has tried to strike a balance in his *Great Crisis in American Catholic History, 1895-1900* (1957).

The history of American Lutherans has been written largely in terms of the consolidation of the numerous national groups. G. M. Stephenson's *Religious Aspects of Swedish Immigration* (1932) and T. C. Blegen's *Norwegian Migration to America* (1931) are the best about Scandinavian immigration. The first volume of a documentary history, *The Augustana Lutheran Church in America, 1846-1860,* by O. N. Olsen, was published in 1950, and a second volume (1956) has continued the story until 1910. E. L. Fevold and E. C. Nelson have traced the ecclesiastical developments of the Norwegian synods in their *Lutheran Church among Norwegian-Americans* (2 vols., 1960), and C. E. Schneider has written a general description of the *German Church on the American Frontier* (1939). The Missouri Synod has drawn several accounts, among them W. O. Forster's *Zion on the Mississippi: The Settlement of the Saxon Lutherans in Missouri, 1839-1841* (1953) and W. A. Baepler's official *Century of Grace: A History of the Missouri Synod, 1847-1947* (1947). Studies of colonial Lutheranism include L. P. Qualben's *Lutheran Church in Colonial America* (1940) and P. A. Wallace's *The Muhlenbergs of Pennsylvania* (1956). *The Journals of H. M. Muhlenberg* were translated and edited in three volumes by T. G. Tappert and J. W. Doberstein in 1942, and in 1955 A. R. Wentz attempted a comprehensive survey in his *Basic History of Lutheranism in America,* although, as for Roman Catholicism in America, the groundwork had not yet been laid for a definitive history.

One might argue that the treatment of the church from the viewpoint of social history was the most widespread method in this generation. If Sweet and the Schlesinger school were the chief representatives, Sidney Mead, Sweet's successor at Chicago, might be taken as the systematizer. Apart from his dissertation on *Nathaniel William Taylor* (1942) Mead published no major new researches, but turned his energy to the critical assessment of various interpretations of American church history. Far more self-conscious and with more analytical power than Sweet, he really wrote but one book in the 1930-60 period. *The Lively Experiment* (1963) assembled about half a dozen articles that had appeared in *Church History* and the *Journal of Religion* between 1953 and 1956. Mead acutely criticized Sweet (see his "Professor Sweet's *Religion and Culture in America*," *Church History,* 1953, pp. 33-49), but all qualifications made, he followed Sweet and Schlesinger in focusing on the sociological pattern of the churches and in explaining it in terms of what Case called "environmental factors." Mead carried the argument further than his predecessors in his analysis of the American denomination as the characteristic product of the American Christian experience. In this analysis, as well as in his account of the achievement of religious liberty, Mead's tendency was to minimize the innate dynamism of the specifically religious motives and to stress the role of external, nontheological pressures.

But if Mead set the capstone to this kind of interpretation, the original manifesto might be sought in Richard Niebuhr's *Social Sources of Denominationalism* (1929). Here was a program of the range of social and cultural factors whose formative influence on Christianity might be profitably explored. The frontier thesis, class, national and racial interests and predispositions were all sketched out in advance for Sweet, Schlesinger, Mead, and their many followers. The theological context of the work is also that of social idealism. The first chapter poses the problem of "the ethical failure of the divided church" and the conclusion is an exhortation to realize the ideal of the brotherhood of all Christians. Niebuhr himself did not long remain satisfied with this approach to church history, but most of the generation did.

Before noting Niebuhr's later proposals we might well glance at the work of one of his Yale colleagues. In some ways the best book-length account of American church history is to be found in the pertinent sections of Latourette's *History of the Expansion of Christianity*. Nearly three hundred pages in Volume IV (1941) are devoted to "the great century" between the American Revolution and World War I, while the colonial and most recent periods are more briefly treated in other volumes. If this material had been separately printed, with the necessary revisions, it might well have competed successfully with Sweet's *Story of Religion in America* as the most useful text on the subject.

Latourette's theme of missionary expansion is certainly central in American church history, and possibly the best theme around which to organize a unified account. No European church can be viewed so satisfactorily from this perspective, and one might argue that Latourette's whole orientation and method were peculiarly rooted in the American Christian experience. His book is, moreover, more definitely *church* history than are the products of the environmental influences school.

The methods were, to be sure, complementary rather than mutually exclusive, and Sweet's source collection especially can be read as documents of the history of the Christian mission. The focus in the one case is on the religious dynamism of the movement and in the other on the reciprocal influence of the environment on reshaping the churches.

Many monographs and theses class themselves in the history of mission or church extension. W. C. Barclay has written at greatest length in his multivolume *History of Methodist Missions* (1949-   ). Similar are C. B. Goodykoontz's *Home Missions on the American Frontier* (1939) and C. M. Drury's *Presbyterian Panorama* (1952). The Roman Catholic expansion into the Mississippi Valley has been described in M. R. Mattingly's *Catholic Church on the Kentucky Frontier, 1785-1812* (1936) and J. H. Schauinger's *Cathedrals in the Wilderness* (1952). Sweet's frontier series does not give equal attention to the lower Mississippi Valley and here W. B. Posey has filled out the picture wtih books on the Methodists (1933), the Presbyterians (1952), and the Baptists (1957) in that region in the period after the Revolutionary War.

Church extension passes naturally into the founding of educational institutions, and here too I can mention only representative works. In 1932, D. G. Tewkesbury set forth a broad account of *The Founding of American Colleges and Universities before the Civil War,* and in 1944 Albea Godbold made a similar effort in *The Church College of the Old South.* The related topic of religious activities in colleges and universities has been developed by Clarence P. Shedd, first in *Two Centuries of Student Christian Movements* (1934) and then in *The Church Follows Its Students* (1938). The student movement and the missionary enthusiasm are alike distinctive manifestations of American Christianity and naturally attract historians. The Y.M.C.A. celebrated a centennial in 1944 and, several years later, published, among other things, C. H. Hopkins' *History of the Y.M.C.A. in North America* (1951) and Latourette's *World Service: A History of the Foreign Work . . . of the Y.M.C.A.* (1957).

The most profound interpretation of American church history made in 1930-60 has come not from a professional church historian, nor even from a historian of American literature, but, as perhaps one ought to expect, from the greatest American theologian of the generation, Richard Niebuhr. One might indeed do worse than to read the story of the best American thinking on church history in this generation in the passage from *The Social Sources of Denomina-tionalism* (1929) through *The Kingdom of God in America* (1937) to *Christ and Culture* (1951).

The Social Sources, as we have seen, served as a model for the larger number of historical writers of the generation, but when Nie-buhr published *The Kingdom of God in America* he prefaced the work with the observation that he was dissatisfied with his earlier at-tempt to illuminate the complexity of American Christianity "by ex-amining the influence of social forces on faith and by tracing the so-ciological pattern of race, class and sectional interests." This kind of analysis was indeed very helpful in interpreting the specific institu-tional diversity of American Christianity, but left unexplained the character, power, and unity of the religious movement that had con-gealed in these particular channels. This was no longer an idealist's history of an idealism. The reader met instead a new and deepened awareness of the reality of the church catholic as the subject of church history and of the power of the religious impulse in itself, to-gether with full recognition of all the corruptions, manipulations, and abuses to which it was subject. This was a reading of American Christianity and culture on "the basis of faith in a sovereign, living, loving God."

Niebuhr's work is comparable to that of Max Weber insofar as he sought to set beside the recognition of the effect of sociological fac-tors on religion the inverse movement, the influence of religion as an autonomous power on culture. But he has not been content like Weber to settle for the theory of an indeterminable confluence of causal factors in history; he has held to a radical relativism, indeed, but in relation to a radical monotheism. In the American setting, overwhelmingly Protestant for most of its history, this meant the interpretation of historical movement in terms of the continual reign of the living God. This was the way the actors of this history—the Puritans, the evangelicals, the social Christians of the nineteenth century—understood their own situation, and in this way only the church historian could adequately interpret their experience. Nie-buhr traced the idea of the Kingdom of God through three phases or nuances: the Puritan view of God's universal sovereignty, the evan-gelical concept of the reign of Christ in the individual soul, and the hope for a redeemed communal life of the social gospelers. But while he sketched with suggestive subtleties the history of the concept, his greatest hope was "that such a work as this may serve 'even as a stepping stone' to the work of some American Augustine who will write a *City of God* that will trace the story of the eternal city in its relations to modern civilization instead of to ancient Rome, or of Jonathan Edwards *redivivus* who will bring down to our own time the *History of the Work of Redemption"* (*The Kingdom of God,* p. xiv).

One cannot see much evidence of the influence of Niebuhr's book in the publications of American church historians of the Thirties or Forties. It was treated, to be sure, with universal respect. But what was to be done with it? Niebuhr's concise style, the compression and profundity of his thought, and the whole theological context in which it is set was puzzling to men who had not come in sight of the questions he was trying to answer. And the work is but an essay, a sketch of two hundred pages that lifts but a few figures and episodes from the vast panorama of American Christian experience. It was at once too much and too little, an unassimilable and alien formulation, a monadnock of harder rock rising high above the surrounding clay of sociological observations on the religious aspects of American culture. If this was the way to conceive American church history what were they all doing? It had all seemed relatively straightforward, but here were all kinds of problems, depths and heights that put unaccustomed demands on the historian's insights, judgment, and comprehension. Were there historians in America with the capacities to execute history after this manner and on these dimensions? Was there a public to read them with understanding? Hardly in the Christian community described in Sweet's works. Here was a vision of the history of American Christianity treated as part and parcel of the sweep of universal Christianity and with the power of the great church historians. But American Christianity had no great church historian yet.

In *Christ and Culture* Niebuhr set forth his analysis in relation to the classic interpreters of the Christian church, Augustine, Aquinas, Luther, Calvin, Tertullian, Tolstoy, and Maurice. No American figure or movement played a central role. Such was the architecture of his argument, however, that brief passing references to a Jonathan

Edwards or a Roger Williams or a Walter Rauschenbusch opened long and striking perspectives on great areas of American church life. The work is implicitly an interpretation of American Christianity, as written by an American who had thought deeply about the church in America and saw it always—as did so few American church historians—as an organic part of the total life of the church catholic. In form it is not a history or a narrative. It is a study in the sociology of Christian faith and obedience. As such it suggests themes that a generation of historians might clothe with flesh.

The influence of Niebuhr's thought is to be discerned in the work of Winthrop Hudson, Mead's former colleague at the University of Chicago. In Hudson's *Great Tradition of the American Churches* (1953) there is a sense of the tension between the claims of Christ and culture, an interest in the distinctive witness of the church apart from culture as well as in its vocation to society. In 1961 came Hudson's brilliant sketch, *American Protestantism*, in which these themes are evident. It is perhaps the most illuminating and judicious of the brief interpretations of American church history.

One last topic should be mentioned as a significant theme of the church history written by the generation at work during 1930-60— the reconsideration of the history of church and state relations in the United States. For a long time there had been little discussion of this question, since the general assumption was that America had found a happy and permanent resolution to the problem. But the rise of European totalitarianism and of the welfare state in the English speaking world and the ecumenical discussion of Christians on the implications of these developments posed many new questions. The new aggressiveness of the American Roman Catholic community set a challenge to the American constitutional pattern, a pattern devised and hitherto interpreted on Puritan Protestant assumptions.

E. B. Greene has set forth an able outline of *Religion and the State* (1941) but the most comprehensive work is Anson Phelps Stokes's three-volume compilation *Church and the State in the United States* (1950). Stokes has assembled conveniently most of the pertinent materials, but seems to have been unable or unwilling to clarify the issues of principle. Mark De Wolfe Howe, the jurist, has published a valuable collection of *Cases on Church and State in the United States* (1952); Leo Pfeffer has set forth a historical analysis from the point of view of a strict separationist in *Church, State and Freedom* (1953); and R. Freeman Butts has taken a similar position in *The American Tradition in Religion and Education* (1950). The opposed Roman Catholic view of the history is perhaps best stated in J. M. O'Neill's *Religion and Education Under the Constitution* (1949). Much of the debate focuses on the Revolutionary generation. The deeper and earlier grounds of the constitutional formation in the tradition of the Puritan denominations has been analyzed in two articles by J. F. Maclear, "The Birth of the Free Church Tradition" (*Church History*, vol. XXVI, pp. 99-131) and "'The True American Union' of Church and State" (*Church History*, vol. XXVIII, pp. 41-62).

The most important and controversial of the church and state issues are those related to education. Since the law of education lies more in the constitutions and statutes of the several states than in those of the federal government, historical inquiry has concentrated especially on church and state relations in various key states, e.g., Massachusetts (J. C. Meyer, 1930; R. B. Culver, 1929), New York (E. M. Connors, 1951), and Connecticut (M. P. Mason, 1953). Several of these studies are theses from Catholic University. R. J. Gabel's *Public Funds for Church and Private Schools* (1937) assembles a mass of material on that problem. In general, Protestant historians have been far less active in this area than the Roman Catholics and have even exhibited here a blind spot; the publication in 1932 of Lewis J. Sherrill's *Presbyterian Parochial Schools, 1846-70* was a surprise to many.

Certain other aspects of American Christianity have been surprisingly slighted by the historians. The theology of the Puritans down to the Unitarian controversy has received considerable attention in the last generation, but little of this has been from men in sufficient command of the whole sweep of Christian thought to be able to place and evaluate the American thinkers with much confidence. On the theology of the postcolonial period very little work has been done, especially on writers outside New England. H. Shelton Smith has opened a cut through the forest with his *Changing Conceptions of Original Sin* (1955) and J. H. Nichols' *Romanticism in American Theology: Nevin and Schaff at Mercersburg* (1961) offers a cross section of views of church, ministry, and sacraments. A Swedish visi-

213

tor, George Hammar, has attempted one of the few surveys of the whole development in his introductory section of *Christian Realism in Contemporary American Theology* (1940).

It is similar with the history of worship and of the sacraments and of biblical interpretation; there are prize topics in interdenominational relations and ecumenics going begging. The most notable achievement here is C. E. Silcox's *Church Union in Canada* (1933). The great interest in social ethics has largely overlooked sex and the family, although in this realm there is E. S. Morgan's *Puritan Family* (1944) and Emil Oberholzer's *Delinquent Saints* (1956).

The basic problem of the historian of American Christianity can be bluntly posed by Professor Pauck's proposition that there is no American church to write about. In the major European countries church history is normally written as denominational history, as the story of one or two or three great ecclesiastical institutional traditions, with perhaps an appendix on miscellaneous minor religious groups. The historian traces the fortunes of prelates and theologians, of canon law and endowments, of cathedrals, preachers, church schools, and colleges on the assumption that they are the locus of the life of the church. Each of these national church histories can be plausibly stitched to accounts of the early church to provide a unified account. But in America all these diverse European traditions are living side-by-side with a few indigenous newcomers. One must deal with at least a dozen church bodies, including all major European churches, for even an outline of the comprehensive history of Christian institutions and activities in America. And their changing interrelations and relative prosperity in America seem to be governed primarily by "nontheological" social and cultural trends. How is one to conceive and organize a coherent pattern of the life of the church amid these tumultuating varieties?

One might argue that the historian of American Christianity faces the common problem of all church historians, which is to discern where the "church" is to be found in the profusion of ecclesiastical institutions and rites, of social life, and of theological ideas. It is just that the various approximations and assumptions that are the stock-in-trade of European historians seem much less plausible in America. Professor Trinterud—in "The Task of the American Church Historian," *Church History*, XXV (1956), 3-14—argues that this

American situation, moreover, is also that of the "younger churches" of Asia and Africa, and probably will be increasingly that of the European churches. The problems that now baffle American church historians may become the inescapable problems of all church historians. One suspects that all of us will be forced in practice to a more radical relativizing of church traditions, and to a more radical, critical, and continuous reference to the Lord of the church as the criterion.

~§~
Summary

1. American scholarship in church history does not bear comparison with that of the chief European countries in either quality or quantity.

2. The better part of American production in the field is contributed by men with training and responsibilities in other disciplines, especially the history of literature.

3. The productive scholars among the church historians proper are largely confined to half a dozen university-related faculties. With a few exceptions the church historians of the denominational seminaries and college departments make negligible contributions to scholarship.

4. The last generation witnessed a migration to America of European scholars in church history and related fields extensive enough to overshadow the native-trained men in scholarly writing.

5. A highly disproportionate section, nearly half, of the resources of personnel, is confined to American themes. Here alone American scholarship in church history constitutes a continuing coherent discussion. This scholarship, however, has been characteristically crippled by inadequate knowledge of the history of Christianity generally, and by a lack of theological capacity.

6. Of major areas the most striking points of concentration in the last generation seem to have been Puritanism, English and American, and to a lesser extent, the left wing of the Reformation.

7. Of types of themes, American scholars seem to have been frequently drawn to studies of the social and political teachings and influence of the church, and infrequently to studies of theology proper, or worship, or religious art.

8. Other recurring themes such as missionary expansion, religious liberty and toleration, seem to reflect American interests and experience.

9. There has been a frequent tendency to sociological interpretations of religious movements of a quasi-Marxist variety, of explanations in terms of "nontheological factors" and "environmental" determinants. Americans have been less able to identify and exhibit convincingly the inherent dynamic of the faith.

10. The older schemes of progress and development as patterns for organizing the history of Christianity as a whole have ceased to command uncritical allegiance and have found rivals in "typologies."

11. The ecclesiastical pluralism and social fluidity of the American scene, which baffle the church historian, are becoming increasingly common everywhere. They will probably compel a redefinition of the nature of the subject matter of church history.

THEOLOGY

೪ఫ

CLAUDE WELCH

BERG PROFESSOR OF RELIGIOUS THOUGHT
UNIVERSITY OF PENNSYLVANIA

Prefatory Note

In this essay, *theology* refers to that kind of reflection commonly called systematic or constructive theology. It may be distinguished from *philosophy of religion,* which is treated elsewhere in this volume, and from *biblical theology* insofar as the latter means the internal analysis of biblical categories in their historical contexts. Obviously the lines of distinction are fluid, the more so in the latter case as recent theology has become more biblically oriented, with a heightened sense of the validity (or authority) of biblical concepts and perspectives (see below).

The assessment of "scholarship" in this field inescapably involves appeal to such subjective criteria as profundity and creativity of thought, power and persuasiveness of argument, clarity in analysis, and extent of influence. Further, it is necessary to take account not only of works of prime scholarship but also of those typical expressions that epitomize a pattern or movement and disclose the character of a "body of scholarship." An attempt is made here to interweave designation of truly decisive works with typological analysis of trends. The "development" of scholarship in respect to particular doctrinal areas is subordinated to the discussion of major figures and theological styles.

It should be noted, further, that no attempt is made to analyze Roman Catholic or Jewish thought. Quite apart from the difficulties that might attend an effort to treat Jewish, Roman Catholic, and Protestant thought in a unified discussion, it must be said with regret that neither of the former two traditions has as yet produced in America a major body of scholarship in *theology* in the strict sense of the term. In American Roman Catholicism no major systematic work, comparable for example to that of Michael Schmaus in Europe, has appeared. The summaries of dogmatics have been reworkings or translations of familiar manuals. Nor have there been special studies comparable to the recent work in Europe of Rahner, Congar, Küng, de Lubac, Mersch, and others. Authoritative Roman Catholic analyses of recent theology are marked by the absence of reference to American scholarship. It seems fair to say that, doubtless in large part because of the sociocultural situation of the Roman Catholic Church in the United States and its distinctive relationship to the church in Europe, the possibility of a powerful theological development has appeared only in very recent years. The burgeoning of scholarship was to come first in the areas of historical studies, church and society, and Thomistic philosophy. Insofar as this development of scholarship involves active communication with non-Catholic thought, it is not surprising that the area of dogmatics should be the last to be affected. Yet the past decade has been marked by an increasing self-consciousness (and self-confidence) of American Roman Catholic thought generally, by a growing ferment in theology proper (in close relation to

221

newer currents in European theology), and by the beginning of serious theological dialogue between Roman Catholic and Protestant scholars. The results of these developments have not yet taken the form of major publications, but there is here clearly the prospect of the emergence of a body of significant scholarship.

The creative thought of contemporary American Judaism has been of a basically nontheological character. The work of Martin Buber has claimed considerable attention in America, and the mystical emphasis of Abraham Heschel (see *Man Is Not Alone*, 1951, and *Man's Quest for God*, 1954) is important. Further, one might view various reinterpretations of Judaism as analyses of the nature of religious community. Nonetheless, it remains true that American Jewish scholarship has been devoted not to the systematic or speculatively theological, but to questions of religious practice, of cultural identity, of the relation of the religiocultural heritage to commitments of faith, to Zionism, etc. And of course the development of *theology* has historically been of far less importance for Judaism than for Christianity.

‌‍‌‍ঙ৩৯

Introduction

In the election year of 1932, the issue of fundamentalism/liberalism (or orthodoxy/modernism) still seemed to dominate the problem setting of American scholarship in theology. True, the fundamentalist controversy was at an end as a significant theological debate, and the protagonists of the "fundamentals" were clearly put to flight. There were signs of an impending storm in which liberal theology itself would be thrown back hard on the defensive: the name of Karl Barth (and even that of Kierkegaard) was already thought worthy of mention by a few, though the flurry of excitement over his theology in Germany was written off as an epiphenomenon of postwar despair; a new member of the faculty of Union Theological Seminary in New York was publishing a book called *Moral Man and Immoral Society*, in which the fallacy of the liberal dreams about man and society was to be devastatingly exposed; and within the liberal camp itself were already indications of reaction against the drift to subjectivism and anthropocentrism.

Yet the march of liberalism did not seem significantly impeded. The putative contrast was still between a faltering and outdated orthodoxy and a new and vital reconstruction of Protestant thought built on firmer foundations and given strength by the new materials of modern science and philosophy. The tensions in liberal theology exposed in Germany by Troeltsch and Schweitzer—tensions among its interests in personal faith, in history, and in ethics—were not yet felt in America. Rather the theologies of liberalism seemed in full flower. William Adams Brown had retired in 1930 as Roosevelt Professor of Systematic Theology at Union but was to continue for over a decade as a highly respected elder statesman among theologians. Harris Franklin Rall of Garrett was in the midst of developing a theology that was to be at once empirical and Christian. Albert C. Knudson of Boston was midway in the publication of the works in which he climaxed his long-formed purpose to rethink Christian theology in the light of the philosophy of personalism. D. C. Macintosh of Yale and Henry Nelson Wieman of Chicago were articulating theologies intended to be rigorously scientific. Edward Scribner Ames and Shailer Mathews of Chicago had just offered significant reinterpretations of the role of religion in human life. Humanism was being hailed as the new religion by Albert Eustace Haydon of Chicago and Charles F. Potter of New York.

Within the complex of liberalism were certain commonly acknowledged problems and concerns. Theological inquiry had to proceed from the realities of religious experience rather than from external and supernatural revelations. Religion had to be certified as integral to the general human quest for understanding. The problem of soteriology and ethics was that of harnessing and ordering the good in man for the realization of recognized social goals. The great question of theology was that of the existence or the "meaning" of God, and the dominant answers focused on the immanence of God in the world process. Theology and philosophy of religion were difficult to distinguish.

By the end of the 1930's, however, a radical reorientation had taken place. The prime questions, if not ultimately different, were at least viewed in a distinctly new light and given strikingly different answers, and other areas of concern came to the fore. The nature of this transition, and the ensuing course of scholarship in theology, will be explored in this essay. But a proper understanding and evaluation of this history requires a look both at the variegated pattern of liberalism and at fundamentalist theology.

❦

The Theology of Fundamentalism

The fundamentalism of the 1920's was not in the main a movement of theological scholarship.[1] Taking its rise around the turn of the present century as a resistance movement to the presumed abandonment of the traditions of classical Protestantism in the theological centers of America, gaining cohesiveness from the publication of a series of tracts *The Fundamentals* from 1910 on, and emerging into violent controversy in the 1920's, fundamentalism was variously a sociopsychological phenomenon reflecting defensive hostility to a changing culture, a political program to outlaw the teaching of evolution (both as threat to the "biblical" picture of the origin of man and as a symbol of the "godlessness" of modern science), and a struggle for control of the denominations with a view to extirpating the errors of modernism. Often the enemy was as much the social gospel as it was the theology of liberalism. Anti-intellectualism, anti-German passions of the war period (now directed against German scholarship as the supposed source of liberalism's heresies), and post-war fears of subversion, together perhaps with rural resistance to the growing dominance of urban culture provided other stimuli. The slogans of fundamentalism—the "Five Points" were not always consistently named, but generally they included the inerrancy of the Bible, the virgin birth of Christ, the substitutionary atonement (in a seventeenth century version), the physical resurrection, and the coming bodily return of Christ—constituted no monument to theological scholarship. With one major exception, the scholarship to which the movement could appeal was that of an earlier day.

That exception was J. Gresham Machen of Princeton, who did not apply to himself the term *fundamentalist,* for his temper was not that of the popular fundamentalist leaders. His own interest was in scholarly defense of the "true Christian faith," based on scripture, expressed in the central stream of the church's life as represented by

[1] Fundamentalism is to be clearly distinguished from such restatements of Protestant orthodoxy as Francis Pieper's rigorous "confessional Lutheranism" in his massive *Christliche Dogmatik* (1917-24; English trans., *Christian Dogmatics,* 1950), which reflect a continuing stream of conservative theology but without participation in the contemporary debate.

Augustine and Calvin, and set forth in the standards of the Reformed faith. This was for him no "ism," but "consistent Christianity." Yet Machen found himself in "the very warmest Christian fellowship" with those who called themselves fundamentalists, and shared their conviction that the theological state of the churches was "fundamentally unsound." Machen's scholarly achievement is doubtless best seen in the biblical analysis of *The Virgin Birth of Christ* (1930), but his more popular works, especially *Christianity and Liberalism* (1923), also provide important guides for understanding the central theological commitments of fundamentalism.

Those commitments involved the judgment that Christianity is definable in terms of doctrine, to be determined from the New Testament and essential to fellowship in the church. This was contrasted with liberalism's "nondoctrinal" religion. Yet not all points of doctrine were equally important. As Machen saw it, the two great presuppositions that liberalism had lost sight of, and that made it an essentially different type of thought and life, were "the awful transcendence of God," "the awful gulf" that separates creator and creature, and the real fact of sin. Only on the basis of these presuppositions could Christianity be properly seen as a gospel, a "triumphant indicative" announcing "a gracious act of God," a religion of redemption from sin by the transcendent God through the atoning sacrifice of Jesus Christ his Son.

But to put the contrast only in these terms, as an affirmation of the theocentric and evangelical nature of Christianity versus the kind of immanentism and confidence in man that was widely prevalent among the liberals of the 1920's, is hardly sufficient—as is clearly shown by the later rejection of Karl Barth and others in the neofundamentalism of the post-World War II period. At least two other sorts of assertions were involved, assertions deemed indispensable for the true statement of the gospel.

The first such principle was the infallibility of the Bible as the word of God preserved *wholly* from error both of fact and of interpretation. In contrast to conceptions of scripture as a human (and possibly erring) record of religious experience or even of God's great deeds, or as in some respects (e.g., faith and morals) inspired but not in others, or as *becoming* God's word to the believing response—in contrast to every such alternative, the Bible must be acknowledged as directly God's word, with an objectively definable content. Difficulties there may be in the scriptural record, but errors none, and none have ever been proved. Allow error at any point, and the whole is suspect, the solid foundation of faith a morass, and the actuality of God's self-revelation given up.

From this way of viewing the problem of biblical authority, it might appear that the infallibility of scripture was the pivot on which the whole theological structure of fundamentalism turned. And that is not altogether wrong, for the other classic points of virgin birth, physical resurrection, etc., as well as special creation in contrast to evolution, have here their warrant. Yet it is a distinctive feature of Machen's thought that without making any concession about the truth of biblical inerrancy, or its necessity for a *consistent* Christianity, he nonetheless could recognize as Christian those who, accepting the supernatural despite their lamentably lowered view of the trustworthiness of the Bible, do find in Christ a real entrance of the creative power of God.

Thus is suggested a second principle at least as important as that of the infallibility of the Bible, namely an insistence on a religious world-view that was cast in traditional supernatural terms and involved an uncompromising emphasis on miracle. This, as much as the scriptural principle, acccounts for the violent defense of the virgin birth, physical resurrection, and bodily return of Christ. "A miracle is the supernatural manifesting itself in the external world"; it is a supernatural event that "takes place by the immediate, as distinguished from the mediate, power of God" (*Christianity and Liberalism*, p. 99). The redemptive acts of God and the creation of man must be understood in such terms. There are real and recognizable intrusions into a natural order, and one cannot be indifferent to the actuality of the biblically recorded miracles. The virgin birth, which Machen powerfully defended both as theologically essential to Christ's deity and as verifiable historical fact (*The Virgin Birth of Christ*), is at the same time, he recognized, a symbol for the whole pattern of truly Christian understanding of the divine redemptive activity. Rejection of the virgin birth is almost always part of a total rejection of the supernatural content of the New Testament, and therefore of the only context within which the gospel can remain really a gospel.

The genuinely theological case for fundamentalism was given a sophisticated statement by Machen. He argued with a firm grasp of issues, with far more historical perspective than most other representatives of the movement, and not without charity toward his opponents. Yet the characteristic spirit of defensiveness is present even in his writings. With him the theological scholarship of fundamentalism seemed to come to an end (as also, by 1931, the movement had been decisively defeated in the attempt to gain institutional control over the major Protestant churches).

◈

Varieties of Liberal Theology

The liberalism or modernism that appeared to be destined for fuller glories at the beginning of the 1930's was by no means a unified movement. There were, to be sure, significant common attitudes and tendencies that make it meaningful to speak of "liberal theology" in the singular. In addition to the "liberal spirit," which meant both the temper of open-mindedness, of tolerance and humility, and the sense of participation in a new era in which all the old truths required and could freely be given thoroughgoing reconsideration, certain other informing principles can be identified: the deep respect (sometimes adulation) for modern sciences and their methods; a tentativeness about the final adequacy of all statements regarding ultimate reality; an emphasis on the priority of religious experience and the derivative character of theological (including biblical) formulations; a preoccupation with continuity, particularly between the natural and the supernatural, and among the means of attaining truth; a confidence in essential human goodness and the possibility of achieving the good society; and a stress on the immanence of God. Yet within the broad tendencies of liberalism the questions were dealt with differently and the informing principles had varying weights, so that in the significant scholarship of the movement, as it appears at the onset of the 1930's, at least four strains of thought may be detected.

The first, not as eye-catching as the others but probably the most widespread, may be termed *evangelical liberalism*—evangelical because it sought to remain Christocentric in its orientation and to

227

rebuild in essential continuity with the Christian experience of all generations. This was earlier the liberalism of the classic texts by W. N. Clarke (*An Outline of Christian Theology*, 1898) and William Adams Brown (*Christian Theology in Outline*, 1906) and of the Anglican William P. Du Bose. About 1930, it was most ably articulated by Brown (*Beliefs That Matter*, 1928; see also *How to Think of Christ*, published posthumously, 1945), by Albert C. Knudson (*The Doctrine of God*, 1930 and *The Doctrine of Redemption*, 1933), by Harris Franklin Rall (his view was best stated later in *Christianity*, 1940), and by John Baillie (*The Place of Jesus Christ in Modern Christianity*, 1929). Here were major efforts to develop a theology that sought to be at once empirical, of faith, and Christian (Rall), or "scientific, philosophical and practical" (Knudson), though only Knudson elaborated this into a full theological system.

For this perspective, the idea of revelation is not to be abandoned, because the God who is personal does not passively await discovery. But it is to be reconceived because historical study shows that the Bible is not an infallible oracle of God, because the traditional idea misconstrues Christianity as a sum of doctrines, and because we have a truer idea of the truly personal relation of God and man and do not view the natural and the supernatural as mutually exclusive. "From one point of view the quest after God is a human search, a human striving, but from another point of view it is a divine revelation" (Knudson, *Doctrine of God*, p. 215). Nonetheless, the emphasis falls on the *how* of the disclosure, on the human side of the communication, and thus revelation has to be set in the context of human knowing in general and to include various ways of knowing God—through tradition, through direct experience in many forms, including morality and saving help, through faith as trust and obedience, and through reason.

It is evident that on this view of the matter the theological enterprise depends upon the validation of religious knowing. Hence the persistent appeal to religious experience (broadly interpreted) as the locus of continuity in Christian history, as the proper religious authority, and as certifying the reality of the divine being. Rudolph Otto's *Das Heilige* (1917; English trans., *The Idea of the Holy*, 1923) was widely received as a powerful buttress for this side of the liberal case. Though the most rigorous efforts toward an "empirical theology" belong to another type of liberal Protestant thought, and though Knudson questions the possibility of a really scientific empiricism in religion, seeking instead to find a sufficient justification and pattern for theology in the personalist philosophy of Borden P. Bowne—the grounding of religious affirmations in empirical data is a persistent theme in this evangelical liberalism. Religious experience is *sui generis* by virtue of its object, but as a way of knowing, it is subject to the ordinary tests of truth.

A crucial element in the experience and in the method is the ethical, which is taken as an almost unquestionable court of appeal. The awareness of the transcendent moral claim is at the heart of genuinely religious experience. The development of religious experience that the Bible records is an increasing ethicizing of the concept of God, through the prophets, the first great exponents of "ethical monotheism," to Jesus Christ, who is the center of revelation because in him the fullness of the divine moral demand is expressed and God is seen as wholly love. Similarly, redemption is centrally moral transformation.

The God apprehended in the highest forms of religious experience is characteristically described as both immanent and transcendent. If the danger of orthodoxy was its exaggeration of the divine transcendence so that God is only externally related to the world, there is the equally great danger of absorbing God in the world process. Certainly God is met in the process, and in such a way that no radical distinction should be made between "natural" and "supernatural" and the category of miracle (as traditionally understood) is no longer of prime importance. But the God so encountered is also the ground and source of the natural order. Because God is immanent he can be found; because he is transcendent he can be depended upon; because he is good he can be trusted. He is creator —which is to speak of the continuing dependence of the natural process on the power and purpose of God rather than of a first moment of finite existence or of a creation *ex nihilo*.

In contrast both to traditional theology, which sought to define God in "impersonal" categories of essence, substance, etc., and to modern naturalism, which makes God only a factor in the world process, the Christian God must be seen as truly personal. If we are

229

to make full use of the data of moral and religious experience, if we are to interpret ultimate reality by analogy from the highest mode of finite existence, and if we are to have an adequate basis for moral and spiritual life, then God cannot be less than will and personal purpose. Obviously the divine transcends the limitations of finite personality, yet the relations of God to man are essentially similar to human interrelationships.

The distinctively Christian element in the understanding of God is found in the concept of universal Fatherhood as known in Christ. God's goodness is defined as righteous love—never an arbitrary and capricious wrath but a steady and patient opposition to evil expressing his mercy toward man (for which again the highest in human love serves as the best analogy). His is a goodness and power that respects the integrity of human personality and its freedom. In the creation of persons God has limited himself in a very important way, yet the whole of history is ordered to the fulfillment of his purposes, for God's power is available to individuals and evil breaks down on the hard facts of moral and spiritual laws, so that history is the proving ground of judgment and grace, and the insights of the prophets and Jesus are vindicated in human experience.

Probably nothing was more important to liberal theology, in its critique of orthodoxy, than the doctrine of man and his sin. For the evangelical liberals this did not mean the abandonment of the ideas of sin and need for redemption, but a renewed emphasis on created goodness and a restatement of the nature of sin. To use Knudson's way of putting it, the idea of creation, leading in an idealistic and optimistic direction in the conception of man, must have priority over the theme of redemption, which makes for a pessimistic and dualistic conception of man, stressing his impotence, misery, sin, and peril of being "lost." (The affinities with William James's "healthy-minded" type of religious experience are obvious.) The prime insistence must be on the supreme value of human personality, the kinship of man to God by virtue of creation in the image of God and by attainment of sonship to God. "We believe in the divine sonship of man because we believe in his essential dignity, quite as truly as the reverse. The two beliefs belong together. One supports the other, and both are parts of a common faith in the ideal" (Knudson, *The Doctrine of Redemption,* p. 90).

Sin, then, refers to the gulf between what man is and what he ought to be, to the failure to realize ideals that are recognized as duties. Sin arises in the willful and irresponsible use of freedom of choice, and is necessarily correlated with guilt and accountability. Man's plight involves *sin* only when it is the result of free and to some extent conscious violation of a moral standard that is binding on conscience. Consequently, the doctrines of the fall and original sin are highly suspect, and the evil and tragedy that are a function of the human situation (of ignorance, of accumulated inhumanity) are to be "understood" rather than "forgiven."

Yet man needs redemption—and that insistence sharply distinguished evangelical liberalism from any secular humanism. Man has to be saved, not by an infusion of grace that would violate his freedom, but by an impulse to conversion that comes from above and elicits his response. Such is the importance of Christ. He is the example and proof of a truly good life and he is the revealer of the true nature and will of God. In response to this pattern the Christian is enabled to live a new kind of life. To be sure, the traditional Christological formulas are no longer very helpful. They were overly intellectual; they tried to state final answers in the language of a particular time; they were cast in substantialist rather than personal categories; they tended to deny the humanity in favor of the deity of Christ. But no disjunction is to be made between the religon *of* Jesus and the religion *about* Jesus. And Jesus is far more than simply an uncommon instance of what men ought to be. The *important* historic answers of the churches to the question "Who is Christ?" remain the same. He is genuinely man, and ideal man. But he is also Messiah, and God incarnate as the one who is the "window" to the divine. "The conviction that in Jesus we meet God . . . is the very heart of our Christian faith" (Brown, *How to Think of Christ,* p. 10; see pp. 267 ff., 282 ff.). Thus the person and work of Christ give, for evangelical liberalism, the unique and decisive impetus to Christian thought and life.

From the standpoint of its proponents, this liberal theology was an attempt to reconstruct the theological edifice in continuity with the central elements of enduring Christian experience and in the light of modern understanding of the Bible and modern thought generally. From the perspective of fundamentalism, the faith had already been abandoned. From more radical liberal views, however, it represented an uneasy compromise, a halfway house, clinging too much to the old and lacking the consistency of a truly scientific and empirical approach.

The demand for a more thoroughgoing revision of theological method found its most important exponents in Douglas Clyde Macintosh and Henry Nelson Wieman, whose work—if one is to judge by rigor and power of argument and by originality—attained a level of scholarship surpassing that of any of the other liberal theologians here discussed. Of the two, Macintosh was the more formally scientific. With care and precision, he sought to work out a theological pattern that, while ultimately faithful to the essentials of the Christian tradition, would embody a strictly scientific procedure and would enable theology to take its rightful place among the sciences. (See esp. *The Problem of Knowledge*, 1915; *Theology as an Empirical Science*, 1919; *The Reasonableness of Christianity*, 1925; "Experimental Realism in Religion," in *Religious Realism*, 1931, pp. 307-409; and *The Problem of Religious Knowledge*, 1940; abbreviations used below are: *TES, RC,* and *PRK*.)

Like other sciences, Macintosh argued, theology ought to proceed on three levels. (1) Religious perception is that in the religious realm which corresponds to sense perception. "In the complex of religious experience . . . at its best, the religious subject is aware, in an empirical situation, of the existence of . . . an Object of religious dependence which proves to be a Source of religious deliverance" (*TES,* p. 91). Hence it must be affirmed that God *is,* though his nature is defined only in a preliminary way. (2) Assuming the divine constant and the variables of the constitution of the self and especially the "religious adjustment" adopted, theological *laws* can be formulated, describing what the divine does on the fulfillment of various elements of the "right" (dependably successful) adjustment, which includes: "aspiration toward spiritual and especially moral ends," concentration on God or religious reality as good and reliable, surrender of self to the divine will, expectancy, willed responsiveness to the moral ideal, and steady persistence in all this. (3) Theological theory, founded on the laws, in turn involves three levels. There are the "fully verified elements," namely the existence of an absolutely dependable divine element and the assurance that this object is "absolutely sufficient for our absolutely imperative needs." Second, there are affirmations that are "practically imperative" but only "partially verifiable," i.e., elements that go beyond empirical certainties but are consistent with them and are based on what a living faith needs to meet the demands of "worthful living." At this level various affirmations are justified: that man, in light of moral obligation, is a free creative agent and is able to assist in the victory of good; that the highest human values, hence the existence of persons, are conserved beyond physical death; and that God is a transcendent, intelligent, and good personal spirit. Finally, theology includes speculative "rational surmises," "the apparently valuable and not yet discredited elements, such as might be gathered from imaginal intuition or respected tradition" (*PRK*, p. 201)—e.g., God as creator, as distinguished from the more fundamental assurance that God controls.

Intrinsic to Macintosh's theological scheme are two further themes. His rigorous articulation and defense of "critical monistic realism" in epistemology, applied to religious perception, justified the assurance that the religious Object is really *there*, yet recognized that "not all that enters into direct religious experience is to be regarded as belonging to the divine reality in its independent existence, nor what is directly experienced of the divine to be taken as all there is of the divine in reality" (*PRK*, p. 178). Since the religious is *appreciative* apperception, value is a crucial criterion. Second, Macintosh's defense of "moral optimism" as "a fundamental attitude of confidence in the cosmos, together with a full sense of man's moral responsibility," was of particular importance for his second level of theological theory and thus for the reasonableness of the "spiritually valuable content" of Christian faith. A permanently courageous attitude of life requires such an optimism, and it is at least as reasonable as alternative beliefs. What is therefore demanded for the full expression of the moral life, and is not precluded on other grounds, is properly to be affirmed as part of a truly rational faith. (See esp. *RC*, pp. 42 ff.)

If Macintosh sought to be more formally scientific in method, Henry Nelson Wieman was more inclined to restrict the realm of permissible affirmation to the fully verifiable (see esp. *The Wrestle of Religion with Truth*, 1927). If one is to avoid devotion to mere ideas, the product of wishes and needs, theological interpretation

233

must leave aside "ultimates" and inquire into the immediacies of experience, seeking to shape the idea of God simply in terms of "objective evidence." This is the scientific method, considered not narrowly as the technique of natural science but as the "combination of observation and reason." The question to be asked is not "What would I like God to be?" but "What in fact is God?" God is more than we can think, but we ought to talk about what is actually observable. The question is also asked in light of values (God is worshiped because of supreme worthfulness), and it is framed with the recognition that all existence is characterized by process (Wieman was a prime agent in the appropriation of elements of Whiteheadian metaphysics for theological use—see below).

From this standpoint, God may be defined and known with certainty as "that Something upon which human life is most dependent for its security, welfare, and increasing abundance"; "growth in meaning and value"; "that activity in our midst which shapes life toward the progressive attainment of mutual support and meaning" —to cite only a few of Wieman's many early definitions. This is God because it is the locus of the greatest value that can be experienced and commands our supreme devotion, creating and carrying personality to whatever heights it can attain.

On the negative side, the restriction of theological affirmation to the observable requires the denial of supernaturalism and of the personality of God. Both are persistent themes of Wieman's early works. God transcends human personalities, but is a part of the total process. Against supernaturalism, therefore, may be affirmed a "theistic naturalism." God cannot be a person but must be more, namely, that interaction or "progressive integration" that generates personality and its values.

A third kind of liberal theology, which in affirmations about God hovered between the preceding view and an explicit religious humanism, was chiefly interested in the role of environment and functional adaptation in the growth of religious ideas. It was significantly developed by Edward Scribner Ames (*Religion,* 1929) and Shailer Mathews (esp. in *The Growth of the Idea of God,* 1931). Ames's basic theme was the understanding of religion as a "natural, social, cultural process": "Religion arises as a phase or quality of the complex life of the human spirit in its idealistic outreach, and is continually subject to restatement under the influence of that flowing stream of life" (p. v). God is "reality idealized" (p. 151). The idea of God expresses "more than the mere projection of human ideals," because the ideals are real and natural. Yet "the order and purpose and moral values in the great Reality which we call Life or the World" (p. 178) have their existence as qualities found in man. Whatever the "more" of the divine nature, our prime interest is in the way in which characteristics of value "are inevitably identified with reality, conceived as God. At any stage of culture, what is good for man is good in his God . . ." (p. 173). Similarly for Mathews, though he was perhaps more definite than Ames in rejecting humanism and holding to the objectivity of God, the important point was the way in which the religious meaning of theological doctrines can be understood through the social (especially political) experience from which the religious symbols derive.

At the farther edge of liberalism was religious humanism per se, in which it was frankly affirmed that man's hopes rest in his own potentialities and that the source and goal of religious thought ought to be explicitly recognized as human life and its concerns. (See esp. A. Eustace Haydon, *The Quest of the Ages,* 1929; John Dewey, *A Common Faith,* 1934; and C. F. Potter, *Humanism, a New Religion,* 1930.) Haydon's approach, from the history of religions, was typical. Religion is "a shared quest of the good life. Seen in the longer perspective, it is the age-old, heroic adventure of earthborn man wrestling for self-fulfillment. . . . Taken thus naturalistically, the religions of the world may be understood as the manifold ways in which human life has sought to mold a cosmic process to the service of man's growing ideal" (*Quest,* pp. ix, xiii). In this quest the enrichment of human life has often been vitiated by the transference of goals to a realm beyond history, by the shifting of the properly human burden to a divine ruler, and thus by the distrust of reason and the subordination of human values to a "glory of God." Modern man's task therefore is to reformulate the religious ideal of the satisfying life and to offer a program for its attainment through the method of science. A religion self-conscious as to the nature of its authorities, and resting the responsibility on man, has at least the possibility of actualizing on earth the goal of "a society in which the personal happiness and the joys of culture may be available to the masses of men" (p. 198).

In Dewey's well-known distinction, the "religious" as a quality of experience can and ought to be freed from the hindrances of the "religions," with their beliefs, practices, institutions, and references to a supernatural power. The religious function can be expressed on a higher level, in devotion to ideal ends presented by the imagination in a continually growing process. There is that in nature that offers possibilities for aspiration and action, yet the uniting of "ideal ends with actual conditions" (which might be called God) is unequivocally a human operation.

The drift toward subjectivism and anthropocentrism, so clearly marked in the two types of thought just noted, was already evoking sharp protest from other liberals in the early 1930's—and not only from the evangelical liberals. One of the chief themes of the group of important theologians who contributed to *Religious Realism* (ed. D. C. Macintosh, 1931) is "the view that a religious Object, such as may appropriately be called God, exists independently of our consciousness thereof . . ." (p. v). Certainly a prime aim of Macintosh's theological program was the countering of purely psychological and subjective views of religion. And Wieman, in spite of his polemic against supernaturalism and a willingness at one point to welcome Dewey as a "theist," nonetheless asserted in his contribution to Ferm's *Contemporary American Theology* (Series I, 1932): "What I am chiefly trying to do in the field of religion is to promote a theocentric religion as over against the prevailing anthropocentric." It is just theocentrism that requires strict attention to "the actuality of God Himself, and not our ideas about God. . . ." (See also E. W. Lyman, *The Meaning and Truth of Religion*, 1933; W. M. Horton, *Realistic Theology*, 1934; and R. L. Calhoun, *God and the Common Life*, 1935.)

Yet it is too much to say that this turn to "realism" formed a major bridge to the acceptance of Barth's theological "objectivism" or Reinhold Niebuhr's "realism" about man and society or Tillich's "belief-ful realism." It does suggest that the impulses of liberal theology in its major forms were not discontinuous with the interests of the following generation; these were to be taken up in quite different

236

contexts, so that the theological complex that may be called liberal theology ceased to be as such a dominant force in American theological scholarship. Not infrequent replies to "neo-orthodoxy" were to appear, complaining of the "irrationalism" or "pessimism" of Kierkegaard, Barth, Niebuhr, etc. (e.g., J. S. Bixler, *Conversations with an Unrepentant Liberal*, 1946; L. H. De Wolf, *The Religious Revolt Against Reason*, 1949; A. C. Knudson, *Basic Issues in Christian Thought*, 1950), and some interpreters have professed to see a more recent turning back toward the "valid elements" of liberal theology. Yet it seems more nearly correct to view the continuation of liberalism's concerns as strands in theological patterns to which other names should be given. The strong empirical thrust has a continuing influence chiefly among those influenced by Wieman, but as a theme subordinate to the relating of Christian faith to the insights of process philosophy. The attempt at a rigorously scientific theology collapsed (Macintosh's hope for disciples was unfulfilled), and religious humanism became explicitly an alternative to, rather than a possible outgrowth of, Christian theology.

Theological Reorientation

The transformation of American theological scholarship (sometimes called a renaissance), which began in the mid-1930's, as a comparable and more radical revolution had occurred in Germany in the previous decade, cannot be described simply, nor can it be accounted for merely by pointing to one or two dominant influences.

A notable series of statements on the theme "How My Mind Has Changed in This Decade," published by the *Christian Century* in 1939, suggests two of the formative factors. First, Karl Barth had become the theologian to be reckoned with. To be sure, it was the Barth reputed for such themes as paradox, "the absolute qualitative distinction between time and eternity," God as *totaliter aliter*, total depravity, etc., that is, the Barth of the 1920's, who was mainly in view, rather than the Barth of the *Kirchliche Dogmatik* and thus of the theology of grace (this later Barth has still only begun to be dealt with in America). And certainly there were few who could be counted disciples of Barth; the reaction included sharp negation as well as appreciation. Emil Brunner's "more moderate" version of the "dialectical theology" was more congenial to the American temper, yet Barth had become the major figure whom the theologian had to take seriously into account.

Second, the Great Depression and the dismal portents of the international scene had effectively destroyed the optimistic illusions of the previous generation. The task of theology could no longer be the Christian understanding of the gradual perfecting of man and society. It had to become instead a problem of interpreting human misery, tragedy, and bestiality. Thus Reinhold Niebuhr, who in 1939 was already becoming the most influential American theologian, confessed "that the gradual unfolding of my theological ideas has come not so much through study as through the pressure of world events" (*Christian Century*, April 26, 1939, p. 546).

Yet these sources of change can hardly be separated from others. The disturbing questions that Albert Schweitzer's *Quest of the Historical Jesus* (1906; 1st English ed., 1910) had raised about the reliability of the liberal picture of Jesus and about the easy incorporation of the actual Jesus into modern perspectives were being intensified by even more radical skepticism, especially in the form critical school of biblical criticism. The relativity of historical perspectives was more widely felt. Kierkegaard was beginning to be read, with his violent protest against the identification of Christianity with "Christendom," against the reduction of Christian truth to rational systems, against philosophies of immanentism. His Christian existentialism was to be of pervasive influence. The collapse of philosophical idealism, already signaled in America by the rise of pragmatism and realism, was complete with the emergence of contemporary philosophies of existentialism and of process, and later of positivism and its successors. Insights of depth-psychology into subrational levels of human motive and desire, and into personal disintegration and disruption, were becoming both threats and aids to the theological analysis of the human situation.

Out of the confluence of these and other streams, some of which will be noted later, the course of American theological scholarship in the past three decades has been marked by profound shifts in interest and emphasis, many of which may be described as reactions against liberal theology. Concentration has been on the transcendence and sovereignty of God rather than on his immanence and the identity of his activity with the progressive realization of human goals. The effort to interpret and justify religious knowledge after the fashion of empiricism has given way to the identification of revelation as the source of the knowledge of God and the basis for all Christian thinking. In this, the relationship of man to God has been characteristically described in the language of personal encounter ("I— Thou," hearing of the word, claim for decision, etc.) rather than religious experience—the difference lies in the connotations of divine initiative and freedom, of a radical and paradoxical coming of God to man, in contrast to the "given datum" of God's presence and availability to discovery. Preoccupation with the possibilities of man and the glories of his accomplishment has been displaced by a far soberer estimate of human virtue and a more vivid awareness of the limitations of historical achievement. The theme of "man" remained peculiarly dominant, but the variations bespeak estrangement from rather than continuity with God. (It is highly significant that Reinhold Niebuhr's *Moral Man and Immoral Society,* 1932, could play a role in American thought comparable to that of Karl Barth's *Römerbrief,* 1918 and 1921, in Germany.) Tendencies toward "culture Christianity" that were powerfully present, though in different ways, in both liberalism and fundamentalism were countered by witness to tension between Christ and culture. (H. Richard Niebuhr, *et al., The Church Against the World,* 1935, is both an important early expression of this and a forerunner of renewed interest in theological interpretation of the church.) And in all of these aspects of change, Protestant theological scholarship was marked by renewed appreciation of classical modes of Christian thought, i.e., by increased sympathy with the creeds and confessions of the church, with the principles of the Reformation, and especially with biblical imagery. Theology was articulated more explicitly from within the church, which was being viewed less as an optional religious institution needing to justify its social usefulness, and more as a unique community of faith with its own raison d'être and responsibility to God.

Within this broad complex, the theological enterprise has not in general been characterized by the formation of "parties" or "schools." Identifiable theological parties might be said to be formed by personalism, carrying on the tradition of Knudson, by a neo-naturalism, principally under the influence of Wieman, and more recently by a neofundamentalist revival. Yet the first of these seems nearly played out as a distinctive pattern, having lost its early creativity; the third remains on the verge of producing a body of scholarship; and the second, in light of its continuing evolution, may be understood as a special representative of a wider theological trend. A more helpful way of analyzing recent scholarship in theology will be found in the identification of broad tendencies or types of thought, which overlap greatly but which do reflect distinguishable styles of constructive theological procedure and by means of which the work of principal scholars can be illumined. I suggest three such major categories: theology that centers in the revival of Reformation insights, theology of correlation, and critical orthodoxy.

Reinhold Niebuhr and the Revival
of Reformation Theology

On the European scene in the period since World War I, the return to the Reformation has taken such definite form that one can properly speak of neo-Reformation theologies. (This is a "critical" return and must be clearly distinguished from the perpetuation of Lutheran and Reformed orthodoxies.) On the Reformed side, it is seen in the work of Karl Barth, Emil Brunner, Wilhelm Niesel, Thomas F. Torrance, and others. On the Lutheran side, it appears especially in the writings of Gustaf Aulen, Anders Nygren, Gustav Wingren, Regin Prenter, and Paul Althaus. No such relatively clear-cut pattern emerges in the American scene. The neo-Lutheranism of Aulen and Nygren receives significant explication in such works as Edgar Carlson's *The Reinterpretation of Luther* (1948) and Nels F. S. Ferré's *Swedish Contributions to Modern Theology* (1939), but the scholarship here is essentially that of interpretation of the work of Lundensian theologians. Important studies of the thought of Luther and Calvin are found in John Dillenberger's *God Hidden and Revealed* (1953) and Edward A. Dowey Jr.'s *The Knowledge of God in Calvin's Theology* (1952).

Yet the revival of Reformation thought is pervasively present in recent American theology, and above all as brought into decisive focus by Reinhold Niebuhr.[2] The sources on which Niebuhr draws are extraordinarily complex, and he is rigidly bound to no predecessors. Powerful strains of empiricism and pragmatism are apparent in his thought, as well as the unquenched passion of the social gospel movement, and these set him distinctly in an American tradition. His continual return to the problems of sin and justification, to the concrete manifestations of the human plight, as well as his effort to bring vividness and feeling to theology, reveal the influence of a Lutheran pietism in the background. His appreciation of the work of Barth and Brunner is expressed in sharp debate with them. The names of Marx, Freud, and Nietzsche, and the whole Western tradition of political and social theory, only suggest the varying sources that must be ranged alongside the explicitly theological background. Yet the tradition of faith to which his thought constantly turns is the Pauline-Augustinian, particularly as this is expressed in the reformers and at decisive points articulated by Kierkegaard. The relevance of Christian faith, for Niebuhr, is to be exhibited by recovery of the Reformation view, for it was the Reformation that rescued the crucial biblical insights into human nature from the medieval synthesis, and those same insights have been disastrously neglected in modern culture. Further, in the areas of his greatest achievement in theological reconstruction Niebuhr has been most clearly dependent upon Reformation theology.

As is well known, Niebuhr has often rejected the claim to be a "theologian." His interests have been chiefly those of ethicist, social critic and theorist, apologete, politician, and prophetic preacher. He has not been much interested in the "nice points of pure theology" (or of the history of theology). So, while the appeal to revelation pervades his theological analysis and construction, Niebuhr has made little effort at systematic explication of a doctrine of revelation

---

[2] Niebuhr's *magnum opus* is unquestionably *The Nature and Destiny of Man* (2 vols., 1941, 1943). Also of importance are *Moral Man and Immoral Society* (1932), *An Interpretation of Christian Ethics* (1934), *Faith and History* (1949), and *The Self and the Dramas of History* (1955). Useful interpretations of his work, and a bibliography of writings to 1956, are found in C. W. Kegley and R. W. Bretall, eds., *Reinhold Niebuhr, His Religious, Social and Political Thought* (1956). Abbreviations used in the text, in order of the titles listed here, are: *NDM, FH, SDH,* and *RN.*

(comparable, say, to his brother's *The Meaning of Revelation*). Even more evidently, Niebuhr has a profound doctrine of God, centering in the biblical view of God as a person who wills and loves—in contrast to impersonal conceptions of God as "rational structure of existence" or "undifferentiated ground of being"—but he has undertaken no technical exploration of this theme. He has not been, and has not wanted to be, an academic theologian, but rather, as one concerned with urgent social and political realities, has sought consistently to elaborate the relevance of theological affirmations to the concrete human situation.

Yet Niebuhr has been in fact the most influential American theologian of the past quarter century. His attitude toward theology has been the source and symbol of a creative approach to theological method and apologetics, and in the focal area of his theological concern, the questions of sin and salvation and of history, his analysis is marked by uncommon precision and technical elaboration and has been the point of departure for much subsequent work. (See, e.g., Alexander Miller, *The Renewal of Man*, 1955, and *The Man in the Mirror*, 1958, and E. La B. Cherbonnier, *Hardness of Heart*, 1955.) Thus without attempting to encompass the full range of Niebuhr's thought, we may designate those points at which he has been of prime importance for scholarship in systematic theology. (Other aspects of his thought are dealt with in James M. Gustafson's essay on "Christian Ethics" in this volume.)

Except as it becomes an explicit program of apologetics, Niebuhr's theological method remains largely unsystematized. It interweaves an appeal to experience with a reliance on "biblical insights" and the apprehension of faith, such that both the relevance and the meaning of biblical doctrine can be established only as they are applied to the facts of experience (see *NDM*, vol. II, p. 107). Apart from this pattern of interrelation, the precise nature of the appeal to scripture is not clearly spelled out. Niebuhr does not engage extensively in exegesis, and he eschews literalism. His characteristic references are to "prophetic religion," "the ethic of Jesus," "biblical religion," and "Paulinism"—permitting considerable selectivity and ambiguity at the point of biblical authority. Biblical categories are regularly contrasted with those of Greek thought and of metaphysical systems generally (so also of mysticism), the greater adequacy of the former being held to lie in their dramatic-historical character, which alone can express the reality of freedom.

A critical feature of the method has been Niebuhr's restoration of biblical myth and symbol to theological respectability. In his famous dictum, the symbols are to be taken "seriously but not literally" in reinterpreting all "ideas dealing with the relation of history and superhistory." "The Biblical symbols cannot be taken literally because it is not possible for finite minds to comprehend that which transcends and fulfills history. The finite mind can only use symbols and pointers of the character of the eternal. These pointers must be taken seriously nevertheless because they express the self-transcendent character of historical existence and point to its eternal ground" (*NDM*, vol. II, p. 289; see also p. 50). Presumably this means that the symbols are ultimately indispensable and untranslatable into other modes of discourse (at least into nonhistorical modes), though to take them in a nonliteral way evidently involves translation into general or universal truths about existence. Yet every translation must itself embody the dramatic-historical. Niebuhr wrote in a brief intellectual autobiography in 1956: "Though I have meditated on these issues for some time, I have only recently come to realize fully why the dramatic-historical account of the Bible . . . should give a truer view of both the nobility and the misery of man than all the wisdom of scientists and philosophers. The fact is that the human self can only be understood in a dramatic-historical environment." "The validity of Christianity is inextricably bound up with the idea of the historical character of man" (*RN*, pp. 11, 18).

At this point a further element of Niebuhr's method becomes clear. In the tradition of Kierkegaard, he is fond of terms like *paradox, contradiction,* and *suprarational,* insisting that religious truths are not subject to the tests of "rational" intelligibility, but it has become increasingly apparent that the foil for the polemic is *rational* in a particular sense. (See esp. "Coherence, Incoherence, and Christian Faith" in *Christian Realism and Political Problems,* 1953, pp. 175 ff.) It is reason as dealing with essences and necessities, and rational schemes of simple coherence, that are inadequate, and supremely so because they cannot adequately encompass "genuine freedom" either in the individual self or in "the total drama of man's existence upon earth."

243

Furthermore, it is the goal of Niebuhr's apologetic to show that the truth of faith becomes a higher wisdom. The method involves at least two stages. First, alternative interpretations, which are mutually contradictory, are shown by their historical outworkings to be inadequate views of the total human situation. (See the "loss of the self" in naturalism, idealism, and romanticism, *NDM,* vol. I, chaps. 2 and 3; the pattern of argument bears an interesting relation to the old defense of religion from the moral consequences of irreligion, though now stated far more subtly and painted on a broader canvas.) Since other views cannot embrace the seeming contradictions of human existence, a "negative proof" of Christian truth results. "Whatever measure of Christian Faith I hold today is due to the gradual exclusion of alternative beliefs through world history" (*Christian Century,* April 26, 1939, p. 546). Second, and positively, the Christian view does in fact illuminate the human situation. "That the final clue to the mystery of the divine power is found in the suffering love of a man on the Cross is not a proposition which follows logically from the observable facts of history. But there are no observable facts of history which cannot be interpreted in its light. When so interpreted the confusions and catastrophes of history may become the source and renewal of life." "Negatively, the Gospel must and can be validated when the truth of faith is correlated with all truths which may be known by scientific and philosophical disciplines and proves itself a resource for coordinating them into a deeper and wider system of coherence" (*FH,* pp. 137, 152). Evidently, the "higher wisdom" does not simply appeal to "rational" understanding, but merges with the power of renewed life.

A prime element of Niebuhr's analysis of the self has already been adumbrated, namely the decisive character of man's "genuine" or "radical" freedom, or self-transcendence, which can be truly understood only in dramatic-historical terms. (See esp. *NDM,* vol. I, and *SDH.*) That theme is one prong of an attempt to counter both the depreciation of the self and the easy conscience that characterize modern culture. Niebuhr is better known for his skill in puncturing human pretensions, for his attack on sentimental views of human nature, on optimistic ideas of progress and the perfectibility of man, and thus on the failure to see that "every growth of human freedom may have evil as well as virtuous consequences" (*RN,* p. 15). But it is equally important to his argument to show how the biblical view preserves the individuality of the self, in a unity of body and spirit, that is destroyed or lost in modern naturalism, idealism, and romanticism. "Both the majesty and the tragedy of human life exceed the dimension within which modern culture seeks to comprehend human existence" (*NDM*, vol. I, p. 122). Thus, in his classic formulation, Christian faith expresses a low estimate of human virtue, but a high estimate of human stature (as created in the image of divine will and personality).

Out of this dual emphasis spring Niebuhr's best-known and most influential contributions to theological reconstruction, in which he reaches the peak of his insights: the analysis of the origin of sin, and the consequent delineation of a morphology of sin (*NDM*, vol. I, chaps. 7 and 8). In refurbishing the doctrine of original sin, he draws heavily on Augustine and especially Kierkegaard, and focuses too exclusively on the individual, but works out his restatement with an acuteness of perception and a wealth of interpretative application unsurpassed in contemporary theological literature.

The human self, on this understanding, is and remains limited, sharing in the necessities and contingencies of nature. Yet man is also free, not simply bound by time, transcending himself in an infinite regression (of self-consciousness), a creature of "infinite" (equals "indefinite"?) possibilities, who can find the adequate goal of his life only in God. He exists "at the juncture of spirit and nature," in the "contradiction" of finitude and freedom. The "inevitable concomitant" of this situation is a spiritual state of anxiety (*Angst*), which is the "internal precondition of sin," "the internal description of the state of temptation" (*NDM*, vol. I, p. 182). Anxiety arises from uncertainty over the limits of freedom and the insecurity of man's not having the basis of his life within himself.

Anxiety is not sin, for it is equally the source and precondition of all human creativity. At least in principle the outcome may be either faith, which accepts the human situation before God, or sin, which denies or seeks to escape that situation. Yet sin always occurs, and this is the force of the symbol of original sin, which cannot refer to a temporal origin but designates a permanent feature of human existence and is a dialectical truth that does justice to the facts. No explanation can be given for sin, since that is to assign it a cause and to deny that it arises from freedom. Niebuhr has been much criticized for the assertion that sin is "inevitable but not necessary" (*NDM,* vol. I, chap. 9), though he evidently means that sin is *historically* inevitable, i.e., universal, and is not produced by any necessities of man's "nature." Nor does sin proceed from "pure caprice of his will" (the oversimplification of liberal theology). Man sins in and by his freedom. Therefore he remains responsible in spite of the inevitability or fatefulness of self-love and self-centeredness. This is attested by the experience of remorse and repentance, the acknowledgment of guilt, pointing to "original righteousness" as the perduring awareness, in the moment of self-transcendence, of the ultimate obligation of man's essential nature as free spirit (*NDM,* vol. I, chap. 10).

Niebuhr has had no peer in modern times in tracing the multifarious configurations of sin, which are all ways in which man attempts "to transmute his partial and finite self and his partial and finite values into the infinite good" (*NDM,* vol. I, p. 122). Sin is basically pride (egotism)—pride of pretension to self-sufficient power and of lust for power, pride of intellect that claims final truth and freedom from all ideological taint, moral pride or self-righteousness, and "quintessentially" spiritual pride. Egotism is also expressed in collective forms, in which even greater pretensions are found. (The distinction that Niebuhr attempts to draw between men's equality of sin in the sight of God and their inequality of guilt, the latter referring to radical differences in the resulting injustice, depending on varying degrees of political and economic power, has been felt to be less successful than other elements of the analysis.) If pride represents an assertion of freedom, then sensuality may be conceived as a flight from freedom, though it also is an act of freedom and involves both self-idolization and flight from self to worship of another god, and is clearly a secondary form of sin. In all its variations, then, sin is at once rebellion against God (idolatry) and denial of the true nature of human existence.

It is in Niebuhr's idea of the redemptive activity of Christ that his theology is most explicitly a reassertion and application of distinctive themes of Luther. Though the breadth of his theological base is exhibited by appeal to the whole Reformation doctrine of justification by faith, and to Roman Catholic theology's effort to do justice to freedom as a valid corrective of the Augustinian-Reformation tendencies, the controlling motifs for Niebuhr remain the recognizably Lutheran *theologia crucis* (rather than a theology of resurrection) and the *simul justus et peccator*. These are to be freshly interpreted by the concepts of "meaning," of suffering and sacrificial love, and of grace as power in and mercy toward man; and in all of these the strongly Christocentric character of Niebuhr's thought is patent.

Niebuhr's writing is filled with reference to "meaning," but the term has at least a dual significance. It denotes illumination, as the full disclosure in Christ of a principle of meaningfulness or ultimate coherence of history. It also refers to fulfillment, as victory over evil. Meaning is that which is to be fulfilled or actualized. Thus the *wisdom* and *truth* in Christ, as "the purpose and the will of the divine sovereign of life and history," is inseparable from the *"power and grace* in Christ," as "the dynamic authority of the divine sovereign of life and history," which divine power "is now established and disclosed in such a way that there can be no question about any other power being able to overcome it" (*NDM,* vol. II, pp. 54 f.).

The content of meaning is characteristically denoted in Niebuhr's theme of suffering divine love. God suffers as an inevitable result of sin and as voluntarily accepting the consequences of sin. The crucifixion discloses the pattern of judgment and mercy in the entire drama of God's working in history. Consequently, sacrificial love is established as the ethical norm that transcends history (i.e., as being unable to "justify" itself in history and as transcending all particular forms of justice and mutuality) and yet illumines and completes what is actual in history.

The grace of God in Christ, for Niebuhr, is then to be understood as both "the power of God over man" and "the power of God in man." It is "over" man as mercy and forgiveness; it is also "in" man as "an accession of resources, which man does not have of himself, enabling him to become what he truly ought to be" (*NDM,* vol. II, p. 99). Only as these complementary elements are both maintained can the complexity of the experience of grace be adequately reflected. Yet the weight of Niebuhr's interpretation falls on the side of mercy, and of wisdom as disclosure; the cross has priority over the resurrection, transcendent meaning and fulfillment over immanent operation. In understanding *simul justus et peccator*—"it happens to be true to the facts of experience that in one sense the converted man is righteous and that in another sense he is not" (*NDM*, vol. II, p. 125)—Niebuhr is closer to Luther than to Calvin. Real fruits of the Holy Spirit can in fact be seen in human life, and ever since *Moral Man and Immoral Society* Niebuhr has found these more readily in the lives of individuals than in large groups. Yet the powerful statement of the disclosure of wisdom, grace, and power in the cross is not matched by an equally powerful interpretation of grace as operative in history.

Even in so brief a sketch, the anthropological orientation of Niebuhr's Christology is apparent. "In the New Testament the Atonement is the significant content of the Incarnation" (*NDM*, vol. II, p. 55; see also vol. I, p. 148). In accord with Luther, and out of his own concern for relevance, the essential starting point for Niebuhr is the *work* of Christ. His interest is in the application of the cross to the actualities of human existence rather than in the *nature* of Christ. Insofar as he has any interest in developing the idea of incarnation, he reflects the view of the Antiochene theologians (emphasizing the relation of human and divine wills) and even more the Reformation insistence on the personal-historical character of the Christ-event. Definitions of Christ as both finite and unconditioned "verge on logical nonsense"; but "it is possible for a character, event or fact of history to point symbolically beyond history and to become a source of disclosure of an eternal meaning, purpose and power which bears history" (*NDM*, vol. II, p. 61).

In his repeated discussions of the meaning of history, Niebuhr has been both a source and representative of much recent theology. As already hinted, the concern of such theology is with history rather than ontology (versus, e.g., Tillich and "process theology"). Drawing inspiration from Augustine, but heavily indebted also to modern existentialism, this theology seeks to state the Christian faith in historical terms rather than in the metaphysical categories that predominated in traditional theology and even in liberalism. The task of theology is to make sense out of human history rather than to draw a philosophical map of being and the universe.

Niebuhr's theology of history may be stated by reference to the symbols of the *center* and the *end*. The former is Christ: "The Christian faith begins with, and is founded upon, the affirmation that the life, death and resurrection of Christ represent an event in history, in and through which a disclosure of the whole meaning of history occurs" (FH, p. 26). But that central event is a pointer to a transcendent fulfillment, lying beyond all events. Therefore it is intimately related to the idea of the end, symbolized in the New Testament concepts of the return of Christ, the last judgment, and the resurrection. Taken seriously but not literally, these express the faith that history "cannot ultimately defy its own norm," that Christ remains the judgment according to which every partial fulfillment in history is known as only partial, and that the richness of historical existence is finally not annulled but fulfilled.

The unity that history may be seen to have is thus perceived in faith in the sovereignty of God (and in no other way). Yet it is a unity and meaning that can take due account of both the possibilities and limitations of history. No limits can be set to the possibilities of creative achievement, but no accomplishment can ever escape the contradictions and corruptions of history. (Here Niebuhr wishes to apply the Reformation perspective even more dialectically than the reformers were able to do—see the striking summary in NDM, vol. II, p. 204.) There is a fulfillment in every moment, which is possible in repentance and faith, but this is also an "earnest" that is "possessed" in hope. Thus the Christian understanding of man, sin, and grace provides the means to an adequate view of the complexities of the life of individuals, of cultures, and of history as a whole.

୶ୡୡ୶

Paul Tillich and Theology of Correlation

Like the new Reformation theology, the pattern of thought here in view exemplifies a spirit and direction of scholarship common to much of recent American theology. In the broadest terms, it encompasses a wide variety of efforts to relate Christian faith explicitly to aspects of its cultural context. These include more or less synoptic explorations of the problem of theology and culture, among the more important of which have been *The Christian Answer* (1945), ed. H. P. Van Dusen, H. Richard Niebuhr's *Christ and Culture* (1951), Richard Kroner's *Culture and Faith* (1951), Bernard E.

Meland's *Faith and Culture* (1953) and *The Realities of Faith* (1962), and several works by Paul Tillich. The past decade in particular has been marked by growing interest in "theology of culture," interpreted either as the attempt to state formal principles of relationship between theology and the arts or as a sympathetic theological commentary on nontheological interpretations of the human situation, as these may be seen to provide points of contact for dimensions of the Christian understanding. The endeavor still remains somewhat formless, especially in the former dimension. Yet a variety of suggestive treatments has appeared. For example, among the fuller works bearing on literature and theology may be mentioned the following: Roland Frye's *Perspective on Man: Literature and the Christian Tradition* (1961), William Mueller's *The Prophetic Voice in Modern Fiction* (1959), Nathan A. Scott's *Modern Literature and the Religious Frontier* (1958), and Amos N. Wilder's *Theology and Modern Literature* (1958).

A more specific expression of this theological motif is seen in attempts to relate theology and psychoanalysis, chiefly at the point of the understanding of man, sin, and redemption. Again, however, it must be said that the investigation is yet in its preliminary stages. In particular, it remains unclear what principles may properly govern the theological appropriation of psychological insights or the correlation of theological with psychological concepts. David Roberts' *Psychotherapy and the Christian View of Man* (1950) and Albert C. Outler's *Psychotherapy and the Christian Message* (1954) are of special importance in bringing this question into the foreground.

Far more extensive treatment has been given to the significance of existentialism for theology, and there is a considerable body of literature seeking to interpret major existentialist thinkers. (See esp. Carl Michalson, ed., *Christianity and the Existentialists,* 1956; and David Roberts, *Existentialism and Religious Belief,* 1957.) The growing attention, within the last decade, to the potential positive significance of analytical philosophy for theology reflects a comparable pattern of thought, though as yet the discussion belongs in the category of philosophy of religion, and the hope that the techniques of linguistic analysis may be used for refining theological concepts remains a hope. (See, e.g., John Hick, *Faith and Knowledge,* 1957; and Frederick Ferré, *Language, Logic and God,* 1960.)

It is evident that a common interest among these varying endeavors is that of theological apologetics or communication. Yet there is also a profound concern for systematic and constructive theological reformulation using categories drawn from diverse nontheological realms. Roger Hazelton, in a perceptive description of the present theological scene, has aptly called this "theology as conversation," in which the work of the theologian is consciously informed by his listening to nontheological voices, especially those of the arts, science, and philosophy (*New Accents in Contemporary Theology*, 1960, chaps. 1 and 2).

Like the neo-Reformation thought, this kind of theologizing reflects a heightened appreciation of the classical Christian affirmations, but it is less self-consciously directed to the revival of Reformation doctrines, exhibiting liberalism's sense of the urgency for new formulations. It is more distinctively characterized by the attempt to restate and revivify the theological tradition by explicit reference to one or another mode of contemporary thought. In this respect of course it stands in important continuity with liberalism, and with the long tradition of Christian thought in which philosophical patterns in particular have served as vehicles for theological construction— Platonic and Aristotelian, idealist and personalist, etc. So too the present program is elaborated most extensively in relation to contemporary philosophies.

Without question the most important representative (and source) of this contemporary theological style, and of the theology of culture movement in general, is Paul Tillich, whose *Systematic Theology*[3] must rank with Reinhold Niebuhr's *Nature and Destiny of Man* in significance for American theological scholarship in the present century. The term *theology of correlation* is drawn here from Tillich's now famous and much emulated "method of correlation."

In broad outline, Tillich's method calls for the correlation of the

---

3 Now completed in three volumes (1951, 1957, and 1963). See also *Biblical Religion and the Search for Ultimate Reality* (1955), *The Courage To Be* (1952), *Dynamics of Faith* (1957), *Love, Power, and Justice* (1954), *The Protestant Era* (1948), and *Theology of Culture* (1959). Useful interpretations of his work and a bibliography of his writings to March 1952 appear in *The Theology of Paul Tillich*, ed. C. W. Kegley and R. W. Bretall (1952). Abbreviations used in the text, in the order of titles listed here, are: *ST, BR, CB, DF, LPJ, PE, TC,* and *PT.*

kerygma—the unchangeable message within the Bible and the tradition, which is the substance and criterion of all theological statements—with the "situation"—defined by Tillich not simply as the present social or psychological state of things but as the totality of the forms of man's creative interpretation of himself and his world at a particular time. For Tillich this involves the widest possible range of relationships, with philosophy, psychology, the arts, science, politics, economics, etc., such that the theologian operates on the boundaries of all these disciplines. Nothing in culture is irrelevant, for "religion as ultimate concern is the meaning-giving substance of culture, and culture is the totality of forms in which the basic concern of religion expresses itself" (*TC*, p. 42; see also *PE*, chap. 4).

Tillich once said that he sought to stand theologically between Barth (representing, as Tillich sees it, an attempt at purely kerygmatic theology and a rejection of culture) and liberalism (often a capitulation to culture). Such an attempt entails synthesis of (1) the appeal to revelation as the basis of theology, recognition of man's estrangement from God and the demonic distortions of history, acceptance of the judgment of the cross and the authority of the scriptures, (2) liberalism's use of critical methods of New Testament study, its recognition of mythical and legendary elements in scripture, its refusal to separate theology from general culture, its acceptance of science, and its rejection of supernaturalism. Comparably, Tillich has resolutely tried to hold together as complementary and mutually corrective the Protestant principle of denying absoluteness to all finite authority and the Roman Catholic appreciation of sacrament and nature, of culture, and of the universality of grace. Separated, the prophetic and sacramental principles become demonic. Protestantism and Catholicism need each other, the former better preserving the indispensable protest, the latter better maintaining the substance of Christianity.

In working out the principle of correlation, Tillich draws on an enormous range of materials, but two types of thought are of special significance for him: existentialism, and the philosophy of identity (or estrangement within ultimate unity) as developed in Schelling's later thought, which Tillich sought to interpret in his three earliest major writings. One may be permitted to oversimplify by speaking of the special prominence of the existentialist element in a threefold way: in the analysis of the basic ontological structure from the self-world correlation (partly following Heidegger, see *ST*, vol. I); in an existentialist approach to sin and redemption through the concepts of anxiety, despair, etc. (see *CB* and *ST*, vol. II); and in the larger sense that valid theology is always "concerned" theology. The identity philosophy, which for Tillich is part of a great tradition of an ontological type of philosophy of religion—including Plato, Augustine, the thirteenth century Franciscans, Boehme, and Schleiermacher—may be said to have particular import for his doctrines of God, creation, and revelation, and for his insistence on ontological analysis. Yet the interweaving of the two modes is such that one might speak of Tillich's program as an "existentializing of ontology" and an "ontologizing of existentialism."

The method of correlation, as stated specifically by Tillich, requires the relating of answers to questions. Systematic theology is always at the same time apologetic theology and philosophical theology, though in a form different from traditional apologetics and philosophy of religion. The questions implicit in the situation are to be formulated by a philosophical analysis independent of theological controls. The theological answers derive from the unchangeable kerygma; they are formulated finally in terms of a norm or central principle taken from the Bible in the light of the situation and made the criterion for the interpretation of the whole of scripture. The answers are genuinely given *to* human existence, their content comes from the revelatory event, yet if they are really to be answers they must be shaped according to the form of the questions. What Tillich apparently means is that the perduring human condition is reflected in varying ways (situations) in different cultural epochs, and that the one ultimate answer requires corresponding formulations. Genuine correlation is the creative, luminous moment in which the truth of the Christian message becomes manifest in valid answers to the questions of human existence. Such a method has in fact been implicit in the history of the Christian theological enterprise, e.g., in the Reformation norm of justification by faith, but Tillich proposes to make it explicit and self-conscious. Thus he appeals deliberately (though not exclusively) to existentialist categories as best suited to formulation of the questions, and proposes the concept of the New Being, which he finds in Paul, as the appropriate norm for our day.

Tillich's program is undoubtedly the most impressive *explicit* theological method that has appeared in the recent American scene, and because of the way in which it concentrates characteristic American concerns and because of the creative power with which he has systematically developed it, it has become a focal point for debate and a decisive influence in theological development. In *Systematic Theology*, Tillich seeks to work out the method in five parts: Reason and Revelation, Being and God, Existence and the Christ, Life and the Spirit, and History and the Kingdom of God. In each is expressed the polarity of question (e.g., "Existence and the Quest for Christ") and answer (e.g., "The Reality of the Christ"). The critic may sometimes ask whether the method is carried out with complete fidelity, particularly with respect to the derivation of the answers from the kerygma, and whether the elements of the system are as interdependent as Tillich thinks, yet certainly in freshness of vision, in fertility of approach, and in the demand for unifying principles Tillich's *Systematic Theology* must be compared with Schleiermacher's epochal *The Christian Faith* and Karl Barth's *Church Dogmatics*.

The conciseness of the system, and the complex interrelation of its parts, make foolhardy any attempt to sketch the whole even briefly. I shall simply adumbrate some of the crucial and distinctive themes. The first is Tillich's attempt to bring together revelation and reason (see *ST,* vol. I, pp. 71 ff., and *BR*). Those who use the appeal to revelation as an excuse for attacking reason, he contends, falsely identify reason with the merely technical or controlling reason that is concerned only with the cognitive, with the relation of means to ends, with logical patterns of reasoning. To be sure, this is the typical modern idea of reason, but it is a narrow and dehumanized reason. In the classical view, from Parmenides to Hegel, an ontological concept of reason dominated, in which reason was conceived inclusively as "the structure of the mind which enables it to grasp and to transform reality." Reason so understood grasps ends as well as means, encompasses both the practical and the theoretical, the aesthetic and the cognitive, passion and detachment, subjectivity and objectivity —in short, the whole range of human existence (compare Coleridge's contrast of Reason and Understanding). Further, reason (*lo-*

gos) can so grasp reality because there is *logos* in reality, a "rational structure of reality" (objective reason) that corresponds to the "rational structure of the mind" (subjective reason). These point to a "depth of reason" that transcends reason's structures and is manifest in them as creative ground and that may metaphorically be described as "truth-itself," "beauty-itself," "justice-itself," "love-itself," and "being-itself," terms corresponding to the various areas of actualized reason.

A "question," however, arises from the fact that the depth of reason is hidden "under the conditions of existence." Reason in existence is involved in both finitude and ambiguity. (The term *existence* for Tillich almost invariably denotes ambiguous and estranged actuality, hence the vigor of his polemic against the idea that God "exists.") The depth of reason is expressed in the symbolic forms of myth and cult. In existence the proper polarities of reason are broken into contradictions, between "autonomous" and "heteronomous" reason, between the static and the dynamic, between the formal and the emotional. Therefore the conflicts of actual reason embody a quest for reintegration in the forms of "theonomy," of the concrete-absolute, and of the union of form and mystery. This is the quest for revelation, which appears not as a stranger to the demands of reason but as the manifestation of reason's own ground.

Second, in the understanding of God Tillich has resolutely tried to find a way beyond naturalism and supranaturalism. (See esp. *ST*, vol. I, pp. 235 ff.; *ST*, vol. II, pp. 5 ff.; *CB*, pp. 182 ff.) Of the two, he sees the greater danger in supranaturalism, particularly as expressed in popular theism, where God is made a highest (yet essentially finite) being alongside other beings, and a world of divine objects is posited. Such a God is met only as a stranger to man's own being, the knowledge of him is uncertain, and his action is conceived as contravening the natural order. Against this "God" the protest of atheism is justified, in the interest of the "God above God." Naturalism is right in its criticisms of supranaturalism. No breach in the natural order is to be allowed. God is rather "being-itself," or "ground" or "power" of being; he is nearer to things than they are to themselves.

Yet the words *God* and *universe* are not interchangeable. "God as the ground of being infinitely transcends that of which he is the

255

ground" (*ST,* vol. II, p. 7). The relation of God to finite beings must be expressed by *both* symbols: substance (indicating unity) and causality (indicating separation), though the distinction is overcome in the more adequate symbol of "creative and abysmal ground of being." The clearest specification that Tillich has offered for transcendence is in the idea of finite freedom: "The divine transcendence is identical with the freedom of the created to turn away from the essential unity with the creative ground of its being" (*ST,* vol. II, p. 8). Yet, paradoxically, the created both "is substantially independent of" and "remains in substantial unity with" the divine ground.

This highly dialectical conception of the relation of God and the world, in which the underlying unity is not destroyed in spite of estrangement, is crucial for many aspects of Tillich's system. It is basic to his view of revelation, for the possibility of knowing God derives from the ultimate unity of the knower with God. It appears in his view of sin, as Tillich speaks of the coincidence of creation and fall, such that "fully developed creatureliness is fallen creatureliness" (*ST,* vol. I, p. 255). To exist is to stand outside the divine life in estrangement from essential being, and such actualization of freedom is "as much a matter of destiny as it is a matter of freedom" (*ST,* vol. I, p. 256). Yet destiny is not the contradiction but the corollary of freedom, and sin is not created. Sin is not a "structural necessity" and the transition cannot be fully demythologized into a dialectical movement.

The dialectic of God and the world is also operative in Tillich's influential analysis of "symbol." (See esp. *TC,* chap. 5; *ST,* vol. I, pp. 235 ff.) He has wavered on the question whether one nonsymbolic statement about God can be made, namely that God is being-itself, but has otherwise insisted on the symbolic character of all religious affirmations. Symbols are never "mere" symbols. While they are living (they are born and die), symbols open up "reality" and the "soul" so as to manifest levels of reality otherwise obscured by the ambiguities and distortions of existence. For example, although the symbol "personal God" cannot be taken literally, it is essential both because persons inescapably use personal symbols in reference to the ground of being and because God is the ground of the personal. The crucial thing is that symbols "participate in" or express the power of the reality they symbolize. They manifest the dimension of the holy and (when not made ultimate in themselves and thereby demonic) point to what transcends them.

Tillich's understanding of God is most inclusively reflected in his view of religion as the "dimension of depth" in the whole of man's spiritual life rather than as a special function. Religion cannot possibly be understood as a matter of relation to a divine being or beings, whose existence the theologian asserts and the scientist denies. It refers to what is ultimate or unconditional in all the functions of life—moral, cognitive, aesthetic, and emotional. Faith is thus properly understood as "concern for the ultimate," which can be expressed even in doubt, since the question of the ultimate could not arise apart from a primordial awareness of it. (See esp. *TC,* chap. 1; *DF, passim.*)

Tillich's Christology is ordered by the concept of the New Being appearing under the conditions of existence. In part this implies a restatement of the classical Christian view of the human condition in generally existentialist categories, i.e., in terms of estrangement, finitude, guilt, suffering, loneliness, doubt, meaninglessness, despair, etc. In the analysis of man's predicament, Tillich finds existentialism "a natural ally" (*ST,* vol. II, p. 27). To speak of the New Being in Jesus as the Christ is to affirm that the conflicts, corruptions, and despair of estrangement are overcome in a personal life. Jesus participated in the tragic element of life but in him finite freedom was actualized in such a way that estrangement from God did not occur. The New Being is thence the power of salvation or healing as men are grasped by and participate in it, accept it and are transformed by it.

On the side of soteriology, then, the novelty of Tillich's elaboration consists mainly in the brilliance and perceptiveness of restatement of classical themes in new language. It is with respect to "incarnation" that he most sharply urges revision. Instead of the idea of a unity of divine and human natures, or the "nonsensical" statement that God has become man, we are to think in "relational concepts" of "eternal God-man-unity" or "eternal God-Manhood" (*ST,* vol. II, pp. 94, 148). Elsewhere Tillich has spoken of the equivalence of God-manhood and essential manhood. The presupposition of this is the underlying unity of God and man in "pure essentiality or potentiality" in the divine life, which is disrupted but not destroyed in es-

257

trangement and which in Jesus as the Christ is actualized in freedom. Thus the prime category for interpreting the work and the person of Christ is that of manifestation, of "transparency to the divine," of the appearance "under the conditions of existence" of the truth of man's essential relation to the ground of being. And the overcoming of estrangement consists finally in Jesus' complete surrender of himself by which he does not lose himself but maintains his unity with God, becoming thereby the bearer of the New Being.

A lifelong problem for Tillich, and a point of no small ambiguity in his earlier writings, has been the relation of faith to the factual element in the story of Jesus. The difficulty seems to be generated especially by two related aspects of modern (especially German) biblical criticism: the paucity of what can be known about "the Jesus of history" and, more basically, the recognition that historical method does not finally permit a separation of the factual element from the interpretative gospel record. Tillich's consistent thesis has been that the certainty of faith cannot be allowed to depend upon the latest conclusions of the biblical critics. (Here he stands with Kierkegaard, though Tillich's ontological and epistemological scheme provides him in another way with a kind of certainty quite lacking in Kierkegaard.) In more recent writings (*ST*, vol. II; see also *PT*, pp. 230 ff.), Tillich is explicit that the New Testament witness does refer to a concrete human individuality that was of such a nature as to support the biblical picture (e.g., the crucifixion of Jesus appears to be essential to faith). Yet the particular traits of that individuality can never be matters of certainty, but only of degrees of probability. The certainty of faith therefore attaches to what is mediated in the biblical portrait, the reality of the New Being: "Faith itself is the immediate (not mediated by conclusions) evidence of the New Being within and under the conditions of existence" (*ST*, vol. II, p. 114). "Faith is based on the experience of being grasped by the power of the New Being through which the destructive consequences of estrangement are conquered. It is the certainty of one's own victory over the death of existential estrangement which created the certainty of the Resurrection of the Christ as event and symbol" (*ST*, vol. II, p. 155). Thus the weight of Christological affirmation is thrown heavily to the side of Christ *for us*.

In this way of dealing with the problem of faith and history in the affirmation about Jesus, a problem that has been a center of much confusion and debate in recent years, Tillich sounds a theme that is a leitmotif of a much more self-consciously existentialist theology. An intensive correlation of theology and existentialism has been most notably developed in Europe, especially by Rudolf Bultmann, for whom the categories of Heidegger are decisive, and by Friedrich Gogarten. In American scholarship, a vigorous and original endeavor to state theology in existentialist terms appears in Carl Michalson's *The Hinge of History: An Existential Approach to the Christian Faith* (1959). To the emphases of Bultmann and Gogarten, Michalson assimilates an imaginative extension of a distinction between "inner" and "outer" history first made popular by H. Richard Niebuhr. The proper categories for Christianity are those of *history* rather than nature or ontology. More specifically, Christianity is uniquely characterized by an "eschatological history" in which the crucial event of the resurrection (and so the entire career of Jesus) has its proper locus in the confrontation of man *in the present.* Interest in happenedness in chronological time is superseded by attention to the present event in which personal existence and history (as a way of viewing things) are transformed or become "authentic." In another vein, Michalson also finds contemporary existentialism useful in exposing the depth of the human predicament and so in propaedeutically destroying the lesser gods and opening a way for acknowledgment of the "God beyond all gods" who makes himself known not as "a being" but as the "source and possibility" of all beings. With this is conjoined a penetrating analysis of the meaning of transcendence and immanence, not as opposites but as mutually involved in the presence of the "hidden" God.

Correlation of Theology and Process Philosophy

A second principal direction of scholarship in which the theme of correlation occurs is evident in a variety of efforts to use elements of process philosophy, particularly that of A. N. Whitehead, for theological construction. Nowhere has this been more marked than in the later development of the "Chicago school," to which Wieman was interpreting the significance of Whitehead as early as the mid-1920's. To empiricism and environmentalism were quite naturally joined the emphasis on process and a metaphysical view in which God and the world are dialectically interrelated. This complex of ideas in turn has been enriched by a growing interest in reappropriating classical Christian concepts of the human problem and its resolution.

Henry Nelson Wieman's later thought reflects this transition. In his best work, *The Source of Human Good* (1946), the polemic against supernaturalism is far less intense than in his earlier writings. That the traditional notions of the ontological transcendence and personal nature of God are mythical is still explicitly maintained, but positive delineation of the immanently real and experienced working of God takes clearer priority over negative circumscription of the mystery beyond. The center of interest is the real truth for which the Christian myth served as a means of devotion, namely the "creative event" or "creative good" itself, and the process by which creative good overcomes the domination of created good (fixed structures of good). "Functionally transcendent" creative good alone is absolute good under all circumstances; it is self-identical, unlimited in demand, not relative to human desire or even to human existence, and therefore absolutely trustworthy. Thus Wieman combines what D. D. Williams has called a "high calvinistic theological vision" with an insistence that the Christian story reflects a real struggle of sin and salvation in which creative event has been victorious from the creation of the living cell to the (so far supreme) creation of the living Christ in history.

From the same general school, Bernard E. Meland, in his writings since 1945 (esp. *Faith and Culture,* 1953), has proposed a "reconstructed liberalism" that finds in the new metaphysics (as developed by C. Lloyd Morgan, S. Alexander, and J. Smuts as well as Whitehead) a more adequate means both of generalizing scientific categories (especially concerning the evolutionary process) and of taking into account the depth and disturbance of experience that faith discloses. Similarly, rapport can be established with biblical imagery. Thus may be overcome the fatal mistake of liberalism, its "disassociation from the Christian myth." Hence a reconstruction is possible that makes significant contact with the revival of Reformation theology, and Meland has attempted such a reconstruction in an analysis of faith as a "motif of culture" and a "resource of psychic energy within the human spirit."

A far more rigorous and explicit use of aspects of Whiteheadian metaphysics for theological reformulation is found in the panentheism of the philosopher Charles Hartshorne. (See John E. Smith's essay on "Philosophy of Religion" in this volume.) In *Man's Vision of God* (1941), *The Divine Relativity* (1948), and *Reality as Social Process* (1953), he counters the traditional (Thomistic) view of God as simply absolute and nonrelative with a conception of God and the world as mutually necessary to each other, of God as supremely related and continually surpassing himself by enjoyment of all values of other individuals. Such a view is urged as logically consistent, metaphysically adequate, and far more appropriate to the religious affirmation of God's knowledge and love.

Strong elements of correlation with patterns of Whiteheadian thought appear in several other major works of theological reconstruction, particularly in respect to the doctrine of God. Nels F. S. Ferré's best writing, *The Christian Understanding of God* (1951), while centrally a part of his effort to interpret the whole range of Christian thought by the category of agape (as the decisive New Testament idea of love), draws much from Whitehead in arguing that love as ultimate being is both "being" and "becoming." W. Norman Pittenger finds "process-thought," with its view of the "continued and intimate relationship" of God and creation, of particular value in shaping a doctrine of incarnation, according to which "it is possible to state clearly and definitively that our Lord is not an intruder into the creation, . . . but is tied in with and expressive of the whole God-world and God-man relationship, even while he is also genuinely new and the saviour from sin" (*The Word Incarnate,* 1959, p. 156).

Perhaps the most illuminating of the works that could be cited here is Daniel D. Williams' *God's Grace and Man's Hope* (1949). In his total perspective Williams is doubtless closer to the attitude of what I shall call critical orthodoxy. He has also consciously and effectively played the role of mediator between liberalism and its critics, and provides important indication of the way in which themes of liberal theology have been taken up in recent styles of thought. Yet he has maintained a special appreciation for the value of process philosophies in theological reconstruction, and in addition to "the principle that all knowledge, without exception, is derived from a critical interpretation of what is given in human experience," he also commits himself to "the conception of God which emerges when God is interpreted in a metaphysics of *process* as over against a metaphysics of static being" (p. 41). In respect to the latter area, Williams' own estimate of the situation vividly illustrates the thrust of scholarship I have been sketching: "Under the impact of modern science our world view has been shifting in the past three hundred years. A new metaphysical orientation has emerged. It finds varied expressions in the philosophies of Whitehead, Bergson, Wieman, Hartshorne and others, in which the concept of process is held to be the most general and fundamental idea which we can apply to anything we know. To be anything is to be an active functioning reality entering into dynamic relations with other things. Now a philosophical theology which takes process as its basic category has one supreme advantage over the metaphysical systems in which Christian thought has traditionally been expressed. This philosophy makes it possible for the Living God, the God who acts, the caring, saving God of the Bible to be made intelligible. . . . To think of God as acting in dynamic relation to His creatures not merely as one actor among many, but as the universal creative power which sustains all things, and without which they could neither be nor act, is true to what our best knowledge of the world tells us. It is true to the insight of the Bible, which the philosophical tradition has tended to obscure behind the impassive mask of absolute, static being" (pp. 41 f.).

Critical Orthodoxy—H. Richard Niebuhr

In our analysis of recently developed "traditions" of theological scholarship, it is easy to see that the lines of distinction do not remain firm or precise. We have been dealing less with self-conscious and consistently articulated schools than with patterns of theological exploration that come into focus in some instances of particular significance but that are also widely diffused throughout contemporary Protestant thought. While it is fashionable among theological students and uncritical observers to speak of "Niebuhrians," "Tillichians," "existentialists," and "process theologians," such captions have only strictly limited validity as symbolizing styles of approach, clusters of problems that appear central, and preferred categories of interpretation. Significant tension does emerge over the relative appropriateness of "metaphysical" or "ontological" versus "historical" categories, in which Tillich and those influenced by Whitehead stand against Reinhold Niebuhr and the more explicitly existentialist thinkers—a tension as yet unresolved and one whose importance should not be minimized. But on both sides of this issue are to be found revivals of Reformation theology and patterns of correlation theology.

The situation is similar for a third sort of theological perspective, which is perhaps more inclusive and less readily definable than those previously described, but not less important as indicative of the character of recent scholarship. Like neo-Reformation theologies, it is marked by vigorous reappropriation of classical Christian themes, but with less strict orientation toward specific Reformation concepts. Unlike the theologies of correlation, it is less easily associated with special contemporary modes of articulation. Yet evidently both Reformation principles and the profound desire to speak to the modern world are co-present components.

This critical orthodoxy, as I shall call it, is characterized by less animus toward liberalism than is present in some neo-Reformation types of thought (especially those of the European variety). Indeed, it includes what some interpreters would prefer to call a chastened evangelical liberalism. Yet the distinctive complex of liberal theology's doctrinal emphases has not persisted (see my discussion of Theological Reorientation, pp. 237 ff.). And where liberalism was apologetic about the creeds and the biblical symbols, this theology is happy to rediscover their meaning and continuing relevance. It is impressed less by the newness of an epoch in which the past formulations must be radically revised and new principles of authority articulated than by the perduring validity of the central theological traditions. In this sense it may be called kerygmatic and orthodox. Yet this is plainly a *critical* orthodoxy, incorporating many of the concerns of liberalism, its historicocritical approach to scripture, its interest in relevance to culture, etc., and there is an openness to new symbols that will not replace but will interpret the classic statements. Further, this critical orthodoxy is distinguished from its European counterpart by much less concern to identify a *depositum fidei* or body of revealed truth or unchanging doctrinal content.

A special role is played in this theology by the ecumenical movement, which, notably since World War II, has become of increasing importance for the context in which theological work (both Roman Catholic and Protestant) is carried on. Thus this theology is markedly a "church" theology.

The most creative and fruitful work reflecting the temper of a critical orthodoxy, both in its commitment to and its freedom from the tradition, has been that of H. Richard Niebuhr.[4] This is not necessarily to say that Niebuhr stands precisely in the center of this movement of thought. Some of his later writings (e.g., *RMWC*) suggest that the term *orthodoxy* is less appropriate to him than the term *critical*. Yet such a judgment must take account of Niebuhr's unusual self-consciousness as a theologian (see below) and his own frequent use of the designation *critical orthodoxy* for a theological tradition with which he patently wished to associate himself.

Like his brother Reinhold, H. R. Niebuhr began his major publication in the area of social criticism (*The Social Sources of Denominationalism*, 1929) and has not been "by profession" a systematic theologian. Rather, as a Christian ethicist he has often approached theological problems explicitly from the standpoint of ethical reflection (see e.g., the exciting Christological statement in terms of the "virtues" of Christ, *CC*, pp. 14 ff.). He is, however, an extraordinarily sensitive interpreter of theological development, as is evident in *Christ and Culture*, in the essay on "Sören Kierkegaard" in *Christianity and the Existentialists* (ed. Carl Michalson, 1956), and in *The Kingdom of God in America* (1937—still the most profound *theological* interpretation of Protestantism in America). And he has been highly self-conscious of his theological "stance," sympatheti-

---

[4] The writings of special significance for our discussion are *The Meaning of Revelation* (1941), *Christ and Culture* (1951), *Radical Monotheism and Western Civilization* (1960), and *The Responsible Self* (1963). In a Festschrift for Niebuhr, *Faith and Ethics* (ed. Paul Ramsey, 1957), are several essays bearing on Niebuhr's thought; see especially the two chapters by Hans W. Frei. Abbreviations used are: *MR, CC,* and *RMWC.*

cally interpreting Barth and the theology of crisis when liberalism was dominant, and more recently reasserting the values of liberalism in face of an apparent return to uncritical orthodoxy. In the mid-1930's, opposing culture-Christianity, he contributed to a manifesto declaring the inner integrity and independence of the church (*The Church Against the World*, 1935); having made that point in the theological scene, he later sought to restore the balance by insisting on the relevance of Christ to culture and by protesting against theological and churchly isolationism and self-centeredness. Niebuhr's concern for balance and wholeness is also reflected in the interplay in his thought of the widest range of theological sources—to the Puritan background of American religion and the German theological tradition from Schleiermacher to Troeltsch and Barth must be added such names as Josiah Royce, S. T. Coleridge, F. D. Maurice, Martin Buber, and Kierkegaard, plus the major Christian thinkers from Justin Martyr through the Reformation.

Out of this has come no system of theology, but a distinctive theological perspective developed in statements on particular themes that are unsurpassed in profundity and originality. The subtlety of Niebuhr's thought and the great care for expression that marks every line of his writing tend to make any summary analysis seem to be mere caricature, even more than similar summaries of Tillich and Reinhold Niebuhr. But an attempt may be made to identify features of prime significance for theological reconstruction by designating several continuing motifs in Niebuhr's writings.

The first is his insistence that theology is relational. This means at least two things (see esp. *MR*, pp. 7 ff; *CC*, pp. 234 ff.). It means historical and social relativity of knowledge, such that every religious affirmation is made from a particular locus in history and experience (here Troeltsch is much in the background). This does not entail subjectivism or skepticism, for what is viewed from a historical standpoint is a reality (God); it entails only that the point of view can never be taken as absolute. Further, there is a "religious relativism." God and faith belong together: "One can speak and think significantly about God only from the point of view of faith in Him" (*MR*, p. 23). Here Luther's stress on God as always God *for us*, Schleiermacher's view of God as the counterpart of the experience of absolute dependence, and a *social* existentialism come together with Niebuhr's defense of a relational theory of value as a clue to theological method. Theology is always "interested," never "neutral."

In view of this, Niebuhr develops a conception of revelation that offers a major alternative both to traditional views and to the vague modern attempts to denote revelation simply as God's personal presence (revelation of "himself" rather than information about himself) or "act" or "event plus appreciation." "Revelation means for us that part of our inner history which illuminates the rest of it and which is itself intelligible" (*MR,* p. 93). In this statement the locus of revelation is identified as history, and more precisely "inner history" as distinguished from "external history." The latter distinction, which has been widely appropriated by others, refers to the difference between history as lived and appreciated, in which value is "worth for selves," and history as viewed from the outside, from the standpoint of the neutral spectator. The difference is not one of "truth" versus "falsehood." It is a matter rather of perspective and value in the relation of persons and events, of a turn to fundamental questions of the self's being or nonbeing. Further, revelation in history is communal rather than private; events are revelatory only as one participates in the community that remembers them as decisive for its life. One moves in a decision of faith "from observed to lived history" and finds in those remembered occasions both the ultimate object of devotion (to be a self is to have a history and a God) and meaning for life.

Thus, finally, revelation is "the discovery of rational pattern" in life. For Niebuhr, the reason that so apprehends is the practical reason (cf. Pascal, Coleridge, and Kierkegaard). It is reason joined with imagination, i.e., reason that employs images in its apprehension and symbolization, especially the images of self and dramatic action. Hence revelation may be described as "that special occasion which provides us with an image by means of which all the occasions of personal and common life become intelligible" (*MR,* p. 109). The occasion of Jesus Christ, for the Christian community, illumines with unity and significance the whole past, including its (our) betrayals and follies. The life and death of Christ becomes the "rational image" for understanding the present and the opportunity for discovering generalized concepts of sin, forgiveness, reconciliation, obedience, the meaning of suffering, etc. And that occasion becomes the means of discerning the "whither" of our existence, the possibility of resurrection and new community.

Among the further aspects of Niebuhr's thought that are intimately involved with his view of revelation, two lie close at hand. One is his consistent refusal to deal with metaphysical questions about God, or to talk about the being of God "in himself." The extent of this rejection is not wholly clear. Obviously, any effort to speak of the being of God apart from the viewpoint of faith, in an uncommited speculative way, is systematically precluded as irrelevant and worse. *God* means an object of loyalty. But whether Niebuhr intends to forbid all attempts to treat of God, from within the context of faith, in ontological terms, or whether he only prefers not to do this himself, is not evident. In any case, the primacy must always be given to a knowledge of God that views him relationally or valuationally.

Second, theology must remain "confessional" and not become "apologetic." Every attempt to speak from a neutral ground erroneously supposes that God can be talked about apart from faith. And every effort to establish superiority for Christian faith reveals unfaithful self-defensiveness and is inherently self-contradictory in seeking to escape from the relational situation of revelation; "revelation and the 'claim of the Christian religion to universal empire over the souls of men' are absolute incompatibles" (*MR*, p. 40). Niebuhr is convinced that "self-defense is the most prevalent source of error in all thinking and perhaps especially in theology and ethics" (*MR*, p. viii). The theologian properly speaks from within the community of faith as one who is justified only by grace.

The confessional form of theology is necessitated even more by the nature of the object of Christian faith, the God who is apprehended in the self-emptying of Christ and who is the only universal sovereign. Any effort to attribute sovereignty to Christianity involves attaching to the point of view of faith an ultimacy that belongs only to him who is viewed in faith. Here is Niebuhr's "radical monotheism" (see esp. *RMWC;* and *MR,* chap. 4). It is the "deity of God" that ultimately demands and makes possible the acceptance of relativities. "Just because faith knows of an absolute standpoint it can therefore accept the relativity of the believer's situation and knowledge." With faith "in the infinite Absolute" men "can make their confessions and decisions both with confidence and with the humility which accepts completion and correction and even conflict from and with others who stand in the same relation to the Absolute. They will then in their fragmentary knowledge be able to state with conviction what they have seen and heard, the truth for them; but they will not contend that it is the whole truth and nothing but the truth, and they will not become dogmatists unwilling to seek out what other men have seen and heard of that same object they have fragmentarily known" (*CC*, pp. 239, 238).

Radical monotheism therefore means for the church a continual process of mutual correction and learning, a recognition of the partiality of the view of each (here Niebuhr finds in F. D. Maurice an especially kindred spirit). It makes imperative a continuing reformation in which tendencies to make faith (or experience or ecclesiastical structures or symbols) the object are overcome by the redirecting of attention to the infinite object, in which the sovereignty of the God of Jesus Christ over the church is again affirmed. Here Niebuhr joins Barth in protest against the subjectivism of liberalism. But at the same time Niebuhr finds in this the warrant for the quest for new symbols. In our period of great religious void—in which there may be a revival of "desire for faith and hope for hope," but not yet of "faith in God and hope of glory"—"our old phrases are worn out; they have become clichés by means of which we can neither grasp nor communicate the reality of our existence before God." Thus Niebuhr looks "for a resymbolization of the message and life of faith in the One God" (*Christian Century*, March 2, 1960, pp. 250 f.).

The reminder of the church to itself is not finally different from its witness to the world. Radical monotheism is contrasted with *all* the "natural" polythesistic and henotheistic faiths of men—whether these be "religions" or faiths in nation or society, etc. In *Radical Monotheism and Western Civilization,* Niebuhr put this especially in reference to the social faiths of modern Western culture. "For radical monotheism, the value-center is no closed society or the principle of such a society, but the principle of being itself; its reference is to no one reality among the many, but to One beyond all the many, whence all the many derive their being, and by participation in which they exist" (*RMWC*, pp. 27 f.). As the "principle of value," the one God is "that by reference to which all things have their value." In language less abstract and closer to our existence as selves, the ultimate is the first person, who is known in revelation less as an essence or principle than as a faithful self to whom fidelity ought to be expressed in every role and relation. The consequence of loyalty to God, so understood, is the transcendence of all partial loyalties in a more inclusive loyalty. Not only loyalty to nation or humanity, but even "reverence for life" is too narrow. "Radical monotheism dethrones all absolutes short of the principle of being itself. At the same time it reverences every relative existent" (*RMWC*, p. 34).

The inclusiveness required by radical monotheism is expressed also in Niebuhr's novel and imaginative reinterpretation of the trinitarian symbol, which seems to have become of increasing importance for him. The trinitarian idea is not a description of the inner divine being but an inclusive denotation of the unity of God in view of varying ways in which he is partially apprehended. In the history of the church, trinitarianism has been a protest against recurrent tendencies to exclusiveness in "practical" unitarianisms: unitarianism of the Father, which is the worship of the creator God of nature and natural theology; unitarianism of the Son, in which Jesus Christ alone becomes God; and unitarianism of the Spirit, in which God is simply the immanent divine spirit in men. Each of these springs from convictions legitimate within the church, but taken alone each is not only partial but distorted. The doctrine of the Trinity is therefore a statement of the inclusive faith of the whole church. It is "a synthesized formula in which all the partial insights and convictions are combined" ("The Doctrine of the Trinity and the Unity of the Church," *Theology Today,* vol. III, no. 3, p. 383).

A special theme of this inclusive trinitarianism is the relation of the power and the goodness of the creator (and in turn the relation of nature and history). Protesting with growing sharpness against "Christomonism," in which everything is purportedly given simply in Jesus Christ and theology becomes only Christology (Karl Barth is seen as a prime example of this, along with much Christocentric theology of the church), Niebuhr insists on the confrontation by God also outside Jesus Christ, since all life is lived in relation to the one God either in trust or in distrust. Apart from Jesus Christ, God confronts us as the creator of nature, as power that is even active hostility, defeating all things. Even in Christ he is met as slayer (the crucifixion). Hence for Niebuhr, theology must in the first instance be theocentric rather than Christocentric. Yet in Jesus Christ that faith in God (as power only) is converted by being united with the conviction of God's goodness. The power that is the source and government of all things is recognized as utterly faithful and loving, loyal even to disloyalty, the Father in whom unequivocal trust may be placed. Thus while insisting on inner *history* as the sphere in which revelation occurs, Niebuhr is unwilling to abandon *nature* as an area of theological concern. And the Trinity is an inclusive answer to the questions of the goodness of the Creator, of the power of Jesus Christ, and of whether there is a *Holy* Spirit among the spirits, hence an answer of radical *mono*-theism.

Yet this is by no means to decry the decisive place of Jesus Christ for Christian faith; he remains the illuminating occasion, the converter of natural religions. In *The Meaning of Revelation* the theme of internal and external history seemed to imply an avoidance of the traditional question of the two natures of Christ in favor of epistemological considerations, i.e., of the ways of understanding a historical occasion. In *Christ and Culture,* however, the suggestions "Toward a Definition of Christ" (pp. 11 ff.) go much further toward a statement of the content of Christology and Niebuhr moves to more direct treatment of the person of Christ than marked his earlier discussion. He proposes to offer only one, a moral, interpretation of Christ, which cannot be claimed to be any better than others (e.g., metaphysical or historical) and needs complementation by them. But just in this, by delineating the virtues of Christ as virtues made radical by being wholly directed to God and thereby making him genuinely mediatorial between God and man, Niebuhr offers one of the few novel and fruitful reinterpretations of Christology that have recently appeared.

Implicit in the motifs so far adumbrated is Niebuhr's conviction that Christianity is *metanoia,* repentance understood as "permanent revolution" or continuing reformation. This may be said to describe the relation of revelation in Christ to cultural faiths. And reformation is repeatedly necessary within Christianity for the sake of radical monotheism, as Christianity tends toward henotheism in the forms of church-centeredness or mere Christ-centeredness.

Niebuhr's understanding of this may be more specifically indicated by the idea, set forth in *Christ and Culture,* of Christ as the "converter." The main point of the book, of course, is the analysis of the variety of patterns of relation between obligation to Christ and obligation to cultural communities that have been affirmed in Christian thinking and acting. These patterns are reflected in a broad range of ideas, including theological conceptions of revelation and reason, of sin, of law and grace, and creation and redemption.

Five general types of ideas are discerned. The two extreme views of the Christ-culture relationship dissolve the tension either by abandoning the "world" as simply opposed to Christ or by seeing Christ as the culmination of cultural aspirations ("Christ Against Culture" and "The Christ of Culture"). Such views have found expression ever since the New Testament and reflect legitimate elements of Christian conviction, but are patently less adequate than the three median types in which the tension is preserved. In the synthetic type —e.g., Thomas Aquinas—Christ is the fulfillment of culture but not simply continuous with it; the supernatural and the natural are related in a harmonious, hierarchical structure ("Christ above Culture"). In the dualistic type—e.g., Luther—the sense of conflict between life in Christ and life in culture is vivid, but the obligation of the latter is acknowledged in a life of continuing tension and hope for eschatological resolution ("Christ and Culture in Paradox"). In the conversionist type—e.g., Augustine and Calvin—while culture is seen as deeply corrupted, the redeemer is recognized as also the creator, and Christ is the converter of man *in* culture and society, in a process of redemption that is partially actual even in the present ("Christ the Transformer of Culture").

Of the mediating answers, Niebuhr unquestionably leans toward the conversionist, yet he is quite unwilling to call it the normative pattern for theology. Nor could he do so consistently with radical monotheism and a relational theology. One's theological conclusions must be arrived at in free decision in a responsible community. At least the three mediating answers are recognizably within the main stream of Christian thought, and all of them Niebuhr traces with profound sympathy and insight into their major manifestations from ancient to modern times.

Nowhere is the temper of a critical orthodoxy better exemplified than in this approach to the theological tradition. Moreover, we see here the fundamentally ecumenical character of a critically orthodox theology—not in the narrow sense of being especially influenced by the modern "ecumenical movement," though that is also a factor for some who share this perspective, but in the broader sense of a theologizing conducted consciously in the presence of, and in responsibility to, the whole community of believers, past and present.

Obviously, no attempt should be made to attribute such an "ecumenicity in time and space" exclusively to one theological style. Yet the mood and intention here indicated do seem to establish a community of interest for a variety of important special studies (as well as a number of relatively popular works). Daniel D. Williams' *God's Grace and Man's Hope* might well be viewed in this perspective. In George S. Hendry's *The Gospel of the Incarnation* (1958) a highly illuminating historical analysis forms the matrix for what is probably the most penetrating analysis of the problem of a modern doctrine of atonement, namely, the question of finding an equivalent for the patristic understanding that work of God in the *humanity* of Christ involves actually (and not merely potentially) the existence of all men, and thence of showing "how that which was accomplished by Christ in the historical work of his incarnate life can be transmitted, conveyed, actualized in the present and communicated to men today" (p. 20). Roger Hazelton, in *God's Way with Man* (1956) outlines an imaginative approach to restatement of the idea of providence, not as an explanation of divine ordering of the cosmos but (in a broadly existentialist way) through the identification of aspects of personal apprehension of the mystery of God's sovereign concern for man, as expressed particularly in divine permission, concurrence or assistance, and approval. Richard Reinhold Niebuhr, in *Resurrection and Historical Reason* (1957), contends for a reconstruction in theological method that, taking the resurrection as the touchstone for an adequate method, can overcome the dichotomies of history and nature, internal and external history, etc., by offering more profound understandings of both history and nature.

Among the studies in which a critical orthodoxy is joined by the distinctive influence of the contemporary ecumenical movement, partly as providing the explicit context for reflection and partly as bringing to the fore certain theological problems (notably the nature of the church and Christology), W. Norman Pittenger's *The Incarnate Word* must be noted again. So also, Walter M. Horton's *Christian Theology: An Ecumenical Approach* (1955), while less a work of theological reconstruction than a summary of consensus and diversity, is symptomatic of the recent importance of the modern ecumenical context.[5] My own book, *The Reality of the Church* (1958), deals directly with a theme of one of the Faith and Order Commissions of the World Council of Churches (the interrelation of the doctrines of Christ and the Spirit and of the church), developing an analogy between the person of Christ and the nature of the church and attempting a positive theological employment of sociological views of the church in interpreting its humanness as sociohistorical community. (Another work of mine, *In This Name,* 1952, also reflects this theology in its attempt at a critical reconstruction of trinitarian doctrine, though with overly great dependence on Karl Barth.)

In a suggestive and fresh study of the idea of tradition, *The Christian Tradition and the Unity We Seek* (1957), Albert C. Outler also speaks explicitly to the problem of the unity of the church as this is posed by the ecumenical movement. With fine historical perspective, Outler cuts beneath the familiar Protestant counterposing of scripture and tradition by a more profound understanding of the total process of "traditioning," as the act of handing over (*actus tradendi*) in history of what was originally "handed over" to the existence of men as the gift of grace in Christ (the *traditum*). Thus it is possible to come to a view of the essential unity of scripture and Christian tradition. Just at this point, a most important contact is made with elements of recent Roman Catholic scholarship. Of particular significance, from the Catholic side, is George H. Tavard's *Holy Writ or Holy Church* (1959), which is principally a detailed

---

[5] It is now hardly possible to theologize without some reference to the ecumenical movement. In contrast, of the twenty-three contributors to Ferm's two volumes, *Contemporary American Theology* (1932, 1933), only two found this worthy of mention.

273

historical study with special emphasis on the Reformation and the Council of Trent, but which has also significant implications for rapprochement of Catholic and Protestant views, by showing that the Council did not, as interpreters have commonly supposed, designate scripture and tradition as parallel individually incomplete (therefore quasi-independent and supplementary) sources, but implied an interpretation of the two as coinherent or concentric.

❧

Neofundamentalism or the New Conservatism

I have suggested that the scholarship of fundamentalism came to an end, or at least faded from view, after the work of J. G. Machen. The past decade and a half, however, has seen a notable renewal of patterns of thought continuous with the central theological commitments of fundamentalism. It is too much to say that this represents as yet a major body of scholarship, but at least there is present here a significant and self-conscious *program* of scholarship that seeks, in the tradition of Machen and B. B. Warfield, a statement and defense of Christian orthodoxy with intellectual rigor. (In addition to the works mentioned below, see, e.g., the *Westminster Theological Journal*.) To call this simply orthodoxy or conservatism, though, would be to use a term far too broad and flexible. The orthodoxy here defended is that of the sixteenth and seventeenth century Protestant (especially Reformed) confessions.

The decisive issues, identified earlier in this essay as the inerrancy or plenary inspiration of scripture and the supernaturalistic conception of God and the world, are again clearly in view. But the program also embodies sharp criticism of the earlier fundamentalist patterns. The defensiveness that found expression even in Machen is replaced by a new self-confidence in a post-World War II situation that is judged more receptive to orthodoxy. The tendencies toward anti-intellectualism and cultural isolation, which infected the earlier movement and even more its subsequent stridently fideistic varieties (epitomized in the summary rejection of the Revised Standard Version of the Bible), are opposed in the interest of scholarship, social responsibility, and active participation in the broader contemporary debate. The divisiveness of the extreme movement, which exalted

274

"truth" at the expense of love and Christian community, is overcome by a broader principle of doctrinal unity and by a growing concern for the unity of the church. Against the rigidity, intolerance, and doctrinaire thinking of radical fundamentalism is set a partial recognition of difficulties in the position, difficulties especially in the relating of science and the scriptural record and in the clarification of the idea of inspiration itself.

Further, the present program is marked by an attempt to unite the important theological emphases of earlier fundamentalism with the continuing strains of Reformed and Lutheran orthodoxy, both in America and in Europe (support has been forthcoming largely from the Calvinist side). In addition to conservative nineteenth century theology and the early twentieth century work of Warfield and Machen, that continuing American orthodoxy is seen especially in the work of Louis Berkhof. Berkhof's *Reformed Dogmatics* (4 vols., 1932-37), while basically a textbook and a comprehensive manual of Calvinist orthodoxy, has nonetheless a breadth of perspective on the development of modern theology and a notably clear awareness of the work of Barth and the incompatibility of his thought at critical points with strict Reformed orthodoxy. H. Orton Wiley's *Christian Theology* (3 vols., 1940-46) may also be mentioned here, though it is a work of far less substance than that of Berkhof.

A distinctive motif of the neofundamentalist revival has been the encounter with the "theology of crisis" or "neo-orthodoxy" and other postliberal developments. These theologies may involve a kind of "return" to "orthodoxy" and a genuine critique of liberalism, but can they be considered adequate? A major attempt to deal with this question is Cornelius Van Til's *The New Modernism* (1946), which is an early landmark of the new conservatism and remains the most significant American contribution to its scholarship. In a detailed analysis of the thought of Barth and Brunner, Van Til argues that the theology of crisis is essentially a "modern" theology, "activistic" and "antimetaphysical." It is informed from beginning to end by the critical philosophy of Kant and therefore has given up the "ontological Trinity," the "self-contained God," and the "temporal" creation (these are Van Til's equivalent for what I earlier called the supernaturalistic conception of God and the world). As in the case of liberalism, everything becomes "for us" rather than the thing-in-itself and rationality-in-itself. Consequently the dialectical principle of Barth and Brunner must be rejected as essentially hostile to historic Christian faith. Some of the words of traditional Reformed faith are used, but finally this is a theology modern in both form and content and it is not a valid Reformation theology in any form. The modern and the classical are comprehensive and mutually exclusive views of God and the world. (E. J. Carnell's *The Theology of Reinhold Niebuhr,* 1951, is a similar critique of Niebuhr, finding in his work a praiseworthy overcoming of the immanentism of liberalism but an acceptance of liberalism's criticism of scripture and its post-Kantian epistemology.)

The insistence on return to pre-Kantian thought is an important theme in a new and aggressive program of apologetics, which takes a highly rationalistic form. This is best seen, again, in the works of Van Til (see esp. *The Defense of the Faith,* 1955) and Carnell (esp. *An Introduction to Christian Apologetics,* 1948), though for Van Til it appears that only a regenerate reason can know the perfect rationality. The program involves both an internal criticism of opposing views, to show their contradictions, and the establishment of an adequate "Christian metaphysic," for the classical Christian position involves a philosophy of science as well as a theology (Van Til). Thus a metaphysical program comparable to that of Protestant scholasticism is called for, through which "biblical theism" may be seen as the most adequate explanation of reality.

Finally, the neofundamentalist movement reveals on occasion a willingness to look again at the problem of science and religion. In part, this involves a concentration on the "essentials" of the biblical picture of creation—origination by the fiat command of a sovereign mind and will, and the establishment of fixed grades of being and life —and a certain flexibility in respect to gaps in the biblical record, to the antiquity of the world and of man, and to the duration of creation. Evolution remains a major problem, and while "total evolutionism" must be rejected, allowance is sometimes made for evolution *within* genera, so long as the special place of man is preserved.

In sum, the neofundamentalist movement reveals a different character from its early twentieth century parent and presents at least instances of significant scholarship within the limits imposed, e.g., by its view of scripture. Nonetheless, while reflecting considerable religious vitality and producing a mass of semipopular studies (among the best are S. G. Craig's *Christianity Rightly So-Called*, 1946, and Loraine Boettner's *Studies in Theology*, 1947), this kind of theologizing continues to appeal, for first-rate scholarship, largely to the works of an earlier day and to contemporary conservative thought in Europe (especially in Holland). (A useful, though often highly uncritical, guide to the literature and some of the problems is *Contemporary Evangelical Thought*, ed. Carl F. H. Henry, 1957.)

⋘§⋙

The State of Scholarship

Reflection on what has been said in the preceding analysis, and what has been passed over in silence, suggests several kinds of judgments on the condition of American scholarship in theology in the past three decades. The first will be obvious: if we are thinking of the level of decisive influence on currents of thought, of unquestioned freshness of vision, of profound and exciting theological construction, and of the truly seminal mind, then only three names have to be mentioned: Reinhold Niebuhr, Paul Tillich, and H. Richard Niebuhr. They have had no peers in their theological generation in America (and very few elsewhere). Roughly contemporary in age, they have come (chronologically) to positions of dominance generally in the order cited above. As yet no successors of comparable stature can be identified (interestingly, the same judgment may be made about the current scene in Germany; no one of the potential impact of a Barth or a Bultmann is yet in view).

To say this, however, is not at all to say that the sum of significant American scholarship in theology consists of the work of these three men. For surrounding their work, often influenced by it or reflecting similar constellations of sources, sometimes running in parallel streams, sometimes developing comparable perspectives in ancillary directions, has been the work of a number of scholars of the second rank (this does not mean "second-rate"). I have attempted to give in brief a reasonably comprehensive indication of the scope, character, and direction of these theological endeavors—though I do not claim

277

this essay to be either an exhaustive listing of those works that may properly be called important scholarship and I have not attempted to exhibit the developments through the relevant periodical literature.

On balance, it seems not inappropriate to describe the past three decades as a period of theological richness and fertility, even of theological renaissance. (The latter term may also suggest the recovery of theological seriousness, or a sense of urgency in the theological enterprise that contrasts with the liberal tendency to suspicion of theology.) With respect both to the creative leadership of the Niebuhrs and Tillich and to the larger body of significant scholarship, such a judgment seems valid. The present epoch compares favorably to previous periods in American theology and to the contemporary scene in Europe as well as to other disciplines.

Yet one must also observe a very considerable unfulfilled potential. It would at this point be unkind and perhaps presumptuous to cite names. But one cannot help being struck by the paucity of major publications on the part of a number of very able theologians. One of the factors involved has doubtless been the diversity of demands under which the theologian inescapably labors. In addition to his responsibilities to students and to the scholarly community, he is subject to a wide variety of pressing claims for service in the church,— among them, the demand for theological popularization, in the form of "theology for laymen" or for the "average" minister. (This in turn is a dismal commentary on the unwillingness or inability of the Protestant ministry in general to come to grips directly with prime theological scholarship.) As a consequence of this, and the eagerness of publishers for religious books for the mass market, much first-rate theological ability has been diverted from creative scholarship into the production of popular or semipopular works; many of these are very good, but they cannot properly be said to have contributed to the advance of scholarship. A further not unrelated feature of the American scene, on which it is perhaps ironical to comment here, has been the amount of energy expended in surveys and analyses of American theology. Quite offhand one can recall at least a dozen volumes published in the past thirty years, most of them excellent works, which have been principally devoted to expounding "contemporary"

American theology or major aspects thereof. Such theological self-analysis obviously has its utility, and it can be a legitimate means of getting ahead with the scholarly job, but it has not in fact often involved creative advances.

A second kind of observation appropriate to recent theological development is that the significant scholarship has been almost entirely of the "occasional" or topical rather than the system-building type. The exceptions to this judgment are quickly noted. Tillich's *Systematic Theology* is the major one. Also several volumes by Nels F. S. Ferré (esp. *Faith and Reason*, 1946; *Evil and the Christian Faith*, 1947; *The Christian Understanding of God*, 1951; and *Christ and the Christian*, 1958) are designed to form part of an inclusive treatment of the whole range of Christian doctrine. To these might be added two works intended as theological texts, Walter M. Horton's *Christian Theology: An Ecumenical Approach* (1955) and L. H. DeWolf's *A Theology of the Living Church* (1953), though the former is more of a summary of the present state of thought and the latter is a handbook of modified personalist theology in the tradition of A. C. Knudson. And from the conservative side, one may recall the works of Berkhof and of Wiley.

Apart from such possible exceptions, the major works of theology have been concerned with particular aspects or problems in Christian thought. Certainly this is true of Reinhold Niebuhr's *magnum opus* and of the writings of H. Richard Niebuhr, as well as of numerous other works earlier identified. There has been much systematic reflection and some suggestions for comprehensive development, but full-scale articulation has been rare. In this respect, recent American theology forms an interesting contrast both to the second half of the nineteenth century, which was marked by the development of extensive (often massive) systems, and to the current scene in European, especially German, theology. (Major systematic statements, either completed or published in part, include those of Althaus, Barth, Brunner, Vogel, Weber, Diem, Elert, Ebeling, Buri, Thornton, Aulen, and Quick.) Further, one may compare the theological scene with the steps toward comprehensive scholarship being taken in other fields of religion, e.g., in biblical studies and in historical theology, though the excellent recent work, *A Handbook of Christian*

Theology (ed. Marvin Halverson and Arthur A. Cohen, 1958) might be said to represent in part a brief move in the direction of a systematic theological encyclopedia.

In noting this characteristic of recent American theology, no negative judgment is intended. What is important is what is disclosed about the present state of the theological enterprise, namely, that 1930-60 has not been a period of system building. Several reasons for this may be suggested. First, this has been a time of unusual ferment and reassessment. Second, and closely related, the present generation, like the preceding era of liberal theology, has been much preoccupied with re-examination of the nature of the theological program and with the reformulation of theological procedures (whether the articulation and justification of theological method must *precede* constructive elaboration is itself a major question; at any rate the latter cannot get along without the former). Finally, the lack of system building seems also to reflect a characteristic conviction that theology's proper expressions are inevitably partial and incomplete, and that theology is not a self-contained enterprise leading to an all-inclusive view, but a continuous dialogue (or trialogue) in which insights of classical faith are interpreted (made relevant) to contemporary culture.

A third major feature of theological scholarship in recent decades is its nondenominational character. In part, this is a reflection of the growing amalgamation of the main streams in American Protestant Christianity, in which the denominations have tended both in structure and in thought to move toward a common pattern. To be sure, under the impetus of theological confrontation in the ecumenical movement there has been a considerable revival of interest in the denominational theological traditions, as well as excellent studies of the reformers and of Protestant orthodoxies, and it is easy enough to detect Lutheran or Calvinistic emphases here and there. But this has not led to major theological works of a distinctively denominational pattern. As conservative Lutheranism has participated in the theological revival, overcoming its previous cultural isolation and becoming less conservative, it has become less narrowly Lutheran. And neo-fundamentalism, though finding its greatest strength in the Reformed tradition, has become more and more a transconfessional movement. Elsewhere, it is even more clear that the theologian does not think of himself in the first instance (if at all) as the representative of a denomination but as a participant in a far broader Christian community. The denominational background of a given theologian can hardly be identified on the basis of his constructive scholarship. The interdenominational theological seminaries have been the centers of theological leadership, and the prime issues have cut across the traditional denominational lines of division.

To put the same point positively, and to carry it further, the course of scholarship shows the formation of a very broad consensus, whose main outlines are apparent from our analysis of major theological types. Although these types represent differences—i.e., distinguishable directions or styles of theology—they are differences within a genuine theological community, and the lines of distinction seem to be growing increasingly less sharp. Important debate continues and new issues are posed, but what is remarkable is the continuity and even convergence of theological concerns. In this connection the question may be raised of the effect on American theological scholarship of the absence of both an inclusive American theological association and a single dominating theological journal. What the existence of either or both of these might mean for scholarship in theology is difficult to judge, but it is a striking fact that none of the various regional or informal theological societies (or the American Theological Society, which is quite restricted in membership) nor any of the journals play the role in theology that is played, for example, in biblical studies by the Society of Biblical Literature and Exegesis and the *Journal of Biblical Literature,* or in church history by the American Society of Church History and *Church History.* Further, very few of the leading theological journals clearly reflect a given point of view or give cohesiveness to a particular type or school of thought. (On the other hand, the multiplicity of journals makes it relatively easy for significant articles to be published.)

It appears that American theology has now entered at least briefly into a period of consolidation and waiting, in which the new perspectives of the past quarter century are being absorbed and diffused. The rising generation of theologians has been brought up on Barth and Bultmann, Tillich and the Niebuhrs, and it is not yet clear what will be the decisively new lines of development.

One may shift the question slightly, however, and ask whether changes are apparent in the focus of attention to problem areas. It is clear that interest in the complex of problems embracing the doctrines of man and sin, grace and judgment, and the theology of history, which reached its climax in Reinhold Niebuhr's *Nature and Destiny of Man,* no longer holds the pre-eminent place. At the same time, especially under the impact of the ecumenical movement, there has been a marked renewal of attention to Christology and ecclesiology, including (for the first time in the American scene) the beginnings of fruitful interchange between Protestant and Roman Catholic thinkers. Questions of religious knowledge and theological method continue to be of pervasive importance, taking on perhaps two primary forms: the problem of the "historical" character of judgments of faith, in connection with which there are at least some tendencies toward a radical existentialism; and the nature of affirmations about the transcendent, at which point the development of analytic philosophy and the more general discussion of symbol and myth have become of increasing significance. The recent thrust toward a "theology of culture," and more generally toward the exploration of the problem of theology and culture, though still rather formless, continues unabated and reflects a kind of return to culture after the earlier sharp withdrawal from the dangers of absorption of the church into the "world." And there are signs of a return to prominence of the problem of theology and science. It is evident that the older liberal view of the rapprochement of religion and science, if not abandoned, is seriously questioned. What may replace it is quite unclear. Only in process theology has a serious attempt been made to take positive theological account of the modern scientific views, and the more radical existentialism has tended to segregate sharply theological and scientific judgments ("meaning" versus "fact"). We have now at least reached the point of recognizing that both from the side of science and from the side of theology new questions must be asked. (See, e.g., the treatment of the problem in Carl Michalson's *The Hinge of History* and in the last part of John Dillenberger's *Protestant Theology and Natural Science,* 1960.)

Finally, we may ask if, in reflection on the past generation of scholarship in theology, it is possible to speak of a distinctively American theology. Certainly some uniquely American patterns may be discerned, the most prominent of which are process theology and the blend of social gospel passion and Reformation theology in Reinhold Niebuhr. But in the larger sense of fundamental theological perspectives, the answer to the question is *No*. The major typology here used to interpret American scholarship is at least equally relevant to the European scene, and indeed the patterns of neo-Reformation theology and of correlation with existentialism are even more sharply defined on the Continent. For the past century and a half it has become increasingly less satisfactory to try to deal with theological construction in national terms. If theology is not ordered by denominational limits, neither is it controlled by national boundaries. The problems at issue have been pervasively present in an international theological community. Our attention here has been focused almost exclusively on American scholarship, but what we have seen are special manifestations and variations of far more widespread movements of thought. (Thus I have little sympathy with pleas for an American theology.)

Yet it may be said that in the United States this tradition of scholarship does have its distinctive nuances, of which two are of special importance. One will be obvious. It is a passion for "relevance," which comes to decisive expression in the wide attraction of "correlation theology" or "theology and"—theology and culture, and existentialism, and psychology, art, literature, music, history, science, etc. But in the larger sense that passion is omnipresent in American theological scholarship. It has something to do with the diversion of energy into theological popularization, reflecting the concern that the church, for all its institutional success, may be or become irrelevant. It is seen in the warmer reception given to Emil Brunner's writing than to Karl Barth's, though Barth is unquestionably a far more powerful thinker. It is a key feature of all Reinhold Niebuhr's thinking and expressed in the continuing attention of both the Niebuhrs to problems of American religious life. It helps to account for the popularity of Tillich—one is tempted to ask whether Tillich could have found acceptance anywhere else than in America, where the correlation aspects of his theology have been strengthened—and the more recent interest in the existentialist theologies of Bultmann and Gogarten. It appears in neofundamentalism's rejection of the anticultural attitude of fundamentalism. That passion, reflecting among other things the continuing heritage of liberalism and the impact of James and Dewey on American thought, has tended to check the revival of classical theological motifs from becoming mere traditionalism (or theology turned in upon itself) and has also prevented the radical polarization of positions (e.g., in Germany between Barth and Bultmann). It is related to the relative absence, in the various recoveries of "orthodoxy," of preoccupation with a body of official doctrine. This broad interest may be put more positively by saying that the proper role and function of theology is understood to be that of a "practical" rather than a "speculative" science, which will maintain an intimate relation of principle and action, will interpret in and from the concrete context of the contemporary situation, and will be truly available for direction of the religious life. Thus H. R. Niebuhr's plea for symbols more adequate to grasp and communicate "the reality of our existence before God" expresses a motif widely characteristic of American theology.

The second nuance, which I should judge to be of even greater importance in the long run, has to do with the sometimes alleged dependence of American theology upon European scholarship. If dependence is certified by the absence of mutual interdependence, then that allegation has substance. But what is most basically involved can be put succinctly (if crudely): the Germans read the Germans, the British read the British and the Germans (sometimes), and the Americans read the Germans, the British, and the Americans— and the reasons for this have little to do with the quality of scholarship. The consequence is that American scholarship is in a uniquely "ecumenical" position, and tends to draw upon a richer complex of traditions than is in practice available to European scholarship. This often makes for diffuseness and even syncretistic thinking, but it also imposes on the American scholar a unique responsibility and opportunity, and may produce more genuinely fruitful perspectives.

CHRISTIAN ETHICS

✥

JAMES M. GUSTAFSON
PROFESSOR OF CHRISTIAN ETHICS
YALE UNIVERSITY

BACKGROUND OF THE CONTEMPORARY PERIOD

Scholarship in Christian ethics in the United States has developed in a particularly American way. Writers have clearly been motivated by concern for the actual state of public and private morality. The dominant intention has been to have some practical effect upon the moral behavior of persons and the public policy of institutions. Thus it is far more characteristic to find theoretical work developed out of practical moral concern than it is to find extensive treatises seeking to resolve theological and philosophical ethical questions in the abstract. This can be contrasted with Protestant scholarship in Europe, where until recently the conversation partners for ethics have been dogmatic theology, biblical exegesis, and philosophy almost exclusively. Few major American writings do not move in the direction of offering counsel on one or a number of actual life problems: sex, foreign policy, war, economic justice, etc. Americans have done little work in the history of Christian ethics; they have done less on the relation of ethical thought to biblical scholarship; only a few scholars have moved with ease between systematic theology and ethics, and too little work has been done on the relation of theological ethics to philosophical ethics. American writers in Christian ethics are fundamentally interested in morals, in moral action and activity. This is not only a Protestant mood, but also a Roman Catholic one.

This tradition precedes the contemporary period; indeed, there are those who argue that the concern for practical morality that found fruition in the social gospel movement and its heirs is rooted in the Puritanism that shaped New England and that in revised forms spread across the land in the westward expansion. Willem A. Visser 't Hooft, in *The Background of the Social Gospel in America* (1928), indicates that some of the roots of the practical moral and social concern of later Christian ethics in America can be found in the Puritan concern for social discipline and for the ideal of a thoroughly Christianized society. H. Richard Niebuhr, in *The Kingdom of God in America* (1936), traces the transformations in the Puritan

287

notion of the sovereignty of God through the history of American Protestant ethics, making clear that throughout there was a concern for social and personal conformation to the current interpretation of God's sovereignty and God's Kingdom.

During the nineteenth century several identifiable movements emerged that continued this practical interest. One was the extensive teaching of "moral philosophy" in American colleges, usually under the direction of churchman-scholars who were also deeply involved in the public life of the time. Wilson Smith, in *Professors and Public Ethics* (1956), delineates some of the major strands of this movement: moral philosophers were really professors and executors of social ethics in America, having in their purview not only analysis of political and economic problems, but also the right to make moral judgments about them. Another nineteenth century phenomenon, the great revivals, had a profound effect not only in the explication of moral discipline in personal conduct, but in motivating and directing important social concerns as well. Timothy Smith, in *Revivalism and Social Reform* (1957), makes the strongest case for the positive impact of American evangelicalism on matters of public morality. Later in the century, and decisive for the shaping of the concerns and procedures of Christian ethics in Protestantism even into the present, was the social gospel movement. In response to urbanization, industrialization, immigration, and their consequent problems on the one hand, and to biblical and theological "liberalism" on the other, a host of writers and reformers emerged on the American scene. Two accounts of this movement are C. Howard Hopkins' *The Rise of the Social Gospel in American Protestantism, 1865-1915* (1940) and Henry F. May's *Protestant Churches and Industrial America* (1949). The movement not only issued in institutional reform in church life, but also evoked a body of systematic literature. Two of the most scholarly books were Newman Smyth's *Christian Ethics* (1892) and Walter Rauschenbusch's *A Theology for the Social Gospel* (1917). Smyth's book draws heavily upon the theology of Schleiermacher and his successors in German Protestantism, and upon English philosophical idealism. Ethics has to do with ideals and their actualization; in Christian ethics the moral ideal has been revealed in Jesus Christ and in his teachings. The task of the Christian community, then, is progressively to realize the Christian ideals in the actual conduct and affairs of the human community. Rauschenbusch's title, *A Theology for* . . . , is itself symbolic of much of Protestant ethics: given in the society and the Christian community is a moral concern that has a high degree of autonomy; what is required is the formation of a theology that supports, sustains, and directs that concern. Indeed, it was at the end of a lifetime as a powerful writer of quite practical moral treatises, such as *Christianizing the Social Order* (1912), that the German-American Baptist Professor of Church History defined the basic principles for his life work.

Parallel to the social gospel movement in Protestantism was the growth of Roman Catholic social theology. In 1891 Pope Leo XIII issued the famous encyclical *Rerum novarum,* which dealt with the fundamental rights of workers to just wages, to organize themselves in "workmen's associations," and so forth, for the sake of the health of the whole social body. This nourished a Catholic social movement in the United States that culminated in the important career of Father John A. Ryan, who became the principal interpreter for American public life of the theological and moral principles of the developing Roman Catholic tradition. The most recent history of this development is Franz Mueller's essay "The Church and the Social Question" (in J. N. Moody and J. G. Lawler, eds., *The Challenge of Mater et Magistra,* 1963). The essential point is that Roman Catholic Christian ethics in the United States also turned some of its most creative intelligence to questions of social ethics and social policy. Aaron Abell, in *American Catholicism and Social Action, 1865-1950* (1960), tells the story of Catholic involvement in public morality.

In the 1920's, the seeds of dissolution of the intellectual foundations of Protestant ethics were sown. The American sower and reaper was Reinhold Niebuhr, who is without doubt the towering figure during the period since 1930. Idealism grounded in theology such as that delineated by Newman Smyth and in the appropriation of the Old Testament prophets and of Jesus that was made by Rauschenbusch and others seemed impossible of realization in economic and social life. What was actually occurring is symbolized by the titles of two excellent studies that deal with the period between the World Wars, and appropriately Reinhold Niebuhr is the pivotal figure in both. Paul A. Carter's *The Decline and Revival of the Social Gospel* (1954) narrates how the social criticism characteristic of the early 1920's did not have the capacity to grapple with more than highly particularized and oversimplified issues, such as the prohibition of liquor, nor was it rooted in an intellectual tradition that could bear the toppling of optimism by crisis events in history. Under the impact of Niebuhr and of the thought of the ecumenical movement, new theological foundations were established that permitted a greater degree of social realism and thus a revitalization of a social gospel that could face the brutal realities of totalitarianism and war. The title of Donald B. Meyer's *The Protestant Search for Political Realism, 1919-1941* (1960) suggests the main thrust of both the reflective and the active side of Protestant ethics. How could Protestantism avoid mere verbalization of social criticism and social goals, and become a shaping force in the critical historical events of depression, totalitarianism, and war? What fundamental theological affirmations were in such error that they fostered illusions about man and society? What reappropriations from traditional Christian doctrine would release Protestants from their optimistic illusions and enable them to penetrate historical experience, to govern the realities of injustice, social evil, and power?

Thus, the earlier 1930's were crucial as a turning point in Protestant Christian ethics. Since the discipline was more practical than academic, it had to face the existence of a depression, the emergence of the powerful Soviet experiment with its radically alternative way to deal with social ills, and the rise of Hitler as grave crises in practical morality. The aspiration to preserve the peace by preaching pacifism, to change the social structure by changing personalities either through conversion or through education, to establish justice by making proclamations or organizing Christian campaigns, was critically called into question. With this, the intellectual foundations of "Applied Christianity" or "Practical Philanthropy," as seminary chairs were named, were also called into question. Had the biblical view of man, a creature of rebellion and sin, been lost in a preoccupation with the possibility of moral progress led on by a high religious moral ideal—Jesus and the Kingdom of God? The discipline of Christian ethics took on a new academic seriousness in response to the social crisis. Inadequate perceptions of what was occurring, inadequate prescriptions for what ought to occur, and inadequate ways to effect what might occur all called for more serious intellectual and academic effort.

The ferment engendered by historical events coincided with the theological ferment that had begun to occur in European Protestantism in the Twenties. "Crisis theology" returned to Paul as well as the teachings of Jesus, viewed the Old Testament prophets as more than religiously motivated social reformers, returned to the Reformation interpretation of man as sinner even while justified, saw the vast distance between God and man, and fed on a newly discovered Kierkegaard. This crisis theology was seeping into the thought of the young American theologians: Christianity was faith before it was morality; it spoke of the Divine-human relation that is perennially in a critical state rather than of a continuous cultural tradition based on the pervasive influence of Jesus, or of the power of the human spirit to transcend and in turn control nature. Jesus Christ was not the revelation of a moral idea; he was the God-man—a paradox. God's grace was not an efficacious infusion of a power moving toward the perfection of man; it was the forgiveness of sins, needed newly in each moment. The Kingdom of God was not a historical possibility in which cooperation would rule out conflict, peace would rule out war; it was rather God's perfect reign, which would come not by the building of men, but by the act of God when he saw fit to bring it. Thus in 1931, the young German-American theologian Wilhelm Pauck could publish a book, *Karl Barth, Prophet of a New Christianity?* The intellectual ferment in Protestant ethics engendered by historical crises was fed by the far-reaching theological ferment created by European pastors and young theologians. The writings of Barth, Brunner, and others found minds ready to take them seriously.

Roman Catholic ethics, more deeply embedded in a stable intellectual tradition, faced the recent decades with greater equanimity. The English manuals of moral theology, such as *Moral and Pastoral Theology* (4 vols.) by Henry Davis, S.J., could be published in 1935 in the United States without a sense of intellectual revolution. Indeed, new developments in some areas of moral life, for example in medical care, required new refinements of casuistry, but the fundamental principles of natural law in its Thomistic form remained unaltered. In matters of social policy, the historical events had to be faced, and were. But this was more by development and application of a continuing intellectual tradition than by agonizing reappraisal of theological foundations. Thus, following World War I, the bishops' Program of Social Reconstruction could bring to bear the principles of *Rerum novarum* on the social needs of America. When Pius XI issued his social encyclical *Quadragesimo anno* in 1931, the American Catholic intellectuals and practitioners had a new basic document from which to launch their fundamental support for such social reforms as were proposed and enacted by the New Deal. New questions had to be faced, primarily with reference to a democratic society founded upon civil liberties in which the Roman Catholic population was a minority. The creative work was to come in that regard. But development, rather than crisis, was the appropriate response.

The fundamental interest in practical morality remains in more recent Christian ethics in America. But it has taken a new academic seriousness. Professorships in the field exist in theological schools and in universities and colleges. New vitality in biblical and theological studies abroad and in the United States contributed to the clarification of both the procedures and the content of the fundamental principles of Christian ethics. The ecumenical movement, earlier within the Protestant community, more recently including Orthodox and Roman Catholic participants, has enlarged the scope of the discourse and argumentation in the field. New philosophical movements have entered the conversation: Christian ethics is related by various scholars not only to natural law, pragmatism, and value theory, but also to existentialism and in a lesser measure to empiricism and linguistic analysis. With the translation of major works of contemporary Roman Catholic moral theologians from Europe, new language begins to appear in Roman Catholic ethics as well—the language of existential phenomenology. (An interpretation of what is occurring in Catholicism can be found in John C. Ford and Gerald Kelly's *Contemporary Moral Theology*, 1958.) The interpretation of the discipline's developments since about 1930, then, requires careful analysis.

≤§ 2 §≈

ISSUES IN THEOLOGICAL ETHICS
IN THE CONTEMPORARY PERIOD

The bulk of this essay is a thematic interpretation of developments in the discipline of Christian ethics since 1930. In this chapter I have selected three themes of theological ethics: the changing interpretation of man, the changing use of the Bible in Christian ethics, and the controversy over the proper procedures of Christian ethical reasoning. These themes draw attention to issues that extend beyond the headings, and thus enable one to describe fairly inclusively what is occurring on the "theoretical" side of the discipline. Basically, these three themes deal with internal conversations between ethics and theology, though subordinately between Christian ethics and philosophy. Chapter 3 is a critical evaluation of contemporary work in Christian ethics in relation to some of its adjacent fields in their own right: biblical studies, philosophical ethics, and historical studies. In Chapter 4, a critical overview of literature on Christian ethics and moral problems is made, indicating again the way in which Christian ethics in America has continued to be dominantly interested in actual moral problems, and thus is in conversation with various fields of the social sciences. I have throughout sought to do justice to Catholic as well as Protestant developments, though it will be obvious to the reader that Protestant material is more familiar to me. It is also the case, however, that until very recent years Roman Catholic ethics has been done in a traditional Thomistic manner, and consequently there is not as much change to report.

The Interpretation of Man

For ethics, whether Christian or non-Christian, the fundamental convictions about man are crucial for understanding the nature of moral achievement. If man is viewed as utterly free, creating himself and his moral world out of his actions, the interpretation of ethics is bound to be different from that that occurs if he is viewed as having

293

within his being an inherent purposiveness or law, an inclination toward the good, that is related to the whole order of being. If man is viewed primarily as curved in upon himself even when he knows God's mercy, there will be a tentativeness about his moral judgment that will not exist if he is viewed primarily as basically restored in his personal moral being by God's redemption. American Christian ethics has moved in several directions during the past decades in its view of man.

Roman Catholic ethics has maintained its fundamentally Thomistic view of man as a creature of appetite, will, and reason, participating in the natural law that gives him a basic inclination toward the good. The signs of a revised pattern of interpretation of man's nature are only currently beginning to appear in Catholic ethics with the growing study of European Catholics who have begun to take the language of existential phenomonology—the language of I and thou, of being for the other, of historicity and temporality—and overlay it upon traditional Thomistic views. American conservative Protestantism, which has not contributed much to academic discussions of Christian ethics, continues to operate with a more individualistic view of man, in which the religious experience of redeeming grace is the principal way for moral reform. In the mainstream of American Protestantism, several trends are discernible. The most obvious is what was popularly called "the recovery of sin" and is identified with the writings of Reinhold Niebuhr. Alongside this has existed a self-conscious effort to resist the impact of Reinhold Niebuhr—this is visible in the writings of D. C. Macintosh and Albert Knudsen, who represent a continuation of an older liberal theology. Two other developments, however, are also noteworthy: one is the appropriation of a social theory of the self, informed not only by such American philosophers as G. H. Mead and John Dewey, but also by the social existentialism of a man like Martin Buber. This development is most cogently demonstrated in the work of H. Richard Niebuhr. Another development might be noted as "the recovery of grace," in which a radical affirmation of God's goodness and freedom issues in a participation in the events of the moral world without much self-consciousness or scrupulosity about man's sin. Such a view is implied in Paul Lehmann's work.

Reinhold Niebuhr: man as nature, spirit, and sinner. The most notable and culturally influential reinterpretation of man, that of Reinhold Niebuhr of Union Theological Seminary in New York, is the obvious point at which to begin. Niebuhr protested vehemently against the excessive expectation of change in moral character that was assumed by religious pietism and by liberal rationalism. The former relied too heavily upon a moral renewal that was assumed to be the consequence of the work of grace and the life of piety, and had unwarranted assurance about its definitions of what the crucial moral issues were and how they could be rather simply solved. Religious and nonreligious liberalism (e.g., John Dewey) relied too heavily upon the re-education of man, on his ability to develop new methods of moral nurture and to shape moral ideals and sentiments. It led also to illusions about the pliability of persons and institutions, assuming, for example, that peace could be achieved by declarations against war and by the growth of the pacifist movement. The biblical myth of the fall, taken seriously as a basis for the interpretation of human existence, enabled Niebuhr to criticize the oversimplifications and pitfalls of pietism and liberal rationalism by stressing the limits of human capacities to know and achieve the temporal good, and the necessity to use coercive power to resist evil.

Niebuhr's interpretation of sin and its consequences for morality has continuity with the moral idealism of American Protestantism, however, at one crucial point: it is delineated in relation to the problem of how *ideal possibilities* of human existence, particularly in society, can and cannot be actualized in history. It assumes a distinction between spirit and nature, between freedom and necessity, between finite and infinite that has roots in the idealistic tradition. "Sin lies at the juncture of spirit and nature, in the sense that the peculiar and unique characteristics of human spirituality, in both its good and evil tendencies, can be understood only by analyzing the paradoxical relation of freedom and necessity, of finiteness and the yearning for the eternal in human life" (*An Interpretation of Christian Ethics,* 1935, p. 76). By virtue of being spirit as well as nature, man knows of higher possibilities in his freedom that cannot be realized in the natural, finite world; he knows therefore the imperfections of the actions that he is forced to take. Indeed, he is constantly under the judgment of these higher possibilities, and out of this con-

trast between ideal and actual comes his moral guilt. The problem
does not rest merely with human finiteness, with the limitations that
are set upon us by the fact that we are bodies within historical processes and contingencies. There is also the religious dimension of the
problem of the will. In man's perversity of will he does not even
achieve that measure of the ideal that is a possibility.

A question necessarily arises, then, about the significance of religious moral ideals (for example, love) that cannot be realized in
human experience. Are they useless? Or how are they to be taken?
Niebuhr, in *An Interpretation of Christian Ethics,* argues for the
"relevance of an impossible ethical ideal" on several grounds.
Against those forms of "liberalism, rationalism, and radicalism" that
insist upon the possibility of the perfect realization of love in human
life, Niebuhr stresses the impossibility of the ideal. Against morally
and socially passive forms of orthodox Christianity, he insists upon
its relevance, that is, upon the necessity to achieve a closer approximation to the law of love, which is possible through the establishment of social equity and other moral values "in an ascending scale
of moral possibilities." With the acknowledgment of sin, and under
the judgment and direction of the law of love, men can participate
in the realities of social power, political strife, and economic conflict
with both determination and contrition.

This basic view of man is refined with great theological sophistication in *The Nature and Destiny of Man* (2 vols., 1941, 1943), the
most important American contribution to Protestant theological
ethics in the first half of this century. Under the influence of serious
grappling with the Bible, the Reformers, Augustine, and Kierkegaard, particularly the latter's *Sickness unto Death,* Niebuhr brings
into his view of man as sinner not merely a moral interpretation of
the inability to actualize ideals because of perversion of will, but also
a religious interpretation of sin arising out of lack of faith. He suggests that the Christian view of man relates three aspects of human
existence to each other: (1) "the height of self-transcendence in
man's spiritual stature," coming from the doctrine of the image of
God; (2) man's "weakness, dependence, and finiteness," his involvement in the contingencies of the natural world, coming from
the doctrine that man is creature and always remains creature; and
(3) the evil of man as "a consequence of his inevitable though not

necessary unwillingness to acknowledge his dependence, to accept his finiteness and to admit his insecurity, an unwillingness which involves him in the vicious circle of accentuating the insecurity from which he seeks to escape" (vol. I, p. 150). Sin is inevitable though not necessary, because man could trust in God but does not, and in turn he seeks to avoid by various escapes his anxiety over being a creature and not God. The forms of escape are the forms of sin: pride, which is basically man's tendency to have more confidence in his power, his knowledge, his virtue, and his religiosity than these things deserve; and sensuality, which is basically man's flight from his responsibility of being spirit as well as nature into sexuality and other forms of loss of "transcendence."

The consequences of such a view of man for morality are evident. Consciousness of human limitation and sin rules out all utopian expectations of the perfect achievement of the social and personal good in history. But two other Christian affirmations qualify the sheer pessimism that might ensue if this were all that could be said. They are the assurance of God's mercy, and love as the law of life. Both refer to the significance of God's revelation in Jesus Christ, and particularly of his crucifixion. The crucifixion reveals the unlimited self-giving sacrificial love of God, his willingness to choose even the death of Jesus as the way to disclose his unfathomable agape. The first affirmation derived from this theory is that even though man continues in creatureliness and sin, he can trust in God's merciful forgiveness and in the final victory of God's kingdom of love. This is an appropriation of a particularly Lutheran emphasis in theology and ethics. Thus while man remains conscious of his sin, the assurance of God's love gives him an inner freedom, an equanimity that removes some of the anxiety and particularly the temptation to pride that corrupt his activities. But he remains a sinner. For Niebuhr, the classical Reformation formula *simul justus, simil peccator* (at once both justified and sinner) is true, but his emphasis is: "To be sure man is justified, but he remains a *sinner."* Niebuhr's stress can be contrasted with Barth's, for whom the same formula testifies to sin rather than love as the "impossible possibility": "To be sure man is sinner, but he is *justified."* For Niebuhr, then, the moral life calls for a sharp awareness of the continuation of human sin even while one pursues the relative good that is achievable in history, though this is done within confidence in the forgiving mercy of God and his final victory.

The second affirmation derived from God's disclosure of his love on the cross is that this very self-sacrificial love is the norm, the fundamental law of life. In the earlier *Interpretation* Niebuhr's view of love was largely based upon the teachings of Jesus, in continuity with the social gospel tradition. In *Nature and Destiny* he avers that Jesus' death disclosed love (agape) even more powerfully than did his teachings. Sinful man is under this law, this norm. Thus a form of moral idealism remains: man is called to achieve the impossible. The impossible remains the light in which all his possible actions are judged, that by which they are informed and qualified. Sinful man is called to approximate self-sacrificial love, and this he does in his pursuit of justice, of equity, and of mutuality, which is the highest form of love that appears to be possible in human experience. His politically realistic actions in the pursuit of justice are to be tempered by mercy and to be conscious of a higher possibility; this is what might distinguish the Christian moral pursuits from those of others. He is to approximate God's agape insofar as it is historically achievable in faithful trust in God's mercy and God's victory, but his sin and creatureliness limit the fulfillment of love.

The attractiveness and influence of Niebuhr's Christian ethics, grounded in this doctrine of man, have been widespread. He has been widely received, it must be noted, for quite American reasons; that is, his intellectual reflection makes sense of human moral experience and enables men to be morally realistic and responsible in very practical matters. To be sure, he resuscitates a doctrine that had been somewhat suppressed, that of sin; he reappropriates biblical, Augustinian, and Reformation motifs; he brings Kierkegaard's existential view of man to bear. He learned from the early writings of Barth, and from Brunner's *Man in Revolt*. But these achievements would not authenticate an American theologian of ethics. His persuasiveness lay in his use of these insights for the interpretation and direction of human moral experience. The validation of ethics rests neither in abstract intellectual finesse, nor in scholarly authority that comes from reference to traditional sources, but in the illumination of human, historical experience. To this Niebuhr brought a virtuosity unsurpassed in this century.

D. C. Macintosh: moral hope in conversion plus science. Niebuhr's view of man did not, however, sweep away the opinions against which he reacted. Liberal Christian views persisted, and to these one must attend. D. C. Macintosh, a Yale theologian who was once Niebuhr's teacher, had confidence in the converting power of grace, the exercise of will, and the information of science to bring in a better moral order. He represents the continuation of the liberal tradition in both its theological and ethical aspects. He believed in the possibility of "empirical theology"—knowledge of God built upon the experiences of men. In ethics, he refused to be shaken by the eschatological interpretations of the New Testament that believed Jesus' teachings referred to the life of perfection that was possible in the present only because the Kingdom of God was expected to come shortly. In piety, he believed that "personal religion" was the foundation of "social religion." "If society is to be saved it must be through saved individuals," he wrote in *Social Religion* (1939, p. 86). Saved individuals are not merely well-taught persons; they must recognize their sin, repent of it, and receive the grace of God. But with this religious experience, Macintosh also affirmed the necessity and ability to pattern life after the spirit of the teachings of Jesus. Whereas Niebuhr had come to believe that men must strive for the historical approximation of love, but not expect its fulfillment in the social world, Macintosh believed that Christians should and could fulfill a faithful loyalty to Jesus, though it would be costly. Man, Macintosh said, must accept the absolute sovereignty of God for his own life, and recognize it as the ideal for everyone else and for the whole world. He must learn to love his enemies—and this he can do when he accepts God's will absolutely and begins to work for the salvation of his enemies. He must avoid doing violence to any man, but live peaceably with all.

Evangelism would bring about the root change in individuals, who in turn would express this new life in society. But there is another human "pre-condition" that makes possible a real achievement of social salvation. Niebuhr did not trust it; Macintosh did. "The one other pre-condition of a steadily progressive realization of the social ideal is an adequate social science and the education of individuals to accept and abide by the findings of genuine experimental science, social as well as material. We may congratulate ourselves that this condition can be more readily fulfilled than in Jesus' day; but even so, it must be admitted that we are still very far from even this nearer goal" (*Social Religion,* pp. 113-14). The mood and temper of this issued in a suggested program for the peace of the world in 1939, which ironically and pathetically was the year that demonstrated how much closer to the realities of human society was Niebuhr than his former teacher. Macintosh's *Social Religion* was fated to be the last great blossom of the pre-1930 tradition, but because of the learning, the intelligence, the piety, and the moral conviction of its author it remains a masterful example of a failing ethos.

Albert Knudsen: good will and high ideals. Another liberal American Protestant tradition that has never been swept away by Niebuhr and other recent currents in theology and ethics is "Boston personalism," identified through three-quarters of a century with the names of Bowne, Brightman, Knudsen, and others. This tradition has made adjustments but has not gone through the revolutions of some others. Its view of man is grounded in a particular understanding of natural law: E. S. Brightman published an influential book called *Moral Laws* in 1933 that has remained something of a landmark for further developments among these Methodist theologians.

Albert Knudsen's *The Principles of Christian Ethics* (1943) represents one systematization of the general point of view. Man has a moral nature, with elements that give content to the moral law: "These are the principle of good will, the conception of a more or less binding human ideal, and the recognition of the sacredness of personality" (p. 76). This native principle of good will is "a manifest basis for the Christian law of love," and the natural human ideal of moral perfection finds content in Jesus. "Natural morality comes first; Christian morality is a later and higher development. But there is no radical difference of kind between them. Christian morality is rooted in the moral nature of man and presupposes both it and the lower expression of it in what has been called natural morality" (p. 83).

How seriously is this moral nature corrupted? For Knudsen most of the traditional interpretation of sin is a "theological fiction." He defined sin essentially in moral rather than religious terms; that is, it is a violation of the moral law (which is also God's law). Conversion, however, makes moral achievement possible. It brings liberation in its release from a sense of guilt; it endows the moral life with a new dynamic, an inspiration; it brings the conviction that man is not left alone in the moral struggle; it brings "new moral insight" through the teaching of Jesus, and even gives "new moral intuitions." Thus the natural moral man, under the power of conversion, moves toward the ideals of love and moral perfection. The Christian moves in life toward the moral perfection of perfect love. Because God is perfect, Christians ought to be perfect. For the Christian, the movement toward perfection involves the "quest after sinlessness," which is the wholehearted devotion to the fundamental principles of love and holiness. Violations of these principles "may now and then occur, but where they are few and not of a serious nature, the moral quality of the life is determined by its obedience rather than by its lapses, and in such a case we may speak of a relative sinlessness" (p. 53). The perfection of man is a moral ideal toward which we move through self-renunciation and through the aid of the divine spirit. Man can move toward the achievement of this in his embodiment of the Christian virtues.

The contrast of Knudsen's view of man with Niebuhr's requires no elaboration. Knudsen represents one of the latter-day forms of Wesleyanism, infused with moral idealism, that Niebuhr found susceptible to excessive self-assurance and pride. For most contemporary students of Christian ethics, Knudsen is easily dismissed as passé. Yet he expressed a Christian idealism that is part of the American intellectual and moral tradition, and is grounded in one strand of the history of Christian ethics.

H. Richard Niebuhr: man as responsible. In the decades of the influence of Reinhold Niebuhr, a less practical interpretation of man's moral nature was being developed by his brother, H. Richard Niebuhr of Yale. His posthumous book, *The Responsible Self* (1963), gives the most concise statement of the position. H. Richard Niebuhr was informed by the social theory of the self that found expression in the writings of the Michigan sociologist Charles Horton Cooley and the philosophers G. H. Mead and Josiah Royce. Mead's *Mind, Self, and Society* (1934) suggested a view of selfhood in which identity was shaped by particular responses to groups and persons, and yet was constantly being reshaped in new responses. But the social determinism imbedded in this genetic view of the self did not permit the kind of freedom for responsibility that Niebuhr's moral interests required. Kant and the existentialists understood the self in terms of radical freedom, but could not account for the socially conditioned self. Martin Buber's thought furnished a notion of the self as both free and significantly related to others, and thus was a contribution to the idea of "social existentialism" that Niebuhr used in *Christ and Culture* (1951). The self is always in relationship to others, and is governed in part by these relations. Yet the relationship is one of responsibility for others and responsibility to God, and thus each being is a center of moral action in relationships.

The distinctiveness of this view for ethics is delineated by H. Richard Niebuhr in *The Responsible Self*. He suggests that three types of ethics emerge out of three types of theory of the self. Deontological ethics, the ethics of obedience to rules of right conduct, emerges from an interpretation of man as citizen. "We come to self-awareness if not to self-existence in the midst of *mores,* of commandments and rules, *Thou shalts* and *Thou shalt nots,* of directions and permissions" (p. 52). In Christian ethics, this takes the form of Christian legalism, but there is also a more existential Christian deontology, such as one finds in Karl Barth's ethics of obedience to the immediate command of God. Teleological ethics, the ethics of conformation of self and world to an image, emerges from an interpretation of man as maker, fashioner, and artificer. "The image of man-the-maker, who, acting for an end, gives shape to things is, of course, refined and criticized in the course of its long use [beginning with Aristotle's *Ethics*], by idealists and utilitarians, hedonists and self-realizationists" (p. 49). In Christian ethics, this has its greatest tradition in Roman Catholic Thomism, where personal life and the order of society are to be shaped in conformation to what "really is," the pattern of their nature.

In contrast to these, Niebuhr offers the notion of responsibility. "What is implicit in the idea of responsibility is the image of man-the-answerer, man engaged in dialogue, man acting in response to action upon him" (p. 56). The pattern of thought becomes interactional; men are seen as "responsive beings, who in all our actions answer to action upon us in accordance with our interpretation of such action" (p. 57). Using this fundamental model, derived from philosophical reflection on moral experience more than from exclusively Christian sources, Niebuhr interprets the Christian moral life. In order to respond to actions taking place, men have to have some pattern of interpretation to bring to bear upon themselves and events. What theology provides is an interpretation of the one who is finally acting upon us in all human and historical actions, and to whom men are finally accountable and responsible in their personal and communal existences. Men are responding to God's actions; they are responsible to God in all their interactions. God is known in his revelation in the history of Israel, in Jesus Christ, and in the life of the Christian community to be our creator, governor, and redeemer. Thus our responsible action in the particularities of what is going on is to be fitting to the creative, ordering, judging, and redeeming action of God.

The effect of this view of man is to multiply the number of places at which the Christian feels moral responsibility, for every relationship is one in which he is to seek the good of the neighbor in his response to him. It is also to expand the sources of moral insight and reflection, for no one or two principles become the exclusive governing ones in conduct. Christians are to respond in love, to be sure, but love is not defined in terms of a moral rule of conduct. They are to respond also in faith and hope; they are to respond in the way that is morally fitting in the particular network of interaction. A new stress is brought to bear by the ethics of responsibility; namely, the necessity to know what is going on in the world, for moral life is no longer defined by a single end to be achieved, or by particular propositions to be obeyed or applied. Less rationalistic and more personalistic factors begin to play a part: the importance of loyalty, of repentance, of fidelity to God and to man are stressed in the relationships. But if the range of considerations and the sources of moral insight are complicated, yet the full force of a sense of responsibility is maintained. To be sure, man responds to what is being done by God through other men, but he is *responsible to God* and to men for his participation in the moral and social interaction.

In H. Richard Niebuhr's view of moral man, a fundamental pattern of thought is introduced to American Christian ethics that is distinguishable from those of his contemporaries. The language of moral idealism is gone: man is no longer trying to realize transcendent norms or moral ideals either in himself or in society. Nor is he seen as a center isolable from the content of his relationships to others. His sin is not his moral failure to fulfill impossible possibilities or to obey the moral law and achieve a model of perfection; it is unfaithfulness and irresponsibility to God and man in his historical existence. He is not redeemed or converted in moral character, but responds to the redemptive activity of God. He is not plagued with the problem of absolute expectations in the relativities of the world; rather he is created in relationships from which he never escapes; he is in time, in history, and in society, and must be responsible within this context. But he is not simply to realize himself within this history; he is obligated to be a restrainer of evil and an evoker of good in the persons he meets and in the ordered relationships of life.

Tillich and Lehmann: the ethics of the antilegalistic conscience. H. Richard Niebuhr's interpretation of man leads to an ethic that is against the legalism that often comes from the stress on norms and rules. But it stresses the obligations that are inherent in the structures of human experience. Contemporary theological currents have given rise to other forms of antilegalistic ethics as well. Paul Tillich, for example, very consciously states that "morality is the self-affirmation of our essential being" (*Theology of Culture,* 1959, p. 136). This means for him that moral law is not a strange law, imposed from outside ourselves, but "it is the law of our own being." All moral rules and laws are conditioned; the true moral imperative is our "essential being" seeking affirmation; it drives us not toward commands, but toward "reality." The best interpretation of conscience is not one that makes judgments according to rules of behavior, but one that judges "according to the participation in a reality which transcends the sphere of moral commands" (*The Protestant Era,* 1948, p. 145). Thus, as man participates in the reality of being, as he overcomes the estrangement between himself and being that is in part caused by the existence of human codes of morality, he will be able to express a true and creative moral life. Legalisms are false idols upon which people rest; they are finally obstructions to the relationships between being and man, between man and man, and prevent true self-affirmation.

Tillich's ethics is one expression of his philosophical theology, but as ethics it has had little impact in American Christian ethical discussion. More important is the view of the self that one can discern in the writings of Paul Lehmann. In a reflection of Karl Barth's procedure for theological ethics—namely, finding what is to be said about man not by looking at him but by looking first of all at Jesus Christ—Lehmann criticizes ethics that have an independent doctrine of man. In relation to Jesus Christ, however, one can make certain affirmations about the moral life of the Christian. Christians belong to the community of faith, the *koinonia*, "where prophetic-apostolic *witness* to revelation and *response* of the fellowship in the Spirit coincide" (*Ethics in a Christian Context*, 1963, p. 51). In this community, Christians come to "mature manhood," which, rather than morality, is what Christian ethics must talk about. This maturity is "the integrity in and through interrelatedness which makes it possible for each individual member of an organic whole to be himself in togetherness, and in togetherness each to be himself" (p. 55). As Christians come to this maturity in faith, they can discern through the gifts of transformed motivation and of clear understanding the direction of God's activity in the world. They can begin to see what God is doing "to make human life truly human," and thus respond in such a way that their action *coincides* with God's action. The point in the self that registers this coincidence is the conscience.

The conscience for Lehmann is not developed by a persistent scrupulosity in the pursuit of moral perfection, nor is it shaped by the casuistry of the church as it seeks to relate abstract moral principles to concrete human behavior. It is "neither libertarian nor legalistic, neither antinomian nor nomian, but whole, i.e., unified and sensitized in the freedom wherewith Christ has set us free" (p. 350). The Christian conscience is not the pursuit of alien norms of behavior (heteronomy), nor does it assume that man has within himself the ability to create the conditions for making and keeping human life human (autonomy). Rather, conscience is to be "theonomous." "The *theonomous* conscience is the conscience immediately sensitive to the freedom of God to do in the always changing human situation what his humanizing aims and purposes require. The *theonomous* conscience is governed and directed by the freedom of God alone" (pp. 358-59). Thus man in Christ, in the community of faith, has the eyes to see what God, in his freedom, is doing in the world, and to be governed and directed by God's activity. The effect is anything but legalism; it is openness to participation in the changes that are going on in the world, with some assurance that in faith one discerns what God himself is doing there.

Paul Lehmann gives a very different view of man from those of his contemporaries: the first thing to be said about man is not that he is a sinner, and continues to be a sinner, nor that he is one who actualizes moral ideals. It is not that he has a moral law within him. Rather the first thing to be said is that he lives in reliance upon what God is doing, and he is enabled in the Christian *koinonia* to perceive with some reliability what he ought to do. He does not need norms of love to guide him or ideals to lead him on. Rather, he involves himself in God's work of humanization. He is free in Christ to respond to what God is doing in his freedom. He is not defined in terms of responsibility to God and to others, but in terms of freedom before God and others. Theology informs man not about his sinful condition, but his radical freedom in faith; not about a pattern for the interpretation of what might be going on in the world, but a knowledge of God who can, for example, freely require strict sexual behavior in one era and permit less strict behavior in another. Human freedom in faith is the coincidence of sensitized imaginations and consciences of Christians with God's freedom.

Roman Catholic views: from a natural-law to a "responsibility" model? Lehmann's view of man must appear to be appalling anarchy to the Roman Catholic moral theologian and philosopher. It minimizes, if it does not abolish, what might be said about the fundamental continuities and requirements of human behavior. It eschews the task of elaborating what really does make human beings human. It seems to deny a stable order of creation and society. And not only to Roman Catholics—a Protestant writer such as Paul Ramsey seeks for the relatively stable principles that can be stated about moral conduct in the human community so that moral counsel can be given with some rational reflection, and with some certainty that it reflects the fundamental characteristics of the created order of life. Roman Catholic ethicists are aware of the danger signals that come from such a situational and contextual view of man,[1] and have basically kept within the traditional Thomistic assumptions of an order of being, a natural tendency toward the good, and reliable knowledge of what the natural law is upon which to make prescriptions and counsels of moral behavior. Man is to actualize what he really is; he is a creature whose actions are directed toward the end of both his natural and supernatural good.

Traditional Protestant criticisms of Catholic interpretations of man have hardly changed the pattern. Even the more liberal views of Jacques Maritain, widely read in America, are basically Thomistic. Protestants have said over and over that the Catholic view assumes too much competence in knowing what the fundamental order of man and his relatedness to other men is, it does not take seriously enough the persistence and depths of corruption in man, and it too easily identifies what it believes man "really" to be with the history of Catholic morality and the society of the medieval period. In the pre–John XXIII period, in America, these criticisms were answered with defense of the tradition.

There are, however, European trends in Catholic philosophy and ethics that have been sowing the seeds of revision in the Catholic interpretation of man. These are being studied in the United States, and what will finally issue from them is yet to be seen. European Catholics have had their own situationalists in ethics; in 1952 Pope Pius XII condemned the trend, and both Americans and Europeans have written about its potential dangers. But apart from the extreme existentialists in Catholicism there is also the work of Albert Dondeyne and others who describe man in terms of historicity, temporality, being for others, and responsibility. (See, for example, Dondeyne's *Faith and the World*, 1963, and Bernard Häring's *The Law of Christ*, 1961.) The scope of human freedom is stressed, and reliance upon the virtue of prudence to respond creatively to new situations is affirmed. (See Josef Pieper's *Prudence*, 1959.) In these works, there is explicit criticism of the rigidity with which the traditional natural-law interpretation of man has been carried out, and

[1] For a rather sympathetic critical account, see Robert Gleason, S.J., "Situational Morality," *Thought*, XXXII (1957), 533-58.

there is often use of modern psychological and existential language. There is also, however, a marked effort to relate the newer language to the older, which looks to Protestant eyes like a somewhat compromising and inconsistent way of working.

The principal journal that has brought much of the new European Catholic thinking into the general conversation in America is *Cross Currents,* edited by laymen, though important articles have been written by American scholars who are priests. There are clear marks of the influence of the new patterns on the writings of such a theologian as Robert Gleason, S.J., and in conversation one finds its penetration into the thought of philosophers and theologians. Behind it lies the work of an earlier generation of philosophers such as Max Scheler, and more contemporary figures such as Maurice Merleau-Ponty. Albert Dondeyne's *Contemporary European Thought and Christian Faith* (1958) is a major bridge-document that critically assesses and selectively absorbs existential phenomenological language into the Catholic tradition. Duquesne University in Pittsburgh seems to be the American center for this mode of thought.

Summary assessment. American Protestants continue to find Reinhold Niebuhr's view of man to be most useful in the interpretation and direction of moral problems in the political, economic, and international spheres of morality. But it is less satisfactory in illuminating the situation of personal responsibility and the responses required in the interpersonal sphere. It is too early to assess the fate of H. Richard Niebuhr's views on the world that knows him only through the printed page; but upon generations of his students teaching Christian ethics in colleges, universities, and seminaries, it has already had a wide effect. Lehmann's view is attractive to a generation of persons also influenced by a popular version of the thought of the German theologian-martyr Dietrich Bonhoeffer, for it counsels deep identification with what is going on in the "secular" world. Whether the virtually intuitive elements in it will finally be able to bear the traffic of moral experience is open to question. Perhaps the most creative avenue opening to future discussions about moral man in Christian ethics is the language of responsibility, historicity, and temporality now shared by many Catholics and Protestants, chastened in its existentialist extremities by a reassessment of the *na-*

ture of moral experience that is grounded in the creation. The kind of moral idealism that was carried into the recent period by Macintosh and Knudsen seems fated to decline in influence in a generation that has undergone a theological revolution and is hardly optimistic about the resolution of moral tensions, though this idealism continues to be a force in American morals through such a distinguished leader as Martin Luther King.

The Changing Use of the Bible

For Christian ethics, the Bible remains the charter document. But what it charters depends upon a number of other things that the Christian ethical thinker brings to it. For some it continues to be a book of morality; that is, its prescriptive statements and patterns of life have morally authoritative character that requires literal obedience. For many more, such a view is no longer possible, for historical-critical scholarship has indicated the relation of much that is said to the time and history in which it was written, and theological scholarship has questioned whether the morality of the Bible can be properly understood apart from such theological themes as eschatology, divine judgment, God's grace, Christian freedom, and human sin. Indeed, for a large part of Protestant ethics, the Bible is now less a book of morality than it is a book giving knowledge of God, his presence and his activity. Among Roman Catholics it has traditionally been relegated to dealing with questions of man's supernatural end, and questions of historical morality have been settled in terms of the natural law, often reinforced by biblical quotations. But this is also changing, for European books dealing with the "law of Christ" are making the biblical witness more central to the whole work of Roman Catholic ethics.

By examining what has happened to the use of the Bible in Christian ethics, we are forced to view other themes as well. Most particularly, we must examine different views of the importance of the work of God, Jesus Christ, and the Spirit that have profound effects upon the content and procedures of Christian ethics. Broader theological use of the Bible is particularly necessary where the Christian community desires to interpret theologically and ethically the importance of Christian faith for the extensive and complex issues of human morality in politics, economics, and other areas, and where the community accepts some responsibility for the temporal good of the whole society. A stricter *moral* use of scripture tends to lead to the development of an exemplary morality of a committed few who witness in their distinct patterns of life to a "higher" way. To use distinctions made by Ernst Troeltsch and Max Weber, where the community takes the high demands of biblical morality with literal seriousness, it tends to become sectarian (clearly defined over against the world) and sees its effect upon the world in terms of "exemplary" prophecy and conduct that might have indirect consequences for the temporal good. Where the community takes the Bible to refer primarily to more universal themes of God's governing and redeeming work, it tends to become "churchly" (blurring lines between the religious community and the world) and accepts broad social responsibility as an "emissary" people whose duty it is to make compromises and accept responsibility for cultural values.

There are no recent American writings of academic repute that assume in a simple way that the Bible provides the rules for the governing of the whole human community as if it were the rational norm and ideal of morality applicable to all regardless of their status in Christian faith. This kind of rationalistic moral idealism, characteristic of Tolstoy's use of the Christian teaching, forgets that the Bible is much more than a moral textbook; it is for writers of various persuasions a source for knowledge of God and a source for God's word of judgment and redemption to man. Thus, the moral teachings are seen within the wider framework of theological affirmations and of the Christian experience of sin and forgiveness through Jesus Christ. The Bible, to put it simply, has a different moral authority for Christians than it has for others. But the variations within this statement are in effect the story of Christian ethics throughout history.

Radical Reformation groups. On the American scene there are Christian groups for whom a literal compliance with the gospel ethic—particularly its commands to love, to meekness, to service— is both an aspiration and a pattern of life. The historic peace churches in the Anabaptist and Quaker traditions, for example, have taken part of the moral teaching to require nonviolence, pacifism, and deeply sacrificial service as the proper expression of Christian life. But there are as yet no American academic treatises that give powerful theological defenses of the Anabaptist view, though in occasional writings such a person as John Howard Yoder promises to be a formidable and theologically informed interpreter and defender of this tradition. Among liberal Quakers, Rufus Jones and Douglas Steere have been more or less faithful to the tradition of a pacifist interpretation of both "inner light" and a Sermon on the Mount ethic. There is no expectation of great worldly success in such ethical teaching; these Christians expect to be a minority representation of faithfulness, and are prepared to suffer at the hands of a more expedient and prudential world.

Evangelical conservative Protestants: revealed morality. A larger segment of American Protestantism is represented by the conservative evangelical position, sometimes the fundamentalist one, in which the "propositional revelation" of the Bible has an authority in matters of both faith and conduct. The words of the Bible are quite literally the word of God, whether they tell us about God and his glory, about man and his rebellion, about the new life that conversion creates, or about the moral conduct that is required of the children of God. This tradition has begun to find new expressions in scholarly work in ethics. The major recent contributor is Carl F. H. Henry, whose *The Uneasy Conscience of Modern Fundamentalism* (1947) opened the way for discussions of social ethics among those groups that had formerly identified that interest with degenerate Christian liberalism. In a very large and ambitious work, *Christian Personal Ethics* (1957), Henry gives more specific expression to his view of biblical authority for ethics. It is framed by his larger conservative use of the Bible in matters of theology. His preference for the moral use of the Bible seems to combine elements of the Anabaptist tradition, which he honors in part because it does not make Christian ethics subjective and humanistic, and the Reformed tradition, which sought within the scripture a design and order for the lives of the members of the Christian church. The reality of Christian ethics comes from the "unique Divine inbreaking" that is recorded in the Bible. "The Christian ethic is a specially revealed morality— not merely religious ethics. It gains its reality in and through supernatural disclosure" (*Christian Personal Ethics*, p. 193). Since Chris-

311

tian ethics is a special and not a universal revelation, it is not accessible to all men; it is the ethics of the believing church. "The ethics of revealed religion therefore divides mankind into two radically opposed groups: the followers of the broad way and those of the narrow way" (p. 203). The divine will is clear: "What God has revealed in the inspired Scriptures defines the content of his will" (p. 264). The historic conviction is "that God has been pleased to reveal his will, and that he has done so in express commands, given to chosen men through the medium of human language, and available to us as the *Word* of God in written form" (p. 265). This will is particularized in the Old and New Testaments, though in a "progressive" way. "A later age is always called upon to 'fulfill' the continuing moral claim, although God may supersede certain positive laws in the newer era" (p. 269). Henry reminds his readers that they are not to take the moral teaching in isolation from the rest of biblical revelation; this is true of the details both of Old and New Testaments. Thus in studying the Sermon on the Mount, Jesus' larger teaching and the whole of the New Testament must be kept in view. But "the Sermon remains an 'ethical directory' for Christians. It contains the character and conduct which Jesus commends to his followers, the demand which the nature and will of God make upon men, the fundamental law of the Kingdom, and the ideal and perfect standard. It is the ultimate formula of ethics for which ideal human nature was fashioned by creation and is destined in eternity. Fallen nature is justified in Christ in conformity to it, and redeemed nature approximates it by the power of the indwelling Spirit of God" (pp. 325-26).

The seriousness with which the moral teachings of the Bible are taken by Henry can best be seen in contrast with Paul Lehmann's view of the Christian life. The way in which the authority of the Bible is understood by these men is, of course, radically different. Whereas Lehmann develops a biblical theology that describes the human maturity in faith in which man in his freedom is sensitive to the freedom of God, Henry is saying that God has declared himself on matters of morals as well as faith in highly particularized ways in the words of the Bible. Henry acknowledges that it is not always easy to move from moral propositions in the Bible to the particular situations in which men must act, but in contrast to Lehmann, he has substantive, authoritative moral propositions from which to begin the process. The Bible is law as well as gospel.

Liberal Protestantism: revealed morality in a different form. One of the characteristics of the ethics of liberal Christianity was its focus on the "spirit" of Jesus and on the authority of his teachings, as these are depicted in the gospel narratives. No intelligent theologians were so simple-minded as to assume that the teachings of Jesus could be immediately applied to the contemporary world, but they did seek the possibility of "translating" them into current needs. Macintosh is typical of this when he wrote, "What we may have to do . . . is to translate into the terms of our best twentieth-century empirical knowledge and world-view the principles of social action normatively present in the spirit and ideal of the Jesus of history and expressed by him, quite naturally, in terms of the concepts available in his day" (*Social Religion,* p. 5). Various aspects of the teachings and deeds of Jesus were used by various interpreters to serve as the basic framework for the fundamental pattern for moving from the authority of the "Jesus of history" to the contemporary world. Some used the notion of the Kingdom of God; some took the command to love the neighbor. Macintosh chose the beatitudes to give the framework to his interpretation of the social content of the gospel. His use of the saying "Blessed are the poor, for theirs is the Kingdom of God" not only illustrates his work, but also suggests the kinds of uses of the Bible that others made.

The Kingdom of God is to be "the rule of God's will in human life, individually, and socially." Thus when Jesus spoke the saying, "he must have meant that when, through the divine initiative and man's response, God's rule was established on earth and God's will was being done fully enough in a sufficient number of human lives for them to revolutionize social relations and make society a genuine brotherhood under the divine Fatherhood, poverty would soon be abolished" (p. 42). A related narrative is Jesus' story of the workers in the vineyard (Matt. 20:1-16). From this narrative Macintosh draws the moral: "From everyone according to his ability; to every one according to his need." "A job for every one, and 'a living wage for every one willing to work.'" In summary, Macintosh is able by the alchemy of his religious thought and feeling to move from these accounts in the Bible to a definition of the social order that is coming through both God's work and man's works. "In the Kingdom the hungry will be fed, not by mere acts of charity, but by a system of justice under which they will be helped to help themselves. When the Kingdom is established, when God's will is being done, people will be brotherly enough to see to it that none hunger in vain, either for food or for social and economic justice" (p. 45).

The use of the Bible typified by Macintosh had important effects upon the work of Christian ethics. It permitted a "translation" of biblical ideas into contemporary language in such a way that a program for "objective ethics"—that is, for the shaping of moral action in the world—could be authorized by the Bible. The Kingdom of God could become a kind of cooperative democratic commonwealth, and thus provide the end toward which man's historical activity is to be directed. The beatitude "Blessed are the poor" could become the basis for proposing a genuinely "Christian communism" as both the ideal toward which men should move and the state of life that will exist in the Kingdom.

But even before Macintosh wrote, the assumptions upon which this use of the Bible was made in ethics were undercut radically by biblical scholars. Much earlier, Albert Schweitzer had suggested that Jesus' ethic was an "interim" one, to be valid until the soon forthcoming Kingdom would arrive. The form critics were questioning the historical authenticity of many of the sayings of Jesus, as well as narratives about him. And historically minded men were raising questions about the easy translation of first century language, with its own particular metaphors, into contemporary social life. If the words of the Bible were to be morally authoritative, the writer in Christian ethics had to find some other way to use them. In America as in Europe, he generally chose to depend upon a summary statement of them, such as in the command to love God and thy neighbor. Or biblical words became first of all a revelation of God, and the morality of the Bible more illustrative of a proper life in relation to God and man than a revealed morality. Certainly, what Carl F. H. Henry suggests as revealed morality is generally rejected or radically qualified, and most recent writers would never try to move from biblical statements to contemporary moral statements in the manner of D. C. Macintosh.

Love: the summary of biblical ethics. The "law of love" became the major summary generalization of biblical morality. Reinhold Niebuhr, it will be recalled, suggested the centrality of love as the distinctive element in Christian ethics. Earlier for Niebuhr the source for this norm was primarily the transcendent morality introduced by the teachings of Jesus; later the crucifixion became the symbol of the highest form of love. In either case, the Bible presents to us an expectation that life is to be governed both inwardly and outwardly by love, both in the intentions of the moral man and in the formation of a state of affairs in the world. Niebuhr's long-time colleague John C. Bennett, whose writings and work in ecclesiastical and ecumenical agencies are of central importance to the story of Christian ethics in recent decades, also fixes upon love as the mark of Christian ethics. "The distinctive element in Christian ethics is the primacy of love, the self-giving love that is known fully to Christian faith in the Cross of Christ" (in A. Dudley Ward, ed., *Goals of Economic Life*, 1953, p. 421). Thus a generalization is made on the basis of the Bible, a generalization that is moral in its language, based upon both moral teachings and example in the New Testament. This view of the Bible builds in a problem of translation, or at least transition, from the general moral propositions given in historically unachievable terms to the realities of the time-bound, historically contingent world. The transition from Bible to contemporary world is then made through the use of less uniquely Christian "values" or terms, such as justice. These terms, and more explicit imperative propositions derived from them, in turn regulate the ends to be sought by moral man and the forms of action he will use to seek those ends. The pure morality of love is always compromised in the movement from the Bible to the world. But there is a sense in which the Bible still contains a revealed morality: it provides distinctive moral norms or values that have authority for the Christian community. These now have a generalized form, rather than the form of the particular propositions given in particular biblical texts. Compromise is required when men who use the Bible in this way wish Christian ethics to inform social and political moral responsibility, and not be merely the "narrow way" for an exemplary Christian community. This use of the Bible is consistent with the preceding generation of liberal theologians, who found in its morality the pattern for contemporary morality; the Bible continued to be in some sense a book of moral teachings with a high level of authority.

The Bible: revealed reality rather than revealed morality. Concurrently, however, a revolution in biblical theology was taking place in Europe and, to a lesser extent, in America. The shift might be overstated as one from ethics to faith, from religion to God, from man to Jesus Christ. Under the impact of the crisis theologians, and particularly Karl Barth, men were saying that the Bible is not the revelation of a morality, but the revelation of the living God; it does not cultivate a human cultural phenomenon called religion that has any significance in its own right, but it points to God and to God's call to men for faith in him; it is not centered upon what men are and ought to do, but upon Jesus Christ as the revelation of God, in the light of whom theological knowledge of men comes. This revolution in theology had much more far-reaching consequences for Christian ethics than did the reassessment of the moral potentialities of men, for it changed the prime point of reference for all thinking in ethics and all moral activity on the part of Christians. In the place of moral teachings, particularized or generalized, the new theology put God in his living, free activity. Thus Christian ethics had to think not about morality reduced to propositions, but about God and how life ought to be rightly related to his power and his presence. The Bible then finds a different use in the thinking of ethics, and its moral teachings are set in a different context. For Carl F. H. Henry both knowledge of God and moral knowledge are authoritatively given in "propositional revelation" in the words of the Bible. For Macintosh the Bible did not give propositional revelation, but its moral teachings expressed the spirit of the "Jesus of history" and thus in turn were a basic blueprint for morality. For Reinhold Niebuhr and John C. Bennett the Bible was not propositional revelation, but revealed God's self-sacrificial love, which in turn was conceptualized in images of commands and love. But for Karl Barth, the Bible first of all points toward the living God, known in Jesus Christ, and thus what is required of ethics is obedience to a Person, not a proposition, or, in the language of H. Richard Niebuhr, *response* to a Person, and not a rule.

H. Richard Niebuhr: response to a revealing God. This change in the fundamental way of thinking, and thus in the use of the Bible, can be illustrated by some of the work of H. Richard Niebuhr. He found too much of Christian ethics trying to find "Christian answers" to problems of morality and culture, rather than being open and responsive to the work of the living Lord. In introducing his great work on *Christ and Culture* (1951), Niebuhr says, "The belief which lies back of this effort . . . is the conviction that Christ as Living Lord is answering the question in the totality of history and life in a fashion which transcends the wisdom of all his interpreters yet employs their partial insights and their necessary conflicts" (p. 2). The crucial point is the stress on the notion that the *"Living Lord is answering"* in the totality of history and life. There are interpretations of what he is doing, but men are not finally to rely upon them, though they give partial insights. This means, it appears, that the Bible itself is of penultimate significance in the work of Christian ethics and that its importance is to enable men to understand and interpret what the "Living Lord" is saying and doing. It points beyond itself; its moral teachings point beyond themselves; the Christian community is to understand its morality in response to God rather than in response to statements about God. The Bible is more important for helping the Christian community to interpret the God whom it knows in its existential faith than it is for giving a revealed morality that is to be translated and applied in the contemporary world. This led Niebuhr to be critical of theologians who use such phrases as "the absolutism and perfectionism of Jesus' love ethic," including his distinguished brother. He retorts, "Jesus nowhere commands love for its own sake"; the virtue of Jesus' character and demand is not "love of love" but "love of God and the neighbor in God." "It was not love but God that filled his soul" (*Christ and Culture,* pp. 15-19). The Christian moral life, then, is not a response to moral imperatives, but to a Person, the living God.

The effect of this transposition in the function of the Bible can be seen in H. Richard Niebuhr's almost lyrical description of the meaning of love in Christian ethics. It is not a norm. Rather, love is an indicative before it is an imperative. "Faith in God's love toward man is perfected in man's love to God and neighbor." "Through

317

Jesus Christ we receive enough faith in God's love toward us to see at least the need for and the possibility of a responsive love on our part. We know enough of the possibility of love to God on our part to long for its perfection; we see enough of the reality of God's love toward us and neighbor to hope for its full revelation and so for our full response." Love is not a law, but "rejoicing over the existence of the beloved one"; it is "gratitude" for the existence of the beloved; it is "reverence" that "keeps its distance even as it draws near"; it is "loyalty," the "willingness to let the self be destroyed rather than that the other cease to be" (*The Purpose of the Church and Its Ministry*, 1956, pp. 33, 35). Love is basically defined, then, in terms of attitudes and actions; it comes into being in the close interrelation of "God's love of the self and neighbor, of the neighbor's love of God and self, and of the self's love of God and neighbor." What the Bible makes known, then, is not a morality, but a *reality*, a living presence to whom man responds. For questions of morality, its authority is "educational," giving men knowledge of themselves and knowledge of God in the light of which they interpret their responsibilities and act; its authority is "corroborative," providing a court of validation that aids the Christian community in seeing its perversities and in verifying its true purposes.

Paul Lehmann: ethics of the biblical indicative. The alteration of the imperative mode in Christian ethics that is present in the writings of H. Richard Niebuhr is even stronger in the work of Paul Lehmann. In a widely acclaimed essay of 1953 ("The Foundation and Pattern of Christian Behavior," in *Christian Faith and Social Action*, ed. John A. Hutchison) that influenced the writing of Albert Rasmussen (*Christian Social Ethics*, 1956), Alexander Miller (*The Renewal of Man*, 1955), and others, Lehmann states that "an ethic, based upon the self-revelation of God in Jesus Christ, is more concerned about 'The Divine Indicative' than it is about the 'Divine Imperative.' The primary question is not 'What does God command?' The primary question is 'What does God do?'" (p. 100). Thus, the importance of the Bible for Christian ethics does not lie in its moral imperatives, but in its delineation of what God is doing to "make and keep life human." "Christian ethics . . . is oriented toward revelation and not toward morality"; and "Christian ethics aims, not at morality, but at maturity. The *mature* life is the fruit of Christian faith. Morality is a by-product of maturity" (*Ethics in a Christian Context,* 1963, pp. 45, 54). The importance of the Bible is what it tells about Jesus Christ. Thus in Lehmann's full-length treatise on Christian ethics there is no significant treatment of biblical morality, even as a guide to the mature life. Rather, the mature man discerns through his transformed motivation and his sensitive imagination what God is doing and, therefore, what man should do in correspondence with what God is doing.

Joseph Sittler: the shape of the engendering deed. In a similar mode is the most significant contribution to Christian ethics in America made by a Lutheran theologian, Joseph Sittler's *The Structure of Christian Ethics* (1958). (Lutherans have only within the past decade begun to produce significant literature in Christian ethics: the work of George Forell, William Lazareth, and Franklin Sherman shows the emerging interest.) Sittler wishes to develop biblical ethics. But he does not do this from the distinctly moral statements in the Bible. Rather, there is a more important structure for understanding Christian morality that can be seen in the fact that God is not defined, but simply is what he does; that a vocabulary of relatedness rather than a vocabulary of substance abounds; that its logic is "the inner logic of the living, the organic." Biblical language is primarily descriptive and indicative. Jesus himself is to be seen in this way: the content of his importance is constituted "by a lived-out and heroically obedient God-relationship in the fire of which all things are what they are by virtue of the creator, all decisions are crucial in virtue of their witness to his primacy and glory, all events interpreted in terms of their transparency, recalcitrancy, or service to God's Kingly rule" (p. 12). The prime importance of the Bible for ethics is that it tells the story of "the shape of the engendering deed," that is, the record of what the living God has actually done in creation, redemption, and sanctification. The living God continues to engender man's involvement in what he is doing. Thus Christian ethics gives an account of the Christian life: "a re-enactment from below on the part of man of the shape of the revelatory drama of God's holy will in Jesus Christ. . . . Suffering, death, burial, resurrection, a new life—these are actualities that plot out the arc of God's

319

self-giving deed in Christ's descent and death and ascension; and precisely *this same shape of grace,* in its recapitulation within the life of the believer and the faithful community, is the nuclear matrix which grounds and unfolds as the Christian life" (p. 36). Christian ethics is the actualization of God's justification of man. It describes life according to a plotted arc; the arc, however, is not the morality given in the Bible, but rather the "shape of the engendering deed."

This indicative mode, with its particular use of the Bible, has not gone unchallenged in American Protestant ethics. It has been criticized in the extreme form for the absence of any procedures of rational reflection about what men are to do. Paul Ramsey, Robert Fitch, Alvin Pitcher, Clinton Gardner, and John C. Bennett have all written critiques on this issue. Indeed, it tends to become what has been called a "contextual" ethics, and against this has been pitted an "ethics of principles," which finds propositional moral imperatives, either directly from the Bible or mediated through the tradition, that are to provide the guidelines of conduct. This issue is reserved for exploration in the next section, "Procedures for Ethical Reflection."

The Bible in Roman Catholic ethics. The use of the Bible has traditionally been the place where the difference between Roman Catholic and Protestant Christian ethics was clearest. Whereas most Protestants have turned to the Bible for the starting point of Christian ethics, whether personal or social, for most questions Roman Catholics have relied upon the natural law that is, in their interpretation, shared by all mankind. The recent American Catholics have shared in that tradition. There is a "science of ethics" independent from revelation. Indeed, the term *Christian ethics* has not been widely used among Roman Catholic writers. For most ethical questions, the distinctively Christian elements have not been of great importance. For example, one of the most widely read recent treatises on matters of American public ethics—*We Hold These Truths* (1960), by John Courtney Murray, S.J.—contains no references to biblical texts that Protestants traditionally grapple with on questions of the state, such as Romans 13:1-7. There is no effort to define what is going on in contemporary society in terms of "what God is doing." Rather, the theoretical foundations are in the Thomistic tradition of natural law. "The doctrine of natural law has no Roman Catholic presuppositions. Its only presupposition is three-fold: that man is intelligent; that reality is intelligible; and that reality, grasped by intelligence, imposes on the will the obligation that it be obeyed in its demands for action or abstention" (p. 109). Most questions of ethics, and particularly public ethics, are dealt with on this natural-law foundation. The more distinctive "Christian" elements of religion deal with the theological virtues and with man's supernatural end, and these relate indirectly back upon the rational moral life. But even here the traditional pattern for interpretation is Thomistic, rather than in the first instance biblical. The morality of saints, with their imitations of Christ, has not been a general expectation for all Christians.

The major American treatise entitled *Christian Ethics* written by a Roman Catholic is remarkably free of biblical references. Dietrich von Hildebrand, in his 1953 publication, makes of Christian ethics a philosophical discipline that is distinct from moral theology. "It is a pure philosophical exploration introducing no arguments which are not accessible through our *lumen naturale* (light of reason), whereas in moral theology faith is presupposed, and revealed truth which surpasses our reason is included in the argumentation. Christian ethics is a strict *philosophical* analysis, starting from the data accessible to our mind through experience" (p. 455). All morality presupposes the existence of God, and the philosophical analysis of Christian morality obviously assumes that many human moral responses and virtues are possible only through Christian revelation. But the analysis does not begin with the datum of revelation in the Bible.

To look for the use of the Bible in Roman Catholic morality, then, one turns to *moral theology* and to the discussions of the Christian virtues. Moral theology presupposes divine revelation "and the proved conclusions of dogmatic theology." In moral theology texts long used in America, such as *Moral and Pastoral Theology,* by Henry Davis, S.J., there is a characteristic structure that brings no surprises. The Bible is used to substantiate the existence of a supernatural, ultimate end for man—namely, that he is to enjoy eternal beatitude in the vision of God. But the bulk of moral theology deals with the natural moral acts of man; here the Thomistic structure asserts itself vigorously as the dominant framework, and the Bible is quoted (so it appears to these Protestant eyes) to proof-text a point already established on principles independent of biblical discussion. Or the Bible is quoted as the divine revealed law that, like the natural law, participates in the eternal law in the mind of God. As particular instances of moral problems come into view, the procedures of casuistry are employed with great rational refinement, in contrast with what Sittler called the "organic language" of the scripture.

There are evidences of a changing pattern in Roman Catholic moral theology, however, that ought to be noted. Two currently widely read texts in moral theology—Bernhard Häring's *The Law of Christ* (2 vols.; English trans., 1961, 1963) and Gérard Gilleman's *The Primacy of Charity in Moral Theology* (English trans., 1959)—and other writings appear to soften the distinction between the natural and the supernatural, and to place Christian love at the center of the whole interpretation of ethics. Indeed, the biblical text that gives these books of European origin their titles is from Romans: "For the law of the Spirit of the life in Christ Jesus has delivered me from the law of sin and of death." Whereas traditional Catholic ethics deals with the natural principles of morality first, and later comes to the higher law of love, Häring, Gilleman, and others begin with the more distinctively Christian and biblical principle of love and seek to keep it at the center of the whole enterprise of moral theology. A few quotations from Häring's Foreword demonstrate the new emphasis. "The principle, the norm, the center, and the goal of Christian Moral Theology is Christ. The law of the Christian is Christ Himself in Person. He alone is our Lord, our Saviour. In Him we have life and therefore also the law of our life." The emphasis here is on a *Christian* ethics, expressing the religious relationship with God in moral terms. "In the love of and through the love of Christ for us He invites our love in return, which is a life truly formed in Christ. The Christian life is following Christ, but not through mere external copying, even though it be in love and obedience. Our life must above all be a life in Christ." "Christian morality is life flowing from the victory of Christ, the hopeful anticipation of the Second Coming of the Saviour in the glorious manifestation of His final triumph on the great day of judgment" (*The Law of Christ,* vol. I, p. vii). Moral theology is reaffirming the biblical tradition, reaffirming those aspects of the Catholic tradition that set Christian ethics in the context of God's loving action and see the norm for every man to be a life sharing in union with Christ and in imitation of him. Häring affirms his purpose to be to expound the most central truths in the light of the inspired word of the Bible. Younger American clergy are quickly beginning to think in those new modes, and no doubt the Bible will find a different place in indigenous American moral theology as a result.

Discussion of the Christian virtues is a second place to see the use of the Bible. Traditionally, Catholics have tended to follow Thomas Aquinas in his distinction between the cardinal virtues and the theological virtues. The latter—faith, hope, and love—are gifts of grace given by participation in the sacramental life of the church. For them, obviously there is a distinctive Christian referent, derived through Catholic interpretation from the Bible. This two-level interpretation, however, is also being altered. A notable American book, Dietrich von Hildebrand's *Transformation in Christ,* is one example of a more biblically centered (though obviously Catholic and not Protestant in exposition) interpretation of the Christian life. Perhaps the text that is central to this book is from 1 Peter 2: "That you may declare his virtues, who hath called you out of darkness into his marvelous light." It is a book that seeks to describe how, through baptism and communion, man is allowed to participate in the life of Christ. The shaping of the Christian life is not so much a matter of external heteronomous norms by which men are to be governed and ruled as it is one of finding the appropriate expression in life for what God has done for man in Jesus Christ. The "supernatural life" is not relegated to achievement by those set apart in the orders, nor is it in von Hildebrand's treatment something to be received in the life beyond death; it is both a reality and a task for the Christian believer (the author is himself a layman) in his present existence.

If a study of more recent Roman Catholic ethics leaves a correct impression, it is clear that the Bible is coming to play a far more significant role and have a more central location in Catholic literature. The traditional distinctions between the ethics of natural law and special Christian morality are being blurred. The biblical witness to God's own presence and action as being both matrix and context for Christian life is being stressed. And the central biblical conception of Christian love is becoming the norm under which all action is judged and directed. Yet no important writers have left the traditional philosophical language behind. What the impact of these mostly imported European writings will be on American Catholic ethics is still unclear, but if it continues to make its way on this continent, men like Father Murray who have reputations in Protestant America for being liberals are likely to appear to be highly traditionalistic.

European influences have been very important among both Catholics and Protestants in altering the place of the Bible in the study of Christian ethics. Between the World Wars American Protestant theologians followed the developments and debates of European theology and biblical scholarship with increasing care. The ecumenical movement, particularly the great 1938 Oxford Conference on Life and Work, provided the occasion for personal discussion and for the influence of Europeans on American ethics. The struggle of the confessing Christians in Germany against the Nazi state provided one of the most significant occasions in modern church history for reflections on the relation of biblical faith to moral concerns. Some of the writings of participants in the "theological revival" in Europe were translated into English. Anders Nygren's *Agape and Eros* was particularly influential in raising issues about the meaning of Christian love.

Since World War II, many important volumes of European theological ethics have become available in English and thus are widely read by students and teachers alike: H. Emil Brunner's *The Divine Imperative,* major volumes of Barth's *Church Dogmatics* that deal with ethics, the writings of Dietrich Bonhoeffer, Kierkegaard, Rudolf Bultmann, Helmut Thielicke, Gustaf Aulen, Gustaf Wingren, Jacques Ellul, and others. The points at issue between these writers are important, and the American reception of them has not lacked in discriminating sophistication. They all do, however, work from an understanding of the high theological authority of the Bible and thus, as conversation partners for American theological ethics, keep the Bible quite at the center of discussion.

Among Roman Catholics, biblical studies have had a new status in all spheres of theological research and discourse since World War II. This is bound to have effects not only on dogmatic theology, but also upon traditional Catholic distinctions between the general science of ethics, moral theology, ascetic theology, pastoral theology, and so forth. Very important also is the way in which the renewal of interest in biblical studies in both Catholicism and Protestantism has coincided with the expansion of the ecumenical discussion. It is clear that one of the directions that scholarship in Christian ethics will take in the next decades is cross-confessional critique and interpretation nourished in part by a common interest in the Bible as the charter document for the Christian movement in history. And one of the questions that will be dealt with is that of the relation between revealed reality (God's presence, his love, his sustaining and redeeming work) and morality (the shape of personal life and social order that is appropriate to faith in God). One aspect of this question is what procedures of ethical reflection are appropriate to the Christian community and to Christian theology.

Procedures of Ethical Reflection

The basic theological convictions of a scholar in Christian ethics deeply affect the manner in which he will delineate the procedures of ethical reflection. If the Bible is a revealed morality, either he will require a literal obedience to its moral teachings or he will design a procedure by which they can be applied to contemporary experience. If moral propositions can be derived from the nature of man's being, these must be brought to bear upon behavior. If man is interpreted as a creature responding to the presence of God and his work in the world, the scholar must describe a way to discern whether one's response is "fitting" or coincides with what God is doing. If the tradition provides viable summary propositions concerning Christian morality, these must be directed to current issues of morality. The scholar's view of the Bible and its importance, of man and his relation to others, and of God and the mode of his involvement in the world will shape the pattern of his ethical thought.

In recent American Protestant literature, advocates of positions sometimes called "contextualism" and an "ethics of principles" have published a series of charges against one another. *Ethics of inspira-*

tion and *ethics of ends* are the terms the English ecumenical leader J. H. Oldham has used to describe the positions. The discussion is grossly oversimplified in its polarized form, but it points to two tendencies present in recent discussion. Paul Lehmann is the contextualist par excellence; H. Richard Niebuhr's thought tends to go toward contextualism, though by a different path. The name is earned by virtue of the stress placed upon doing the right thing in relation to what is occurring. What is occurring has both its empirical aspects (a reading of the events and the times) and its theological aspects (discerning what God is doing). Those who apply the term *contextualism* pejoratively see little place for the use of traditional ethical principles and moral reasoning in this mode of work. They see in it an excessively existentialist posture that relies too heavily upon imagination, intuition, and free response. Paul Ramsey and John C. Bennett have been, in different ways, the defenders of "principles." They have stressed the importance of statements of moral imperatives: in Bennett's case, *goals* derived from the biblical norm of love; in Ramsey's case, *principles of right conduct* shaped by Christian love and natural law. The critics of ethics of principles believe that this view errs in not taking the activity of the living God as the theological starting point for ethics; that it excessively intellectualizes the moral life by reducing it to the logical applications of ethical generalizations; and that consequently it has a hard time closing the gap between principles and actions.

The issues that divide the extremes are hardly theological alone, however, for theologians display in their procedures affinites for certain points of view in philosophy. It is not an accident that Lehmann finds William James to be a congenial philosopher, and that H. Richard Niebuhr is indebted to G. H. Mead, to Martin Buber, and other existentialists. It is clear that Ramsey wants to be identified with the natural-law tradition, with its affirmations of man's capacity to appropriate moral truth and to exercise his reason in the direction of his action. Though he is harder to identify with particular philosophers, John C. Bennett shows the marks of the kind of moral idealism (not with reference to the expectation of moral perfection, but to the distinction between ideal and actual) that informed liberal Protestant ethics.

Roman Catholicism has traditionally been on the "principles" side

326

of this particular polarization, finding laws both in nature and in scripture that are to be applied to the actualization of the inherent purposes in man. But with the new stresses on biblical theology in Catholicism, and with the impact of the language from phenomenological existentialism, one finds movement out of the traditional procedures into a more situational approach. American Catholic writers tend to be critical of situational ethics: this can be seen especially in *Contemporary Moral Theology* (1958) by John C. Ford, S.J., and Gerald Kelly, S.J. In his widely read article "Situational Morality" (*Thought*, XXXII [1957], 533-58), Robert Gleason, S.J., states the issue in the following terms: "The ultimate differences between this new morality and traditional morality come down then to this: in an objective system of ethics the moral judgment is submitted to an extrinsic norm, an ontological norm founded on the principles of being. In situational ethics the moral judgment is measured only by the subjective, immanent light of the individual in question." Gleason gives a more sympathetic interpretation of contextualism than do Ford and Kelly, but in the end he is sharply critical. "The subjectivism and relativism that are in some degree implicit in situational ethics make it quite unacceptable to the Christian mind, even though the excellent intentions and partial intuitions of the system may be admired" (pp. 555, 558).

Contextualists earn the appellation for different reasons. Some, such as Kenneth Underwood, who are concerned with social policy, believe that the moralist must have technical knowledge of economics, political science, urban renewal, or other pertinent areas. For them, one cannot be a good ethicist without knowing the "nonethical" materials about which moral judgments are to be made. Sociological, political, economic, and other kinds of research are necessary for the intelligent conduct of ethical discourse. Social action and policy statements require such information. A recent example of literature that stresses this point is Bruce Morgan's *Christians, The Church, and Property* (1963). This affirmation of the importance of technical knowledge, however, is accepted by such people as Ramsey and Bennett.

Others are called contextualists for doctrinal reasons. If one stresses *the freedom of God* to do and to command different things at different times, a sensitivity to the changing conditions under which moral responsibility is exercised is necessary. There are no fixed rules through which God acts; there are no absolutely clear principles that govern the divine ordering of the world. Paul Lehmann, in this instance following closely upon Karl Barth, invokes the freedom of God as the theological principle of prime importance in the determination of thought and action in Christian ethics—it is more important than God's love or God's law, for example. If the Christian ethical thinker stresses in his doctrine of God the present *creating, governing, and redeeming work of God* in the world, he must seek to interpret the events and situations of which he is a part in the light of these theological affirmations. Thus, in the ethics of H. Richard Niebuhr one finds the dictum "Responsibility affirms: 'God is acting in all actions upon you. So respond to all actions upon you as to respond to his action'" (*The Responsible Self*, p. 126). Each occasion of responsibility requires an action that is fitting to the actions that are occuring in which God is himself acting. The ability to interpret situations in the light of theological principles is stressed.

Contextualism is derived not only from certain doctrines of God but from certain Christological emphases as well. Proponents of an ethics of principles tend to stress Christ as a source of moral norms that stem from both his teachings and his deeds, whereas contextualists tend to stress Christ as the living, reigning Lord. Paul Lehmann, for example, builds his Christian ethics upon the idea that in the lordship of Christ a new humanity has been given. The world is to be regarded in the light of the victory of Christ over the powers of sin, death, and law. Both believer and unbeliever are confronted by an environment "being shaped by Christ's royal and redemptive activity." The moral action of Christians has the symbolic significance of pointing to what Christ is doing for men in the fact of their new humanity that he has given. Thus there are no set principles that define what men ought to do; Christians are to have "imaginative and behavioral sensitivity to what God is doing in the world to make and to keep human life human, to achieve the maturity of men, that is, the new humanity" (*Ethics in a Christian Context*, p. 117). For Joseph Sittler, Christian action is defined in terms of the "re-enactment" in every sphere and realm of life of the "shape of grace" that has been given in Christ. The relation of the moral actor to the world is an organic one; he participates in its life in a way analogical to the way Christ has participated in the life of the world. This cannot be reduced to principles or to rules of conduct, but is a matter of living out our justification in Christ, of "faith-facts" in which the action of men will be appropriate to the occasion.

Certain views of the nature of man also lead to a contextualism. This is clearest in H. Richard Niebuhr's notion of the man living in response to actions upon him. As we have seen, he distinguishes his view from teleological and deontological views. In the Christian form of the first, man is reminded that God has a plan for his life and that he is to shape his life according to a plan. This would lead, in its procedures of moral reflection, to the delineation of what God's plan is, and then to a means-ends scheme to bring the actual conditions into accord with that plan. In the Christian form of deontological ethics, man is reminded that he is to obey God's law in his obedience to all finite rules. This would lead to the delineation of how finite rules are related to God's law and to an assessment of which particular rules are most in accord with God's rule. In contrast to these, the idea that man is characterized by responses to particular actions upon him makes the definition of moral responsibility by means of plans, ends, and rules almost invalid. Man is in a pattern of relationships; he is to do what is fitting in response to what is being done to him.

The effect of these various reasons for espousing contextualism on the procedures of reflection and action becomes clear. The ethical thinker does not design ideal schemes and then propose the procedures by which they can be actualized. For one thing, changing historical circumstances make this impossible. One cannot control the shape of events that are subject to so many different sources of determination. God has not provided some grand plan for the world's moral life; he is not the great designer, but the active being who calls for proper action in the face of new occasions and new opportunities. To be sure, the Christian community is to act in accord with what it believes God to be saying and doing, but the mode of discerning this is not the delineation of a set of goals or rules, but the *interpretation* of events as occasions in which God's humanizing work (Lehmann) or God's governing and redeeming work (H. Richard

329

Niebuhr) is occurring. God is not the lawgiver, and man is not principally the being who obeys rules; God is the active being, and man is the responder to his actions.

To those who are schooled in more traditional procedures of ethical reflection, in the natural-law tradition, the Kantian deontological tradition, or the tradition of moral idealism, this contextualism appears to be a chaotic wasteland, providing no firm basis for the determination of conduct and no clear rational procedures for prescription of action. It appears to rely too heavily on intuitive responses, upon the illumination of the Spirit in the moral life, on the capacity through imagination and sensitivity to discern what God is doing, and how man's action can be coincident with God's action. Not all contextualists are equally culpable on each charge, but on the whole they appear to underestimate the importance of traditional modes of ethical reflection and are in danger of permitting what actually is occurring to dominate morality, of having the empirical *is* overwhelm the moral *ought*.

The tension between ethics of principles and contextualism is not new in the history of Christian ethics. Father Edward Duff, in *The Social Thought of the World Council of Churches* (1956), indicates that these two emphases represent roughly certain Roman Catholic and Protestant tendencies on the history of ethics. Not all Protestants would agree that Protestantism provides an ethics of inspiration, and in the contemporary American scene there have been counterstatements in the face of the emergence of American contextualism. Two important writers, until now only briefly mentioned, can be interpreted as resisters to contextualism and as affirmers of an important place for principles in Christian ethical discourse. They are John C. Bennett and Paul Ramsey. To Protestant writers can be added the continuing tradition of Roman Catholic natural-law ethics, vigorously espoused and widely influential in this country through the writings of the American John Courtney Murray, S.J., and others.

John C. Bennett has had a long career of writing in Christian ethics and of involvement in ecumenical social thought and action. A brief but very influential book that he wrote in mid-career, *Christian Ethics and Social Policy* (1946), illustrates the particular way in which he would use principles in the development of Christian social ethics. Bennett critically expounds four strategies of Christian social ethics—the Catholic, the sectarian, the identification of Christianity with particular social programs (often the error of the social gospel), and the "double standard for personal and public life"—that he finds characteristic of Lutheranism. He proceeds to develop a fifth strategy, which includes a statement of procedure for the formation of social goals. In fairness to Bennett, this goal-forming procedure has to be set in the context of other elements of his fifth strategy: these are the control of the *motives* of Christians by their faith and ethics in making decisions, the self-criticism that is encouraged by Christian humility, the criticism of all proposals in the light of Christian love, and the margin of freedom that is given to Christians in the exercise of any policy or judgment. For purposes of indicating the issues that are drawn between contextualism and principles, however, Bennett's notion of "middle axioms" is of particular significance.

The idea of middle axioms was first expressed in those words by J. H. Oldham in *The Church and Its Function in Society* (1937), a volume written in preparation for the Oxford Conference of 1938 held by the Life and Work Movement. Oldham states that "middle axioms" are "an attempt to define the directions in which, in a particular state of society, Christian faith must express itself. They are not binding for all time, but are provisional definitions of the type of behavior required of Christians at a given period and in given circumstance" (p. 210). Bennett suggests that a middle axiom "is more concrete than a universal ethical principle and less specific than a program that includes legislation and political strategy" (*Christian Ethics and Social Policy*, p. 77). These axioms are to "give a sense of direction" to the activities of Christians. There is no Christian formula that can be given to the particular issues of foreign policy, or economic life, or strategy for race relations, but there are provisional statements that can be made of goals that represent the purpose of God in a particular time.

An example will show how this procedure works. Christian love is a universal principle that cannot be easily applied to the area of economic life. Yet Christians are involved in the debates between free enterprise and social planning, and between particular policy options on particular levels of legislation and bargaining. Bennett proposes two middle axioms that could be a minimum basis for com-

331

mon action by American Christians: "That the national community acting through government in cooperation with industry, labor, and agriculture has responsibility to maintain full employment" and "That the national community should prevent all private centers of economic power from becoming stronger than the government" (p. 81). These axioms, then, provide a statement of consensus (hopefully) that is formed with reference to universal moral principles, and with reference to the American economy as of 1946. They posit goals (full employment), means to achieve them (government action), and rules for the limitation of conduct (private interests must not become stronger than the national interest). These goals, means, and rules can then inform the discussions of particular policies, and can be applied to particular actions.

What would a contextualist response be to this kind of proposal? Those concerned with disciplined knowledge of the facts of economic life and policy would suggest that one has not yet gotten to the real moral and technical issues, if this is where Christian ethics ends. The crucial issues are in the analysis of what constitutes full employment (what percentage of the labor force can be tolerated as "hardcore" unemployment, what rate of growth of national product is needed to achieve full employment, and so forth). The discussion of ethics must be embedded in the analysis of the information needed to make a decision, and in the very concrete formulations of policy.

From Lehmann's point of view, the critical issue is at another point, and can be stated in his own words. "For a *koinonia* [contextual] ethic the clarification of ethical principles and their application to concrete situations is ethically unreal because such clarification is a logical enterprise and there is no way in logic of closing the gap between the abstract and the concrete. Ethics is a matter not of logic but of life, a certain kind of reality possessed by the concrete." The resolution of a problem in economics is not ethical because it has been directed by moral principles. Economic action is ethical insofar "as it bears the marks of God's transformation of the world in accordance with his purposes, of the world's resistance to what God is doing, and of God's ultimate overcoming of the world." An action is ethical "in so far as it is a *sign* of the new humanity" (*Ethics in a Christian Context,* p. 152). The defender of principles asks, "How does one discern what God is doing in the sphere of economic life, if not by the establishment of certain middle axioms or principles?" Lehmann appears to answer, "By the theonomous conscience that is sensitive to what God is doing."

The existence of such contextual ethics has been the occasion for Paul Ramsey to sharpen his polemic against the "wastelands of relativism," and to define a position he has called "Christ transforming natural law" or "faith effective through in-principled love." The crucial stress appears to be on the assertion that whatever transformation of the world Christ enables includes law, and that Christian freedom and love are normally expressed through rules of right conduct, through law. To state it another way, faith is active in love, as Luther and the Lutherans are quick to remind us, but the love through which faith is active is "in-principled." The ethical thinker and actor does not have to rely upon his more or less intuitive response to what is fitting in a particular event; he does not assume that his sensitivity and his theonomous conscience are adequate to discern the coincidence of his own free action and God's free action in the world. For Ramsey, speculation about consequences is hardly adequate to determine what is proper and improper.

Ramsey's view is most systematically worked out in *War and the Christian Conscience* (1961). This book has the merit of being a treatise in the methods of Christian ethical thought that at the same time deals substantively with a critical moral question, "How shall modern war be conducted justly?" This question, which forms the subtitle of the book, is itself stated in a way that indicates Ramsey's way of work. He does not first ask "For what ends can a war be fought?" but *"How* shall war be conducted?" With reference to war, as to other questions, the task of the Christian ethicist is to seek to determine what love permits and requires to be done and not to be done. "Thus, love posits or takes form in principles of right conduct which express the difference it discerns between permitted and prohibited action" (p. 4). For Ramsey, Christian ethics is not another form of utilitarianism, seeking to calculate prudentially the consequences of action according to technical political reason. To be sure, there is a place for consideration of the objectives of war. But one does not reason back from some statement of a calculated end to finding the means to achieve it. Ends and means interpenetrate, and this can be stated as follows: "Limited (or unlimited) means or weapons

333

are available and resolved to be used, and *therefore* limited (or unlimited) political objectives may be thought to be proper goals in war" (p. 7). The decision of proper means of conduct is as important as that of objectives; Christian ethics deals with *right conduct* according to in-principled love, and not just with concern for good and evil consequences.

In his statement of this position Ramsey clearly has various contextualists in view, and might even include John C. Bennett's goal-forming and goal-seeking ethics under the banner of things he wishes to criticize. "Those theologians who most stress the fact that Christian ethics is wholly predicated upon redemption or upon the Divine indicative, and who say that decisive action is made possible by virtue of *justification* in Christ and by God's *forgiveness,* are often precisely the thinkers who strip politics of norms and principles distinguishing between right and wrong action. For them policy decisions are always wholly relative or 'contextual,' pragmatically relating means to ends" (pp. 12-13). The course then is set for Ramsey's consideration of the problems of modern war, as it is for his consideration of questions of sexual morality or any other issue. There are reliable principles given to govern conduct. In the case of war these are the traditional ones of the just-war doctrine developed in Christian thought from the time of Augustine, and particularly the principle of non-combatant immunity. His argument is executed with a great deal of congeniality with Roman Catholic casuistry.

But Ramsey finds the natural-law ethics of the Roman Catholic to be excessively static. The issue between Ramsey's procedure and that of Roman Catholics is not one of whether the principles of casuistry are too refined, but the relation of Christian love as a principle to "nature." He finds in Catholic arguments against abortion, for example, that the moral theologians fail "to allow divine charity any vital role in the matter of morality" (p. 176). Theoretical reflection about wrong and right in concrete cases needs to be "kept open to the impact and guidance of Christian love, rather than smothering the requirements of love under what 'nature itself teaches.'" "Charity enters into a fresh determination of what is right and wrong in the given concrete context, and it is not wholly in bondage to natural-law determination of permitted or prohibited means. These rules are opened for review and radical revision in the instant *agape* controls" (pp. 177, 179). Finally, for Ramsey, as for Edward L. Long, principles of action devised in accordance with love are to be employed "not as a reliance but as a service."

Ramsey's position can be seen more sharply against that of Lehmann. For Ramsey, Christian love generally acts within the law and lays down rules or principles for the guidance of action, but it still exerts "a free and sovereign pressure—since Jesus Christ is Lord— toward fresh determination of what should be done in situations not rightly covered by the law, by natural justice, or even by its former articulation in principle" (p. 190). Ramsey works basically with Christian principles, and allows for the possibility that a more spontaneous act of love might be required. For Lehmann, to work with principles at all tends to become absolutistic, and the first fact is man's response in freedom to God's free action. Even in the determination of man's response there is little development of the place of rational moral reflection in Lehmann's book, though perhaps his theory permits more than in fact he has exercised. Lehmann works basically with open ends—man's freedom and God's freedom—and principles find little or no place.

Indeed, the proper method of reflection is just now a very live issue in Protestant Christian ethics, with Niebuhr's posthumous *The Responsible Self* joining works of Ramsey and Lehmann among the recent publications that address it. It is likely that the extreme poles set by Ramsey and Lehmann will both be subject to critical revision, and that a methodological pluralism will be recognized as valid in Christian ethics. Ramsey, as a previous quotation indicates, moves toward the "context" in which some more free spontaneous act is proper under certain circumstances. Lehmann frequently writes about God's "humanizing work," something that is probably capable of more precise explication in terms of moral principles than Lehmann gives. (See my "Context vs. Principles: A Misplaced Debate," *Harvard Theological Review*, April 1965.)

Perhaps a comparable dialogue is emerging in Roman Catholic ethics as well. At present, American Catholic moral theologians have in print no *radical* revisions of the traditional natural-law foundations or of the procedures of casuistry that have been exercised with reference to them. But the European trends referred to earlier will probably begin to have more effect at this point as well. Josef Pieper,

335

in a widely read essay on *Prudence* (1959), suggests that the excessive refinements of casuistry are a symptom of the human desire to achieve security. "It is rather that the striving for certainty and security can gravitate, by virtue of its own direction and its natural inclination, into the degenerate, anti-natural state of non-human rigidity. Indeed, this danger is all the greater the more powerfully the desire for certainty is concerned with the decision-making center of the spiritual person. Casuistry falls into this trap the very moment it claims to be more than a (probably indispensable) makeshift, an aid for sharpening judgment, a technique for temporary approximation, and more than the manipulation of a lifeless model" (p. 52). The refinements of casuistry have their traditional authority sharply challenged: all casuistry can do is to provide aid, "certainly not . . . an absolute standard for making ethical judgments and performing ethical actions." Pieper maximizes the virtue of prudence, particularly Christian prudence that is molded by charity. This Christian prudence "means precisely the throwing open of [the realm of determinative factors of our actions] and (in faith informed by love) the inclusion of new and invisible realities within the determinants of our decisions. . . . The highest and most fruitful achievements of Christian life depend upon the felicitous collaboration of prudence and charity" (p. 70).

Not only the stress on the virtue of prudence, a possibility that exists within the Thomistic system, but also the introduction of the language of response and responsibility that one finds in Häring and others could radically alter the procedures of ethical reflection in Roman Catholic ethics. The freedom of conscience to determine what is the right action, the responsible action, after being informed by the moral tradition of the church, could lead in the direction of contextualism. The personalistic model in which the relation of the believer to Jesus Christ is now often interpreted could mean a stress on doing what is in accord with the gifts Christ has given, rather than doing what experts in casuistry define as proper conduct on the basis of their reasoning from natural law. The act might be the same, whether derived from one avenue or the other, but the context of meaning out of which it emerges would be different.

✠ 3 ✠

CHRISTIAN ETHICS IN RELATION
TO OTHER FIELDS

Having suggested in Chapter 2 the way in which Christian ethics is related to biblical, theological, and philosophical work, I shall try in this chapter to lift out more clearly some of the relations of Christian ethics to these and other disciplines, and to suggest some of the influences on Christian ethics from other studies.

Ethics and Biblical Studies

In spite of the great interest in ethics in the past thirty years, and in spite of the extensive growth of biblical studies, there is a paucity of material that relates the two areas in a scholarly way. Writers in ethics necessarily make their forays into the Bible without the technical exegetical and historical acumen and skills to be secure in the way that they use biblical materials. But few biblical scholars have provided studies upon which writers in ethics can draw.

One would think, for example, with the renewal of interest in biblical theology and particularly in the Pauline and Johannine parts of the New Testament, that major monographs would have been written on New Testament ethics or at least on the relation of the faith of the early Christian community to its moral outlook. But this is not the case. For Pauline ethics, the best American work available is Morton Scott Enslin's *The Ethics of Paul* (1930), which has recently been reprinted. Amos N. Wilder has written occasional articles that relate New Testament themes to ethics, notably his essay "Kerygma, Eschatology, and Social Ethics," in W. D. Davies and David Daube's *The Background of the New Testament and Its Eschatology* (1956). Occasional monographs, such as Clinton D. Morrison's *The Powers That Be* (1960), bring technical exegetical competence to passages of Pauline materials that are important for ethics, but they are rare.

The ethical teachings of Jesus continue to be of great interest to

337

both biblical scholarship and Christian ethics. The principal movements of biblical interpretation that have brought a reassessment of their historical validity and their place in theology and ethics, however, have been European in origin. Earlier it was the work of Albert Schweitzer; in the contemporary period it is the work of Rudolf Bultmann and other form critics. Amos N. Wilder's *Eschatology and Ethics in the Teaching of Jesus* (1939; rev. ed., 1950) is the major American interpretation of the questions involved, and continues to be an important resource for the study of biblical ethics. A major work by W. D. Davies, *The Setting of the Sermon on the Mount,* has just been announced. Other American scholars who have written very brief but useful studies in the contemporary period are John Knox (*The Ethic of Jesus in the Teaching of the Church,* 1961) and E. C. Colwell (*An Approach to the Teaching of Jesus,* 1947).

The resources of American Old Testament scholarship that contribute to the study of ethics are even more meager. G. E. Wright's *God Who Acts* (1952) provides an overview of a major theological theme that can be appropriated by ethics. James Muilenberg's essays on the prophetic ethics are of some help—for example, his *Way of Israel* (1961). Various books on Old Testament theology provide analyses of key terms in Hebrew ethics (for example, Miller Burrows, *An Outline of Biblical Theology,* 1946) or interpretations of key events in Israel's history, but no major treatises on Old Testament ethics, as a whole or in part, have been provided.

Thus, for the biblical background of Christian ethics, one turns primarily to the work of European scholars. For Old Testament, the influence of such writers as Eichrodt and von Rad is beginning to be felt; for New Testament background, the works of Manson, Bultmann, and Cullman are particularly influential.

Work in Christian ethics is dependent upon biblical scholarship to some extent, but obviously moralists can never have the competence in the documentary and historical work that biblical scholars have. Further, the ethicist cannot adjudicate the competing interpretations within the biblical field, and therefore must make choices about the use of that material with reference to his own terms and interests. But it is not unfair to say that biblical scholars have provided a very limited amount of writing in ethics. More exegetical works like Edwin Larsson's *Christus als Vorbild* (1962) are needed.

Ethics and Philosophical Studies

The parallels between the problems dealt with in Christian ethics and in non-Christian philosophical ethics are notable. Questions of the authority of moral claims, of the nature and locus of the good, of the moral self—its motives, intentions, and actions—and of ethical reasoning are pervasive in ethical discourse, whether the language is particularly Christian or not. Some of this has been indicated in Chapter 2. Here I shall limit my comments to designated points of view in philosophy, and the ways in which Christian ethics has or has not been related to them.

Logical positivism and, more particularly, linguistic analysis have swept across American philosophy with great rapidity in the contemporary period. Curiously, they have been largely ignored by writers in Christian ethics. This is easily understandable with reference to the work of A. J. Ayer, but the writings of such persons as Charles Stevenson, R. M. Hare, Patrick Nowell-Smith, Stephen Toulmin, H. D. Aiken, and Stuart Hampshire provide a less dogmatic way of working with the uses of language and with the relations of language, thought, and action. With some revision, the metaethics of these philosophers could well be pursued or paralleled in the areas of theological ethics. The effect might be a clarification of the logic of Christian moral discourse, an opening of new ways to pursue problems within systematic theological ethics, and a pedagogically significant approach to students schooled in such philosophy. As yet, however, there are no works written by Christian ethicists that seek critically to appropriate the philosophical procedures of linguistic analysis.

A brief example indicates what could be done. H. D. Aiken, who is more complex than the appellation *linguistic analyst* indicates, has an essay on "Levels of Moral Discourse" in his *Reason and Conduct* (1962). In this he suggests that moral discourse takes place on four levels: the "expressive level," the "level of moral rules," the "level of ethical principles," and the "post-ethical level." The last-named deals with the question "Why be moral?" The level of ethical principles asks whether the rules and convictions that govern conduct are really right, and why they are right. The level of moral rules

339

asks what patterns of conduct and rules of behavior are appropriate under particular circumstances: the question is "What ought I to do?" The expressive level is more emotive in character, giving vent to moral approval or indignation. Surely the literature in Christian ethics works on all of these levels and on the relation of these levels to each other. I would suggest that Aiken's simple pattern could provide a way for clarifying the logical movement within Christian ethical thought, and could provide a framework for "unpacking" many hidden issues in Christian ethics. This is an area in which important work can be done in the future.

The other new movement in philosophy that has not been used significantly in Christian ethics, either by appropriation or in polemics, is existential phenomenology. This is identified with the names of Husserl, Heidegger, Merleau-Ponty, and perhaps Sartre. Since this movement is only currently getting wide introduction in America, particularly in its latter-day European forms, it is not surprising that it has been largely ignored. I have previously suggested the ways in which it is influencing Roman Catholic philosophy and indirectly moral theology. In American Protestantism its transmuted influence can be detected in the phenomenology of moral experience provided by H. Richard Niebuhr in *The Responsible Self.* Some of this work, together with writings such as Stuart Hampshire's *Thought and Action* (1959) and John MacMurray's *The Self as Agent* (1957) and *Persons in Relation* (1961), could provide a pattern for the construction of a phenomenology of Christian moral experience. This could take the shape of an analysis of the patterns of thought and action that are characteristic of Christian moral life. From this, in turn, a constructive interpretation of how the moral life ought to be conducted might be forthcoming.

Value theory seems to be passing from the scene in philosophical ethics, but it has had some importance in theological studies. The works of Hartmann, Urban, Scheler, and Perry come to mind, each with its own point of view. In Catholic ethics, Dietrich von Hildebrand's *Christian Ethics* is obviously indebted to objective value theory in ethics. Indeed, in a crucial point in his argument he suggests that an ethics derived exclusively from the "nature of being" (natural-law ethics) has "mere factual and neutral character," whereas moral norms are rooted in values and thus "possess an outspoken importance and relevance." Norms derived from the immanent logic of being have only a hypothetical character, whereas those derived from objective values have a "categorial obligation" (pp. 180 ff). Von Hildebrand takes value theory as his primary philosophical stance, and the traditional philosophy of being is secondary in his development of Christian ethics.

In Protestant thought, H. Richard Niebuhr was most concerned to come to grips with value theory. This he did in several essays, but primarily in "The Center of Value" (reprinted in *Radical Monotheism*, 1960). There he develops a "relational value theory" that asserts that value arises when beings are related to each other. God is the center of values, and finally all values emerge in relation to him. Niebuhr shapes his view in argument against both subjective (Perry) and objective (Hartmann) value theories.

It is doubtful whether discussion between Christian ethics and value theory in the forms that it took during the decades 1920-40 will continue to be a major interest in Christian ethics. Yet, this might well be reopened if phenomenology becomes important, for such a value theorist as Hartmann conceived his task to be the delineation of a phenomenology of moral experience, and thus he was driven to deal with the ultimate status of "value"-experience.

The language and thought of existentialism has been pervasive in a great deal of contemporary theology and ethics, even when it has been metamorphosed so that its effects are not obviously clear. Certainly one of the elements of the contextualism now current is the influence of existentialism, stressing the personal responsibility of the free self to accept accountability for the shaping of the moral world by his individual action. The European theologians who are now influencing American Christian ethics have strongly personalistic models at the heart of their work: this is certainly true of Barth's hearing the command of God and responding to it in obedience; of Brunner's view of the existence of the truly Christian and moral community in the relationship of I to thou; of Bultmann's whole interpretation of the New Testament, and particularly of his view of faith as free obedience; of Bonhoeffer's stress upon obedience and suffering. On the American scene the impact can be seen in Reinhold Niebuhr's appropriation of Kierkegaard's views of finitude, anxiety, and sin, and his concern for the "dramatic" view of selfhood in *The Self and the*

Dramas of History (1955); in H. Richard Niebuhr's "social existentialism" that he describes in *Christ and Culture* and in his notion of the self as "responding"; in Lehmann's stress on imagination, sensitivity, and freedom in the moral life; and in the lesser known works such as George Forell's *Ethics of Decision* (1955) and Gordon Kaufman's *The Context of Decision* (1961).

The American concern for social ethics, however, keeps the existentialist influence at a distance, or at least severely qualifies its appropriation in dealing with questions of public morality. The language of existentialism is more appropriate to the discussion of the individual's decision-making and the realm of interpersonal relations than it is to complex social policy. Americans have been concerned with large moral problems like the conduct of war, full employment, racial integration; they are concerned with policy, strategy, and tactics in these areas, and to these existentialism does not readily relate. Perhaps also, the existentialist posture is not attractive to much of the mood of American Christianity. Roman Catholicism particularly provides a mode and style of ethics that does not readily incorporate motifs from existentialism.

Older and more traditional philosophies have had a wider impact on Christian ethics. This is symbolized in the one contemporary book that seeks to relate theological and philosophical ethics as part of its major contribution, George Thomas's *Christian Ethics and Moral Philosophy* (1955). Thomas suggests that moral philosophy must be "transformed or 'converted'" before Christians make use of it. He goes on to discuss, then, mostly classical and historical writers: Plato, Aristotle, Kant, Paulsen, Sidgwick, Bradley, Nicolai Hartmann, and others. Paul Lehmann expounds various philosophies in his recent publication, including linguistic analysis, but obviously he is more at home with Aristotle, Kant, and particularly William James. Paul Ramsey's first book, *Basic Christian Ethics* (1950), shows his indebtedness at that time to philosophical idealism; his more recent writings show his indebtedness to the natural-law tradition. Surely Kant remains *the* philosopher of greatest impact on European Protestant ethics—Brunner and Barth particularly—just as Thomism is dominant in Catholic ethics. The Boston theologians acknowledge their continuation of a tradition grounded in German idealism. And pragmatism and utilitarianism, if only culturally absorbed, abound in the writings of the contextualists, of Reinhold Niebuhr and John C. Bennett, and almost all the publications that seek to deal with social policy.

This obvious deference to traditional philosophies provokes speculation. One reason for it could be simply that theological ethics is always out of date, because it takes at least thirty years for the Christian thinkers really to absorb what is going on in secular philosophy. Another reason could be that theologians working in ethics have been so preoccupied with actual moral problems and their solution that they have not consciously defined themselves in relation to current fields of philosophical study. A third might be that those philosophies that were more impregnated indirectly by theological modes of thought—Kantianism, Thomism, idealism—are naturally more congenial to theologians. Perhaps there is something correct about each of these reasons. In any case, it is clear that if Christian ethics is to be in conversation with contemporary movements in philosophy, a great deal of work needs to be done by theologians.

Ethics and Historical Studies

In addition to writing Christian ethics in response to biblical work and philosophy, it is quite appropriate to study Christian ethics as history. This can be done in several ways. A systematic Christian ethicist turns to historical figures to find insight on the questions he is dealing with in the present. This is the most common approach to history among Christian ethicists. Or a scholar might relate a particular ongoing tradition to contemporary problems: Roman Catholics interpret new issues out of a Thomistic background; Lutherans bring characteristic distinctions of law and gospel, two realms, and so forth, to bear on the present. Or Christian ethics can be studied as a field with its own history; that is, methods of historical research can be used on materials in ethics.

The most common use of history is turning to historical figures to see how they met certain perennial problems. One sees this in Ramsey's uses of Augustine, Thomas Aquinas, and others in the development of his own position on the just war; in Lehmann's frequent references to Luther and Calvin in the exposition of his theological foundations for ethics; in Reinhold Niebuhr's forays into Augustine, the reformers, and Kierkegaard; in H. Richard Niebuhr's reflections on the problem of Christ and culture in relation to a typology of historical solutions to this question.

Historical research on the development of Christian ethics is a rare thing in American scholarship. Histories of American Christian ethics have been done as often by "secular" historians as by church historians. Books by Meyer, Carter, and Robert Miller on the period from 1918 to 1940 are cases in point. H. Richard Niebuhr, in *Christ and Culture* and in *The Kingdom of God in America*, has provided us with the most competent historical work done by a man whose major concern is ethics. By and large, however, Americans must continue to rely upon European works for the history of Christian ethics, most of which are written to defend a thesis: K. E. Kirk's *The Vision of God*, Anders Nygren's *Agape and Eros*, Newton Flew's *The Idea of Perfection*, Troeltsch's *History of Christian Social Teachings*, and Luthardt's *History of Christian Ethics*.

It is understandable that a scholar trained in ethics may not have the historical knowledge and the method to deal with the history of ethics. Roland Bainton, a church historian, has provided the most competent material written by an historian in his *The Travail of Religious Liberty* (1951), *Christian Attitudes Toward War and Peace* (1960), and *What Christianity Says about Sex, Love, and Marriage* (1957). William Cole has done a survey of teachings on sex in a book that has another purpose, *Sex in Christianity and Psychoanalysis* (1955). There are monographs on historical figures hidden in the archives of Ph.D. dissertations, but, in the main, historical research in Christian ethics has been badly neglected in America.

It is important for ethics that more be done. This is the case not merely to fill in lacunae on library shelves, but also to make contemporary writers and students aware of changing patterns of ethical thought and moral action, and some of the reasons why these shifts have occurred. Some of this occurs in general surveys of western morals by Crane Brinton and William E. H. Lecky, but more work of the sort done by Bainton is obviously required in future years.

Comparative Religious Ethics

A totally ignored area is that of comparative religious ethics. There are in a number of volumes both careful and not so careful differentiations between Protestant ethics and Catholic ethics, between Christian ethics and Jewish ethics. But careful comparative studies on particular figures are yet to be done even in these cases. Beyond that, there are in comparative religion texts some general remarks about the differences between Hindu, Islamic, Taoist, Buddhist, and Christian ethics, but nothing of major significance has been published in this regard. Again, the competence of a theologian working in ethics is quickly exceeded when this type of research and writing is engaged in, but certainly for the future more will need to be done. Perhaps the comparative sociologists of religion, building from Max Weber's studies of the religion, ethics, and cultures of Judaism, Protestantism, Chinese and Indian religions will provide the literature needed in this area.

This rapid overview of the literature relating Christian ethics to biblical, philosophical, historical, and other religious fields indicates that there is ample opportunity for further research and publication. It calls for persons trained in more than one discipline in most instances, i.e., in Bible and ethics, or in Hindu and Christian ethics. But because of the nature of the field of Christian ethics, it is important that such persons be trained.

⊷§ 4 §⊷

CHRISTIAN ETHICS AND MORAL PROBLEMS

This essay began with the contention that the dominant characteristic of American Christian ethics is its concern with practical moral issues. That theme has occasionally reappeared, but a full substantiation of the continuing importance of practical morality has now to be made. A survey of the literature indicates that the bulk of writing and thus the preoccupation of the teachers and scholars in Christian ethics continues to deal with Christian ethics in relation to particular moral questions. This is as true of the contemporary period as it was of earlier decades.

This becomes clear when the many general textbooks on Christian ethics are brought before review. The pattern is almost stereotyped: a brief section on biblical ethics, a brief section on historical ethics, particularly the Reformation, and then chapters that deal with politics, economics, international relations and war, sex and marriage, race, church and state, "cutlure," etc. Indeed, if there is a surplus of one kind of literature in the field it is of survey textbooks that try to treat large and complex subjects in short and simple chapters, and thus do not do justice to the biblical and theological problems involved, nor to the particular moral problems, each of which deserves several monographs rather than a brief synoptic treatment. These chapters often are so generalized that their intention to clarify moral issues in behavior is not achieved; often they are sprinkled with dubious empirical as well as moral generalizations. But the practical concern that is central to the American way of work in ethics seems to require that the bulk of the textbooks be addressed to moral questions that the authors seem to believe the readers face.

This practical intention requires that the energies of many able writers be given to the preparation of books and pamphlets that are more oriented to pedagogy than to research. Not only textbooks, but also a vast number of "study books" are prepared for use in churches and college discussion groups. Some of these are prepared by ministers; but many are prepared by men who might better spend their energy exploring undeveloped areas of the subject matter. The practical books are important in a "moralistic" nation, and in religious communities, Protestant and Catholic, that take moral responsibility seriously. But all too often they are of ephemeral value in the development of an academic discipline.

The practical orientation also dictates that professors of Christian ethics be more conversant with materials from fields such as economics, politics, race relations, and other parts of sociology, sex, etc., than with philosophy, biblical studies, and history. Thus there is a sizable amount of literature that appropriates, necessarily and properly, the theories, information, and insights of the social sciences for the resolution in theory and, hopefully, in action of moral issues that are detailed in the languages of these disciplines. Indeed, interest in social ethics led to significant empirical research in sociology of religion, such as Liston Pope's *Millhands and Preachers* (1942), Kenneth Underwood's *Protestant and Catholic* (1951), and Paul Harrison's *Authority and Power in the Free Church Tradition* (1959). Some of these areas deserve comment.

The concern for economic life goes well back into the social gospel period when Protestantism faced the injustices that accrued from urbanization and industrialization. In that time socialism (loosely defined) became almost a panacea for economic ethics. In the 1930's some ethicists were still socialists, and most supported organized labor and the New Deal. As the problems of economic ethics became more complex and the ethical thinkers more sophisticated about them, a particular literature on economic ethics began to emerge. One example is Walter Muelder's *Religion and Economic Responsibility* (1953), which is still couched largely in big ideological terms rather than in terms of the technical data of national income analysis and economic growth. Indeed, the literature has tended to be rather simply concerned with the problems of equitable distribution of wealth rather than with issues of monetary and fiscal policy. In the 1950's the National Council of Churches gathered scholars in ethics and in economics and other fields to develop an extensive series of books, usually called "The Ethics and Economic Life Series." Persons of technical competence wrote texts: e.g., Kenneth Boulding on *The Organizational Revolution,* Howard Bowen on *The Social Responsibilities of the Businessman,* several economists on the uses of Ameri-

347

can income. This series was a step in the right direction, but the considerations of ethics and those of technical economics remain rather unconnected in some of the material. American Protestantism has yet to produce a Denis Munby, the English economist and lay theologian who combines both interests in his *Christianity and Economic Problems* and *God and the Rich Society* to develop a kind of Christian and Keynesian commentary.

Part of the Protestant difficulty in approaching economics and other particular areas is the lack of consensus within the tradition as to *how* one goes about this task. Theological foundations and procedures of ethical reflection are in dispute. Roman Catholics at this and other points have more consensus, and thus a more coherent body of literature. They have been able to move from the social encyclicals of the popes, with their concern—grounded in natural law—for working conditions, just wages, and the right of labor to organize, to the issues that face contemporary society. Notable writers in America during the contemporary period are John A. Ryan and A. J. Cronin, plus many more. Catholics have moved with certainty to a position favoring the involvement of the state in welfare and other related questions, while Protestants have been trying to decide whether the Christian interpretation of life supports limited government and laissez faire (there is a strong Protestant right wing, though no scholars of Christian ethics of any reputation belong to it) or some form of welfare state.

Two other broad areas have received much attention in recent decades. One is the general problem of social justice in American life, and the political means for implementing it. The other is the area of international relations. In many respects Reinhold Niebuhr in his voluminous occasional writings and his books on political problems has been at the center of the discussion.

Beginning with his *Moral Man and Immoral Society* (1932), which, in fact, had been preceded by many articles in popular journals, Niebuhr began to interpret the social problem in terms of balances of power, rather than in more "sentimental" terms. Groups must organize and exercise coercive power through various means in order to achieve their due in the human exchange. This was true for Negroes (for whom Niebuhr suggested boycott, etc., at that time), for labor, and for other groups. He applied his fundamental theories with great specificity to particular problems through many decades of writing for the *Christian Century, Radical Religion, Christianity and Society, Christianity and Crisis,* and liberal secular political journals. Many of these occasional writings have been collected in *Love and Justice* (1957) and *Essays in Applied Christianity* (1959), and in them one can recapture some of the force that his polemic had on less realistic Christians and others. In *The Children of Light and the Children of Dark* (1944), an essay on democratic theory, he coined the famous statement that gets at the heart of his political philosophy: "Man's capacity for justice makes democracy possible; but man's inclination to injustice makes democracy necessary" (p. xi).

Niebuhr's thought and activity led many other scholars and teachers of Christian ethics into active participation in political parties and in voluntary associations that sought to establish "rough justice" in American life through the use of political means. Thus most Christian ethicists consider themselves to be "political realists," and though there are disputes about the methods and assumptions of Niebuhr's position, almost no one writing in Protestant social ethics could deny the heavy influence of his thought.

Prior to World War II, and of course since, war and international relations has received a great deal of attention, both from Protestants and Catholics. For Protestants the intellectual process of the late 1930's was one of being weaned away from a pacifist tendency that aspired to see war abolished. The rise of Hitler and the articulation of a theology and ethics that saw the need for coercive power to restrain evil brought most American Protestants into the war with a sense of being involved in a "just and mournful war." There continued to be the traditional dissenters: the historic peace churches, and others, including a few important theologians. The literature about the war took more the form of articles in journals and reports by ecclesiastical commissions than it did major books. For Catholics, whose ecclesiastical consensus on the just war tradition remained, the agony of the decision to participate in the war did not exist. Both, however, had theologians who were concerned enough with the problems of the right conduct of war to express regret at the breakdown of certain just war principles, particularly the bombing of noncombatants. Yet even some Christians were overcome with the crusade mentality, and justified the use of the atomic bomb in 1945.

Since the war, the ethics of international relations has drawn more attention of talented Christian ethicists than any other problem. In this discussion there has been more Catholic-Protestant dialogue than in any other area or in any other time in the United States. Fathers John C. Ford and John Courtney Murray have been among the leading participants on the Catholic side; among Protestants Reinhold Niebuhr (whose *The Structure of Nations and Empires,* 1959, is his most recent major book), John C. Bennett, and Paul Ramsey have done important writing. There are hundreds of pages in books, pamphlets, and journals by other authors as well. Nontheological writers who are informed by Christian ethics, such as Kenneth Thompson, Paul Nitze, and Thomas Murray, have participated. The consensus of this main line of thinking in recent years can be expressed in terms of a movement toward a view of limited war for limited purposes.

The knowledgeability of the theological moralists in the materials produced by military strategists, political scientists, and others is remarkable. Hans Morganthau, Herman Kahn, Henry Kissinger, Oskar Morgenstern, Robert Osgood, William T. R. Fox, and many others have written books and essays on problems of international relations and military strategy that have been carefully studied by the writers in ethics. Writings by Christian ethicists, Catholic and Protestant, take into account the arguments produced by these men in a serious and learned way.

There continue to be those for whom the consensus to support limited war as a means of foreign policy is a dubious one from a Christian perspective. Among these are "nuclear pacifists" as well as traditional pacifists.

More has been written in the area of international relations about war than about some other facets, such as economic assistance programs and the revolutions among the younger nations. There are theologians of note, however, who tend to identify themselves with the aspirations of anticolonialist powers. The World Council of Churches studied issues in this nest of problems, and the report volume, *The Churches and Rapid Social Change* (1961), was written by an American staff member, Paul Abrecht. While the major figures in American Christian ethics have tended to be anti-anti-Communists in their critiques of the crusading mentality that informs the American right wing, they have also been "realists" about Russian expansionism, and at the same time sympathetic to the emerging new nations. One of the most important interpretations of Protestant Christian ethics to appear in recent years deals with the problems of Christianity and communism and has the new nations sympathetically in view; it is Charles West's *Communism and the Theologians* (1958).

The issues of civil liberties were much in the minds of the Protestant writers during the period of McCarthyism, when many earlier and current leaders were under the attack of the right wing. A major research study that digs into the facts of the matter is Ralph Roy's *Communism and the Churches* (1960). We have, however, no major theological treatises that are focused upon the area of civil liberties—either their theological ground or the rationale for them within law and custom—except John Courtney Murray's *We Hold These Truths* (1960). Symptomatically, one finds almost no distinguished Christian ethics professors on lists of leaders in the American Civil Liberties Union, and those who are there tend to be regarded as liberals in theology, whereas Americans for Democratic Action is well supplied with distinguished Protestant names.

The question of church and state emerges larger and larger as Americans come to grips with religious and cultural pluralism. This is at present a major concern. Symbolic is the fact that a recent review article in the *Christian Century* dealt with five books pertaining to the question that had been published within a few months. Among Roman Catholics, the major theoretician has been John Courtney Murray, whose "Contemporary Orientations of Catholic Thought on Church and State in the Light of History," published in *Theological Studies* in 1949, is a landmark of American Catholic thought. Murray's view can be called dyarchical, in that it seeks to avoid the dominance of either over the other. He states that "in the native structure of the American system the citizen-of-religious-conscience is placed in the mediating position between Church and state. The Church is free to form the consciences of her members; and they as citizens are free to conform the life of the City to the demands of their consciences." The unity is not in the power of either church or state, but in "the oneness of man as Christian and as citizen." Murray continued his contribution in the collection of essays, *We Hold These Truths.* Certainly not all Catholics agree with Murray, but with the discussions on religious liberty and freedom that are occurring in the Roman Catholic Church as a whole, it is likely that his view will win wider and wider acceptance.

Protestants continue, as usual, to be fragmented. There is the hardline separation principle, represented in the Protestants and Other Americans United for the Separation of Church and State. The views of this group have distinct tinges of anti-Catholicism. There are also Protestants who feel at home with the writings of the American Jewish Committee lawyer Leo Pfeffer, who is deeply involved in cases that seek to get all traces of particular religions out of the public life. But in more recent years a more moderate "wavy line" between church and state is being drawn by others, such as John C. Bennett in his *Christians and the State* (1958). Denominations are taking positions; the United Presbyterian Church is particularly active in this regard, recommending that churches give up all special tax-free and other privileges in order fully to emancipate themselves from special status in the state. "Church and state" is one of the most crucial areas of continuing discussion, and perhaps out of many more books and pamphlets, dealing with law cases, theology, historical factors, and social conditions, a consensus will emerge in Christian ethics, Protestant and Catholic together.

The question of civil rights is currently in the foreground. On this issue there is significant consensus among writers in Christian ethics, Protestant and Catholic, arrived at by diverse theological and ethical paths—namely, that segregation is wrong, and that integration is right. A number of essays and books have helped to shape and express this consensus, such as Liston Pope's widely read *Kingdom Beyond Caste* (1957) and Kyle Haselden's *The Racial Problem in Christian Perspective* (1959). Leadership of clergy in the struggle, both the notables like Martin Luther King and many lesser lights, indicates that on this point there is enough assurance of the moral rightness of the general position to prompt men to participate actively in its actualization. There are disagreements on questions of strategy and tactics, and some of these have issues of ethics at their roots (see, e.g., Ramsey's *Christian Ethics and the Sit-in,* 1961), but pluralism of action substantiated by pluralism of theories and convictions seems to be the state of affairs that will continue.

Ethical problems of medical care have received far more extensive treatment by Roman Catholics than by Protestants. The manuals of moral theology discuss problems of sterilization, euthanasia, abortion, birth control, the "patient's right to know," prolongation of life, etc. There are also particular books on medical ethics—for example, Father John P. Kenny's *Principles of Medical Ethics* (1952; 2nd ed., 1962). Another recent Catholic study of great importance is Norman St. John-Stevas's *Life, Death and the Law* (1961). The only comparable Protestant book is Joseph Fletcher's *Morals and Medicine* (1954). Paul Ramsey has given some attention to these questions, and Richard Fagley, in *The Population Explosion and Christian Responsibility* (1960), deals with one of the big issues in which medical and vast public ethical questions come together. On questions related to both population control and issues of medical care, Catholics tend to take a firm stand against man's right to take life and prohibit it from coming into being, though the occasions for discussion of crucial marginal cases are increasing. Dr. John Rock's *The Time Has Come* (1963) and the writings of Father John A. O'Brien of Notre Dame indicate new openness particularly on the control of birth. Certainly Protestants need to do more work in relation to the host of issues involved in medical care, and in public policies in which medical action is required.

The work that has been done on sex ethics by Protestants has largely been directed to a student population. There are a number of books by Peter Bertocci, William Hamilton, and others that seek to speak to the actual problems of the young unmarried person. There is also the literature that takes a large historical or biblical approach, such as books by William Cole, and Otto Piper's *The Biblical View of Sex and Marriage* (1960). Currently American Protestants are reading *The Ethics of Sex* (1964), by Helmut Thielicke, a German theologian and preacher. On the whole, we have far from an adequate discussion of this important area in Protestantism. Roman Catholicism continues to instruct on questions of sex in the manner of traditional manuals of moral theology, though here as elsewhere account has to be taken of new medical possibilities, of the changing cultural ethos, and other factors.

Any survey of literature on Christian ethics and moral problems that sought to be complete would require much more extensive development than has been given here. But the vastness of material is important to visualize, both because of its intrinsic importance and because it indicates the extent to which Christian ethics in America has been occupied with questions of practical morality. This has been the genius of American work, particularly in Protestantism: ethics has not been done here as exclusively in relation to dogmatics, to exegesis, and to philosophy as it has in Europe. But this preoccupation has also left large areas of fundamental importance inadequately explored.

PHILOSOPHY OF RELIGION

JOHN E. SMITH
PROFESSOR OF PHILOSOPHY
YALE UNIVERSITY

⊷ 1 ⊷

INTRODUCTION

There is no need to disguise the fact that many different, and not always compatible, enterprises have been carried on in America under the banner of the philosophy of religion. The entire subject is marked with a certain confusion. Not even the enterprise of philosophy itself has been more variously conceived. For some, the philosophy of religion has meant a predominantly psychological study, embracing the nature of religious belief and its function in the total life of the person. For others it has meant a phenomenology or description of religious forms aimed at capturing the essence of religion as it reveals itself in human history. For still others it has meant the interpretation of religion from a definite metaphysical point of view or the inclusion of certain religious insights within the compass of a general theory of reality (so-called religious philosophy). Nor are these possibilities exhaustive; some have taken the philosophy of religion to mean concentration upon religion as a "natural" phenomenon to the exclusion of God or as the development of a "natural" theology based not on revelation but on man's general experience and knowledge. Most recently, and in keeping with the dependence of much American philosophy on British thought, the philosophy of religion has become identified with the analysis of so-called religious language.

It seems likely that an adequate philosophical treatment of religion, including distinctive ideas and doctrines about God, salvation, history, and similar topics, will have to encompass all of these alternatives with some difference in emphasis marking a given system of thought. And in any case, an account that faithfully reflects what has transpired on the American scene in recent years must not be selective and identify the philosophy of religion with any one of these conceptions to the exclusion of the others. The plurality of approaches has been dictated in part by differing conceptions of what philosophy is as well as the singling out of different facets of religion for special attention. It is important to notice that at present, and indeed for at

357

least a decade among certain religious thinkers, strong objections in principle are raised against the philosophy of religion. In addition to the claim that theology (or more frequently, Christianity) is *sui generis* and hence not to be treated philosophically, there are those who regard the philosophy of religion as no more than a name for "unorthodox theology" and for them the discipline becomes a masquerade. Objections of this sort prove that apparently innocent names may take on pejorative meanings so that it becomes possible to express a critical judgment upon a system of religious thought by saying that it represents no more than "a philosophy of religion." [1]

This is no place to settle the question of the "real" meaning of the philosophy of religion; such a discussion might well turn out to be an academic exercise. Philosophical treatments of religion and religions have abounded in America for some time and to these we must turn. Insofar as it is necessary and helpful to distinguish the philosophy of religion from theology proper, the following working distinction based on actual practice will suffice. Whereas the theologian has as his primary task the formulation and elaboration of ideas and doctrines about God, man, nature, creation, redemption, etc., which stand as revealed within a historical religious tradition such as Christianity or Judaism, the philosopher confronting religion will focus more particularly upon the *nature* of religion and its relation to knowledge and the forms of secular culture, and he will do so from some philosophical standpoint different from that of any historical religion. Overlap of interest and content there will be, but this fact supplies no warrant for the often expressed but quite erroneous opinion that the theologian talks about God while the philosopher of religion talks only about religion.

According to an ancient philosophical tradition the only way in which we can ever hope to encompass a multitude of fact is through the unifying force of a principle. In attempting to describe the work done by American thinkers in the philosophy of religion over recent decades, we must have recourse to a typology, for we cannot hope to

---

[1] The problem is not an academic one; it has a direct bearing upon the divisions of the present volume. Paul Tillich's writings, for example, are considered, as they should be, under the title "Theology" but it is no secret that some of his critics would prefer to see him classified as a "philosopher of religion" with the implication that his thought omits or radically transforms some favorite doctrine in the theology of the critic.

treat in detail all the relevant works in the field. The following positions may be distinguished: Idealist and Rationalist Interpretations; Empirical Philosophies of Religion; Personalism; Mysticism; Existential and Ontological Approach; Philosophy of Religion and Process Philosophy. As will become clear, the last two positions, represented respectively by Tillich and Hartshorne, mark the two focal points of current discussion. The above approaches define the chief lines of thought; in the course of developing them their boundaries will at times become indistinct because of overlap in both content and approach.

This study does not undertake to include developments within Roman Catholic thought or the traditions of Judaism. There is, however, room for one exception, especially since it throws further light on the relations between philosophy and religion at the present time. An original and provocative interpretation of religion has been offered from within the Jewish tradition by Abraham Heschel in *Man Is Not Alone* (1951). This volume, a unique combination of analysis and proclamation, of philosophy and poetry, aims at making the modern man aware of the meaning of religion as a phenomenon centered entirely in God. Heschel is critical of those accounts of religion according to which it is seen as a response to man's need. "Religion," he writes, "is for God's sake. The human side of religion, its creeds, rituals, and institutions, is a way rather than the goal" (p. 237). We have here the echo of Buber's insistence that God does not care for religion as such, but for the righteousness of the individual soul, which, in turn, is righteous through caring for God. The similarity between Heschel's approach and that of Barth is striking. Both treat "religion" in man's experience as ephemeral and subjective. Only God is real. The major difference is that Heschel leans in the direction of mysticism, maintaining the primacy of experience that eludes expression, whereas Barth is a rationalist in the theological sense of upholding the priority of a doctrinal system.

Heschel skillfully exposes the shortcomings of reductive explanations of religion in terms of causes. At times his treatment is insufficiently dialectical. After criticizing other alternatives because they seek to reduce the divine to conceptual terms or because they take religion to be no more than man's response, he himself goes on to interpret God as "the holy dimension of all existence" and piety as

359

the "subjective correlate" of God's activity. To maintain that it is impossible to have religion in the form of purely human experience —without, that is, God or a reality worthy of absolute devotion—is true enough, but insistence upon this truth must not make it impossible for us to analyze religion in terms familiar to us in our own experience.

Of major importance in Heschel's analysis is his treatment of religion not only in its generic sense, but as it is understood in the Jewish tradition. Here the ancient doctrine of the covenant is recovered. Distinctive of the Jewish tradition, in his view, is the idea of reciprocity in the covenant between God and man. Man is committed to God (this commitment defines his being as a reality not limited to time, space, and historical life) and God has an interest in man and his life. God is, in fact, in need of man in the special sense that God has made man a partner in creation and has a concern that man shall become righteous. Heschel speaks of the divine "pathos" expressed in the prophetic writings and the Psalms as the sign of God's concern.

The main consequence of this doctrine of God for man's life and self-understanding is that man, instead of surveying his needs and seeking to fulfill them by manipulating reality, should ask instead: What *ought* I need? The decisive answer is: God. Man, that is to say, should understand his need for God in the light of God's concern for the righteousness of every man. The aim of this novel dialectic is to avoid what Heschel takes to be the subjectivism involved in interpreting religion simply as man's need. Religion, instead, must be viewed as a need only in the sense that we ought to seek and feel the need to love that reality truly worthy of worship.

ঙ্গ 2 ৪৯

IDEALIST AND RATIONALIST INTERPRETATIONS

Although William James's work antedates by several decades the period to be covered in this study, we cannot afford to ignore his pragmatic theory of religion. His *Varieties of Religious Experience,* the Gifford Lectures for 1901-02, was a pioneering work; it is impossible to overestimate its influence on the American scene. As the author tells us, it was his aim to give first a description of "man's religious appetites" and then to supplement it with an account of their satisfaction through philosophy. James's empirical bent, however, intervened and the entire work was finally given over to the description and analysis of various forms of piety. Particularly valuable are the descriptions of conversion experiences and of mystical encounters, the elucidation of the difference between the "once born" and the "twice born" frame of mind and the bearing of the distinction upon religion, the phenomenon of the divided self and the interpretation of salvation as the power to unify that self. More important than this invaluable treasure of detail was the general drift of James's thought and approach. He was focusing on religion as it is found in the soul of the individual believer; he was finding, in his own words, the "cash value" in terms of living experience for a whole spectrum of theological concepts. Sin, guilt, salvation, atonement, and many other concepts were taken from their more austere setting in theological treatises and given experiential meaning. Whether this approach was called "psychology of religion" or "philosophy" did not matter in the end. James's contribution is that he showed the "actual working" of religious belief in the life of the person. Although the expression of his own philosophical outlook and conclusions was postponed to a section at the end of the book, his doctrine that belief in God has actual consequences in the life of the individual came to be regarded as the watchword of an empirical interpretation of religion. In addition, his "piecemeal supernaturalism" and the idea of a finite God struggling against evil considerably influenced later thought.

361

Despite the strong empirical and pragmatistic orientation to be found in James's thought, the objective idealism of the German tradition powerfully represented by Josiah Royce and, to a lesser extent, Charles Peirce became dominant in the first decades of the present century. One of the chief reasons behind this fact was the preservation by the idealist tradition of a *metaphysical* interpretation of religious truth. To many it seemed that while James had given a clear and cogent analysis of the *function* of religious belief in experience, he had paid insufficient attention to its *truth*. The pragmatic approach made it appear that religion is useful for man's life even if it is not true in a more abstract sense of the term. Since this way of defending religion in an age of science was open to the charge of evading the central question, the idealist interpreters pleaded instead for a return to metaphysical analysis as the only way of showing how religious doctrines could be true of a real world.

To the background of the idealist interpretation belong Royce's works *The Sources of Religious Insight* (1914), *The World and the Individual* (2 vols., 1900-01), and *The Problem of Christianity* (2 vols., 1913). In these writings Royce set forth an original, voluntaristic version of absolute idealism in which God is interpreted first as absolute subject and finally as the unifying spirit of the beloved community, a conception consciously patterned after the classical Christian doctrine of the Holy Spirit. To the line inaugurated by Royce belong W. E. Hocking (*The Meaning of God in Human Experience,* 1912; *Living Religions and a World Faith,* 1940; and *The Meaning of Immortality in Human Experience,* 1957) and W. M. Urban (*Language and Reality,* 1939, and *Humanity and Deity,* 1951). Hocking's approach is experiential, and his thought represents an original synthesis of idealistic and pragmatic elements. It also embodies many insights derived from the tradition of phenomenology initiated by Husserl. By comparison, Urban's interpretation is much more dialectical, somewhat lacking in imagination and thoroughly dependent upon the tradition of the German idealists. Both defended versions of the ontological argument, a fact that further supports the view that idealism in America has been the heir of the Platonic–Augustinian strain of thought in Christian theology.

Though indebted to both James and Royce, Hocking refused to be bound by either. He acknowledged the truth in the pragmatic demand that religious faith "make a difference" and he saw that religion must lose its life if it consists in nothing more than the wholesale consecration of the world as it is without visible effect on the course of events. Against a simple pragmatism, however, he urged what he called "negative pragmatism" or the thesis that unless a doctrine has identifiable consequences, unless it makes a difference in the lives of men, unless it enhances our resources for meeting the exigencies of life, it is false. But this is not the same as saying that whatever meets these conditions is true. The will to believe, he thought, has its place in the world of action; it is not a sufficient principle for knowledge. What fails to interest us, excite us, sustain us, and engage our devotion cannot finally be true, but it does not follow that a doctrine capable of doing all these things is on that account true. Hocking parts company with pragmatism at this point; truth is not determined by the demands of practice alone. The truth about God must arise out of human experience, taken as a liberal and generous encounter with the world, and not as a tissue of sensible data. Religious truth, however, is not confined to the world of encounter; reason must enter in to interpret and reveal the connections of things. Hocking more than once expressed his approval of Hegel's dictum that the proof for God's existence is found in lifting the mind from secular business and preoccupation with routine to those present but neglected aspects of man's experience in which God is truly to be found. God is not merely in a world beyond; he is found in what is open to us if we know where to look and how to develop the original experience in a rational way. Experience is not devoid of reason.

Hocking follows Royce most closely in adopting his voluntarism —the doctrine that the truth must have the character of satisfying the rational will. With this idea as a guide, Hocking argues for the need of God as the power able to transmute the evil of the world, because divine power is not one competing force besides others in a finite realm. It is our will to find a harmony beyond the disharmony marking our common lot that directs our attention to the supreme power, to an other not subject to internal defect. The problem is to discover the reality of that other that man's will demands.

If God is to be found in human experience, experience must be capable of revealing selves as well as things. In a fashion that anticipates very recent developments in a remarkable way, Hocking argued for a view of experience rich enough to include all the relations involved in meetings between selves. For he saw that if we are to understand how God can possibly be a matter of experience we shall have to understand how experience of selves is possible.

The quest for God, though it begins in elemental experience, finds its culmination in a rational apprehension. Following the consequences of this approach, Hocking developed his own original form of the ontological argument for God. Unlike similar attempts in the past, his does not lose sight of nature. It is noteworthy that Hocking demands a God of nature as well as a God of spirit. He held fast to Royce's idea that a world of common objects and of selves in communication with one another requires an other self as a unifying term. In knowing ourselves, the world, and other selves, we come into relation with God at the same time.

The journey of the soul to God is divided into three stages, each flowing into the other. The primordial experience of God comes through the sense that in knowing the world we are judged by it; there we come up against the other self for the first time. This more or less dim awareness becomes the subject of further thought and we develop the idea of God as the necessary condition for all knowledge. Finally, as if to enter the most inner recess of both thought and reality, the mind must be directed to God in the ultimate fashion of showing that God is *literally* there. In anticipation of a point that Tillich was later to make with considerable force, Hocking shows the fundamental difference between the ontological way to God and the various forms of the cosmological argument. The latter starts with the solidity of the world and argues that because the world is and is incomplete, therefore God must be as its cause and ground. In this case we argue *away from* the world that appears, to a God who does not appear but who is nevertheless demanded by what appears. In the ontological way, the mind moves in the opposite direction. *God must be* because, in a peculiar sense, the *world is not.* Since neither the world nor the finite self can furnish the starting point, some deeper foundation must be found. Hocking will not allow the validity of the standard form of the argument that starts with the abstract idea of "the all-perfect being" and moves from there to existence. He demands instead that the idea of God with which we begin already have roots in experience; we do not pass from "mere thought" to existence but rather from the experience of ourselves, the world, and other selves to the knowledge that in all these is also included the experience of God. The ontological proof is but a tracing out, a reminder to the soul, of what was already present at the beginning but not known as such. It leads us to see that God is the only really ultimate foundation; by themselves neither the world nor the self can provide final satisfaction.

Unlike some other thinkers, Hocking was not content to resolve the philosophy of religion into the discussion of God's existence alone. He went on to develop the implications of his position for worship, prayer, death and immortality, the mystical consciousness and the historical order. As a result of his wide learning and his many-sided approach he came to consider the problem of the world religions and their relation to the dominant Judeo-Christian tradition in the West. In *Living Religions and a World Faith* Hocking deals in an incisive way with a problem that has increased in importance with the passing of the years. The existence of powerful and comprehensive non-Western religious traditions must be understood in their opposition to the unique claim of Christianity. Starting with the thesis that religion must be universal in its scope and yet historically rooted in a concrete community and a culture, Hocking classifies the major religions according to their concern for preserving both features in some sort of balance. He sees Buddhism, Christianity, and Islam as the three religions aiming at the synthesis. The next question is: Can a world religion be achieved by "the way of radical displacement" or the traditional missionary zeal that sweeps aside as false and inadequate the old faith in order to gain converts for one of these religions as the potential world religion? Hocking was keenly aware of the support that the displacement approach receives from the hands of a purely revelationist theology; if God has spoken in specific historical acts and circumstances, it is not for us to suppose that we can do other than obey and propagate the faith accordingly. While not unmindful of the truth in the approach through historical revelation, Hocking will not sacrifice the universal element. What is to be true for all men must reveal itself in the total fabric of things and thus be, to a degree at least, open to all. The radical displacement approach is not the final answer. The fact is

365

Christianity, though *ideally* it may embrace the full character of genuine religion, does not *actually* include within itself all the religious values, and it has not yet succeeded in applying its principles in the areas where it is dominant. This means that it is not yet ready to become the world faith. Hocking, nevertheless, rejects the idea that a "least common denominator" amalgam of religious values, drawn from different religions and marching under the banner of humanism, can be a solution. If we are to have a world religion in the end, we must have a particular religion in the beginning. Hocking follows the wisdom of Hegel: to achieve universal form without sacrificing concrete embodiment, we must begin with a particular religion *that has within itself the capacity for becoming universal*. Christianity in his view can do this if it is able to overcome its defects, through what Hocking calls the way of reconception.

Taken in its total sweep, Hocking's thought provides us with an important insight into the American religious situation. On the one hand the ultimate roots of his position are found in an older idealism that no longer has the position of dominance it once enjoyed. On the other hand, the fact that his conception of experience is closer to the pragmatic, radical type of empiricism, capturing at once overtones of Bergson and of Husserl, has served to give to his thought a remarkably contemporary flavor. The two sides are not unconnected. Insofar as Hocking's idealism retained connections with the tradition of broad empiricism, he was able to keep in touch with all those thinkers whose aim it was to rescue experience from the narrow limits of British empiricism. For, after all, the appeal to experience that we associate with phenomenology and existentialism at present has its ultimate source in the rich and many-sided conception of experience that Hegel introduced into Western thought. Hocking followed in that line.

W. M. Urban's idealistic interpretation of religion differs from the approach of Hocking in a most fundamental point. While Hocking remained sensitive throughout to the need for experience at the heart of religion, Urban was more interested in an epistemological and dialectical treatment, emphasizing the problems of language and logic. If Hocking developed the latent empiricism in the modern idealist outlook, Urban brought out its rationalism.

There are three basic points essential to an understanding of Urban's philosophy of religion. He wanted first of all to refute positivism and the theory of language and meaning that eliminates metaphysics and robs religion of its claim to truth. Second, he claimed that there is an intimate and indissoluble connection between the meaning and truth of Christianity and what he called the *philosophia perennis* or "natural metaphysic of the human mind." Finally, he rejected as untenable the dualism between a religion of pure humanity in which all transcendence is sacrificed and a religion of pure deity according to which God is "wholly other" and effectively beyond comprehension in any rational dialectic.

In *Language and Reality* (1939), Urban developed an original synthesis of ideas and theories about language stemming from Kant, Hegel, Humboldt, Cassirer, and others. Maintaining the indissoluble unity between language and expression, he attacked the exhaustive dichotomy put forth by the older positivist thinkers between "indicative" and "emotive" language. He saw that to allow this distinction to stand unchallenged means the end of any truth-claim for religious utterances. For with the natural sciences taken as the model of "indicative" language intended to convey information, which alone can be "true" or "false," all other forms of language are reduced to the status of emotional expression. Religion, no less than art and morality, loses all prospect of harboring truth, for what does not indicate anything does not make a claim that can be regarded as cognitive.

Urban was especially concerned with the approach to language through the study of its *origin*. He saw that theories of origins are both unavoidable and apt to be misleading. He tried to prove that practicalistic, behavioristic, and positivistic theories of the intrinsic character of language are based not on an empirical study of actual languages, but rather on the demands of a naturalistic metaphysics. By contrast, Urban rejected naturalistic explanations; language and meaning are indissoluble and meaning is not a "natural" fact. Consequently he could not accept any view that tries to state the *present* nature and function of language in terms of theories that hold that human speech developed from animal cries, or that meaning genetically understood is but a name for cues to behavior.

Following Cassirer and his theory of symbolic forms, Urban developed a theory of religious symbolism that he called *realistic* in the sense that a genuine religious symbol has a real referent and hence is something more than a bearer of pragmatic meaning. Religious symbols are said to be *evocative*, especially in the act of worship, where praise is the proper response to the holy; but they are *invoca*tive as well, calling upon the divine as a reality beyond human consciousness. Urban carefully distinguished between the mythical and dramatic language of religion and the creedal language of theology. The latter, though necessarily connected with metaphysical language because it seeks to express what surpasses sense experience, must retain its dramatic or poetic character. Theology always has something of the character of numinous poetry. Urban held that the justification of the religious symbol as one of the tasks of theology requires in turn the defense of a metaphysical interpretation of symbolic meaning. Since the material but not the entire meaning of the religious symbol is drawn from sensible experience, verification in any narrow empirical sense will be impossible. Instead we have to interpret the symbol in metaphysical terms; its validity then becomes a matter of the general validity of the metaphysical system. For Urban this means the validity of the *philosophia perennis*.

Urban's high regard for medieval theology and his deep involvement in the tradition of Anglican religious thought are both clearly revealed in his claim that there is a "natural metaphysic of the human mind" that represents a synthesis of Greek and Christian ideas. The body of ideas associated with the philosophical doctrine called "the great chain of being," or the internal unity and continuity of nature, man, and God, is one way of expressing the perennial philosophy. It means the primacy and reality of the good and the denial of a world of mere "things" devoid of value. It means also the primacy of being and substance over becoming and process. Just as the voice of philosophy is heard speaking of the good as the highest goal of thought, so the voice of religion is heard saying the same thing about God. The truth is the synthesis of the two lines of thought. Urban saw the formidable problems raised for Christianity by the loss of the traditional metaphysical background against which its ideas could be understood. He attempted to give current reinterpretation to the ancient tradition through the medium of his symbolic theory, and in the end he tried to establish metaphysics as a "symbolic form." But he remained uninfluenced by more recent thinking that raised critical objections against the type of metaphysics he found essential.

In *Humanity and Deity* (1951), Urban gave clearest expression to his philosophy of religion. His main aim was the vindication of a rational theology that can do justice to the claims of religion as well as those of reason. He objected to the tendency of the neo-Reformation revival to oppose the "God of the philosophers" to the "God of Abraham, Isaac, and Jacob." He was as critical of this separation of theology and philosophy as he was of every attempt to interpret religion in wholly human terms, retaining moral values while denying God. He revived and reinterpreted the classical arguments for God's existence in "axiological" fashion, starting with the idea of perfection as a valuational concept, and regarded them as providing mutual support for each other in a *"consilience of proof."* He was particularly critical of the Kierkegaardian influence on modern religious thinking because to him it meant the end of metaphysics and a return to primitive faith and uninterpreted experience. He never wavered in his devotion to the Platonic tradition and his belief in the power of dialectic to lead the mind to God.

⚜ 3 ⚜

EMPIRICAL PHILOSOPHIES OF RELIGION

One may well ask exactly what is meant by an "empirical" philosophy of religion, especially in view of the notorious ambiguity in the concepts of experience and of empirical.[2] Two characteristics of the empirical approach and temper may be cited. First, an insistence on basing all claims to knowledge, and all interpretations, on what is actually encountered or met with by the self; second, an insistence on a method of inquiry that is public in character or accessible, in principle, to every intelligent being. The first demand may be taken more narrowly to mean that the data of sense constitute the only material of encounter, or in a more liberal sense, encounter may embrace all that is "enjoyed and suffered" to use the favorite phrase of John Dewey. In addition there is the question of the legitimacy of including "value" within experience.[3] The second demand—the requirement of a public method—is satisfied for some only by a procedure strictly analogous to that of the natural sciences. The so-called empirical theology illustrates this view. Or the demand may be satisfied by a more dialectical treatment rooted in experience understood after the fashion of Hegel.

The full meaning of the empirical philosophy of religion can be given ultimately only through the thought of those who developed such philosophies. Some further light, however, is thrown on the general position by the contrast between empiricism and its two chief rivals—absolute idealism and various forms of realism. Absolute idealism refuses to rest the claim of religion on experience in the end, because of its demand that all critical assertions be rooted in an ideal

---

[2] See J. A. Martin Jr., *Empirical Philosophies of Religion* (1945) for a judicious review of the alternatives, especially as they are illustrated by the same thinkers considered in this essay. The bibliography contained in Martin's book (pp. 138-46) is valuable both for empiricist and related points of view.
[3] This question is well focused for the philosophy of religion by Peter A. Bertocci in his *Empirical Argument for God in Late British Thought* (1938); cf. *Introduction to the Philosophy of Religion* (1951), pp. 347 ff. Bertocci is developing the basic position of personalism in new and fruitful directions.

of rational coherence that ultimately satisfies the intellect in its quest for truth. From this perspective, experience in the sense of encountering is too "immediate" to be an ultimate critical ground. Realism, on the other hand, suspects the appeal to experience because of its supposition that experience means subjectivism or "mentalism"— the doctrine that the object of knowledge is made identical with the content of personal consciousness and that it is real only for mind. To both criticisms, empiricists had replies. Absolute idealism, they claimed, loses first-person experience, especially in religion, because of its tendency to identify reality with a system of ideas or conceptions. Realism, on the other hand, underestimates the value of experience in a rich and full sense because it supposes that experience means no more than "sense data" or private mental content.

We may doubt whether the full dimensions of the problems surrounding the appeal to experience were understood by those who made that appeal central. There was a sufficient recognition, by those who refused to sacrifice the experiential foundations of religion, of the impossibility of getting along with an experience confined to sense qualities or sensible objects alone. On such a view, the experience of God or the holy is ruled out in principle. But while the narrowness of classical empiricism was grasped, the radical implications of some broader conception of experience were not always understood. The awareness that bare sensible fact is inadequate to express the richness of experience does not of itself make clear in what way a more adequate interpretation can be achieved. One is tempted to say that we need do no more than supplement the inadequate theory of experience by adding to sensible fact something called "value" as if a mere external addition could remedy the defect. Unhappily, this is not so. If classical empiricism—the reduction of experience to sense —is inadequate, nothing less than a radical reconsideration of the nature of experience is called for. The proposal to add value to experience when the latter is still conceived after the fashion of the old sensationalist empiricism, shows that the underlying problem has not been understood. Those who, like Hocking, followed the line of radical empiricism saw the issue more clearly than others who retained the old empiricism and then introduced value in order to make room for God. The puzzling aspect of the situation is that idealists like Hocking understood better than narrower empiricists why a fresh analysis of the nature of experience is necessary and why it is not sufficient to leave the old empiricism standing while demanding only that a value dimension be added to it.

We must not forget that James had been most critical of the tradition of German idealism and that he was skeptical of metaphysical constructions. He was bound to have as his followers men who kept more closely in touch with the empiricist side of his thought. D. C. Macintosh and H. N. Wieman may be taken as the main representatives of the empiricist approach. Not that either would have subscribed to James's pragmatic theory of truth; they had epistemological theories of their own. But each in his own way tried to carry out an empiricist program with a starting point in religious experience, determined not by interest in metaphysical interpretations but rather by concern for religious epistemology and the issues raised by the claims of religious knowledge in a world dominated by science. Macintosh relied heavily on common sense and an exhaustive account of other alternatives in order to give some plausibility to his own position. Wieman's thought developed against a background of evolutionary and process philosophy and he sought in many ways to describe facets of experience that might be interpreted as instances of divine integration or growth. Despite fundamental differences, the two are the heirs of James in that they developed the most comprehensive interpretations of religion based on experience as they understood it. Wieman was more open to the many aspects of experience, and he was consequently more vague in his formulations; Macintosh fell back on a more conventional empiricism and tried to construct an empirical theology based on "data" of a religious sort that he regarded as the exact counterpart of basic facts in the natural sciences.

Distinctive of Macintosh's position (his more distinctively theological contribution is treated elsewhere in this volume in Claude Welch's essay on "Theology") is the claim that we have direct perception of God, which, however, is *not* sensory. The exact character of this perception is not as clearly expressed as it might have been (despite Macintosh's many statements of it) because of his tendency to confuse his own constructive thought with the exposition and criticism of a bewildering variety of other positions. "Religious perception," he says, "is a special case of perception in a complex"

(*TES*[4], p. 31); this means the awareness of a power that produces certain results in our lives when we have achieved what Macintosh called the "right religious adjustment." Religious perception belongs to what he called "experimental religion" or actual dependence upon a God believed to be actual and capable of influencing men. Religion in this form differs from what is called "fundamental religion" or devotion to an ideal or set of values regarded as divine. The two religious forms are distinguished and compared in several places; the clearest statement of the relationship is found in the claim that in fundamental religion the religious object must be regarded as ideal, though it may also be taken as real, while in experimental religion that object must be believed to be real, although it may also be regarded as ideal. At times fundamental religion is said to belong to what is "appreciated" or "valued" by the self, while the experimental type is described as having to do with "knowledge."

Macintosh took the claim to knowledge in religion very seriously; it was at the root not only of his constant concern with epistemological questions but of his refusal to accept the thesis that religion has the fundamental status of mythology or that it can be defended on pragmatic grounds. In an arresting comparison (*PRK,* p. 2) between the natures of science and religion, Macintosh claimed that agnosticism or skepticism concerning the physical object does not prevent the scientist from gathering data as he would if he held a quite different theory of knowledge, whereas a similar skepticism in religion or the doctrine that God is unknowable leads invariably to the supposition that we actually know God to be nonexistent and religion a tissue of falsehoods. The theory of religious knowledge had, for Macintosh, a vitally important function in the life of religion itself; it was not a theoretical exercise for him despite the fact that he treated it in an academic way. He made his point most forcefully in criticism of the humanism upheld by such thinkers as E. S. Ames, A. E. Haydon, and M. C. Otto. Macintosh claimed, contrary to what he took to be their attempt to preserve religion without God, that religion cannot survive unless there is belief that religious doctrines are true.

Religion, however, is not entirely an affair of knowledge. In a

[4] *Theology as an Empirical Science* (1919). In the following pages, Macintosh's *The Problem of Religious Knowledge* (1940) and *The Reasonableness of Christianity* (1925) are abbreviated as *PRK* and *RC.*

manner reminiscent of James's doctrine of "over-belief," Macintosh distinguished between knowledge and belief in religion. Through experience we have knowledge of and acquaintance with God as a "divine value-producing-reality" (*PRK*, p. 164) or "a divinely functioning reality" (*PRK*, p. 165), but this knowledge needs to be supplemented with a body of "reasonable belief" about God. Such belief turns out to be a body of truths about God insofar as he is transcendent and not merely immanent in experience. Macintosh's position is admirably clear; it can be stated succinctly without danger of misrepresenting his fundamental intention. Defending what he called the doctrine of "critical monistic realism" Macintosh held that there is a partial identity between what is immediately experienced and the independently real in religion. This enables us to say that God is real beyond human consciousness and that not everything in subjective consciousness is to be ascribed to him. Conversely, there is also a partial duality between experience and the religious object in the sense that God is not made fully manifest in experience. God is more than we can know through the medium of religious experience. There is a transcendent dimension in the divine nature, apprehension of which is dependent upon religious intuition or faith. The latter is a supplement, in the form of "normative theology," to the empirical theology rooted in experience. The criterion for judging normative theology—which remains in the sphere of belief and not knowledge —is the conception of the "divine" developed in the empirical theology. Consistency between the two sets of affirmations is demanded. This is made clear in the following strong claim:

> Now it is important to observe that in the divine value of the spiritual processes dependably promoted in human experience by the divinely functioning reality on condition of the right religious adjustment we are in possession of a norm by which to measure all that is claimed to be divine, whether immanently and open to direct inspection or transcendently and such as can only be affirmed in faith. [*PRK*, p. 359.]

To understand the full import of the criterion advanced, it is necessary to have recourse to the concept of the "divine" as elaborated in connection with the experience and knowledge of God. Macintosh, though he later restated some of his earlier views differently in order to take account of criticisms and the insights of others, did not waver on this point. What he meant by "divine" in human experience was consistently stated in several works and the several statements, though differing slightly in terminology, give expression to the same view. By "divine" Macintosh meant certain absolute and eternal values "qualitatively" considered. There are certain processes in human experience that are recognizable as the presence of the divine by virtue of the fact that they exhibit the same characters that "spiritual religion tends to ascribe to its ideal object" (*PRK*, p. 164). These processes are those in which divine ideals are being realized and divine values produced. God literally causes the emergence of human personality and at the same time educates humanity to understand the divine character of the processes in which God is present. The divine reality is identical neither with man nor with reality as a whole, for God is beyond man and not every aspect of reality represents a realization of the values called divine.

It is to be noticed that the divine, though objective in the sense underlined by Macintosh's "realism," is related to the human subject in at least two specific ways. First, and more important, the divine factor in reality works for the bringing about of divine values on condition that there is what Macintosh called a "right religious adjustment" on the part of man. And second, the doctrine of critical monistic realism in religious knowledge means that there is but a partial identity between what is directly experienced by the subject and what is independently real. That the identity is only partial means that there is something in our experience that does not belong to God and, on the other hand, there is much in God that has not yet become matter of experience for man.

The right religious adjustment is a necessary condition for knowledge; this condition represents the involvement of the subject in such a way that he is more than a passive spectator. Macintosh was able to use the concept in his interpretation of faith as something that is both a gift of God and a matter of human responsibility and freedom at the same time. That the adjustment is essential is clearly stated: "When this subjective condition of adjustment to the religious Object is fulfilled, revelation of the reality, presence, and activity of a divine Factor in human experience is dependably experienced" (*RC*, p. 237). The adjustment itself is complex and includes a variety of

375

acts, attitudes, and ideas. The person must *aspire* toward a thoroughly ethical and spiritual ideal; he must *concentrate attention* upon the religious object taken as real and striving for the realization of the ideal; he must *surrender* himself to the reality of God; he must have *faith* that the ideal is beginning to be realized in him; he must be ready to *respond in a voluntary way* to the divine and be ready to follow the best judgment we can make as to the true will of God; he must *persist* in seeking to make the right adjustment a habitual way of life.

The subjective conditions of religious perception and revelation play a major role in Macintosh's thought. He sought to interpret them in such a way that the twin evils of agnosticism and dogmatism might be overcome. Agnosticism he could not accept because it meant a sacrifice of religion to skepticism and to some wholly practical faith. On the other hand dogmatism attracted him even less. He described it as a position based on a vicious circle, a criticism that formed the basis of his rejection of recent neo-Protestant theology—described as "reactionary irrationalism" (*PRK*, pp. 326 ff.)—as a reason-destroying approach to the problems of religion. The vicious circle is that if one already has faith, revelation becomes a possibility, but faith itself is possible only on condition of revelation. Macintosh's charge is that a relation of mutual implication is established that makes it impossible to criticize the content of revelation from a rational point of view.

We need not consider whether this characterization does justice to all the thinkers—Barth, Berdyaev, Kierkegaard, Tillich—whom Macintosh lumps together under the category of irrationalism. It is enough that we understand his charge that dogmatism shares with agnosticism an identical character; each renders it impossible to make critical judgments about the content of revelation. The death of critical judgment, whether through the claim that reason is incompetent to judge revelation or because rational judgment is believed to be irrelevant, comes to the same thing in the end. It means dogmatism. By contrast, Macintosh aimed at a mediating position that makes a place for the critical function of reason. He sought to break the circle not by denying the legitimacy of subjective factors but by interpreting them in a way that preserves freedom. "Trust" he regarded as necessary for actually recognizing the experience of God, but trust, often described as the right religious adjustment, requires a genuine act on the part of man. It is not a state that descends upon man as if he were a star or a stone, capable of being acted upon but not of acting in his own right.

Taken as a whole, Macintosh's position is valuable chiefly for the insight it furnishes into the American religious situation. On the one side it stresses the need for personal experience and freedom in religion; on the other hand it shows a proper respect for the limits of empiricism and the need to have critical standards for evaluating the deliverances of experience. It is characteristic of the piety of the earlier part of the present century that these critical standards for evaluating religion were most often drawn from morality; consequently insufficient attention was paid to the problem of criticizing religion in terms appropriate to its own nature. Macintosh was overly concerned with the task of making religion "scientific," and while he was on sound ground in demanding that religion evaporates unless it seeks to support the claim that it is true, he overrated the parallel between an empirical theology and the empirical sciences. He underestimated the extent to which the truth-claim of religion is bound up with the truth-claim of metaphysics.

Macintosh appears to have overlooked the eclectic flavor imparted to his own position by his basically academic attempt to expound, refute, or assimilate the views advanced by others. His own positive position stands out less clearly as a consequence. He seems, moreover, to have minimized his closeness to a pragmatic outlook; his interpretation of religious experience as a matter of *functioning* and his emphasis upon the right adjustment of the individual to the divine reality are both cases in point. In the end, however, he saw the limitations of the practical approach and he refused to go along with the various humanists who, though equally eager to follow in the line of Jamesian empiricism, tried to preserve religion without God. Macintosh was as critical of these attempts as he was of every position that aimed at eliminating rational criticism from the consideration of religious beliefs.

The thought of H. N. Wieman represents another development of the religious empiricism we must forever associate with the name of William James. Though also concerned with the problem of truth in religion and with the reconciliation of religion and science, Wie-

377

man did not concentrate on religious epistemology after the fashion of Macintosh. His approach is more experiential, psychological, and even sociological. While the main drift of his position is clear enough, Wieman was not always consistent and careful with regard to detail, and in the end his thought appears to be more valuable for its suggestiveness than for its analytic precision. A lifelong proponent of an experiential approach, Wieman was sympathetic in his earlier thought to a metaphysical approach to religious problems. The speculative philosophy of Whitehead, especially, provided him with basic notions for the development of his idea of God as creative activity and purposive growth (e.g., in *Religious Experience and Scientific Method,* 1926, and *The Wrestle of Religion with Truth,* 1927, esp. chap. XI). Later on, however, Wieman became more critical of attempts to find metaphysical foundations for religion. His criticism of Tillich, Hartshorne, and even Whitehead, together with his surprising attack on Paul Weiss's *Modes of Being* (see *Intellectual Foundation of Faith,* 1961, pp. 174 ff.) point to a disillusionment about metaphysical analysis. It appears to him as too abstract and inadequate for faith, and he even regards it as opposed to an empirical approach.

Wieman distinguishes religion, theology, and the philosophy of religion. Religion is the ultimate subject matter of inquiry. Religion means the perception of God, belief about God, worship, and the sincere attempt to live a creative life in accordance with what is supremely valuable. Like James, Wieman always understood religion as existent in the life of the individual person. Theology means formulation of the beliefs that enter into the religious life, especially the clarification of their content. Theology is always rooted in a historical religion. Wieman regarded Christianity as part of the cultural heritage of Western civilization and he took its traditional beliefs for granted, but his writings do not show a close acquaintance with the classical Christian concepts, and he appears to have used such terms as *sin* and *atonement* with some embarrassment. He was more concerned with religion in a generic sense as defined by his own theory of religion. Philosophy of religion, as distinct from both religion and theology, means the analysis and clarification of concepts that enter into religion and are presupposed by theology. Philosophy of religion is twice removed from religion itself because it has to do with the analysis of what Wieman calls "formal concepts" presupposed by theology.

The point is a basic one, and different views about it divide contemporary thinkers into two camps. Wieman claims that every specific doctrine of God or belief about him—such as the doctrine that God is love—presupposes a formal concept of God that is not itself a belief about God but rather an inescapable generic concept expressing what it means to be God. The intention to speak about God, the assigning of attributes to God, and the formulating of insights about God to be found in a positive religion such as Christianity or Hinduism, all presuppose the generic idea of God. On Wieman's analysis this idea means that God is the same as that feature of the total environment that vitally affects human welfare and to which we must adjust. This formal or generic concept enters into all formulations of the nature of God. It follows that theological beliefs are not self-contained and wholly unique to one historical tradition, but that they require for their formulation some generic concepts that derive their meaning from a philosophical analysis of reality. Wieman, in short, asserts exactly what Karl Barth denies. While the latter would hold that when a Christian says "God" he means what no one outside Christianity could mean were he to use the term, Wieman argues that every specific theological belief about God has, as part of its meaning, the formal concept of God. The specific belief is not reducible to the generic concept, but the concept is always part of what the belief means. It is in this sense that theology presupposes concepts developed within the philosophy of religion; far from being illegitimate, as some maintain, the philosophy of religion becomes inescapable.

On the whole, those theologians in recent years who have rejected the philosophy of religion have not replied to arguments of the sort Wieman advanced. The tendency has been to invoke instead the superiority of revelation and to attack philosophical analysis on the ground that it is irrelevant, incompetent, or both. Dogmatic theologians, as can be seen clearly in the critical discussion raised by the philosophical theology of Paul Tillich, are on sounder ground in their criticism of the philosophy of religion when they point to the neglect of ideas *distinctive* of Christianity. There has been confusion and misunderstanding on both sides. Many theologians, seeing that a philosophy of religion developed on the basis of generic concepts alone fails to do justice to doctrines peculiar to Christianity, have drawn the conclusion that philosophy must be rejected. They have sought to secure their view by withdrawing into the history of the dogmatic tradition, hoping to achieve a contemporary expression of their faith *without making use of any generic categories.* This way of thinking gives rise to such statements as that Christianity is not a religion or that the Christian doctrine of revelation is not to be understood as merely a special case of a general concept of revelation derived from the general phenomenon of religion. On the other hand, many thinkers like Wieman who developed philosophical accounts of religion failed to understand the extent to which they had neglected the task of reinterpreting classical Christian ideas because of the supposition that whatever is essential for religion has already been summed up in their theories of religion in its generic form. There was, moreover, a tendency to substitute the general theory of religion and the formal concept of God for Christian faith, a tendency that led to the condemnation of the philosophy of religion by those who came to believe that it is, by nature, a substitute for historical religion and theology.

Quite apart from the controversy about the validity of the philosophy of religion as a distinct enterprise, Wieman's position may be expressed in two main theses. First, the claim that God is really present in perceptual experience and, second, the claim that God is to be understood as an activity that is the source of all that is "supremely worthful" in reality. Though based on Wieman's own reading of the facts, these claims are directed against two doctrines he consistently rejected. God must not be understood as a "mere concept" or system of ideas, and he must not be identified with reality as a whole. Wieman's contention is that if we stress the presence of God in perceptual experience, we avoid reducing him to an idea or conceptual scheme, and if we identify God with value and understand him as the creative power and source of all good, we avoid confusing the divine with the whole of reality.

The claim that God is present in *perceptual* experience has been the occasion of much criticism. Urban, for example, supposed that this made God into a sense object and it is clear that Wieman's concern to avoid identifying God with a concept led him to exaggerate the need for sense experience. His position is not entirely clear. It is compounded from a desire to follow James's view that religion always rests on immediate experience and a willingness to accept the alternative that God must be either an object of sensory experience or a system of concepts. Wieman seems not to have seen that the appeal to immediate experience was intended to avoid just that exclusive alternative. Since he accepted it, however, and came down on the side of sense, Wieman had to show how a position resting on immediate experience could be scientific in character.

By understanding *scientific* in a broad sense to mean critical discrimination between true and false and by claiming that sensible experience is not itself knowledge but furnishes the material for knowledge, Wieman aimed to show that the truth about God is to be found in *interpreted* experience. Experience is essential, but a scientific approach requires critical interpretation and empirical tests. Our grasp of God is of a reality present in sense, but only through critical concepts tested in the experience of living the religious life can we have knowledge of God. For Wieman there is no problem of God's reality; religious experience is a fact and all experience is experience of something. Although he often tried to pattern his thinking after the method of the natural sciences (his writings abound with such terms as *data, hypothesis, test, experiment,* etc.), Wieman was not proposing a "scientific" argument for the existence of God. For him the problem is found in the interpretation; we have the experience and our task is to interpret it correctly and critically.

Wieman's doctrine of God finds its best expression in his contribution to *The Growth of Religion* (1938), which he wrote with W. M. Horton. Although Wieman frequently used the term *object* in referring to God, it is clear that for him God is more properly an activity and a process. God he characterized as the being upon whom depends the accomplishment of the religious aim of reorganizing the world into a system of mutually sustaining activities leading to an endless growth of meaning and value. That this being is more accurately described as a becoming is clear from Wieman's demand that our definitions be "operational," that is, that they enable us to shape conduct in accordance with them. Understanding God in terms of growth and creativity makes it possible for us to find the effects of the divine creativity within the lives of religious persons.

While Wieman regards God as the origin of human personality, he is reluctant to describe God as a personality. That category, on his view, is too restricted; God is rather "superpersonal." Wieman insisted that God is not "impersonal" but something more than can be summed up in the idea of person. There are hints in Wieman's writings that he envisaged God as a community of creativity, a doctrine reminiscent of Royce, and one that was later developed by Hartshorne under the title of a "social" conception of God.

The most serious problem facing the type of position Wieman held is the avoidance of a total naturalism. Although he vigorously maintained the transcendence of God, most critics regarded his position as basically naturalistic. In the attempt to avoid identifying God with all reality and escape supernaturalism at the same time, Wieman repeatedly spoke of growth and creativity within nature and man's life as the true locus of the divine. The result was that God became but a name for the humanization of the social order and the process of growth in value experience, both individual and social. Wieman rejected supernaturalist doctrines and he seems not to have felt any opposition between the acceptance of naturalism and his own view of God. Participating in a symposium on "The Present Outlook in the Philosophy of Religion" in 1936, Wieman looked forward to the birth of a more adequate naturalism in which mechanical and materialistic interpretations of nature would be replaced so as to permit a closer bond between religion and science. His prediction at that point was that the only alternative to naturalism—supernaturalistic revelation—will be unable to sustain itself because of its exclusively "prophetic" appearance on the American scene. To Wieman it appeared that the theological revival represented by Karl Barth, Paul Tillich, and others was no more than a reaction lacking organic connections with American life and experience.

In *The Source of Human Good* (1946) Wieman seeks to analyze the contemporary social scene and man's predicament by reference to a comprehensive theory of value. While not precisely a philosophy of religion, the book has much to say about the nature of religion and its place in modern life. Wieman finds modern man in a most desperate situation; catastrophe will be the inevitable outcome of our technological ingenuity unless we can find ways to direct the course of events through *creative* (not *created*) values. He acknowledges the fact that man is beset by limitations—the narrowness of his perception of value, the tendency to pervert value through self-interest, the resistance to change where fundamental values are concerned. Insofar as these limitations actually attach to human life, man confronts and is forced to live in the midst of a genuine predicament. A way out is sought; and while Wieman does not ignore the contribution of religion, he is most critical of those religious thinkers who, in his opinion, make the situation worse by claiming that the source of human good is beyond the reach of reason. Wieman, in short, is opposed to those who hold that God transcends the boundaries of reason.[5] And the main ground of his objection is that the eternal becomes unavailable to us in our present predicament if it is completely beyond both our power to understand and the changing world in which we live.

In a turn of thought surprising for its originality, Wieman argues that with Jesus a new creative power—"the source of all good in human existence"—came into reality and that the true salvation for man in his present predicament can be attained only if man can be transformed by this power. Man, in other words, has to be transcended, but in terms continuous with his own understanding. The authority of the "source of human good" cannot reside in man, not even in the man Jesus, but only in God. And if the transforming power of the creative source really is the true salvation, it must show itself as intelligible in terms of human experience.

Despite his attack upon the neo-orthodox theologians, Wieman shares with them the classical Christian view that man must receive resources from beyond himself if he is not to be destroyed by his own misuse of freedom and knowledge. The influence here of Reinhold Niebuhr's thought is unmistakable. The basic difference, however, between Wieman's views and those of some of his opponents is found in his persistent refusal to accept the idea that God is "wholly other"; Wieman demands continuity of religion, science, and philosophy. It is important, however, to notice that Wieman's rationalism is of a peculiar sort. His argument is not aimed against religion in the name of a purely rational morality based on

[5] See *The Source of Human Good,* p. 33 n., where the proponents of the view Wieman rejects are identified.

the facts of human nature and society. On the contrary, he argues in behalf of a religious power that man himself cannot create, but in so doing he asks that the source of this power not be interpreted as so completely beyond all existence that its actual appearance in the world of time and change becomes a mystery that cannot be understood.

In view of the importance of pragmatism as a philosophy on the American scene and especially its close connection with empiricism, it will prove helpful to add a brief general assessment of the effect pragmatism had on religious thought.

The influence of pragmatism on the philosophy of religion is difficult to overestimate. It extends far beyond the original work of William James and the introduction of the concept of religious experience. The emphasis upon action and the need to translate belief into conduct that characterized the pragmatist position were well in accord with the already established tendency on the American scene to think of religion in wholly practical terms. Pragmatism provided an intellectual justification for the conviction that religion means essentially a way of living; for many it served to reinforce the idea that creeds and theological formulas are secondary in importance. The pragmatic outlook gave new impetus to the belief that "organized religion" is incurably stereotyped, conventional, hypocritical, and dogmatic, while "genuine religion" is to be found only in good conduct and simple belief. The "simple belief" usually consisted in the formula—conventionalized among the supposedly unconventional by overuse—"the Fatherhood of God and the Brotherhood of Man." There is no necessary connection between pragmatism as a philosophy and this formula, as is shown by the thought of Charles Peirce, but the two were often joined by association even if they are not to be connected in a more intelligible way.

More important even than the effect pragmatism exercised on the conception of religion was the revolution brought about by its theory of truth when applied to the problem of religious knowledge. In an age demanding proof of an experimental sort as a necessary condition for knowledge, and for a people either unable or unwilling to accept the reality of what does not appear locally to the senses, the pragmatic doctrine that belief or knowledge might be estimated by an appeal to the conduct and type of life exhibited by those who hold religious beliefs was a welcome development. Reference to consequences and practical results meant an escape from the purely immediate or intuitive positions so much criticized by the proponents of science and scientific method. Religious beliefs had acquired for themselves a critical test. The dictum that "by their fruits shall ye know them" was uttered with conviction by many who could not say for sure whether it was Jesus, Paul, or William James who had first given expression to this "pragmatic" maxim.

The subtleties of pragmatism were generally not explored by religious thinkers and for too many of them pragmatism meant no more than the slogan that the idea that "works" is true or, if not true, at least sufficiently justified to be accepted by the circumspect. A typical example is found in E. A. Cook's *Christian Pragmatism,* published over fifty years ago, in which the author maintained that Christians believe in God and are justified in so doing because it makes them better, happier, and more equipped to perform their duty. Unhappily, the metaphysical and cosmological elaboration of pragmatism exemplified in the writings of Charles Peirce had little influence on the earlier religious pragmatists. In the end, pragmatism turned the philosophy of religion in the direction of psychological, sociological, and historical analysis. It had the merit of keeping alive the connection between religious faith and direct experience, a connection sometimes denied both in the attempts of rationalists to show that religious knowledge is not inferior to science and in the efforts of skeptics to take religious ideas as essentially causal explanations in order to condemn them as either meaningless or unverifiable. Against these errors, pragmatism was a bulwark. But with this advantage went liabilities.

The emphasis on the "success" of religious beliefs (for example, Wieman has described how, through prayer, he improved his memory and was able to keep all of his appointments) and on the "function" of religion in life (though an important category for analysis, *function* came to mean in practice the "use" to which religion might be put) diverted attention from more fundamental issues. Most recently there has been a mounting feeling that a pragmatic foundation for religion is not entirely adequate, first, because the identification of moral norms and religious principles with human interest and desire sacrifices their authority, and, second, because the

385

pragmatic approach has been so exclusively humanistic that it stresses the centrality of man and his experience to the neglect of both God and nature.

It is of some importance to notice the fluid character of the pragmatic influence; pragmatic foundations were used to support very different philosophies of religion. A few typical examples will clarify the point. John Dewey, who brought the pragmatic tradition to its fullest expression, set the pattern for a variety of humanistic and naturalistic religious philosophies and philosophies of religion. His *A Common Faith*, the Terry Lectures delivered at Yale in 1938, is an attempt to lay hold of "the religious" in human experience and to reinterpret the idea of God as an active unification of the ideal and the actual. E. W. Lyman (*Theology and Human Problems*, 1910; *The Meaning and Truth of Religion*, 1933), who was engaged in the very different enterprise of reinterpreting Christian faith for the mind of the Thirties, welcomed the pragmatic conception of knowledge as a means of overcoming the ancient struggle between reason and faith. For Lyman, pragmatism had succeeded in showing the element of faith present in every form of knowledge, thus leading us to reconsider the traditional separation of the two. J. E. Boodin (*God*, 1934; *The Religion of Tomorrow*, 1943), a thinker who is as original as he has been neglected, sought to bring about a new synthesis of Platonic and Christian ideas, starting with the principle that beliefs are true to the extent to which their acceptance enables a person to realize his highest potentialities. Although both Lyman and Boodin transformed their positions in the course of time—the former moved to a kind of religious intuitionism and the latter developed a more mystical outlook emphasizing a "sense of the presence of God"—neither completely abandoned the pragmatism with which he began.

Dewey's position, as stated in *A Common Faith*, is representative of many attempts made during the past twenty-five years to reinterpret religion in order to free it from a supernaturalistic position. Distinguishing between "religion" as an institution based on an organized system of beliefs propagated with authority, and the "religious" as an attitude or a way of approaching the world and experience, Dewey sought to preserve the values he believed inherent in the latter and to free them from connections with the supernatural taken as a realm apart from and above nature. Central to Dewey's view is the denial of a special or psychologically specific "religious experience." For him the "religious" is a quality that may belong to many experiences; as such it has to do with an *effect,* a more satisfactory adjustment to life and its conditions, rather than with a feeling or a state within which the self can dwell. By adjustment to life, Dewey meant a change of will, a reorientation in life, a harmonization of discordant tendencies in the self by becoming related to the universe in imagination and devotion. The self is drawn and harmonized from beyond itself through devotion and activity guided by imagination. Dewey made a sincere effort to reinterpret the idea of God through his analysis of the religious. Reflection upon the world and ourselves teaches us that there are ideals of which we can say neither that they are already fully realized nor that they are rootless, completely cut off from connection with existence. There is, in short, an *active relation* disclosed in experience between the ideal and the actual; for Dewey, God is to be understood as that relation. The union, as Dewey says, between the ideal and the actual, the force bringing it about, is an active one and thus we should speak rather of a *uniting,* a process and a function, rather than of a unification already "given" as completed.

It is not always noticed that Dewey aimed at staking out a middle ground between the extremes of dogmatic supernaturalism and "militant atheism." On his view both extremes share the error of isolating man from nature and of taking him as a being apart, a being living in an alien world. Supernaturalism locates religion in the drama of the human soul, cut off from both nature and other men. Atheism on the other hand conjures up a picture of man as the defiant being, once again cut off from nature, hurling epithets against the alien world and protesting his superiority in the face of a universe growing cold.

The feature in Dewey's interpretation of religion that was found most attractive by his followers was the emphasis on *activity.* The self demands unification and the world needs to be civilized or controlled so that life becomes not only possible but good through the neutralization of the unfavorable factors in the environment. Religion becomes an ally in the conquest of nature and of man. Although there remained an element of manipulation and control in the conception, Dewey's view was well suited to attract those eager to see God as a power producing effects in man and the world rather than as a "substance" transcending nature and oppressing man through authority.

4

PERSONALISM

No account of the development of the philosophy of religion in America would be complete without consideration of the basic doctrines of personalism, a name first made current by Borden P. Bowne at the turn of the century. The position was later to be elaborated with skill and conviction by such thinkers as A. C. Knudson, E. S. Brightman, and most recently by Peter A. Bertocci. Personalism, sometimes called theism by Brightman, means basically the doctrine that personality is the only ultimately creative reality and that it is the controlling power in the universe. This way of thinking has occupied a peculiar position on the American scene because it furnishes us with an example of what is essentially a philosophy of religion (and even a comprehensive metaphysical system) taking on the status of theology for a Protestant denomination. While not all personalists had the same religious affiliations, the fact is that the position established and maintained connections with Methodism in America, an unusual example of an intimate relationship between a philosophical interpretation of God and religion and a living religious tradition.

E. S. Brightman has given the most careful, learned, and comprehensive statement of the position. For him personalism was more than a philosophy of religion, although he developed a coherent interpretation of God and religious experience from that standpoint; the doctrine of personality as the heart of reality was made by him into the coping stone of an idealistic metaphysic. Influenced by Hegel's view of experience to an even greater extent than either he or his contemporaries were aware, Brightman was sensitive to the subtle interconnections of philosophy, theology, and religion. Unlike many others, he was not satisfied with an interpretation of religion that regards it as just one more subject to be explored like science, morality, and art. For him the doctrine of God at once raises questions about the nature of reality and what we say about God does not belong in a sealed compartment of "religious experience" but

389

must be related to a comprehensive theory of the nature of value and existence. This means that if there is to be an explanation of religion—the primary task of the philosophy of religion—that explanation must be achieved from a standpoint more inclusive than religion itself. If, in short, there is to be a philosophy of religion, there must be, in Brightman's view, a philosophy or metaphysic as well. Such a metaphysic draws on religious experience as part of its initial data, but it returns in the end to the interpretation of religion with categories and principles derived from the whole range of experience and reality.

Brightman's approach is that of idealistic empiricism; the proper criterion of philosophic thought is coherence, and coherence is more than logical consistency since it must include and express an actual world. Like Hegel, Brightman took experience to be as wide as the content of consciousness; knowledge is the most coherent account of that experience. Religion is a universal phenomenon in human experience; philosophy of religion understands its subject in a sense broad enough to include religions other than Christianity. Philosophy of religion is distinguished from theology in that theology has to do with the beliefs of the historical tradition in which the theologian stands. There is no difference in principle between the two studies, only a difference in scope. Brightman anticipated the problem that would later arise for the philosophy of religion with the advent of the view that God can be considered only from the standpoint of revelation received through a historical community so that analysis of religion as a universal phenomenon is made to appear as beside the point. By contrast, Brightman defended the rational consideration of religious belief and distinguished between theologians who accept the philosophy of religion (i.e., rational articulation and critical discussion of religious doctrines) and those who rely so exclusively on revelation as authoritative that philosophical reflection is excluded.

Like so many others at the time, Brightman defined religion through the concept of value; religion is concern about experiences that are regarded as of supreme value and it includes, besides concern, devotion to the supreme object of value experience and expression of this concern and devotion in worship. In summarizing what the study of "religion as a fact" reveals, Brightman offers three fundamental beliefs: (1) there is an objective source of values in the cosmos (God); (2) human beings experience values; (3) religious value is the experienced relation of the human to the divine. As will become clear, the tendency to suppose that beliefs such as these, allegedly derived from religion generally, represent the essence of the Christian religion, became a major offense to theologians working under the influence of the neo-Reformation revival.

The two pivotal conceptions in Brightman's thought center on the doctrine of God—the view that God is a person and the theory of the finite God. The former view expresses the essence of Brightman's personalism and the latter represents his original attempt to deal with the problem of evil. Brief consideration of both ideas will furnish us with the key to his comprehensive scheme.

Brightman interpreted the classical Christian doctrine that "God is a spirit" to mean that he is the being whose essence is to be conscious—to experience, to think, to will, and to control the universe by rational purpose. As person, God is no "psychophysical organism" such as popular imagination and sophisticated skepticism invariably construct. The doctrine of a personal God demands metaphysical sophistication; it means first that man is not the only consciousness in existence and second that matter and its organization cannot produce consciousness and values. Starting with the fact of conscious experience and citing the evidence of law and order, of purpose, and of value, Brightman argued that only a cosmic person could explain experience coherently. Neither the blind force of the naturalists nor the absolute of the idealists is adequate for such an explanation. An empirical approach demands a personal God; the only argument to the contrary as Brightman saw the problem is the fact of evil. He attempted to remove that obstacle with his doctrine of the finite God.

Many thinkers representing different schools of thought raised their voices in protest against what Brightman called theistic absolutism—the doctrine that God is omnipotent and unchangeable in every respect. Several factors in the intellectual climate of the late nineteenth and early twentieth century were responsible for the protest against the traditional view. The theory of evolution, having the effect of establishing change and becoming at the heart of reality; the new concern for time and growth, signalized by the philosophy of Bergson; the special emphasis placed by voluntarists on the hu-

391

man will and human activity; the "process philosophy" of Whitehead—all these focused attention on the facts of growth, change, creativity. The classical identification of God with being now appeared as the equating of God with the static and the exclusion from the divine nature of all relation to a world of change and creativity. In place of the view that God is absolute and unchanging—the one in "whom there is no shadow of turning"—there appeared various versions of the doctrine that God is "finite." Although this view may be taken as representative of a position adopted by others, personalism itself must not be identified with the doctrine of the finite God, since neither Bowne nor Knudson accepted it.

The problem of evil was the most important factor determining Brightman's theory, but he urged five considerations against the absolutist view as a preliminary to arguing for his own. By the "absolutist view" Brightman meant a combination of classical Aristotelian theology and absolute idealism. First, absolutism is in error because it appeals to ignorance as the only explanation of "surd evil" in the world. It appeals, that is, to an inscrutable will into which we have no insight. Second, absolutism is led to ascribe surd evil to the divine will, and thus endangers the goodness of God. Third, absolutism leads to moral confusion through the doctrine that apparent evil is really good. Fourth, absolutism makes moral endeavor irrelevant or unnecessary through its doctrine of the unreality of time and an optimism that declares that God is already perfect in himself (cf. James's "moral holiday" made possible by the nature of the absolute). Fifth, absolutism ignores experience in order to defend an a priori view at all costs.

Against this view, Brightman urged the thesis of "theistic finitism" according to which "the eternal will of God faces given conditions which that will did not create, whether those conditions are ultimately within the personality of God or external to it" (*Person and Reality*, p. 313). If the conditions are taken to be external, a dualism results; if they are within divine personality, we have a type of idealistic personalism. The arguments for finitism are parallel to the objections to the absolutist position. By contrast, finitism does not (1) derive its evidence from ignorance, but from present experience and knowledge; (2) ascribe surd evils to the will of God; (3) obliterate the distinction between good and evil within man's experience; (4)

paralyze moral endeavor, but, on the contrary, requires it because we must take part with God in the creative struggle to increase value and overcome evil; (5) neglect experience, because finitism proceeds from what is known to the conquest of the unknown.

It is clear that Brightman's doctrine of the finite God is aimed chiefly at resolving the problem of evil in the form of the ancient dilemma proposed by Epicurus according to which God cannot be both all powerful and all benevolent at once. Acknowledging the facts of futility and waste in the evolutionary process along with the reality of "surd evil" in human affairs, Brightman argues that "there seems to be evil in the universe so cruel, so irrational, so unjust that it could not be the work of a good God" (*Person and Reality,* p. 318). The hypothesis that God is finite is intended to meet this difficulty. The goodness of God is infinite, but God is limited in power. Brightman regarded this as the best way of resolving the dilemma because he rated goodness higher than power; means exist for the sake of ends and derive their value from the purposes they serve.

If God is to be understood as finite, what is the nature of the conditions of limitation and how are they related to the divine personality? In answering this question, Brightman clarified his position and tried to avoid the misleading connotations of the expression *finite God* by speaking instead of a "God whose will is finite." As personal consciousness, God is primarily eternal, active will. According to finitism, that will is limited and the limiting factor is called the given. At every moment God finds the given within the divine consciousness; Brightman speaks, somewhat surprisingly, of God as "controlling" the given. What is the given? It is a complex factor consisting of the uncreated laws of reason (logical and mathematical relations) and uncreated nonrational consciousness—disorderly desires, pains, suffering, and indeed all sources of surd evil. The given is a realm of necessity; Brightman's view is reminiscent of those hierarchical theories of reality originating in the ancient world in which sense and matter stand at the bottom of the scale, totally apart from the divine principle, the source of evil and of all that opposes the good. The given is eternal within the experience of God, but it is a product neither of divine will nor of God's creative activity.

Brightman's description of God as the "controller" of the given may sound strange in view of what has already been said about its nature. The point, however, is readily explained. Brightman's view is a modern version of the doctrine that there is an uncreated or eternal "material" upon which the divine power works; this "material" serves as both the means and the ultimate obstacle to the divine creativity. The "control" that God exercises consists largely in shaping the given and in finding new avenues of creativity. That God's will is finite means that God's plans will on occasion be thwarted. But, Brightman argued, no such defeat is final because the divine goodness is infinite. As some have pointed out, this can only mean that the problem is postponed. No defeat is final for God and yet God is always subject to the given. That no defeat is "final" can mean no more than that there is an infinite future and an endless process. The very nature of the given makes it clear that nothing that happens in the cosmic process can alter the given in a fundamental way. That no defeat is final is to say that *every* defeat is, in a sense, final, unless there is a basic drift in both the divine consciousness and the cosmic process toward conquest of the given itself.

Brightman's doctrine of God as conscious, rational will or cosmic person is important not only for his personalism but also because his development of the view shows how clearly he saw the distinction between personalism as a metaphysical position and as an account of religion. Brightman's last book, *Person and Reality* (1958), contains the fullest discussion of the point, although it was considered by him in other works. He understood that religion, and especially the idea of God, demands metaphysical interpretation if we are to escape from sheer dogmatism at one pole and from a skeptical dissolution of religion at the other. Personalism as a doctrine embraces an idealistic interpretation of the status of value in existence and the ultimate identification of the God of worship with the "supreme experient" of the personalist metaphysic. There is a mutual connection between metaphysics and religion. To be comprehensive, a metaphysic must take account of the phenomenon of religion; religious value is part of the total experience that a theory of reality must interpret and explain. The analysis of religious experience, moreover, provides a touchstone for the principles and categories constituting the metaphysical position. A metaphysic unable to deal successfully with the problem of God is inadequate. We are reminded here of Whitehead's insistence that God, so far from being an exception to the principles of a speculative scheme, must embody them in a supreme way unsurpassed by any other creature. Religion, on the other hand, cannot sustain itself in naïve or uncritical fashion. If a general theory of reality must take account of religion, religion must also be interpreted in terms of a general theory of reality. What is said about God, for example, must be subject to critical discussion in experiential terms. If we speak of knowledge in religion, we cannot mean by knowledge something entirely different from what is meant in other spheres of thought.

In a final metaphysical summary, Brightman posed the problem of religious knowledge in a novel way. In what he called the "dialectic of religious experience," he offered an antinomy between a thesis asserting the autonomy of religious experience in providing knowledge of God and an antithesis denying that autonomy and dissolving religious experience into something other than itself. Arguing in Hegelian fashion, Brightman sought to resolve the antinomy in a third position that combines the element of truth in each side. Religious experience is seen as a valid starting point, but as incapable of sustaining itself without critical support. The view that God is to be found simply as a datum of direct experience needs to be argued for. On the other hand, the view expressed in the antithesis—that all religious values are illusory—will not survive the test of coherence. The fact of the antinomy shows that a more adequate approach to God is needed. In the end, metaphysics must mediate between science and religion.

The philosophical origins of the so-called analytic philosophy of religion are to be found in the British tradition of empirical philosophy. Much more has been done in England under the aegis of this way of thinking than has been accomplished in America. To attempt a general characterization of the analytic approach to philosophy would be rash indeed, especially in view of the protestations by analytic philosophers that one just "does" philosophy and does not indulge in general formulations of what one is doing. Those engaged in the analysis of religion from this vantage point have not changed the pattern. The essential feature of the approach is that one begins with language, and the general assumption seems to be that this is a necessary (in the sense of inescapable in practice) starting point because everyone must use language in order to express his ideas or talk about the world, God, or himself.

Apart from the type of analysis carried on by G. E. Moore and, before him, by McTaggart, the analytic tradition in philosophy had a largely positivistic outlook. This was expressed in the narrowest possible version of classical British empiricism, the positivism of A. J. Ayer's *Language, Truth and Logic* (1937). The primary question was always "What does expression X mean?" and the answer had to be given in terms of immediate sensory data or by specifying a method for arriving at such data that would be encountered if the given expression were true. Thus the meaning of an expression came to be identified with the data themselves or with the operations to be carried out in reaching such data. The Continental versions of this doctrine, stemming originally from the Vienna positivists, did not differ in principle from the position of Ayer, although the Continental positivists such as Carnap and Schlick had a much higher regard for logic, mathematics, and formal systems than ever existed in the more commonsensical English tradition.

It is not difficult to see that for original positivism, religious statements, insofar as they purported to refer to a transcendent reality, were strictly meaningless since they cannot be translated into sensory terms nor is there any process by which they can be "verified" in sense. The only "meaning" that religious statements could possibly have on the classical positivist position was that of "emotive" meaning, i.e., a sheer *expression* of emotions, or an *assertion* to the effect that one actually has or is having certain emotions when he utters a religious statement. In the latter case the "meaning" of the statements is the emotions themselves. It should be obvious that little of a creative sort in the philosophy of religion is possible on such a basis. Original positivism aimed, in the end, not at dealing constructively with the issues of religion and metaphysics, but at eliminating them once and for all.

Although original positivism is not as dead as contemporary analytic philosophers would have us believe, the fact remains that it is an error to identify current analytic philosophy with the old positivist outlook. Not only has there been an internal development in positivism itself resulting, among other changes, in the abandoning of the original "strong" meaning-criterion, but there has been as well the decisive and still puzzling impact of Ludwig Wittgenstein. At the risk of oversimplifying a complex picture, we may say that Wittgenstein transformed the linguistic approach in a radical way by claiming that we should ask not for the *meaning* of a term but for the *use* to which the term is put in some actual communication between persons. The interest in actual use, and especially the tendency to distinguish different functions of language have the merit of bringing a wider range of experience into view; language in actual use reflects what is actually encountered and believed. By contrast, emphasis on formalized languages results in loss of experience.

Leaving aside the problem of determining exactly the meaning and authority of so-called ordinary language, the consequence of Wittgenstein's work for the philosophy of religion was to stimulate the investigation of religious language. Whereas the older forms of analysis had taken the language of natural science as a model and standard for judging every form of language, after Wittgenstein analytic philosophy has shown the tendency to regard all uses of language—aesthetic, ethical, religious—as equally legitimate and open to consideration. The aim of the analytic philosophy of religion is to avoid both speculative interpretations of basic concepts and questions about the "truth" of religious statements in order to concentrate on the discovery of what people who use religious language mean to say. There is a most striking similarity between the attempt of the analytic philosophers to arrive at the meaning of religious utterance without the distortion of theory and prejudice and the program of phenomenology. Both have the goal of sheer disclosure or clarification of meaning.

The aims of a fairly large number of philosophers seeking to employ the methods of linguistic analysis to religion are admirably summed up in *Religious Language* (1957) by Ian Ramsey of Oxford University. While Ramsey's work obviously does not belong to the development of American scholarship in the field, it is important because of the influence it has had on the American scene. Starting with the assumption that a kind of "logical empiricism" can make a contribution to theological thinking, Ramsey suggests that the demand for clarity that played so large a part in the displacement of the older idealism in British philosophy might profitably be invoked as a means of bringing theology within hailing distance of current analytic philosophy. Ramsey's view is that there are characteristically personal situations that are *religious* in nature because they involve a peculiar kind of discernment and require a commitment engaging the total person. To speak about these situations requires a religious language that is "logically odd" vis-à-vis the languages of science and ordinary life and experience. It would perhaps be more accurate to speak of the "religious use of language" rather than "religious language" in view of the fact that, as Ramsey repeatedly points out, in religion we employ object or observational words and then assign them a "strained" meaning so that they can perform their task.

Basic to Ramsey's position is the claim that no attempt to make biblical language conform to "straight-forward public language" ever succeeds. In accordance with this claim he criticizes the existential type theologies aimed at using the language of history no less than the eighteenth century type theology using the language of science. Religious language remains in the end unique, not to be identified with the language used to express public, impersonal fact. The language of the Bible, for example, is not the language of either science or history; it has instead the special function of so presenting the situations in which the word *God* becomes appropriate, that they are discerned by us or "dawn upon" us. Ramsey thus accepts an "existential" type approach to the meaning of religion, but he expresses it through his theory of religious language rather than through historical, ontological, or phenomenological categories.

In addition to what might be called the primary religious language, characterized by a "riotous mixture of phrases," there is also the language of Christian *doctrine*. Ramsey is well aware of the circumstances that gave rise to the need for a form of expression somewhat more reflective and analytical than that to be found in the initial language. The need to communicate to a wider audience in a critical way became paramount. Theology or doctrine aims at systematizing and putting some order into the variety of religious phraseology. To this end use was made of interpretative ideas such as that of the *logos* or of the divine Sonship. Christian doctrine is rooted initially in disclosure-situations; theology has the task of elucidating these situations in language of higher order complexity and of preserving the ultimate religious mystery by clearing up misunderstandings arising from failure to grasp the logical oddity of all discourse about God.

Turning to the development of this approach to the philosophical interpretation of religion in America, we may cite two works—very different in form but both written from a philosophical vantage point analytical in character—John Hick's *Faith and Knowledge* (1957) and Willem Zuurdeeg's *An Analytical Philosophy of Religion* (1958). Hick describes his approach as analytic on the philosophical side and neo-orthodox in theological perspective. His discussion concerns itself largely with epistemological problems and is much less exclusively occupied with the problems of language than similar works written from an analytic point of view. Hick's main aim is to analyze faith as "putative knowledge or awareness of God" and this he seeks to accomplish without becoming involved in the ontological question about the existence of God. The separation is characteristic of the approach; a direct attack upon the substantive question is set aside in favor of an analysis of faith as something "given." Faith is considered according to a voluntarist interpretation (James), the moral argument approach (Kant), and the theory of assent developed by Newman. Hick criticizes these views and then offers a synthesis of his own, drawing elements of truth from each. Distinguishing natural, ethical, and religious orders of "significance," Hick develops the idea that significance is apprehended in "interpretation" a form of explanation and recognition. Religious interpretation sees all experience in terms of a divine purpose. Religion is a "total interpretation" that does not admit of probabilities based on appeal to some wider context. Hick's concern to relate his view to the "world of contemporary philosophy" with its overweening empiricism leads him to search for the meaningfulness of Christianity in some form of immediate experience. In order to meet the demand that the truth of theism make a difference in fact, Hick falls back on the view that the survival of bodily death represents the "experiential crux" in the issue between theism and naturalism. If we do survive bodily death we shall know that we have done so. Verification in religion is a matter of eschatology and not of present experience. On the other hand, life *in via* presents us with the problem of deciding between alternative interpretations of the universe; this we do, not as a matter of compulsory perception, but of voluntary interpretation. In the end, Hick is led back to an "innate bias" in human nature leading or "inclining" us to interpret the universe religiously.

Zuurdeeg's book provides us with the clearest example of the attempt to combine philosophy conceived as neutral analysis with Christian convictions. Analysis does not involve any form of evaluation or judgment, according to this view, although Zuurdeeg does not bother to tell us exactly what analysis is and what we do when we "analyze" religious language. His conception of the philosophy of religion is wholly determined by his view of philosophy. The latter does not have the aim of establishing the truth of anything; it is not preaching, it cannot ascertain the "real" nature of good and evil (and indeed philosophy cannot even raise the question properly see *An Analytic Philosophy of Religion*, p. 15), and it is not ontology. Philosophy is, in short, the enterprise of "analyzing" language. Among the languages it is to treat is the language of religion —convictional language—and the aim of the philosophy of religion is to restrict itself to such analysis avoiding entirely any attempt to defend some form of Christianity or to connect it with the "truths" of science, art, or philosophy. Zuurdeeg, moreover, regards analytic philosophy as ideally suited to the task he sets for it vis-à-vis religion, because it eschews metaphysics and ontology and thus affords no rival to the Christianity he espouses. Zuurdeeg does not consider the possibility that ontological categories may be inescapable for *any* philosophical analysis, and he totally disregards the metaphysical assumptions of analytic philosophy. He fails to see how easy it would be, adopting his own method in "exposing" ontological philosophies, to carry out a similar exposé of analytic ontologies by capitalizing the terms *Sentence, Proposition, Fact, Language, Use, Meaning*, etc. and then banishing them as illegitimate "entities." The fact is that Zuurdeeg, like so many analytic philosophers, never gets to the task of philosophical interpretation because of the belief that all that is required is for us to "analyze" or "clear up" the language in which religious truth is already fully contained and dogmatically expressed.

It is important to notice that though Zuurdeeg makes many evaluations of other views and even characterizes linguistic philosophy as a "correction" of language, he wants to dissociate himself from the

Oxford school of analysis on the ground that they want to attack or defend Christianity by means of analytic philosophy whereas analysis on his view precludes all forms of evaluation and judgment. What is needed instead is an analytic philosophy of religion that shall treat the language of religion in the same way that the languages of mathematics and empirical science have been scrutinized by analytic philosophers. Zuurdeeg, on the other hand, criticizes the analytic approach for not taking seriously enough what he calls the *language situation* or total context within which language, especially religious language, is used. Overcoming the deficiency means an excursion into the phenomenology of religion and the bringing to bear of much material from the history of religion as well as some recent religious thought. The analytic philosophy of religion, it would appear, embraces much that has little to do with analytic philosophy. The catholic scope of analytic philosophy in Zuurdeeg's view is nowhere better illustrated than in his claim that in selecting courage as a topic for analysis, Tillich has made a significant contribution to the understanding of modern man and "therewith to analytical philosophy."

Zuurdeeg defines religious language as "convictional language," which he describes as close to Tillich's idea of ultimate concern. In a distinction reminiscent of Whitehead's comparison between arithmetic and religion, Zuurdeeg claims that while we *use* the languages of mathematics and science, we *are* the convictional language in the sense that such language requires the unity of word, thought, and person. Convictional language correlates with faith as indicative language correlates with cognition. This essentially positivistic philosophical outlook does no damage to religion from Zuurdeeg's standpoint because philosophy makes no evaluations and is incompetent to determine the nature of things.

Since, however, every analysis involves interpretation that is both more and less than a sheer repetition of the expressions to be analyzed,[6] the analytic philosopher cannot avoid introducing some idea of what a given expression *might* or *could* mean; he cannot confine himself merely to what it *does* mean in the intention of the one who

[6] The question of the nature and extent of interpretation in every analysis depends for an answer on another question: Is exact synonymity possible in natural languages?

actually uses the expression. It should be obvious enough that the supposition of what an expression might or could mean, whether the supposition is explicit or not, requires a general philosophical perspective. When it comes to the matter of determining what this perspective is in the case of analytic philosophy of religion, it remains uncertain to what extent the old sensational empiricism still survives. That it does survive is strongly suggested by the antimetaphysical character of analytic philosophy and the belief that it is possible merely to "analyze" religious language without becoming essentially involved in the critical metaphysical and theological problems implicit in such language. There is, moreover, the further evidence of the curious alliance that is developing at present between analytic philosophy of religion and conservative, dogmatic theology.

This type of theology rejects philosophical *criticism* on the ground that theology belongs entirely within the church or religious community and can be developed in its content without external influence. That content, moreover, as part of revelation, is not subject to secular judgment. It seems unlikely that an analytic philosophical approach would be acceptable to such a standpoint unless it did in fact remain "neutral." Unless, that is, it appeared to be engaged only in "clarification" of meaning without in any way claiming to contribute to the theological content. It is perhaps too early to be sure that this characterization of the analytic approach is adequate; other and different developments may be forthcoming. It is clear, nevertheless, that the alliance between the analytic philosophy of religion and dogmatic theology represents a modern form of an ancient phenomenon seen more than once in the history of Western Christianity. That phenomenon is the joining together of a formalistic philosophy with a dogmatic theology in the common effort to eliminate the explicitly metaphysical type of interpretation that would disturb the secure foundations of both enterprises. For in the alliance itself neither side is actually confronted by the positive claim of the other. Analytic philosophy is not forced to a critical reflection on its own foundations such as it would be if, instead of regarding religious language as one more area for the use of analytic tools, it actually took seriously the problem of God as posing a crucial test for all philosophical categories and principles. Dogmatic theology, on the other hand, is not driven from its own encapsulation by intercourse with a philosophy that, instead of initiating critical exchange by proposing alternative possibilities for theological doctrines, aims only at "clarifying" theological content without adding to it.

Whatever the future of analytic philosophy of religion may be, it must be pointed out that current developments in the analytic tradition have made possible at least a philosophical treatment of religion that could not have taken place at an earlier time. And if some analysts are disturbed by the fact and have an uneasy feeling that, after the modification of the old positivist program, the "bars are down," that is a problem that will have to be worked out among themselves. On the other hand, it must not be supposed that the philosophy of religion represented by Hartshorne and others previously mentioned has been dependent on any "relaxation" of philosophical standards. Those who do not share the analytic viewpoint have kept the enterprise alive without interruption, preferring to challenge the implicit metaphysics of positivism rather than to attempt to think about God within the narrow and impossible limits set by the verifiability theory of meaning. For Tillich, Hartshorne, and Stace, the philosophy of religion is an essential and unavoidable discipline not wholly subject to philosophical fashions. Their work is no return to a task that can now be resumed because "the bars are down"; for them no bars were ever up in the first place because they never accepted narrow empiricism. All view philosophy as a substantial enterprise involving construction, synthesis, and interpretation as well as analysis.

5

MYSTICISM

It has often been said that piety in America is largely of a practical nature emphasizing the ethical and political implications of religious belief to the exclusion of the contemplative aspect that we customarily associate with the mystical. While this view has much evidence behind it, it does not express the whole truth. To a surprising extent, some form of mysticism has maintained itself on the American scene in every period. To avoid confusion it is necessary to distinguish between *mysticism as a total or comprehensive form of religion* that excludes other and different forms and mysticism in the form of a *mystical element* such as immediate experience that is present in every religious form to a greater or lesser degree.

Total mysticism, seen in historical perspective, has appeared in two fundamental forms—a practical and a contemplative. The primary basis for differentiating the two is found in the attitude to the "world" of secular concerns. The contemplative form tends to neglect the world of time and change as "inferior" and as a passing reality that we are justified in "overlooking" because of the importance attached to the object of mystical union. The practical type, on the other hand, views the mystical way as primarily a source of power for transforming personal and social life in the world.

Mysticism in the sense of a mystical element means the aspect of immediacy or direct experience that may accompany other types of piety such as the prophetic, the priestly, the practical, and the aesthetic. Total mysticism fully established as a way of life has not been a widespread phenomenon in America. The belief, however, that every description of religious experience must include a mystical element has exercized considerable influence.

James's *Varieties of Religious Experience* gave a place of primary importance to mysticism and the living presence of one type of practical mysticism in the tradition of Quaker piety has served to keep it before us as a vital religious form. In many books and studies, Rufus Jones developed a philosophy of mystical piety of the sort generally associated with the Quaker tradition. Jones was, in fact, the foremost philosophical interpreter of a mysticism of the inner light. His mysticism, like that of the Quakerism he represented, was of the practical type. This means that the world is not denied or life in it depreciated; on the contrary, Jones held that true power for existence in the world can be secured only from mystical experience, from the opening of the self to the divine influence. Nor is the orientation purely individualistic; Jones was fond of emphasizing the "social" character of Quaker silence. His account of mystical experience as it figures in Quakerism confirms both points:

> This new mysticism wrought out with others is not "a flight of the alone to the Alone," not a moveless ecstasy in which the lonely soul attains a passive union with a super-reality yonder. It is a vital discovery of the divine Life revealing itself here and now in and through a group of persons who are bent on transmitting that Life. It is mysticism not of solitude and self-seeking; it is practical mysticism of life and action. God is not sought as an Infinite beyond all finites, but rather as the inward sap of a living Vine where His life and our lives bear spiritual fruit together. [*New Studies in Mystical Religion,* 1927, p. 170.]

Jones was especially sensitive to the problem of relating a mystical approach to religion to a community of believers organized as a church. As a matter of historical interpretation, he regarded the organization and polity of the Christian church in its formative period as growing out of essentially *nonreligious* needs. The point requires some interpretation. By *religion* Jones always meant "firsthand experience of God" and he invariably contrasted that with *religion* taken in the sense of the transmission of grace through an ecclesiastical *institution* conceived as divinely appointed. Thus when he described the organization of the ancient church as having developed to fit the institution for its role as "a divine instrument of salvation," he regarded this as a nonreligious function. At the time of the Reformation, a new opportunity presented itself—recovery of the importance of first person experience in religion focused the problem of finding a type of organization genuinely expressive of individual experience. While Jones saw the seeds of the proper solution in Luther's idea of the "communion of saints" he maintained that Luther was unable to realize this ideal under adverse historical circumstances. Calvin, moreover, in seeking to realize the theocratic ideal, did not seek to find a type of organization that could remain sensitive to the religious experience of each man. Jones saw Calvinism as an imitation of the Roman Catholic approach in Protestant terms. For him, then, classical Protestantism did not solve the problem. He found no solution save in the organization characteristic of the Society of Friends.

In emphasizing the invisible bonds of community in common experience—the Holy Spirit—as the essence of the church, Jones thought of his view as a return to New Testament foundations. He drew the contrast between the primitive communities and the later world historical church as a contrast between religion as immediate experience and religion as acceptance of theological doctrine. This contrast runs throughout the thought of Jones; his was not a speculative mysticism nor one arrived at through philosophical dialectic. His was a religious mysticism in pure form.

If we take the thought of Jones as representative of the practical religious type of mystical religion, the approach of W. T. Stace represents in striking contrast the metaphysical form of mysticism. Whereas Jones thought within a religious framework and sought to show the superiority of immediate experience of God over other types of piety, Stace develops his philosophy of mystical religion in response to criticism against every form of religion advanced from the side of skepticism and secular thought. Stace, moreover, is sensitive to the problem of being, and he sees in the mystical insight the only way to solve the problem and retain the element of truth in modern science at the same time. While we must not exaggerate the differences, Stace's position represents something very different from a practical piety. More informed by the tradition of philosophical mysticism, and especially by insights derived from both Buddhist and Hindu mysticism, Stace's view must be placed alongside those of Hartshorne and Tillich as forming an indispensable part of the current situation in the philosophy of religion. Obviously much closer to Tillich than to Hartshorne in outlook, Stace has his own positive and clearly expressed alternative to propose. He has neither a rationalism based on process nor an existential ontology, but rather a theory of mystical experience alleged to be compatible with the conclusions alike of modern science, naturalistic metaphysics, and positivist theories of knowledge. His understanding of mysticism and its peculiar place on the current scene can best be grasped if we attend not only to his analysis of the nature of mystical experience but also to those problems posed by modern thought to which Stace believes mysticism can furnish the only defensible answer.

Stace has long been interested in mysticism as a philosophy, and his recent work, *Mysticism and Philosophy* (1960), aims at elucidating the properly philosophical characters of mysticism by emphasizing the fact that not all of its forms are religious. Stace's involvement in the philosophy of religion dates particularly from the fall of 1947, when he published an article, "Man Against Darkness," that was widely attacked as "atheistic." While that article expressed a naturalistic position that, as Stace claims, is reaffirmed in *Time and Eternity* (1952), there can be no doubt that the two writings reveal two very different evaluations of religion. The article implies a rejection of religion as outmoded and rooted in a "failure of nerve," while *Time and Eternity* no less than *Religion and the Modern Mind* (1952) are positive defenses of mystical religion in opposition to positivism and reductive naturalism. The obvious shift in position is not so important as the deeper identity in outlook to which Stace quite correctly points. Mysticism seems able, abounding as it does in expressions that can appear only as paradoxes if one insists on maintaining an ordinary or "common-sense" point of view, to embrace a naturalism that has no place for God and a conception of God that requires no "beyond" because the divine reality is everywhere present. Stace compares this synthesis of pantheism and atheism with the duality of being and non-being in which the writings of mystics abound.

Stace's defense of mystical religion may be viewed in its own right and also as essentially a response to the problems posed for religion by the scientific outlook on the world. *Religion and the Modern Mind* outlines the problem by tracing the impact on the religious view of reality made by the development of a purely scientific view of the world. It is Stace's view that, whereas the heritage of the Western religious tradition led to a medieval world picture in which religious conceptions were dominant—especially the idea of a world purpose rooted in God and a moral order deriving from his will— the modern scientific picture of the universe runs counter to and must

407

finally exclude the classical religious outlook. Rejecting the widespread belief that the conflict between religion and science is found in the contradiction of specific religious propositions by verifiable scientific statements, Stace says:

> The real antagonism lies much deeper. It is not between particular discoveries of science and particular dogmas of religion at all. It is rather that certain very general assumptions which are implicit in the scientific view of the world conflict with basic assumptions of the religious view . . . [p. 56].

In particular he singles out the fundamental shift in outlook that is involved in going from the classical Christian picture of reality to the modern scientific world view. We are to move from a vision of a God who has purposes for the world that are manifested in the world and who sustains a real moral order within which man has a purposive life to a picture of the universe in which there are no purposes and all events are explained in terms of mathematical physics and the science of mechanics. It is with this view of the conflict between "world-pictures" in mind that Stace seeks a way of reconciliation. His version of mystical religion represents the solution. By interpreting God as the sacred nothing that is the truly infinite because it is beyond all finite distinctions and cannot be described adequately after the fashion of "things" in the world, Stace hopes to preserve a religious world view and at the same time avoid having to deny the validity of the modern scientific picture of the world of physical things. The "sacred nothing" is, of course, the "all" of pantheistic mysticism; it is not really the void but it must be expressed in this paradoxical way in order not to be reduced to one thing besides others. Not being a thing, the sacred does not interfere with the world of things or our knowledge of that world.

Stace is acutely aware of the fact that the intellectual results of the sciences do not synthesize themselves into a unified picture, but that rather what is called the scientific outlook is a philosophical construction of the nature of reality as seen by the intellect aiming at the interpretation of everything in causal terms. This means that the conflict is not between science and religion as such, but between religion and skeptical or positivistic philosophies. The majority of skeptical objections to belief in God, he says, have come from philosophical criticism. Stace's solution is to effect a radical disconnection between the literal knowledge contained in science and the symbolic affirmations of religion. Scientific knowledge is incapable of either proving or disproving the existence of God, and even philosophical dialectic is in the same position. Adopting a position not unlike Kant's, Stace argues that while rational arguments for the existence of God are all invalid, no rational knowledge is capable of showing the nonexistence of God. This means that the whole case of religion is thrown into another court. Religious affirmations are not literally true; the proper form of expression for religion is not concepts but symbol and myth. All religious truths are symbolic in character.

Not unlike Tillich, whose ideas he acknowledges with sympathy, Stace appeals to the mystical tradition in support of a conception of the divine that stands against both the traditional theistic conception of God and the atheistic dissolution. To think of God as comprehensible, at least to a degree, and as existing in a literal sense belongs to the beliefs of traditional theism. Stace denies both the comprehensibility and the literal existence of God. He does so, however, in the name of neither positivism nor atheism, but in the name of mysticism —"the negative divine." For Stace the incomprehensible mystery of the divine is disclosed in the experience of the true mystic. Such disclosure does not dispel the mystery or produce comprehension; rather it confirms, and indeed is, experience of the mystery itself.

6

EXISTENTIAL AND ONTOLOGICAL APPROACH

A complete account of the influence of existential philosophy on religious thought in America cannot yet be written because we are still in the midst of the development. The existentialist influence started with the introduction of the writings of Kierkegaard, made available in English through the devoted scholarship of David and Lillian Swenson and Walter Lowrie. In addition, the writings of Berdyaev, Sartre, Marcel, Heidegger, and Jaspers have made their impact and there has arisen a debate between the so-called atheistic and the religious versions of existentialism. The anti-ontological cast of some existential thinking, its concern for the interior life of the individual and its emphasis on freedom, choice, commitment, and responsibility have all worked to bring existentialism into close relation with current religious thought emphasizing the primacy of faith over all forms of speculation.

David E. Roberts' *Existentialism and Religious Belief* (1959) has furnished an excellent account of the interplay between the various forms of the philosophy of existence and recent treatments of religious issues in both philosophical and theological terms. In addition to his illuminating analyses of the basic ideas set forth by the major existentialist thinkers, Roberts attempted to assess the relevance of existentialism for Christian faith. He sought to determine the proper response of religious people to the existential outlook and concluded that neither a total rejection nor an unqualified acceptance would be justified. The existential approach correctly warns against excess rationalism and the denial of human freedom often following in the wake of extreme scientism. From existentialism we learn in phenomenological terms the facts of guilt, anxiety, despair, and the sense of nothingness. These facts, according to Roberts, are of the utmost importance for the religious life of America because they form a realistic counterweight to the optimism, the moralism, and the activism of much contemporary Christianity. Roberts also pointed out the extent to which the criticism of rationalism, thought to be exclusive with the existentialists, was in fact shared by others such as James, Bergson, Dewey, and Whitehead—philosophers who certainly are not to be numbered among the existentialists. Finally, and in some ways most important, Roberts underlined the contribution that the existentialists have made to our understanding of skepticism and unbelief. Instead of viewing this understanding simply as a means of providing the Christian apologist with ammunition for the fight against secular positions, Roberts demanded that Christians use it to become more aware of their own unfaith and despair in an age that has lost God. Such awareness can become a pledge of good faith in an honest dialogue between religious and nonreligious points of view.

The impact of existentialism on the philosophy of religion has made itself felt not only through studies of the existentialist philosophers, but in a more direct use of the point of view for the reinterpretation of Christian doctrines. Here Paul Tillich's thought must be seen as basic. For in his method of "correlation," according to which the doctrines of theology are seen as answers to philosophical questions raised by rational analysis but not answerable on grounds of reason alone, it is clear that the philosophy involved must be of an existential sort. Theology furnishes answers to existential questions; like Berdyaev, Tillich believes that if there is to be a rapprochement between philosophy and theology at present it can come about only if the philosophy involved is oriented toward existence and away from past substantialisms. Yet we must not overlook the extent to which Tillich, in contrast with some of the existentialists, has developed an existential *ontology* and a theory of being to be used as a means of reinterpreting the concept of God.

The impact of Tillich on the course of religious thought in America has been enormous; this fact would be acknowledged by critics and supporters alike. His influence extends to theology as well as to the philosophy of religion (see Claude Welch's essay on "Theology," elsewhere in this volume). Coming to America in 1933 to escape the Nazi tyranny, Tillich brought to the religious situation of the time a unique combination of philosophical and theological learning. His arrival coincided with the high point of liberalism in theology and the dominant ethical orientation of the social gospel. Tillich's viewpoint represented an effective synthesis of Lutheran Christianity and the mystical religion of the Rhineland Mystics with the existential philosophy of Schelling. As became clear, this was a formidable combination on a religious scene filled with a philosophy of activism and a practical faith. However, unlike so many others from Europe who came to America either before or during the war, Tillich was open to American ideas and experience. He was not content to repeat old doctrines. Though schooled in Reformation theology and in the tradition of German idealism, Tillich did not follow standard patterns in the interpretation of either. Where others were content to graft idealism onto Christianity, or vice versa, he developed a realistic standpoint aimed at showing how religion had greatly weakened its influence among the industrial masses through its connection with a conservative idealism; where others were content with the value theology of Ritschl and an optimistic outlook on the world, Tillich was deriving insights from Schelling's metaphysic of experience and developing his doctrine of the demonic in human life.

At first, Tillich was classified along with Karl Barth as one of the "neosupernaturalists" who aimed at the establishment of a purely dogmatic theology of revelation. This initial judgment was based largely on a few articles and an early work, *Die Religiöse Lage* (1926; English trans., *The Religious Situation*, 1932, by H. R. Niebuhr). Two of Tillich's doctrines were responsible for the conclusion that he belonged to the school of "irrationalistic supernaturalism" [7]

[7] The expression is due to Macintosh. It is most instructive to compare current interpretations and judgments of Tillich's philosophical theology with early reactions to his thought stemming from a time when his system was not yet completed and when only a few of his writings were available. The reader is directed to the following: *American Philosophies of Religion* (1936), ed. H. N. Wieman and B. E. Meland, esp. pp. 88-92; E. S. Brightman's *A Philosophy of Religion* (1940), esp. pp. 172-74. Brightman had noticed Tillich's defense of philosophy and he did not make the mistake so often made of confusing Tillich with Barth, but Brightman was critical of Tillich's use of the concept of revelation, regarding it as a challenge to philosophy. Macintosh's brief account of Tillich's ideas (*The Problem of Religious Knowledge*, 1940, pp. 348-50) is based on more sources than any other early appraisal. Macintosh rightly emphasized Tillich's Kantianism, but he interpreted it as a strictly "agnostic" tendency. Unsympathetic with any form of "dialectic," Macintosh could not make sense of Tillich's attempts at the reconciliation of opposites in the treatment of theological problems. For a good indication of the early reaction to Tillich among theologians, see W. M. Horton's *A Realistic Theology* (1934). This book nicely illustrates the enthusiasm with which Tillich's "realism" was received. Tillich's own account of his initial reception in America should also be consulted: "Autobiographical Re-

—first, his retention of the concept of revelation, and second, his doctrine that God cannot be said to "exist" because the divine is beyond the contrast between essence and existence. The appeal to revelation aroused suspicion because the dominant philosophy of religion of the time could understand the concept only in the ancient sense of a body of doctrine delivered to man in a wholly supernaturalistic way. That Tillich was attempting to interpret revelation in a philosophical way was to become clear only at a later time. The denial that God "exists" appeared to many as a confusing paradox, and it served to create the belief that for Tillich God is so transcendent as to be entirely beyond man's capacity to make intelligible statements about him. Again, that Tillich meant no more than what is meant by saying that if *exist* means exactly what it does in the case of tables and chairs God does not exist is something that became clear only later on. But the premature identification of Tillich with the new European supernaturalism had the effect of obscuring the profound differences between his position and that of Barth, especially on the place of philosophical criticism in the theological enterprise. That Tillich defended the indispensability of philosophical principles and categories for the theological task was a factor that, as Hartshorne points out in *The Logic of Perfection* (1962), p. 10, has kept alive the communication between philosophers and theologians in recent years.

Every creative thinker has the effect of transcending and therefore of obscuring the categories through which we have become accustomed to classify intellectual endeavor and schools of thought. This is particularly true in Tillich's case. He does not attempt a philosophy of religion in the sense in which it had been understood in the American tradition. Tillich is primarily a theologian seeking to reinterpret for the modern situation the basic ideas of Christianity in its Reformation version. For this enterprise he uses the term *philosophical theology,* and it embraces both a philosophy and a phenomenology of religion as a prelude to the treatment of more specifically theological issues. For this reason Tillich's thought has to be considered under more than one category. Tillich distinguishes a philosophical theology from what he calls a kerygmatic theology, which is developed

flections of Paul Tillich" in *The Theology of Paul Tillich* (1952), ed. C. W. Kegley and R. W. Bretall.

413

from within the religious community and which has as its aim the systematic presentation of the Christian faith without special regard for secular disciplines, especially the doctrines of philosophy. While not unmindful of the need for the kerygmatic type, Tillich has devoted his major effort to philosophical theology. He seeks through what he calls the method of correlation to relate theological doctrine to philosophical questions by showing that questions posed from a primarily existential standpoint can be finally resolved only from the standpoint of Christian faith.

Tillich's entire system is dependent on the "correlation method." Each theological concept is set in relation to a philosophical problem arising out of an analysis or diagnosis of the human situation. Thus revelation is the religious answer to reason's quest for a solution to the problems posed by the limitation of human reason: revelation discloses the "depth of reason" at the point where reason's own finitude becomes apparent; God as the Unconditioned is the answer to the question of the meaning of being; Christ as the New Being reconciling man and God is the answer to man's quest for a reality overcoming the tragic distortion of historical existence; the Holy Spirit as the Divine Life sets the pattern for balancing the polar elements—dynamics and form, individualization and participation, destiny and freedom—so as to allow for the fullest self-realization.

It should not be difficult to understand why this original way of presenting the Christian position fails to fit neatly into familiar categories. Philosophers wonder if it is philosophy and theologians are puzzled by the intricate ontology. The affinity, however, of Tillich's intellectual endeavor with the efforts of such classical philosophical theologians as Augustine, Abelard, and Aquinas would, if taken more seriously by Protestants, lessen the sense of strangeness with which Tillich's thought is often received. His combination of philosophical and theological ideas could not fail to elicit a striking variety of response. Theologians have tended either to set his thought down as "speculative" and without adequate roots in the biblical tradition,[8] or they have praised it as a contribution to the philosophy of religion which is, for some, the same as saying that as theology it need not be taken seriously. Philosophers, on the other hand, have been wary of

[8] *Biblical Religion and the Search for Ultimate Reality* (1955) is Tillich's answer to this charge.

the theological orientation evident in his treatment of philosophical issues and, in view of the antimetaphysical character of recent philosophy, Tillich's continued use of metaphysical language adds to the suspicion. Both sides have been slow to take note of the novel character of Tillich's scheme.

Prior to Tillich, American philosophers of religion, with but a few notable exceptions, did not start with distinctively Christian concepts, but began instead with religion in some generic sense or religious values and tried to arrive at a religious view of reality without being careful to show the relation of that view to Christianity in a systematic way. This is not to say that Christianity played no part in their thought; it is rather to say that Christianity often played no explicit or clearly focused role. Side by side with this failure of philosophers to put the Christian doctrines in the center of their thought, theologians were countering with the concept of a wholly biblical theology developed on a dogmatic basis within the confines of the church. One group minimized Christianity and the other excluded philosophical criticism. Genuine exchange based on mutual encounter was lost. Tillich's philosophical theology was aimed at destroying this radical separation. Theology is to be subject to rational canons and it is under obligation to take metaphysical problems into account in the development of theological doctrine. Philosophy is not to remain within the safe limits of analysis and formal systems; it must take seriously the religious claim of revelation and recover, through critical reflection on theological issues, the classical philosophical issues abandoned in the face of positivistic criticism. The arresting character of Tillich's thought and one of the chief reasons for its catalytic affect on the American scene is found in the claim that Christian revelation and philosophical interpretation can and must be taken seriously together. This claim has proved deeply disturbing to those determined to keep the two in separate compartments.

Tillich defines religion as "ultimate concern," by which he means the response of the entire person to God defined by the biblical injunction "Thou shalt love the Lord thy God with all thy soul and with all thy heart and with all thy mind." Ultimate concern directed to the Unconditioned as ground of all reality is distinguished from proximate concerns for family, occupation, and success in the world.

415

Tillich holds that when we have a genuinely ultimate concern we have at the same time a concern for the really ultimate. He has been unwilling to admit the possibility that a really ultimate concern can be directed to an idol or finite reality that is not God. The full justification of this claim is bound up with his doctrine of God no less than with the nature of concern itself. Like the phenomenologists, Tillich understands concern to be part of the ontological structure of human life; it is more than a "subjective" or "psychological" complex. A person manifesting that concern is at the same time in the presence of the Unconditioned, for were it not so, the individual would have no power to will that concern into being himself. This is Tillich's version of the Augustinian standpoint in theology. Following this tradition, Tillich starts with the idea of truth as the power making possible all finite truth. The individual apprehends the presence of the Unconditioned when he apprehends the necessity of truth in critical reflection. This apprehension gives immediate certainty. Religion, however, is not speculation; it requires in addition to the reflective apprehension, a concrete manifestation of the Unconditioned in existence. Religion requires the unity of the Unconditioned and the concrete. Risk enters at the point where the transition is made from the certainty of the Unconditioned to the concrete form of the divine in a historical religious tradition. In Christian terms this would mean identifying the Unconditioned with Jesus as the Christ encountered through the Bible and the church.

The key to Tillich's doctrine of God is found in the idea that the divine—the Unconditioned—is present in the form of "depth," that is to say, in the form of a power that sustains every reality and makes it what it is, even though this power may not be recognized for what it is. Filled with a profound sense, which he shares with the prophetic and mystical traditions, that a "god" who merely "exists" as one more reality beside others is nothing but a finite idol, Tillich tries to recover the sense of God as transcendent reality, beyond the logical contraries—finite-infinite, existent-nonexistent, etc. In this way he hopes to avoid what is for him the religious idolatry implied in thinking of God as an "object" the existence of which is open to doubt and discussion. Instead he identifies God with "being itself" or "the power of being" and insists that this conception is thoroughly in accord with the God of whom the Bible speaks as demanding our unqualified love and worship. Much of the critical discussion of Tillich's thought in recent years has centered on this doctrine. Difficulties stem in part from Tillich's rather too abundant vocabulary; *power of being, being itself, ground of being, unconditioned, abyss* are all used by him in either naming or describing God. Another source of controversy is the strangeness of the conception of being on the current philosophical scene. For so many contemporary thinkers, *being* is taken to mean the emptiest universal shared by everything that "is," and consequently in their view to identify God with being in this sense appears to be saying nothing at all. Criticism comes not only from the opponents of metaphysics; the proponents of process philosophy are also set against the concept of being because they suppose it to mean the "static" and timeless and, they argue, a world of change and development, of becoming and creativity cannot be understood in terms of being.

If Tillich's doctrine of God has provoked critical discussion, his insistence on the symbolic character of religious discourse has met with an even more vigorous reaction. He maintains that religious meaning can only be expressed through religious symbols, and that the religious life is structured by means of these symbols. It is noteworthy that a sacramental conception of reality results from the theory of religious symbols. To be religiously significant, the materials of nature and history must point beyond themselves to the divine reality. Or, conversely, in order to be made manifest the divine must have a medium of revelation; the Spirit needs flesh. Tillich's insistence that the affirmations about God, Christ, and the Spirit that form the center of Christian faith must be understood as symbolic has met with determined opposition. The struggle continues on the current scene and the problems are not yet resolved. Accepting as valid Kant's analysis, which he takes to imply that God cannot be literally described by means of the same categories legitimate for the theoretical explanation of natural objects, Tillich holds that the only way we can speak about God is through symbols. In order to provide a root in actuality for the theory of symbolism, Tillich asserts that "God is being itself" and takes this not in a symbolic sense but as the one literal statement in the scheme.[9] All else must be understood

---

[9] Central to any theory of symbolism is the answer to the question: What is the logical contrary of *symbolic?* If the answer is *literal* then it becomes necessary

symbolically. This means that since the media through which religious meaning is expressed—words, images, events, persons, objects —are drawn from finite things and human experience, some transformation of their finite meaning is required if they are to express what is *not* a finite object—God. Tillich's historical sense makes him aware of the ancient character of the problem; since the period of pseudo-Dionysius, theologians asked "With what names can we speak of God and how are they to be understood?" Tillich's solution has affinities with the answer proposed by the defenders of "negative" theology as well as with the theology of "eminence" that dominated the later Middle Age. In reply to criticism, Tillich describes his *via symbolica* as the unity of the *via negativa* and the *via eminentiae*. He claims that while the one approach depends exclusively on negations and the other on affirmations, his view combines both features. How this can be is still the subject of much discussion.

Two sorts of objections have been advanced. First, there is the charge that a symbolic approach sacrifices the reality of God, reducing him to human consciousness; and second, there is the charge that the very adoption of the symbolic approach means the acceptance of skepticism in the use of human reason and the "agnosticism" of the Kantian critical philosophy. Tillich's answer to the first objection rests on his distinction between a symbol and a sign. Symbols are connected essentially with the reality to which they point, whereas signs are not. The total character of Jesus, for example, is what enables him to disclose the divine nature, or as Tillich puts it, to be "transparent" to the divine. To claim that "Jesus is the Christ" is to employ a symbolic expression that says that Jesus in his nature manifests or points beyond himself to the nature of God. Jesus is not "merely a symbol," Tillich argues, because a "mere" symbol would be only a sign and not a symbol in the proper sense at all. A sign is connected only externally with its object and it does not "participate" in the reality that it means. This is why signs are always partially conventional while symbols, especially religious symbols, can-

---

to show that there actually is "literal" discourse devoid of every "symbolic" element. On the other hand, if the "literal" itself is a special way of symbolizing reality, the contrast between literal and symbolic cannot be maintained and we must introduce the idea of different kinds of symbolism. It is not clear in Tillich exactly what the contrast term is. His most extended discussion of religious symbols and symbolism is in *Dynamics of Faith* (1957).

not be created by human will. Tillich has repeatedly denied that his theory of symbols has anything in common with the view of the nineteenth century "symbolists" for whom religious symbols replaced the religious reality in which men no longer believed.

More serious than the charge of subjectivism is the denial of the need for symbolism entered from the side of speculative rationalism.[10] According to this view, to speak of symbols is confusing and presupposes uncritical acceptance of the Kantian and empiricistic limitation of the scope of reason. Hartshorne prefers to speak of analogical concepts, distinguishing them from both literal and formal concepts; all three can apply to God and there is even a sense in which the analogical concepts have a "literal" meaning. The issue between Tillich and Hartshorne is not merely verbal, although the use of different terminology does obscure their points of agreement and exaggerate their points of difference.[11] The difference between them, however, is serious enough to touch the central question of the nature of God. We may pose the issue (or at least one aspect of it) as follows: for Tillich God is beyond the subject-object distinction, and therefore any concept whose meaning is derived from the sphere in which that distinction is valid cannot apply literally to God but must be understood symbolically. Hartshorne, on the other hand, rejects this idea of God and holds that, far from being beyond rational categories, God is the supreme exemplification of them. This view, though it has affinities with the analogical position taken by Aquinas, stems from Whitehead's well-known dictum that God is not to be

---

[10] Hartshorne's criticism may be taken as typical of this denial. The issue is so complex that I can do no more than pose it here; there are, moreover, statements by both Tillich and Hartshorne that suggest that neither is certain about the extent of their agreement or disagreement. The reader should consult Hartshorne's paper, "Tillich's Doctrine of God," in *The Theology of Paul Tillich,* pp. 164-95, and Tillich's reply, pp. 333 ff. Tillich has set forth his position at greater length in *Systematic Theology,* vol. I (1951), vol. II (1957), and in *Dynamics of Faith.* See Hartshorne's comment in *The Logic of Perfection* (1962), p. 9 n4, and cf. pp. 140-41.

[11] It is clear, for example, that what makes some concepts analogical for Hartshorne is precisely what makes the same concepts symbolic for Tillich. One who uses the expression *analogical concept,* however, is likely to suppose that what he is saying means "logical," "rational," "clear," etc. as compared with the expression *symbolic,* which smacks of "poetic," "confused," etc. But these rhetorical considerations are irrelevant to the main issue and should not be exploited merely to gain the point.

taken as an exception to all the rational categories, invoked merely to save the collapse of a metaphysical scheme, but rather that he is the perfect embodiment of the categorial system. To express the difference in an example, we may say that from Hartshorne's perspective the assertion that God is a person means that only God is literally and fully a person in the "eminent" sense and by contrast all human persons are persons in a derivative sense, through diminution and negation. Hartshorne has referred to this as "negative anthropology." Tillich holds that to speak of the perfect exemplification of a category in the assertion, to continue the example, that God is a person, is to understand the category of person in a sense other than that derived from experience of finite things. The category cannot, when used to characterize God, retain the same meaning that it has in polar contrasts characteristic of finite experience. Tillich takes this to be the meaning of the classical doctrine that in God all attributes are identical. Consequently, he argues, the categorial terms used to describe God, since they are drawn from finite experience, and this meaning is determined by the natures and relations of finite objects to each other, can be used only in a symbolic way. The truth is that both Hartshorne and Tillich are at one in holding that *negation* is required in regard to the finite or human; the crucial difference between their views is that while Hartshorne believes we know what the eminent or perfect sense of the category means, Tillich does not. For Tillich what we know is the finite meaning of the category, and while we may speak of the "perfect" realization of this category in God we do not know what this means in "literal" terms. Hartshorne, on the contrary, holds that we do know the eminent meaning and even asserts that in the case of the divine knowledge it is "simple" to know what perfect knowledge means. He admits, however, that knowing what the eminent sense means can result only from a *quantitative* negation, i.e., we know what fallible knowledge means and we have but to remove the restrictions in order to arrive at the concept of infallible knowledge; we *sometimes* make mistakes whereas God *never* does. The difference between Tillich and Hartshorne, expressed in more immediately religious terms, is that the mystical tendency of the former leads him to attempt to preserve the divine mystery while the rationalistic bent of the latter results in a bolder conceptual penetration. Whatever reconciliation of their views is possible will depend upon further analysis of the sense in which each understands the operation of negation, for while both appeal to it one employs it starting with the side of God and the other with the side of man.

One of the striking features of the religious situation in recent years has been the development of an interplay between religion and depth psychology. The emergence of this relationship has been marked by both tension and cooperation. Tillich's contribution here is sizeable, although considerable literature now exists in this field of thought and a fuller understanding requires that we pay attention to such works as David Roberts' *Psychotherapy and a Christian View of Man* (1950), Fritz Kunkel's *In Search of Maturity* (1943), Erich Fromm's *Psychoanalysis and Religion* (1950), Carl Jung's *Psychology and Religion* (1938). Tillich has not only employed psychological insights for the reinterpretation of classical religious beliefs, but he also has led many depth psychologists to reconsider the grounds for the traditional antireligious bias stemming from acceptance of the Freudian outlook. The discussion is not confined to theologians and philosophers; it reaches down into the depths of the religious life of every man. Tillich's most widely read work, *The Courage to Be* (1952), gives clear evidence of the point. There he aims at the reinterpretation of the Christian concepts of faith, hope, and love by setting them in relation to the most intimate problems of human life. Starting with the fact of man's anxiety in the face of a world filled with evil, uncertainty, and failure, he seeks to assess the ways in which man has attempted to affirm himself in the face of these obstacles.

One result of Tillich's analysis is the clarification of the meaning of being in religious terms. Here the being of man as a finite creature is interpreted in terms of self-acceptance and self-affirmation in the face of forces, both in the world and in man himself, that stand in the way of self-realization. The religious problem of salvation is seen as the problem of receiving and accepting a source of *courage* (embracing faith, hope, and love) that enables man *to be* who he essentially is despite the distortions of historical existence.

The approach also has important implications for the doctrine of God. Tillich here discloses most sharply his opposition to "theism" understood as the doctrine that God is a being beside other beings within the subject-object framework. God is understood instead as the power beyond the subject-object distinction, the "power of being" able to bestow the "courage to be" upon those who accept this courage in faith. Tillich is led to speak of "the God beyond God," meaning thereby that the God of traditional theism is but a finite being, albeit the highest one, not to be identified with being itself, which alone is the true power able to overcome the distortions of existence.

Roberts in *Psychotherapy and a Christian View of Man* (1950) presents a clear and cogent case for the mutual relevance of psychology and theology. He attacks the twin evils of "psychologism" and "theologism." The former outlook fails to see that since true and false beliefs can both alike enter the nexus of personal character, the question of truth and validity cannot be determined on the basis of psychological considerations alone. Roberts criticizes depth psychologists for following the Freudian lead uncritically and for assuming, frequently without awareness of how such issues should be discussed, that belief in God is all projection and that theology is all false. On the other hand, Roberts is equally critical of theologians who claim to be aware of the developments of science, but who show no evidence of the fact and pay no attention to the disclosures of psychology, anthropology, and sociology in framing their views of man and his nature.

Roberts maintains that neither Protestant fundamentalism nor Roman Catholicism is likely to revise any essential elements in their positions in the light of new secular knowledge. He finds, however, that the Protestant situation is complicated by the opposition between liberalism and neo-orthodoxy. This opposition was, of course, more in evidence in 1950 than it is today. The liberal theology took science so seriously that extrascientific sources of insight were ignored; the neo-orthodox revival, on the other hand, so completely eliminates man and indeed the whole natural order from making any contribution to the redemptive process that empirical investigation into the actual state of man and society becomes irrelevant. Roberts hoped instead for a new alliance within Protestantism between theology and the insights of the sciences of man, especially depth psychology.

Central to Roberts' analysis is his interpretation of the redemptive process. Contrasting static and dynamic views of salvation, he argues that the former regard the status of the individual before God as already determined and without possibility of alteration. By holding before men a vision of perfection in relation to which man is always ashamed of himself, the static view sets up an obligatory pattern against man and totally fails to take the facts of human growth into account. Roberts assesses this approach by citing various characteristic responses it has called forth; self-righteousness results from identifying ourselves with the vision of perfection; unresolved despair leads to the rejection of God; self-repudiation takes the form of viewing every assertion of the self as evil and as something to be avoided.

A dynamic conception of salvation makes way for a decision on the part of man and it allows us to understand the religious meaning of salvation in relation to the facts about the structure and growth of human personality. Roberts saw that the major problem for any theory of salvation admitting a contribution from the side of man in the saving process is to avoid any hint that man is thus able to save himself. On the dynamic view, man's action is one of self-acceptance based on his faith that he is accepted of God despite the fact that he is, in terms of merit or "acceptability," not worthy. The act stemming from the human self is thus one of reconciliation to God and not of self-assertion in the sense that man would replace the divine power.

In the decade of the Fifties much progress was made in the direction of bringing about an understanding and an exchange of ideas between theologians and depth psychologists. Initial hostilities have been overcome and, while a naturalistic standpoint still predominates among psychiatrists and psychotherapists, there is better communication than was the case in previous years.

The thought of Reinhold Niebuhr must ultimately be treated in the context of theology, which is its primary focus. This remains true even though his thought is too prophetic to be called theological in the classical sense, and too theological to be called prophetic, again in the classical sense. In view, however, of the uncertain boundary dividing theology from the philosophy of religion in American thought, there is good reason for including Niebuhr in this discussion. One aspect of his thought particularly has been important for the general interpretation of religion—his attack upon ontological thinking based on the argument that historical and dramatic modes of comprehension are more appropriate for grasping religious truth than purely rationalistic or conceptual schemes. Despite his criticism of Barthian revelationism, and his demand that religious ideas be kept in creative relation to cultural life and secular knowledge, Niebuhr has been consistently suspicious of ontological rationalism. He has so vigorously pointed out the shortcomings of reason that to many his position appears as an explicit irrationalism. This conclusion is not warranted by the evidence, but one can readily understand how the impression is created.

There are four basic considerations determining Niebuhr's negative judgment on ontological interpretations of Christian faith. The four, though distinct, are interrelated. First, he identifies ontology with being in the sense of the "static" structure of things imposing a "necessity" on all things that is incompatible with their freedom. Second, he sets the Hebraic historical and prophetic approach to God against the Greek interest in speculation and the rational comprehension of the divine nature. Third, he supposes that an ontological defense of religious truth must mean the replacement of faith by reason and a consequent overintellectualization of religion. Fourth, he believes that every claim to comprehend God and the cosmic scheme in a rational system means an illegitimate penetration of the divine mystery and the exaltation of the "wisdom of this world" beyond its true status.

Although the motives behind his view are different, Niebuhr's complaint that to speak of being is to speak of the static or timeless coincides precisely with the criticism of philosophers of becoming like Hartshorne who hold that the concept of being is inadequate. If, of course, being is identical with static being, the critics have a point. But it is not at all clear why being must be understood in this way. With regard to the charge that an ontology, any ontology, imposes a "necessary" structure on all reality, including God, Niebuhr stands with the philosophers of existence and freedom who try to give the priority to existence over essence and who stress the transcendence of power or the dynamic side of things over rational structures. This charge is more serious and it raises several questions, philosophical and theological. That freedom and creativity cannot be made intelligible wholly in terms of the fixed and necessary is now generally admitted; but whether, like the identification of being with the static, it is legitimate to identify ontology as an enterprise with one particular kind of ontology, is surely debateable. The issue is bound up with the problem faced by the existentialist philosophers who are uncertain whether it is possible to speak of an existentialist ontology or whether the existential standpoint sets itself, after the fashion of Kierkegaard, against *all* systems of ontology. Niebuhr, it is clear, wants to preserve freedom, and especially some mystery in the divine freedom in his criticism of the ontological enterprise. That this aim is incompatible with all forms of ontology is open to question.

Niebuhr rightly sees that the Hebraic approach to God, forming as it does a portion of the Christian inheritance, differs from certain emphases in the Greek approach to religious and metaphysical topics. The Hebraic prophetic tradition, so heavily dependent on religious insight into the course of historical events, appears to be very different from the speculative and analytic approach to God that we associate with the names of Plato and Aristotle. Accordingly it seems legitimate to mark a sharp separation between the "Hebraic" and the "Greek" way of thinking, exalting the former as closer to Christianity and rejecting the latter as an alien intrusion of "rationalism." That the Greek thinkers, on the whole, undervalued and even failed to understand the historical nature of reality is true. In this regard the Hebraic contribution is unique. It will not do, however, to identify the entire Greek tradition and way of thinking with theoretical rationalism. As Jaeger has pointed out in his studies of early Christian thought and of Greek *paideia,* by the time of Clement of Alexandria the traditions of Greek philosophy had to adjust themselves to the dominant moral and religious interests of the time. The high point of Greek speculation had passed; the demand was now for a philosophy of personal life such as was found in stoicism and the Epicureans. Attention has also been called to the fact that at the time of the most serious confrontation between Greek thought and Christianity in the third century the dominant Greek concept of reason was that of *gnosis,* a mystical type of apprehension that represents something very different from the analytic rationalism of Aristotle. Niebuhr is justified in wanting to preserve the prophetic type of thinking and the historical consciousness that accompanies it. But whether the achievement of this result requires us to identify the Greek philosophical tradition with a nonhistorical rationalism may well be questioned. The encounter between Christianity and Greek philosophy was complex; there were positive gains for Christianity as well as problems, and it remains doubtful whether, without the aid of the philosophical language of the Greek thinkers, the earliest Christian theologians would have been able to transcend the limits of Hebraic interpretations. The devaluation of the philosophical tradition is, therefore, difficult to sustain. Moreover, Niebuhr's attempt to present his own original and creative interpretation of Christian faith as a position that avoids the errors of naturalism on the one hand and idealism on the other actually pays more attention to philosophical issues raised by the critical mind than his many criticisms of philosophy seem to indicate. Tillich is right when he protests against the description of Niebuhr's thought as "irrationalist," because in fact *The Nature and Destiny of Man* reveals a stubborn attempt to argue for the superiority of the Christian outlook over both idealism and naturalism.

Niebuhr's contention that an ontological elaboration of religious faith must result in the replacing of faith by reason raises a complex question. Everything depends on how reason and faith are understood. Niebuhr inclines toward an interpretation of faith that sets it in opposition to reason. For all of his Augustianism, Niebuhr does not seem to make nearly enough of the ancient formula "faith seeking understanding." He stresses instead the idea that faith is a mode of apprehension transcending reason and that faith puts us in possession of a kind of insight that cannot be expressed in rational terms; the insight of faith is "foolishness to the Greeks." On his view the need for the divine wisdom and its superiority over philosophies of coherence and rational system stem from the fact of incongruities both in man and in human history. More important are the mysteries of the divine nature—the relation between justice and mercy, the trinitarian conception—that defy the reach of reason. Reason lives in coherences; faith exists in repentance.

It would, however, be an error to overlook the fact that Niebuhr's thought has a curious twist in it at just the point where it appears to coincide most completely with the irrationalist tradition in theology. Instead of denying that there can be any intelligible connection whatever between human knowledge and religious insight, Niebuhr tries instead to present Christian truths as "made plausible when understood as the keys which make the drama of human life and history comprehensible." Thus in the end the idea of critical validation or justification of Christianity is not abandoned. Justification, however, does not take the form of invoking the evidence of an ontological system but of appealing to a more "existential" criterion. Like Berdyaev and others, Niebuhr looks to history as the heir of the old metaphysics. If we are to make sense of the realities of freedom, process, and creativity—of which human history and the individual self are the best examples—we are in need of an insight that can survive paradoxes and incongruities. What this means is that Christian truths can be seen as valid when they are made to appear as solutions not to the problems of ontology or cosmology, but to the perplexities of historical life. Though faith, on such a view, stands in a certain opposition to reason, rational validation is not denied. Niebuhr's view is thus different from that of Kierkegaard and Barth.

True to the Reformed tradition from which he comes, Niebuhr places considerable emphasis on the hiddenness, the mystery, and the otherness of God. God appears as confounding the wisdom of the wise and as expressing himself in ways that disappoint rational expectations. Niebuhr is concerned to protect the divine mystery against reduction to an ontological scheme. Niebuhr has held consistently to this position starting with his well-known paper of 1937, "The Truth in Myths"; the same position is upheld in "Coherence, Incoherence and Christian Faith" (1951). In the first paper he maintains that the transcendent meaning of life cannot finally be expressed in terms of either immediate experience or rational form. Distinguishing between primitive and permanent myth, Niebuhr defends the unavoidability of myth as a vehicle of religious meaning by pointing out that, while certain myths purporting to give scientific explanations can be set aside as outmoded, there is a permanent need for myth in the expression of value and religious truth. Christianity, depending as it must upon the myth of creation in which the goodness of the world is affirmed, and upon the myth of the fall in which the sin of man is revealed, is superior in its wisdom both to science and rational metaphysics. For science in its reduction of reality to causal sequences loses the element of human responsibility and denies the reality of sin, while rational metaphysics (sometimes identified by Niebuhr with "philosophical idealism") is said to result in refusal to take seriously those aspects of experience that cannot easily be conceptualized.

The key to Niebuhr's position on every issue is found in the attempt to represent the Christian answer as a third position transcending the extremes of naturalism and idealism. While the two extremes are said to represent interpretations based respectively on natural science and speculative construction, the third position expresses itself in the form of myth and paradox. His claim for the superiority of the third position is that it is able to avoid the errors of the extremes while at the same time standing beyond them as a genuinely distinct position and not merely as an amalgam.

An important and far reaching consequence of the Nazi tyranny in Germany during the Thirties was the emigration of many scholars and men of learning to Britain and America to take up residence and participate in the intellectual life of their adopted nations. Richard Kroner, formerly of the University of Kiel and a leading exponent of classical German idealism, was among them. Since coming to America in 1940, he has transformed his former idealism—a synthesis standing between the ethical idealism of Kant and the panlogism of Hegel—into a religiously oriented philosophy aimed at overcoming the gap between philosophy and theology, culture and faith.

In a remarkable little book, *The Religious Function of Imagination* (1941), Kroner argues for the superiority of religious truth expressed in an intuitive or imaginative form over the conceptual thought of philosophy and science. Attacking both Aristotle and Hegel who believed in the primacy of purely conceptual over all other forms of expression, Kroner defends the indispensability of the religious imagination as a form of inspiration and revelation. He draws on Kant's important but neglected distinction between the *productive* and the *reproductive* imagination for his theory. The productive imagination, though required (as the link between sense and understanding) even for theoretical knowledge, has a practical function as well in the moral and religious life of man. Religious truth, Kroner claims, is more adequately expressed in the vivid images of the Bible than in the conceptual schemes of philosophy. Kroner set this thesis in a larger philosophical perspective in the Gifford Lectures delivered in 1942 and published in America under the title *The Primacy of Faith* (1943). There the attempt is made to drive a middle course between Barth's rejection of natural theology and Kant's restriction of religion to rational faith.

Kroner's views are further elaborated in *Culture and Faith* (1951), which represents a transformation (made on the basis of his experience in confronting the American scene) of an older German work on the development of *Geist*. More recently Kroner has been engaged in a large-scale work—*Speculation and Revelation in the History of Philosophy*—dealing with the relations between philosophy and theology in Western civilization. The third and concluding volume, *Speculation and Revelation in Modern Philosophy* (1961), interprets the problems raised by the autonomy of philosophy since Descartes and the ever widening gulf that has opened between philosophy and theology in the modern era. Two previous volumes considered the role of speculative philosophy against the background of pre-Christian thought among the Greeks, and the interplay between philosophy and theology in the Christian Middle Ages.

7

PHILOSOPHY OF RELIGION
AND PROCESS PHILOSOPHY

Ever since the end of the last century—the century dominated by the idea of evolution and the conception of history—time and change have come to be recognized as irreducible features of reality. In contrast with older outlooks that emphasized the priority of perfection over becoming and of the fixed over the changing, a powerful trend in modern thought has sought to reverse the order and to install process at the heart of the real world. Religion and the idea of God have not escaped this trend. The powerful influence of James, Whitehead, and Bergson has made itself felt in theology no less than in other fields of thought. The work of Charles Hartshorne and others at present represent this philosophical trend. To a very large extent it was fostered on the American secne by Whitehead's later philosophy, developed since his coming to this country. The influence of his process philosophy has, in fact, been so important that I must attempt to give a brief exposition of his fundamental philosophic vision.

To provide a complete account of Whitehead's philosophy and its religious implications in a study of this size is out of the question. This limitation, however, must not lead us to minimize the importance of his contribution to the philosophical and religious thought of the twentieth century. There have been two distinct periods of influence—an earlier one in which Whitehead's idea of creativity led men like H. N. Wieman and others to reinterpret God as the value producing and conserving power in nature, and a later period, not yet concluded, in which a more precise knowledge of Whitehead's system has been achieved and the metaphysical and religious implications better understood. In the first period, Whitehead's process philosophy was used largely to reinforce a philosophy of religion based on values. His speculative philosophy and its categorial scheme were not fully exploited. More recently the intricacies of the philosophy of organism, the concepts of time, of nature, of actuality, of abstraction, and of God have been explored, with the result that a more explicitly metaphysical and cosmological treatment of God and religious problems is possible. The work of Hartshorne signalizes the second phase, although this does not imply that his thought is merely an exposition of Whitehead.

Whitehead's doctrine of God as found in *Process and Reality* (1929), *Science and the Modern World* (1925), and *Religion in the Making* (1926) especially commands attention. His novel and comprehensive interpretation of the cosmic process demanding God as a principle of limitation and conservation appeared to many as an oasis in a dry philosophical land. For here was a thinker who no one could dismiss as prescientific or unscientific in his approach who yet could speak of the importance of speculative philosophy and of the inescapability of God. While his emphasis on process served to disturb and uproot old ideas, and the suggestion that God may himself be involved in becoming has caused great concern, there is no denying that Whitehead's philosophy has provided a stimulus to philosophical thinking about religion.

Impossible as it is to do justice here to Whitehead's metaphysical scheme, it is essential to set forth briefly several ideas that have shown themselves to be of special importance for the philosophy of religion. These are: the definition of religion, the attempt to synthesize the conclusions of speculative philosophy with the deliverances of religious insight, and the idea of God in relation to the creative advance of the cosmic process.

In an arresting comparison between religion and arithmetic, Whitehead aimed at bringing out the intimate connection between religion and history on the one hand and the relation of religion to the being of the individual person on the other. "You *use* arithmetic, but you *are* religious" (*Religion in the Making,* p. 15), said Whitehead. Religion has to do with what the self *is,* its nature and character, its source of identity in time. Arithmetic is something known, presupposed, or taken for granted and it can be used successfuly because there is a sense in which it is independent of historical happenings. For practical purposes, arithmetic can be regarded as finished; religion, by contrast, is always in the making because the ultimate matters with which it deals have to be confronted anew by every individual and by each succeeding age in the light of fresh experience. Religion is so comprehensive in scope and so intimately connected with human life that we must turn to the history of religion to understand what it is. By contrast, the history of a science like arithmetic sheds little light on the truth of its fundamental theorems.

Although Whitehead placed considerable emphasis on the need for rational formulations and the justification of religious belief, he never lost sight of the peculiar function to be performed by religious doctrine. Religion is neither science nor metaphysics; the truth of its basic affirmations must "cleanse the inward parts" and thus have a character-transforming effect on the person. While Whitehead was critical of attempts to rest religion on pragmatic foundations, he did not, in his demand for rational support, turn religion into a merely speculative knowledge.

Religion is said to stand between abstract metaphysics and its pure generality at one pole and particular principles governing a limited region of life and experience at the other. Through its middle position, religion shares features of both extremes. Since it is based on the insights of prophetic personalities living under historical conditions, religion is limited and appears as one part of life besides others. But in view of the fact that religion claims universal validity for these insights they must, like metaphysical truths, be relevant for the interpretation of everything that happens. The following formula expresses the point precisely: "Rational religion appeals to the direct intuition of special occasions, and to the elucidatory power of its concepts for all occasions" (*Religion in the Making,* p. 32). Religion is always moving in two directions at once; it continually draws its life from historical experience. (Hebraic religion, for example, is rooted in the insights of Moses and the prophetic personalities), but since it makes universal claims for its principles, it is forever seeking to find language rich enough to express their cosmic import.

Whitehead's famous characterization of religion as "what the individual does with his own solitariness" (*Religion in the Making,* p. 16) has been much quoted and much misunderstood. This saying, like many of Whitehead's, is a dark one, but properly interpreted it expresses an important point. Whitehead tells us that the statement was intended to deny the claim that religion is primarily a *social* fact. It is not that religion is unrelated to the social character of every reality, but rather that religion has to do with the person considered *in himself.* The formula expresses more than the vague sense that religion demands quiet and solitude; it directs attention to the fact that a person has a worth solely in himself. The reference to what one "does" with his solitariness means the manner in which he *responds* to the consideration of himself as having being in his own right. Every person takes on a universal character in the sense that, having a worth in himself, he does not derive it from being a member of some special group.

Whitehead was greatly concerned with the problem of evil and he showed his profound grasp of living religion when he described Christianity and Buddhism as the two great traditions that begin by acknowledging the facts of tragedy in the world and then go on to propose a means of "escape." By this Whitehead did not intend to explain religion away as an "escape mechanism"; rather this was his way of describing salvation. Both religions confront human life with a grand strategy for overcoming the force of evil in the world and for establishing good in its place. In an arresting set of comparisons, Whitehead described Buddhism as relying on metaphysical doctrines and Christianity as appealing to "elucidatory facts" in order to accomplish their goal. While Buddhism finds the root of evil in the illusion of individuality itself, Christianity accepts the individual as such and finds evil in man's limitations and his ability to misdirect his powers.

Religious experience for Whitehead meant primarily the intuition of a "character of permanent rightness" (*Religion in the Making,* p. 61) in the universe; the object of this intuition is a *character* modifying the course of events rather than a person or individual. Religion, as a vital factor in human life, means reverance and duty. The latter stems from our power to control events while the former arises from our sense that the present is the model of eternity. Whitehead denied that we have an intuition of a personal God; a personal God is a matter of inference and interpretation. Whitehead's reason for this conclusion is that there is no general consensus in experience leading to the idea of the personal God. That idea is essential, but it enters through the door of rational reflection; it is not "given" in the original religious intuition. Starting however with the intuition of a permanent rightness in things, we can go on to ask whether a metaphysical analysis of the world and man's experience does not lead us

433

in the end to that same rightness. This is in fact what Whitehead believed. A thorough analysis of the generic categories required to describe the cosmic process will lead us ultimately to God as the reality that sustains and conserves the order of permanent rightness. We have here another example of the classical Augustinian tradition in which religion and philosophy interpenetrate.

In order to understand its own insights, religion must have recourse to metaphysics for a scrutiny of its terms. In this sense religion requires metaphysical backing. On the other hand, religion contributes insights that metaphysics must take into account in the framing of a comprehensive theory of reality. Whitehead refused to accept the view that says that religion can be interpreted in practical terms, leaving the field of theoretical knowledge to science and metaphysics. Religion has its own insights into the nature of man and the world and it seeks to express them in the form of rational doctrine. In so doing, however, it is forced to make use of concepts such as "person," "actual," "God," etc. that require metaphysical analysis. It was Whitehead's contention that such analysis will provide religion with its intellectual justification. His metaphysics of process and creativity demands God as a cosmic principle that is the metaphysical counterpart of the initial deliverance of religious experience.

To understand Whitehead's conception of God it is necessary to grasp his general metaphysical outlook. This requirement holds in the case of any comprehensive philosophical interpretation; it is especially true for Whitehead because of his demand that "God is not to be treated as an exception to all metaphysical principles, invoked to save their collapse. He is their chief exemplification" (*Process and Reality*, p. 521). This does not mean, as some have supposed, that God is here subordinated to a general metaphysical scheme, but rather that God, in what Whitehead calls his "consequent" nature, is the realization of conceptual possibility and actuality in one divine unity. As "primordial" in nature, God embraces the infinitude of conceptual possibility; as "consequent" in nature God is the conscious realization of the actual world, transformed by his wisdom. In both aspects of his nature, God embodies the conceptual order and structure that make the creative process of the world intelligible; it is in this sense that God exemplifies and does not overturn the metaphysical principles. While Whitehead was critical of the traditional doctrine of God's "eminence" as implying a static perfection omitting the world of time and change, his own doctrine of the consequent nature implies that God is the chief or "eminent" exemplification of the categorial structure.

Following in the wake of Bergson and James, Whitehead sought to do full justice to time and change in his conception of reality. The actual world is never unrelated to time. This does not mean that everything actual is in time, only that what is actual is somehow related to time. Actuality is characterized by creativity or *directed change* issuing in the novel. Rejecting mechanical models for the cosmic process, Whitehead maintained that an organic process always contains novel elements. In addition to creativity, the actual world exhibits ideal elements or eternal objects that are the source of form and knowledge. We can understand the nature of carbon, the erosion of the land by the sea, or the Battle of Waterloo because each exemplifies universal, recurring features. The ideal elements are ingredient in actuality, but considered in themselves they are abstract and incapable of making up a creative process. For such a process we are in need of the actual but nontemporal entity that is God.

God is the guiding factor who gives form to all the limited processes of creativity that make up the world. The order of the universe comes from God as the principle of selection directing all the limited processes and guaranteeing a sufficient harmony to keep the total process from lapsing into a sheer, chaotic change. Every creative advance depends both for its form and its direction on the divine wisdom; the proper relations between the eternal objects must be determined so that the resulting creativity will conserve value and contribute to the realization of the stable order that is the good.

Whitehead had a remarkable sensitivity for the images used to depict the divine nature. In *Religion in the Making* he distinguished three principal types of concept used to characterize God: the concept of impersonal order, the concepts of a definite personal reality, and the pantheistic concept (in one of its senses) according to which all is one and the world is part of God. In *Process and Reality* he referred instead to three images: the image of God as imperial ruler, as the personification of moral energy, and as an ultimate philosophical principle. For Whitehead, Hume's criticism was fatal to these traditional images. He regarded the insights of Jesus into the nature of love as superior.

> There is in the Galilean origin of Christianity yet another suggestion which does not fit very well with any of the three main strands of thought. It does not emphasize the ruling Caesar, or the ruthless moralist, or the unmoved mover. It dwells upon the tender elements in the world, which slowly and in quietness operate by love; and it finds purpose in the present immediacy of a kingdom not of this world. Love neither rules nor is unmoved; also it is a little oblivious as to morals. It does not look to the future; for it finds its own reward in the immediate present. [*Process and Reality,* pp. 520-21.]

The idea expressed in the above image dominates Whitehead's ultimate conception of God. God as love outweighs in importance the other images used to apprehend the divine nature. Instead, however, of developing the point on the basis of religious intuitions, Whitehead turns to the implications of his own metaphysical system. Since that scheme aims primarily at a description of the cosmic process as an organically connected course of actualization, creativity, and novelty, its implications for the doctrine of God will emphasize the mutual interplay between God and the world. This relationship is in fact the key to Whitehead's entire theory. Above all else, he rejected every form of the view that contrasts God taken as unchanging or static perfection and possessed of superior reality with the world taken as fluent change and possessed of a lower or deficient reality. For Whitehead there is a mutual relationship (*not* symmetrical in every respect) between God and the world. God exhibits primary action on the world, but there is also a reaction of the world on God.

The novelty and even daring of Whitehead's view consists in the fact that he tried to express the sense in which a real, creative novelty in the cosmic process enters into the divine life and experience. God is not only *with* the world at the beginning (primordial nature) but he is also the end (consequent nature) and, as such, he shares in the novel elements resulting from the ongoing cosmic process in time. The doctrine implies that God's primordial nature as conceptual is "deficient" because it lacks the actuality and the union with physical feelings that only the creative advance of the world can bring about.

One of the principal consequences of this doctrine is that there is an "advance" in God. There is the transition from the eternal, infinite but unconscious primordial nature to the consequent nature that is fully actual, conscious, and everlasting.[12] God as consequent integrates the creative advance of the world with the completeness of the divine nature as primordial, i.e., as conceptual. God, as Whitehead says, "does not create the world, he saves it" (*Process and Reality,* p. 526), and this by guiding the cosmic process in accordance with a vision of the good. God appears not only as the principle of selection (in Whitehead's official terminology, "the principle of concretion") determining the relevance of the eternal objects so as to produce a definite and intelligible outcome at each moment of the cosmic process; God is also, in traditional religious language, the "sustainer" because he has a "tender care that nothing be lost."

The doctrine that God sustains and preserves in accordance with his wisdom has, as one of its consequences, the permanence of individuality and the details of the temporal world. There is within the unity of the divine prehension a multiplicity of individuals. The polarity of God and the world and the interaction between them leads to various correspondences; in God the temporal reality has counterparts. In the temporal world, for example, there is the fact of an enduring personality as a "route of occasions" and the counterpart of this same actuality in God is the "transmutation" of that successive

---

[12] The reader should consult the excellent study of William A. Christian, *An Interpretation of Whitehead's Metaphysics* (1959), esp. pp. 283 ff. Christian holds that there is no transition or "passage" in God according to Whitehead because that relationship holds only between an actual entity that perishes and another that comes into being. This will not do for God. Christian is correct if we take seriously the idea of "concrescence" and God's "experience" as requiring duration but not transition (see p. 394). On the other hand, if Whitehead is to attack successfully the traditional conception of God as always fully complete and without "any shadow of turning," we must not shy away from interpretations that involve an "advance" in the divine life. Unless we are to take the position that God is beyond categorial description, we cannot avoid something like a transition when we consider the "realization" involved in going from God as "deficient" to God as fully actual. And yet the idea of "going from" may be misleading. If the two aspects of God are considered as *polar* elements, then the sense of a *linear* advance disappears.

route into "a living and ever-present fact." The person "in the world" has as counterpart the person "in God." The realizations of the temporal world thus enter into God's experience and consequent nature without being reduced to a static or undifferentiated unity in which individuality is lost.

Most important for Whitehead's attempt to show how the detail of individual life may be preserved in God is the concept of "relativity." Against the doctrine that God is "absolutely unrelated" in his *aseity* or transcendence, Whitehead sees God as the "eminent" individual who is supremely related to all the individual occasions that go to make up the temporal world. No other individual exemplifies universal relatedness to the same degree. This idea, as we shall see, was taken up by Hartshorne and made central to his interpretation of the "divine relativity." Relatedness, as Whitehead says, does not stop even with the consequent nature of God, as can be seen from his brief summary of the four phases distinguished within the cosmic process in its march to actualization. In the first phase, we have conceptual orgination, which, though devoid of actuality, involves valuation among the eternal objects (similar to Leibniz' idea of "compossibility"); in the second phase, physical feelings and temporal, individual actualities are present but the unity of the many individuals remains deficient; in the third phase, this deficiency is overcome in the unity of God's consequent nature where all individuals are everlasting in their identity; in the fourth phase, the divine love actualized in the previous phase passes back again into the world. Whitehead describes this as "the love of God for the world" and as the meaning of the classical religious belief in the *presence* of the kingdom of heaven. The move back to the world is the final form of *relatedness,* so that the completion of the divine life includes the individuals constituting the universe.

Inspired by several basic Whiteheadian theses, Charles Hartshorne has taken up the task of reinterpreting religion generally and Christianity in particular in terms of process metaphysics. If Tillich's thought represents a theological position elaborated in philosophical terms, the writings of Hartshorne manifest the opposite development. They represent a philosophical outlook applied to the resolution of theological issues in terms that remain at the same time sensitive to the facts of actual religious insight. Hartshorne's work shows the influence of Peirce's metaphysics, the thought of Bergson and Fechner, modern mathematical logic, and, to a high degree, Whitehead's philosophy. The connection with Whitehead is at certain points so close that it is difficult to distinguish one view from the other. An important difference in approach is to be found in the fact that while Whitehead was not a close student of the Western theological tradition and was interested mainly in drawing the religious implications of his metaphysics, Hartshorne comes to his task with first-hand knowledge of the classical theologians and their problems.

Like Leibniz, Hartshorne has unbounded faith in logic (especially current mathematical logic) and he is impatient with those doctrines that stress the limitation of reason or imply agnosticism of any kind. For Hartshorne, logic is logic and any subject matter is equally open to analysis and interpertation in logical terms. Unlike Leibniz, however, he has an involuted style that sometimes obscures the main point. A certain fear of overlooking a possible objection or of omitting an alternative leads to what is frequently an excessive complication in the expression of central ideas. Hartshorne's position is a speculative rationalism in which a metaphysics of becoming is made into a foundation for a type of theism called "panentheism." There are several stages in its development, unified by the doctrine that God includes all and is distinguished from all at the same time. This doctrine is contained in *Man's Vision of God* (1941) and it receives further elaboration in *The Divine Relativity* (1947) and *The Logic of Perfection* (1962).[13] The central or unifying conception in his philosophical treatment of religion is the idea of perfection. Although this concept receives its most detailed treatment in connection with

[13] In *Man's Vision of God* Hartshorne develops a dialectic of theistic positions according to the logically possible conceptions of God derived from the concept of "surpassibility." In an "Epilogue" (pp. 347 ff.) he uses the term *panentheism* for what I believe is the first time—he does not use it in the text itself to describe the position and there is no entry for it in the index. In the Preface to *The Divine Relativity*, *panentheism* is used as the name for the central position expounded in the book (along with *surrelativism*). *The Logic of Perfection* does not mention *panentheism* and it appears that Hartshorne decided to abandon the term. But see also the article "Panpsychism" in *A History of Philosophical Systems* (1950), ed. Vergilius Ferm, for the idea that the panpsychist view contributes to a "new synthesis" of theistic and pantheistic insights. This new synthesis is in fact what Hartshorne means by *panentheism* although he does not use the term.

the ontological argument in Chapter 2 of *The Logic of Perfection,* it actually stands behind all that Hartshorne has written about religion and the idea of God. Reflection on the meaning of the divine attributes and the sense in which God can be said to be perfect and to possess the characteristic attributes in a perfect degree led Hartshorne to ask about the relation between perfection and contingent reality—man and the ongoing cosmic process. For Hartshorne, traditional theology was committed exclusively to the concept of being, with the result that God had to be identified with static perfection, complete and self-sufficient. The world of change and especially of man's growing experience seem to stand unrelated to a God conceived as fully complete and final perfection. The problem of how to understand perfection so as to relate it to process and creativity on the human level has been persistently in the center of Hartshorne's thinking.

For reasons very different from those of Tillich, Hartshorne also attacks traditional theism. While Tillich criticizes the position for making God into a being besides other beings, Hartshorne objects to the static perfectionism of the classical theology of being and to the consequent neglect of becoming, which means creativity, the realization of value, and the novelty logically connected with future time. Contrary to what might be supposed, Hartshorne finds the primary basis of his criticism of past theology not so much in philosophical considerations as in the religious ideas themselves. In setting forth his conception of the "two strands in historical theology" (*Man's Vision of God,* chap. III), Hartshorne points to a fundamental inconsistency between the religious idea of God and the primary philosophical concepts that have been used to interpret that idea. More specifically, the alleged inconsistency is between the idea of God as love—as the all-understanding and everlasting individual who has concern for all *existent* creatures—and the concepts of pure actuality, immutability, impassivity, and uncaused causality that have been used to express the divine nature in past systems of theology.[14]

---

[14] It should be pointed out that Hartshorne has invariably chosen as his model for "classical theology" the Aristotelian–Thomist tradition. Despite his own involvement in the Platonic mathematicological tradition, Hartshorne tends to neglect the Augustinian line. It is not necessary to maintain that the Augustinian position is immune to his criticisms in order to point out that Hartshorne will find more to his liking in that tradition than he seems to be aware.

It is Hartshorne's main contention that the religious idea of love is not adequately expressed in the "secular" concepts employed to express it in traditional theism. The chief problem concerns the relation of God to human life and welfare; more specifically, the question is to understand how man's acts and his realization of the good in particular instances can *contribute* to God's experience. We recognize this at once as a current form of the old problem of "accidents" in God. That the experiences and actions constituting human life make some contribution to the divine nature is required, according to Hartshorne, by the religious strand in theology. But the theological concepts of *immutability, impassivity,* and *maximal perfection in all respects* make no allowance for that contribution because we cannot see how, if we interpret God through them, the world passing in time can possibly make any difference to the divine experience. No concern is possible for an impassive being; no change is possible for an immutable being and no increment of value arising from a real, temporal process of individual self-realization can be added to a being already maximally perfect in all respects.

Hartshorne's main conclusion is that a revision in the metaphysical concepts is required if we are to express the religious content adequately. What he calls "simple perfectionism" in theology fails to do justice to the love of God. He also raises the question of whether the traditional metaphysical concepts do not involve us in theological contradictions because they are "self-contradictory in themselves." A pure actuality, Hartshorne claims, means an absolute realization of potency where all potency is transcended; a pure unity means the complete unification of elements where all complexity is transcended. How can this be? Hartshorne, in short, is raising the question of how the meaning of the positive attributes of God can be independent of the contrasting concepts implied by them. Actuality cannot be independent in its meaning from the contrast between the possible and the existent; unity requires the uniting of a complexity. The contrasts, moreover, cannot be eliminated from God's experience for then the divine experience would be poorer than our own. Although Hartshorne is generally critical of "negative theology" he points to the problems raised for simple theism by the "hidden complexity" in God brought forward by the criticism of the negative theologians.

From the inconsistency of the metaphysical concepts Hartshorne does not conclude, as do many contemporary theologians, that all philosophical interpretation is to be rejected. On the contrary, he asks for a new reflective analysis of the philosophical concepts previously employed in theology. The secular concepts need not be thought of as unqualifiedly wrong; they must be employed instead in a twofold way—positive and negative—in order to express accurately the two aspects, *abstract* and *concrete,* that it is necessary to distinguish in God. In the abstract aspect, God is immutable and impassive; in the concrete aspect, God is eminently mutable and passive, surpassing all other beings infinitely in these respects. Hartshorne wants to assert the synthesis of the two aspects without resort to paradox or confusion. What changes also has an aspect that does not change—in enduring *all* change, God exhibits all possible permanence. Though suggestive of a dialectical or polar analysis, Hartshorne's view is different from both. Change and permanence, unity and complexity, he regards as complementary concepts, not as polar opposites. Complementarity, however, is not symmetrical. Asymmetry enters the relationship, for example, in the fact that the abstract aspect is included in the concrete as a partial derivative, while the converse relationship does not hold. This is true as well of the complementary concepts change and permanence; the changing can include an aspect of permanence, whereas the permanent all by itself is incapable of including change. Hartshorne uses the argument from asymmetry to establish the claim of becoming to be the "all inclusive category" rather than being. Taking the latter to mean the static, the argument is that while the dynamic can include a static aspect, the converse does not hold: becoming can include being but not vice versa.

Hartshorne's aim in the philosophical interpretation of religion is to find a metaphysical scheme adequate for expressing the religious idea of God—the idea that God is primarily love and concern. To this end he avails himself of a philosophy of organism according to which the world is a vast complex of temporal processes issuing in novel results and related to God in such a way that while he remains unsurpassable by anything in the world, he is surpassable by himself.

The best presentation of panentheism (also called surrelativism) is found in *The Divine Relativity* (1947). This work develops in clear and concise form the type of theism first expressed in *Man's Vision of God,* and it introduces a way of thinking about perfection and the ontological argument that is brought to completion in *The Logic of Perfection* (1962). Of special importance for the current scene is the synthetic function that Hartshorne claims for his position. Panentheism, he claims, embraces the insights, while avoiding the errors, of existentialism, crisis theology, and the older tradition of metaphysical theology. God, according to panentheism, has qualities that are accidental in the sense that they do not follow from any necessity in the divine essence. This, together with acceptance of the view that man is, to a degree, self-created, is in agreement with the existentialist insight. Panentheism's stress on the personal nature of God involving self-relationship to creatures in a fashion that demands "encounter" not to be anticipated by rational necessity accords with the major contention of crisis theology. Hartshorne's complaint, however, is that present-day neo-Reformation theologians revel in the "arbitrariness" of these relationships and do not see that it belongs "necessarily" to the essence of a personal God of love to act in this way. Panentheism preserves, among other doctrines of classical theology, the realistic theory of knowledge according to which a particular or actual knowing of an object by God must be internally related to the object known without the object itself becoming dependent upon any particular act of knowing. This doctrine is stated more formally as the thesis that not every actual relation (a R b) has an actual converse (b R a); the knowing relation might be taken as internal from the side of the knower while remaining external from the side of the object.

Taken in itself, the panentheistic view means primarily that God is concerned for all existence and that this concern is best expressed in the idea that God is "supremely relative" to all that is. The divine nature has two aspects, relative and absolute: God as supremely related to all creatures and God "in himself." A synthesis of the two is required and the key to the relation between the two aspects is furnished by the contrast between abstract and concrete. The concrete embraces both itself and the abstract in a unity. Similarly, the relative includes itself and the absolute aspect in a unity. Hartshorne accepts a doctrine of polarity according to which these contrary determinations are co-present in mutual dependence. This view differs

443

from some polarity doctrines because more emphasis falls on the complementary character of the polar elements than on such tension as may result from their coexistence.

It cannot be too often repeated that the chief aim of Hartshorne is to express the *religious* idea of God in metaphysical terms, and to show that an adequate philosophical account of things brings us back in the end to the God of religion. This means that the ideas of personality and of love are required by the cosmic scheme. Starting with the reality of relations (i.e., that the relatedness of things to each other is an "absolute" truth), Hartshorne argues that sensitivity —the ability to care for and adjust to—and the power to sustain relations go together. An animal stands next to an inanimate object; while the animal is able to take note of and adjust to that object, the converse does not hold because the object remains in itself unaffected. The animal is more relative in Hartshorne's view because it has more ability to respond to the objects it meets. Applying this to the knowledge relationship, realism is defined as the claim that the knower becomes internally related to the object, while the object remains externally related to the knower. Hartshorne commends medieval realists for holding to this doctrine. He, however, not only objects to their failure to apply it consistently to God's knowledge but also to their actual reversal of the relationship in God's case. God should, Hartshorne contends, become supremely relative to all creatures in knowing them. As the supreme reality, God has the maximal sensitivity. Traditionally, however, there has been the greatest reluctance to speak of God in this way because becoming internally related in knowledge to finite, contingent creatures means the introduction of accidents into the divine nature. To avoid the consequence, God's knowledge of the contingent was made external.

Hartshorne's solution is to distinguish two aspects in God—an "absolute" and a "relative"—and to show how the two are combined. If God is unqualifiedly absolute and complete in himself, then it is difficult to understand how he can love and how he can care. As perfect in the simple sense, God can be immutable substance but not person. To be the God of religion, it is necessary to be absolute in some sense, but it is equally essential to embrace what is not absolute but imperfect. To be perfect means to surpass all the imperfect beings in excellence, but also to be able to surpass self as well. This is

Hartshorne's bold stroke in philosophical theology—to say that "being perfect" in the sense of excluding the imperfect is inferior to a perfection that includes both. In being internally related to the world, including man and his tragedy and evil along with his progress in self-realization, God surpasses himself in the sense of abstract, eternal, nonrelative perfection. This does not mean that contingent reality is coequal with God. God confronts a world that is neither prior to him nor alien in nature—whatever "influences" God in the creative process is created reality that has been influenced by God initially.

The concept of the social takes on new theological import. To be the God of love is to be supremely related in a vast society of relationships to all finite and suffering being. "Love," says Hartshorne, "defined as social awareness, taken literally, is God" (*The Divine Relativity*, p. 36). But if this is so, the traditional glorification of God as the absolutely independent cannot be correct. Hartshorne sharply criticizes those who rejoice in the aloofness of God. The true God is instead the eternal sympathizer who is concerned for man and the struggle in which he is engaged. God is not a spectator of all time, but the redeemer of all time through love. Far from being unrelated to human actions and decisions, God is all-inclusive in his relatedness. The uniqueness of perfection is found in the fact of superrelativity; God has power to sustain relations beyond that of all other beings.

The most obvious objection to this line of thought is that it introduces accidents into the divine nature and thereby destroys the absolute majesty of God. Hartshorne acknowledges the difficulty and seeks to overcome it. The key to the solution has been given before. The "absolute" character of God Hartshorne takes to be the non-relative, eternal, and unchanging aspect; this character is abstract because it leaves out the supremely relative nature of God as the one who loves all creatures. The result is the reverse of an old formula. It was often asserted that the "absolute" is the true God and the "personal God" of religion is an "appearance" or concession to the human imagination. Hartshorne maintains, on the contrary, that the true God is the personal deity while the "absolute" is the abstraction since it expresses only the identity of God and not the actual knowledge of contingent reality that makes God supremely relative. The relative includes the absolute, but the converse does not hold. The supremely relative being includes "something absolute" and since inclusion is taken as an external relation, the "absolute" aspect is a feature for the divine subject but is not the divine subject as such. God can be taken as independent of (and thus as "absolute with respect to") this or that actual embodiment, but not of embodiment as such.

Despite considerable emphasis on the cosmological aspect of theology, Hartshorne is more concerned ultimately for the ontological and religious dimensions. Interest in the ontological argument runs throughout his writings and it is completely in accord with his logical rationalism. In *The Logic of Perfection* (1962) the ontological argument is given one of the most exhaustive treatments in terms of formal logic that it has ever received. There Hartshorne seeks to reinterpret the argument in two respects; first, he claims that the traditional idea of perfection (the *nature* of God) has been ambiguous and needs to be redefined; second, he approaches the question of the divine existence in terms of modal logic, holding that the issue posed by Anselm's argument has to do not with the alternative of contingent existence or nonexistence but with necessary existence and impossibility. Hartshorne's reinterpretation of the idea of perfection is based on his "neoclassical" metaphysics. Starting with the reality of time and process as ingredient in the divine knowledge, Hartshorne argues that the traditional conception of perfection allowed only for the identity and completeness of God without regard for his relation to the order of contingent events. This view will be seen at once to be an extension of the divine relativity idea. Instead of being "perfect" in the sense of being complete and unrelated to the world of time and change, God becomes related to all contingencies through his knowledge and concern for the world. Hartshorne believes that his conception is required no less by the religious belief in a living God than by the metaphysical demand that perfection be capable of surpassing itself. The latter doctrine means that, while no reality greater than God can be conceived, God can surpass himself in the sense that his actual state at any given time in the course of events is not the greatest possible. With this idea Hartshorne aims at reflecting the actual realization of persons and things in the divine knowledge. Stated in other terms, divine perfection, though necessary, can embrace the contingent in the form of knowledge and concern for the world of finite and developing things.

From the purely logical side, Hartshorne restates the ontological argument in terms of modal logic, relying on the postulate that modal determinations—determinations of possibility, impossibility, necessity, existence, etc.—are predicated necessarily. Central to his discussion is the contention that Anselm's ontological argument does not pose the issue of the existence versus the nonexistence of God in the contingent sense, but rather the alternative between necessary existence and impossibility. Thus, according to Hartshorne, all "refutations" of the argument based on considerations drawn from the domain of contingent existence alone are misdirected. A decision as to the validity of the ontological argument requires a theory of possibility as a basis for judgment; merely claiming that "existence is not a predicate" will not do. The core of his reinterpretation is found in his doctrine of "modal coincidence" according to which perfection turns out to be coincident with possibility in general. This is the main line of Hartshorne's argument; the details are beyond our present scope. Suffice it to say that the position underlying the essays in *The Logic of Perfection* is a further development of the "panentheistic" or "surrelativist" conception of God outlined in previous works. Hartshorne remains true to his persistent belief in a metaphysical theology that can do justice to religious no less than to philosophical demands.

As we move further into the second half of the twentieth century, one fact stands out: thinking about religious doctrines and issues is receiving a new stimulus. Prompted by a sense that neither a purely technical philosophy nor a purely fideistic theology will suffice, philosophers and theologians are once again reflecting in a speculative spirit about the doctrine of God, the ontological argument, the relation between religion and science, the doctrine of creation, and related topics. The widespread conviction that such problems are beyond our rational powers no longer goes unchallenged. The narrow empiricism that forced metaphysical issues out of the sphere of reason is becoming increasingly a matter for re-examination. Although there is more talk at present of a "philosophical theology" than of the philosophy of religion, the fact remains that the issues long asso-

ciated with the encounter of philosophy with religion are now coming to be discussed in a fresh way. It is to be hoped that the resources
of the American tradition will not be neglected and that we shall
find ourselves able to learn from the philosophical record just surveyed.

◆§◈◆

BIBLIOGRAPHICAL NOTE

In view of the need to confine the foregoing study to basic trends and points of view, it has not been possible to make mention of every work by an American scholar in the field falling within the period covered. It will therefore be in the interest of completeness to note some hitherto neglected titles and to suggest, through brief descriptions, the place they should occupy in the total picture.

Bixler, J. S., R. L. Calhoun, and H. R. Niebuhr, eds., *The Nature of Religious Experience* (1937). Essays in honor of Douglas Clyde Macintosh by many hands aimed at critical discussion of the themes in the philosophy of religion that most interested Macintosh —the relation of religion to experience, the problem of religious knowledge, religious realism, etc.

Burtt, E. A., *Man Seeks the Divine* (1957). A philosophical treatment of the basic concepts and doctrines of the major religious traditions, East and West. The author attempts to show the essential nature of religion through a comparison of classical religious forms. The position of religion on the current scene is also considered.

Collins, James D., *God in Modern Philosophy* (1959). A perceptive study by a Roman Catholic scholar focusing on the place of God and religious issues in the systems of modern philosophers. The point of departure is the fifteenth century and the study is carried to the present. The book provides an illuminating background for understanding the current situation.

Ducasse, C. J., *A Philosophical Scrutiny of Religion* (1953). A philosophical inquiry into the nature of religion and the problems of religious faith and knowledge. Special attention is given to the problem of a life after death; the author here makes use chiefly of material gathered under the aegis of parapsychology.

449

Ferré, Frederick, *Language, Logic and God* (1961). An attempt to show the relevant connections between recent analytic philosophy, largely of the type developed in Britain, and theological discourse. Narrow positivism is criticized and an effort made to show how the linguistic approach helps us to understand and articulate the nature and functions of theological language.

Ferré, Nels F. S., *Faith and Reason* (1946). A brief study drawing on many points of view aimed at setting forth a theory of the proper relations between science, philosophy, and religion. The author is better known as a theologian; this book focuses on more strictly philosophical issues.

Greene, T. M., *Moral, Aesthetic and Religious Insight* (1957). An original reworking of some themes first suggested by the Kantian philosophy. Most rewarding for the philosopher concerned with religion is the concept of "synoptic rationality" developed for the purpose of showing the place of reason in religion.

Moore, John M., *Theories of Religious Experience* (1938). A critical exposition and evaluation of the theories of religious experience developed by William James, Rudolf Otto, and Henri Bergson. The author aims at providing a general estimate of the validity of the empirical approach in religion.

Randall, John Herman, Jr., *The Role of Knowledge in Western Religion* (1958). A learned, penetrating, and spirited attempt to estimate the proper place of knowledge within the life of religion and the enterprise of theology. Adopting a functional interpretation of religion, Randall seeks to show the proper relations between philosophy, religion, and science, and especially to reinterpret the tension between science and religion as two different ways of understanding what religion really is.

Wild, John, *Human Freedom and Social Order: An Essay in Christian Philosophy* (1959). An original treatment of the problems connected with the perennial task of relating faith to reason. The author defends the idea of a Christian philosophy and draws on the insights of phenomenology and existentialism for its development. Particularly illuminating is the attempt to connect the basic ideas of a Christian philosophy with social, ethical, and political problems.

INDEX

112159